LITERATURE AND MASS CULTURE

Communication in Society, Volume 1

LITERATURE AND MASS CULTURE

Communication in Society, Volume 1

LEO LOWENTHAL

Transaction Books
New Brunswick (U.S.A.) and London (U.K.)

Library of Congress Catalog Number: 83-17888
ISBN: 0-87855-489-0 (cloth)
Printed in the United States of America

Library of Congress Cataloging in Publication Data
Lowenthal, Leo.
  Communication in society.

  Contents: v. 1. Literature and mass culture.
  1. Interpersonal communication—Philosophy—Addresses,
essays, lectures. 2. Popular culture—Philosophy—
Addresses, essays, lectures. 3. Literature—Philosophy
—Addresses, essays, lectures. 4. Sociology—Philosophy
—Addresses, essays, lectures. I. Title.
HM258.L675 1984   302.2   83-17888
ISBN 0-87855-489-0 (v. 1)

CONTENTS

ACKNOWLEDGMENTS

The essays in this volume originally appeared in the following publications:

"Historical Perspectives of Popular Culture," *American Journal of Sociology,* vol. 55, January 1950, pp. 323-32.

"The Debate over Art and Popular Culture: A Synopsis" was written as a research memorandum commissioned by the Ford Foundation's Implementation Committee on Television, and was completed in 1954.

"Notes on the Theater and the Sermon," *Transactions of the Sixth World Congress of Sociology,* vol. IV, 1970.

"The Debate over Art and Popular Culture: Eighteenth-Century England as a Case Study," *Common Frontiers of the Social Sciences,* ed. Mirra Komarowsky, Free Press, 1957. Coauthored with Marjorie Fiske.

"The Debate on Cultural Standards in Nineteenth-Century England," *Social Research,* vol. 30, 1963.

"The Reception of Dostoevski in Pre–World War I Germany," *Zeitschrift für Sozialforschung,* vol. 3, 1934 (in German).

"The Biographical Fashion," *Sociologica,* ed. T.W. Adorno and Walter Dirks, Europäische Verlagsanstalt, Frankfurt/Main, 1955 (in German).

"The Triumph of Mass Idols," *Radio Research 1942-43,* ed. Paul F. Lazarsfeld and Frank N. Stanton, Duell, Sloan & Pierce, 1944.

"Some Thoughts on the 1937 Edition of the *International Who's Who,*" *Studies in Philosophy and Social Sciences,* vol. 8, 1939 (in German).

"On Sociology of Literature (1932)," *Zeitschrift für Sozilaforschung,* vol. 1, 1932 (in German).

"On Sociology of Literature (1948)," *Communication in Modern Society,* ed. Wilbur Schramm, University of Illinois Press, 1948.

"Humanistic Perspectives of David Riesman's *The Lonely Crowd,*" *Culture and Social Character,* ed. Seymour Lipset and Leo Lowenthal, Free Press, 1961.

"Popular Culture: A Humanistic and Sociological Concept," *The Human Dialogue,* ed. Floyd W. Matson and Ashley Montague, Free Press, 1967.

"Some Thoughts on the 1937 Edition of *International Who's Who*" and "On Sociology of Literature (1932)" have been translated from German into English by Susanne Hoppmann-Lowenthal for publication in this volume.

PREFACE

The essays collected in this first volume of my writings on communication in society, though written at various times ranging from the 1930s to the 1960s, have an underlying theme closely related to my long-term intellectual concerns.

During my university training in Germany, immediately after the end of World War I, I devoted four years to the study of the social sciences and another four years to that of literature and history; throughout this period I was also engaged in the study of philosophy. By now, I have lived for almost half a century in the United States, and my professional affiliations here and abroad have been that of a sociologist. These bare facts may indicate that I can neither confess nor boast adherence to an unequivocally defined specialization. I believe this to be an advantage.

Approaching sociological research from a humanistic angle while retaining a sociological view of the humanities has helped clarify my concern with cultural phenomena (which, for me, also means with political morality). I came to focus my research on the issues of the individual and individualism—concepts which in my lifetime have undergone a dramatic change from the ideological heights of unquestioned supreme values to the gloomy relativism which questions any meaning of history and human coherence. Obviously, except for the genius and the charlatan, no one individual can undertake the task of tackling all aspects and data in such a problematic field. My own approach—partly by accident, partly by predilection—has led me to narrow down this overriding theoretical interest to research on literary production. In the sociologist's idiom, it is the area of communication; in the parlance of the humanist, it is the area of literature (artistic or otherwise).

The French philosopher and political theorist Charles de Bonald once said: "Were one to see the literature of a people whose history one does not know, one could tell what this people had been, and were one to read the history of a people whose literature one does not know, one could assume with certainty which one had been the basic trait of its literature." That is to say, literature is a particularly suitable bearer of the fundamental symbols and values which give cohesion to social groups and its members—in nations and epochs as well as in special social subgroups and particular historical situations. Perceived in this way, literature embraces two powerful cultural complexes: art on the one hand, and a market-oriented commodity on the other.

Popular commodities serve primarily as indicators of the sociopsychological characteristics of the multitude. By studying the organization, content, and linguistic symbols of mass media, we learn about the typical forms of behavior, attitudes, commonly held beliefs, prejudices, and aspirations of large numbers of people. At least since the separation of literature into the two distinct fields of art and commodity in the course of the eighteenth century, the popular literary products can make no claim to insight and truth. Yet, although they have become a powerful force in the life of modern man, their symbols cannot be overestimated as diagnostic tools for studying man in contemporary society.

Literature as art is another matter. It is the creation of individuals and is experienced by individuals qua individuals. It thus seems to be as remote from the concerns of the social scientist as the physician-patient relationship is from the interests of the research biochemist; it is not surprising that social scientists usually have made a detour around it—at least in their professional work. Yet it is my profound conviction that particularly since the dawn of our era in the Renaissance, creative artistic literature presents one of the essential sources for the study of the relation between man and society. On a previous occasion I compared the creative writer with the authors of personal documents such as memoirs, autobiographies, diaries, and letters, and commented that it is the artist who portrays what is more real than reality itself. (This is a broad, if not grandiose statement; it will be the underlying theme of the second volume of *Communication in Society*.)

The present volume deals primarily (but not exclusively) with popular literature as commodity, a field where social science research has flourished for some time. It has, however, been so preoccupied with research techniques and methodological devices for refined data processing that a paradoxical situation has developed. One of the many professional specialties of our day, the study of the mass media—the most visible, audible, and time-consuming social institutions—has not attracted much attention from the literate public at large. This is due to the reluctance of the theorists and research specialists in the mass media field to relate their work to the general intellectual discussion of modern mass culture on the one hand, and to its historical antecedents on the other.

An investigation does not have to start with a *tabula rasa*. One of the first tasks is to make clear that much has been written on the tablet which now has to be deciphered and read. Modern communications research, like so many other specialized activities in the social sciences, has led an ascetic life—limiting itself to closely defined problems of content analysis, effects, audience stratification, problems of inter- and intro-media relations, and so on. Outside of this world of diligent and conscientious specialized research, a literary discussion has been raging, led by more or less sophisticated conributors to literary and highbrow magazines, namely social philosophers, artists, educators, and other agents of institutionalized and noninstitutionalized public policy. Each group treats the other side with irony or contempt: the writers by poking fun at the specialists, who do not see or want to see the forest because of their jargon, and the specialists by denying any dignity of evidence to the theorizing or moralizing literati. The real victim in this battle is not the literary guild, which has gone on setting its own standards of proof and speculation unruffled by the methodological headaches of the specializing disciplinarian, but the very social scientist who increasingly has felt the need for placing his studies, projects, and plans in a context of socially useful theoretical orientations. Being a scientist and not a theologian or a metaphysician, he will not gain or regain such orientation without recourse to a historical continuum.

Indeed, popular culture has a history of many centuries, and is probably as old as human civilization. We have only to think of the differentiation between esoteric and exoteric religious exercises in early oriental and occidental civilizations, of the dichotomy between high and low tragedy and comedy on the stages of ancient Greece and Rome, of the gulf between philosophizing elites at the estates of Roman emperors and the circuses promoted by the very same elite, of the organized medieval holidays with their hierarchical performances in the cathedral, and the folksy entertainments at popular fairs, to which the crowd surrendered immediately after participation in the services.

Popular art is not a specifically modern phenomenon. But until the modern era it did not give rise to intellectual or moral controversies; these arose only after the two domains had come in contact. The process that led to the change was gradual, and was associated with broad social and technological changes which ushered in the beginnings of a middle class. The artist, traditionally dependent for his subsistence on the direct consumers of his art, no longer had to please only one rich or powerful patron; he had now to worry about the demands of an increasingly broader, more "popular" audience. Though the process took place in all great European nations with varying speed, there has arisen in each of them, since the end of the eighteenth century, a class of writers and playwrights who cater to the needs of these broader audiences. During that century the controversies about popular culture began to rage in earnest. We owe an even earlier formulation, in terms that have stayed with us, to Montaigne, who was one of the most profound students of human nature of all times. His psychological analysis of entertainment as a means of meeting a universal human need applied to *both* domains of culture, and he thus unwittingly fired the opening shot in the battle of ideas that followed.

Montaigne's ideas on the psychological and social function of entertainment contrast with those of Pascal. His century—the seventeenth— marks the consolidation of modern national states following the breakdown of the medieval supranational political, economic, and cultural hierarchies. The intellectual task of the period was to reconcile the individual's religious and moral heritage and his basic human needs with the requirements of the national and capitalist economy that was replacing the feudal system. It is therefore not surprising that the philosophers of this period discussed the individual's cultural efforts and personal needs in relation to his spiritual and emotional well-being, nor is it surprising that it was the philosophers who played leading roles in these discussions. Today these discussions may sometimes present a bewildering play of speculation around the question of whether the individual should ever be allowed to indulge in any leisure-time activities except those that may be construed as contributing to the salvation of his soul. However rambling and general these philosophical speculations may be, they nevertheless juxtapose, for the first time in modern history, serious against relatively frivolous leisure-time pursuits, and in so doing implicitly pose a problem.

Some of the milestones in the history of this debate on popular culture are discussed in this volume. It is my hope that the interpretation of the social role of artistic and nonartistic products in literature will eventually be amenable to theoretical formulation. For the time being, they remain a series of isolated concepts and basic, as yet largely unresolved, questions.

I do not have an all-embracing formula to offer for the study of popular culture. Indeed, I find myself here (more so than in the area of artistic literature) caught between the prerogatives claimed by the social sciences and the humanities. Yet despite considerable confusion, competition, and occasional bitterness, there is probably more agreement among the two groups than either is at present aware of. Students entering one or the other field may have preconceived ideas, sometimes contemptuous ones, about what students in the other area are doing (indeed, this is an area that should be well-worth exploring), but they often speak in each other's terms without knowing it. When social scientists who work within an academic framework draft rationales for studies of the social aspects of mass media, they are usually guided by the same sense of responsibility and concern for cultural and moral values that are part and parcel of the humanists' approach to the same problems (in contrast to the notion that the social sciences are mere bagatelles of commercial and political merchandising). Actually, both groups share a concern with the role of the arts and their counterparts in modern society, both seek standards and criteria for judgment with regard to media output and its social role, and both believe in the importance of studying the transmission of values through time and space. Such emotional involvement and tension in itself suggests that there are many concerns common to the two fields but that they have not yet worked out efficient means of communicating with each other.

Some chapters in this volume deal with literature as commodity, while others deal with problems of literature as art. There is, however, a certain overlap, since the historical material, in discussing the issues of popular arts, is quite frequently taken from the writings of leading literary figures. An attempt has been made to refer to historical as well as contemporary phenomena and to select sources from a number of countries including England, France, Germany, Norway, Russia, and the United States. The material on popular culture as offered here is primarily centered on the study of intellectual debates over the arts and its popular counterparts; however, the two papers on popular biographies offer examples for an analysis of the popular commodities themselves.

By way of a postscript, a word on the essay on the reception of Dostoevski. I believe that this study was the first attempt to open up the area of the history and aesthetics of reception (the essay was written in the early 1930s), which has lately become a lively field in literary theory and criticism. The two versions of "The Sociology of Literature" are to demonstrate my own maturing process from a traditional Marxist in 1932 to what I hope is a more sophisticated version of a cosmopolitan intellectual who has not given up the moral tenets of critical theory, to which I profess a lifelong commitment from my youth to my present old age.

The material in this first volume of my writings is organized according to subject matter rather than chronology. Part I presents a number of studies that should be considered a contribution to an applied theory of mass culture even though they are self-contained pieces of research. All essays appear in their original form and have not been "brought up to date."

I am grateful to the staff of the Book Division of Transaction for professional assistance, and above all to its president, my friend and colleague, Irving Louis Horowitz, who has had the great courage to engage in a unique publishing venture and to enable a scholar to present the entire record of his academic work while still alive and thus nurturing an old man's impulse to remain productive for a little while longer.

Fall 1983

Part I
HISTORICAL AND EMPIRICAL STUDIES

Part I

HISTORICAL PERSPECTIVES

Chapter 1
HISTORICAL PERSPECTIVES OF
POPULAR CULTURE

This chapter was written to be provocative, by one who has been engaged in empirical research for a considerable number of years and who has recently been charged with the administration of a large-scale research program. The author has taken it upon himself to act as the spokesman for an approach to popular culture which some will call "social theory" and others "obsolete, abstract criticism." Specifically, this chapter deals with aspects of the historical and theoretical frame of reference which seem to me to be a basic requirement for the study of mass communications and yet a blind spot in contemporary social science. I know of no better statement with which to highlight this blind spot in contemporary analyses of mass phenomena than De Tocqueville's remarks on the fact-finding obsession of the American mind a century ago:

> The practice of Americans leads their minds to fixing the standard of their judgment in themselves alone. As they perceive that they succeed in resolving without assistance all the little difficulties which their practical life presents, they readily conclude that everything in the world may be explained, and that nothing in it transcends the limits of the understanding. Thus they fall to denying what they cannot comprehend; which leaves them but little faith for whatever is extraordinary and an almost insurmountable distaste for whatever is supernatural. As it is on their own testimony that they are accustomed to rely, they like to discern the object which engages their attention with extreme clearness; they therefore strip off as much as possible all that covers it; they rid themselves of whatever separates them from it, they remove whatever conceals it from sight, in order to view it more closely and in the broad light of day. This disposition of mind soon leads them to condemn forms, which they regard as useless and inconvenient veils placed between them and the truth.[1]

My plea on behalf of these "veils" takes the form of five rather unsystematic groups of observations: (1) I shall indicate that the discussion of popular culture has a century-old tradition in modern history; (2) the historical locus of popular culture today will be fixed; (3) an attempt will be made to evaluate the over-all approach of empirical research to the social function of contemporary popular culture; (4) the current philosophical, qualitative, nonresearch analysis of popular culture will be summarized briefly; and (5) some programmatic notes will be offered on the relationship between social criticism and social research.

POPULAR CULTURE—AN OLD DILEMMA

In a survey recently undertaken of radio-listening habits in a foreign country, one of the respondents remarked:

> Radio is the companion of the lonely. It has made gigantic strides for almost half a century. Women in particiular, especially those with small pensions and without other resources, who are completely isolated, are now in touch with the whole world thanks to the radio. They have undergone a regular transformation; they have found a kind of second youth. They are up-to-date and they know the stars of the headlines, of the theatre, the movies, the world of sports, etc. I have heard village people, discussing the merits of Mozart and Chopin, refer to what the radio had said.

In quite the opposite vein another woman revealed that she did not have a radio set in her home. Asked to explain why, she answered: "Because once there is a set in the house, one cannot resist. Everybody listens idiotically, the kids and the others too. When we stay with my friend G., my husband plays with the radio all the time." Her view was supported by a male respondent, who also refuses to permit a radio in the house. He believes that studies, conversation, and activity around the house provide enough interest, that the indiscriminate outpouring of music and talk over the radio lowers everyone's intellectual level.

These spontaneous remarks reveal two leitmotifs which have run continuously through the modern era: on the one hand, a positive attitude toward all instrumentalities for the socialization of the individual; on the other hand, a deep concern about the inner fate of the individual under the impact of the leveling powers of institutional and other organized forms of leisure activity. This basic dilemma concerning man's existence beyond the requirements of biological and material survival, the vital question of how to live out that stretch of life which is neither sleep nor work, can be said to have found its classic intellectual expression in a philosophical dialogue that never took place. Montaigne in the sixteenth century took stock of the situation of the individual after the breakdown of medieval culture. He was particularly struck by the phenomenon of loneliness in a world without faith, in which tremendous pressures were being exerted on everyone under the conditions of a postfeudal society. To escape destruction by these pressures, to avoid becoming lost in the horrors of isolation, Montaigne suggested distraction as a way out:

> Variety always solaces, dissolves, and scatters. If I cannot combat it, I run away from it; and in running away I double and change my direction. By changing place, occupation, company, I escape into the crowd of other thoughts and diversions, where it loses my trace, and leaves me safe.
>
> Is it reasonable that even the arts should take advantage of and profit by our natural stupidity and feebleness of mind? The barrister, says Rhetoric, in that farce they call pleading, will be moved by the sound of his own voice and his feigned emotion, and will suffer himself to be cozened by the passion he is acting. He will affect a real and substantial grief in this mummery he is playing, to transmit it to the jury who are still less concerned in the matter than he. Like those men who are hired at funerals to assist in the ceremonial of mourning, who sell their tears and grief by weight and measure; for, although they are stirred by borrowed emotions, it is certain that, through the habit of settling their countenance to suit the occasion, they are often quite carried away and affected with genuine melancholy.[2]

It is significant that quite a few basic concepts which we have been accustomed to regard as very modern emerge as early as the sixteenth century: escape, distraction, entertainment, and, last but not least, vicarious living.

The reply to Montaigne came a century later. Commercial culture had developed in the meantime, and the waning influence of religion, pre- or post-Reformation, had made itself felt much more strongly in the average way of life. Restlessness, the search for relief everywhere and anywhere, had become a major social phenomenon. It was then that Pascal spoke up against the complete surrender of man to self-destroying restlessness:

> Men are entrusted from infancy with the care of their honor, their property, their friends, and even with the property and the honor of their friends. They are overwhelmed with business, with the study of languages, and with physical exercise; and they are made to understand that they cannot be happy unless their health, their honor, their fortune and that of their good friends be in good condition, and that a single thing wanting will make them unhappy. Thus they are given cares and business which make them bustle about from break of day.—It is, you will exclaim, a strange way to make them happy! What more could be done to make them miserable?—Indeed! what could be done? We should only have to relieve them from all these cares; for then they would see themselves: they would

reflect on what they are, whence they came, whither they go, and thus we cannot employ and divert them too much. And this is why, after having given them so much business, we advise them, if they have some time for relaxation, to employ it in amusement, in play, and to be always fully occupied.

How hollow and full of ribaldry is the heart of man![3]

Again and again he warned against what he called "diversion" as a way of life which could lead only to permanent unhappiness:

When I have occasionally set myself to consider the different distractions of men, the pains and perils to which they expose themselves at court or in war, whence arise so many quarrels, passions, bold and often bad ventures, etc., I have discovered that *all the unhappiness of men arises from one single fact, that they cannot stay quietly in their own chamber.*

They have a secret instinct which impels them to seek amusement and occupation abroad, and which arises from the sense of their constant unhappiness.[4]

Thus the attitude toward leisure which, for Montaigne, guarantees survival means self-destruction to Pascal. And the controversy is still going on. Each side has its partisans on all intellectual levels in everyday life, as illustrated in the study on radio as well as in learned treatises. On one side there is the benevolent analyst of a mass medium who seems to say that, while everything is not yet wonderful, it is getting better every day:

For in the old days the artists and writers and craftsmen were not writing at the behest of the people, but to please small powerful groups, the kings and lords and chieftains, who drew the talent of the time inward towards them and kept it circumscribed within the bounds of their castles and baronies. Much of the fine art of today remains alive only through a similar connection.

Yet, taking civilization as a whole, this ancient process is now in reverse. There is an outward movement. Pictures, entertainment, fun, are beginning to be seen as the rightful possession of all, and the comics join in and reflect this spreading democratization. And if the people's standards are at present lower than those which were set by workers around the seats of the mighty, the people's artists will have the satisfaction of knowing that they are identified with a vast and forward movement, which is giving to everyday folks their right to laugh and flourish under the sun.[5]

On the other hand, we find the nonconformist social critic who connects the loneliness of modern man with his interest in mass media as a setup of utter frustration:

> The conditions of earning one's bread in this society create the lonely modern man.
>
> Such conditions help explain the need, sometimes feverish, for an entertainment that so repetitively presents the same reveries, the same daydreams, the same childish fables of success and happiness. So much of the inner life of men is dried up that they tend to become filled with yearnings and to need the consolation of these reveries about people who are happy, healthy, and always successful.
>
> Hence, parallel to the retrogression of consciousness in, say, the Hollywood writer, there is a more widespread and also more pernicious retrogression of consciousness in the motion-picture audience. Social and economic conditions have established the basis for this; the motion picture further enforces it.[6]

The differences in the verbalization of the dilemma are obvious. The language of the sixteenth and seventeenth century philosophers is still deeply steeped in religious terminology; that of the modern writers in sociological terms; that of the nonprofessional radio listeners or nonlisteners in the ordinary words of everyday life. But beneath these differences in nomenclature the dilemma remains the same: perhaps it could be called a conflict between the psychological and the moral approaches to popular culture.

THE HISTORICAL LOCUS OF POPULAR CULTURE

This section of my discussion will be somewhat dogmatic in character, partly for the sake of brevity but also because it ought to be permissible to pause from time to time in our sociological routine and to speculate about the secular trend in which we, together with our objects of research, find ourselves.

The counterconcept to popular culture is art. Today artistic products are losing the character of spontaneity more and more and are being replaced by the phenomena of popular culture, which are nothing but a manipulated reproduction of reality as it is; and, in so doing, popular culture sanctions and glorifies whatever it finds worth echoing. Schopenhauer remarked that music is "the world once more." This philosophical aphorism throws light on the unbridgeble difference between art and popular culture: it is the difference between an increase in insight through a medium possessing self-sustaining means and mere repetition of given facts with the use of borrowed tools.

A superficial inventory of the contents and motivations in the products of the entertainment and publishing worlds in our Western civilization will include such themes as the nation, the family, religion, free enterprise, individual initiative; and in the Eastern orbit, higher production achievements, national cultures, the moral corruption of the West. The topical differences are not very decisive and, in any case, considerably smaller than the political differences which keep these two worlds apart. Saint-Simon, the great French pre-Marxian socialist philosopher, whose life extended from the *ancien régime* through the Revolutiuon and the Napoleonic era into the days of the reactionary Bourbon restoration, once remarked that, while he had experienced the most contradictory political systems, he realized that consistent, deeply rooted social tendencies which were completely impervious to political change made themselves felt in those decades. The very concept of society rests in this insight. Rigidly and consistently different as political systems are from one another today, there is also a complete inconsistency in the content of popular culture within a given political system—and popular culture is an element of society of the first order. The yardstick is expediency, within the total social situation, of course, and particularly the distribution of power.

Nietzsche, who may be called the discoverer and matchless critical analyst of modern popular culture, has formulated its relativism with respect to content:

> Modern counterfeit practices in the arts: regarded as necessary—that is to say, as fully in keeping with the needs most proper to the modern soul.

> Artists harangue the dark instincts of the dissatisfied, the ambitious, and the self-deceivers of a democratic age: the importance of poses. . . . The procedures of one era are transferred to the realm of another; the object of art is confounded with that of science, with that of the Church, or with that of the interests of the race (nationalism), or with that of philosophy— a man rings all bells at once, and awakens the vague suspicion that he is a god.

> Artists flatter women, sufferers, and indignant folk. Narcotics and opiates are made to preponderate in art. The fancy of cultured people, and of readers of poetry and ancient history, is tickled.[7]

What Nietzsche expressed in the general terms of the philosopher of culture has its spokesmen today. In an analysis of cartoon films a modern writer has pointed to the criterion of social expediency in the selection of their materials:

> It is just Disney's distinguishing characteristic that he is uncritical of what he reflects. He is quite artless. If the values by which the society lives are still serving, if the prevailing outlook is relatively brightfaced and aggressive, he will improvise from that—and give us Mickey Mouse. If the time is

one of crisis, and these values will no longer serve but are in conflict and in question, if the prevailing state of mind is a deep bewilderment, he will improvise with equal lack of inhibition. His particular talent is that he does not embarrass himself. This makes his dreams sometimes monstrous. But it gives them a wide reference.[8]

It may be noted in passing that in the present postwar period disillusionment over the lack of definitive cultural and moral solutions has become prevalent. It finds expression in an artificial permeation of entertainment products with religion. In the average movie the pursuit of love almost invariably means the appearance of the clergyman. Nietzsche had already commented on the artificial respiration administered to religion in an era of decadence and nihilism. When he said, "God is dead," he meant that the frenzied activities of modern life produce popular culture in an attempt to fill a vacuum which cannot be filled. Nietzsche linked the precarious role of religion with the pressure of civilization and its neuroticizing influence on people:

> *In the Neighborhood of Insanity.*—The sum of sensations, knowledge and experiences, the whole burden of culture, therefore, has become so great that an overstraining of nerves and powers of thought is a common danger, indeed the cultivated classes of European countries are throughout neurotic, and almost every one of their great families is on the verge of insanity in one of their branches. True, health is now sought in every possible way; but in the main a diminution of that tension of feeling, of that oppressive burden of culture, is needful, which, even though it might be bought at a heavy sacrifice, would at least give us room for the great hope of a *new Renaissance.*[9]

With this quotation we return to the differences between popular culture and art, between spurious gratification and a genuine experience as a step to greater individual fulfilment (this is the meaning of Aristotle's catharsis). Art lives on the threshold of action. Men free themselves truly from the mythical relation to things by stepping back, so to speak, from that which they once worshiped and which they now discover as the Beautiful. To experience beauty is to be liberated from the overpowering domination of nature over men. In popular culture, men free themselves from mythical powers by discarding everything, even reverence for the Beautiful. They deny anything that transcends the given reality.[10] This is exactly what De Tocqueville meant, I think, in our opening quotation. From the realm of beauty man walks into the realm of entertainment, which is, in turn, integrated with the necessities of society and denies the right to individual fulfilment:

Under the absolute sway of one man the body was attacked in order to
subdue the soul; but the soul escaped the blows which were directed against
it and rose proudly superior. Such is not the course adopted by tyranny
in democratic republics; there the body is left free, and the soul is enslaved.
The master no longer says: "You shall think as I do or you shall die"; but
he says: "You are free to think differently from me and to retain your life,
your property, and all that you possess; but you are henceforth a stranger
among your people. You may retain your civil rights, but they will be
useless to you, for you will never be chosen by your fellow citizens if you
solicit their votes; and they will affect to scorn you if you ask for their
esteem. You will remain among men, but you will be deprived of the rights
of mankind. Your fellow creatures will shun you like an impure being; and
even those who believe in your innocence will abandon you, lest they should
be shunned in their turn. Go in peace! I have given you your life, but it
is an existence worse than death."[11]

Men no longer surrender to illusions.

SOCIAL RESEARCH AND POPULAR CULTURE

The problem is whether, and to what extent, modern social science
is equipped to deal with modern social culture. The instruments of
research have been brought to a high degree of refinement. But is this
enough? Empirical social science has become a kind of applied asceticism.
It stands clear of any entanglements with foreign powers and thrives in
an atmosphere of rigidly enforced neutrality. It refuses to enter the sphere
of meaning. A study of television, for instance, will go to great lengths
in analyzing data on the influence of television on family life, but it will
leave to poets and dreamers the question of the actual human values of
this new institution. Social research takes the phenomena of modern life,
including the mass media, at face value. It rejects the task of placing
them in a historical and moral context. In the beginning of the modern
era, social theory had theology as its model, but today the natural sciences
have replaced theology. This change in models has far-reaching implications. Theology aims at salvation, natural science at manipulation; the
one leads to heaven and hell, the other to technology and machinery.
Social science is today defined as an analysis of painstakingly circumscribed, more or less artificially isolated, social sectors. It imagines that
such horizontal segments constitute its research laboratory, and it seems
to forget that the only social research laboratories that are properly
admissible are historical situations.

This has not always been the case. Popular culture, particularly as
represented by the newspapers, has been a subject of discussion for about
a hundred and fifty years. Before the naturalistic phase of social science

set in, the phenomena of popular culture were treated as a social and historical whole. This holds true for religious, philosophical, and political discussions from the time of Napoleon to Hitler. Our contemporary social science literature seems completely void of any knowledge of, or at least of any application and reference to, the voluminous writings produced on both the left and the right wings of the political and cultural fronts in the nineteenth century. It seems to ignore Catholic social philosophy as well as Socialist polemics, Nietzsche as well as the great, but completely unknown, Austrian critic, Karl Kraus, who tried to validate the notion of the crisis of modern culture by a critique of popular culture. Kraus focused attention on the analysis of language. The common denominator of his essays is his thesis that it is in the hollowing-out of language that we can see the disintegratrion, and even the disappearance, of the concept and existence of the autonomous individual, of the personality in its classical sense.

Studies of the role of the press, even of such specialized problems as readership figures, would do well to go back to the nineteenth- and early-twentieth-century analyses of the press in Germany. There they would find, in the different political and philosophical camps, illustrations of the fruitfulness of studying social phenomena in context—in the case of the press, the relationship of the modern newspaper to the history of the economic, social, and political emancipation of the middle classes. A study of the modern newspaper is meaningless, in the very exact sense of the word, if it is not aware of the historical framework, which is composed of both critical materials like those of Karl Kraus, writing at the end of an epoch, and optimistic attitudes like the following, from the work of the German publicist, Joseph Goerres, at the beginning of the nineteenth century:

> What everybody desires and wants shall be expressed in the newspapers; what is depressing and troubling everybody may not remain unexpressed; there must be somebody who is obliged to speak the truth, candid, without reservation, and unfettered. For, under a good constitution the right of freedom of expression is not merely tolerated but is a basic requirement; the speaker shall be looked upon as a holy person until he forfeits his right by his own fault and lies. Those who work against such freedom leave themselves open to the charge that the consciousness of their own great faults weighs heavily upon them; those who act justly do not shun free speech—it can in the end lead only to "honor be to whom honor is due"; but those who are dependent on dirt and darkness certainly like secretiveness.[12]

This is not to say that the whole field of sociology has been given over to historical ascetism. Quite a number of leading scholars in social theory and social history have kept alive the conscience of a historical civilization. It is worth our while to read again the following remarks by Robert E. Park:

> In fact, the reason we have newspapers at all, in the modern sense of the term, is because about one hundred years ago, in 1835 to be exact, a few newspaper publishers in New York City and in London discovered (1) that most human beings, if they could read at all, found it easier to read news than editorial opinion and (2) that the common man would rather be entertained than edified. This, in its day, had the character and importance of a real discovery. It was like the discovery, made later in Hollywood, that gentlemen prefer blonds. At any rate, it is to the consistent application of the principle involved that the modern newspaper owes not merely its present character but its survival as a species.[13]

His point of view finds confirmation in an excellent study in the history of mass culture by Louis B. Wright: "If it is desirable to trace the pedigree of the popular culture of modern America, it is possible to find most of its ideology implicit in the middle-class thought of Elizabethan England. The historian of American culture must look back to the Renaissance and read widely in the forgotten literature of tradesmen."[14]

One of the difficulties which have occasionally arisen in intellectual intercourse between people of American and European backgrounds is perhaps due to the antihistorical allergy of the former and the historical oversensitivity of the latter. I can illustrate this point by a very recent example. When I received the first two volumes of the outstanding work by Samuel A. Stouffer and his staff, *The American Soldier,* I was curious to learn how the authors would place their research within the context of the social theories about the soldier that have been developed from Plato on. To my amazement, I could find no historical reference beyond a solitary quotation from Tolstoi, who wrote somewhere in *War and Peace:* "In warfare the force of armies is a product of the mass multiplied by something else, an unknown x." The authors added the following comment: "Thus for perhaps the first time in military history it is possible to present statistical evidence relating to the factor x described in the quotation from Tolstoi's *War and Peace* at the beginning of this chapter."[15] They seem to have been fascinated by the mathematical symbolism of Tolstoi's sentence, but they successfully resisted the temptation to compare the social situation of armies in the time of Napoleon with modern conditions. In the face of such heroic restraint, it seems appropriate to quote the following flippant remark of a fellow-sociologist: "In this respect I speak of the failure of modern psychology. I firmly believe that one can learn more about the *ordre du coeur* from La Rochefoucauld and

Pascal (who was the author of this term) than from the most up-to-date textbook on psychology or ethics."[16]

It seems to me that the splendid isolationism of the social researcher is likely to reinforce a common suspicion, namely, that social research is, in the final analysis, nothing but market research, an instrument of expedient manipulation, a tool with which to prepare reluctant customers for enthusiastic spending. Only twenty years ago, social scientists were well aware of the dangers in the mass media, and they did not consider it beyond their duty to concern themselves with the negative, as well as the positive, potentialities of these mass media. In the pioneering article on "The Agencies of Communication," 1933, Malcolm M. Willey and Stuart A. Rice wrote:

> The effects produced may now be quite unpremeditated, although the machinery opens the way for mass impression in keeping with special ends, private or public. The individual, the figures show, increasingly utilizes these media and they inevitably modify his attitudes and behavior. What these modifications are to be depends entirely upon those who control the agencies. Greater posibilities for social manipulation, for ends that are selfish or socially desirable, have never existed. The major problem is to protect the interest and welfare of the individual citizen.[17]

Today, manipulation is taken for granted as an end of social science. A publisher can now dare to praise an outstanding sociological work with the following blurb on the jacket of the book:

> For the first time on such a scale an attempt was made to direct human behavior on a basis of scientific evidence, and the results suggest the opening of a new epoch in social studies and in social management.
>
> It is the editor's hope that the value to social science will prove to be as great as to the military, for whom the original research was undertaken.
>
> The problems were Army problems, for the most part peculiar to wartime. But the implications are universal.[18]

Expediency and the lack of a historical or philosophical frame of reference make a sorry marriage of convenience.

SOCIAL CRITICISM OF POPULAR CULTURE TODAY

No systematic body of theories is available. The situation has been characterized very aptly by Frederick Laws:

It will hardly be denied that the *condition of criticism today is chaotic,* especially when it is applied to the products of these immense distributing machines, *the new media.* Much reviewing is unselective in its enthusiasm and can with difficulty be distinguished from advertising copy. . . . *There is a lack of clearly expressed and generally recognized standards of value.* We believe that this confusion is partly due to a failure to realize or accept the fact that *the social framework in which works of art are produced and judged has changed fundamentally.* It is nonsense to suppose that the means of distribution or the size of social origin of the audience wholly determines the quality of art or entertainment, but it is stupid to pretend that they do not affect it.[19]

There is a literature on popular culture today which is thoroughly critical. I shall try to summarize the findings of this body of writings in a few brief generalizations. Some direct their critique against the product, but many turn it against the system on which the product depends. In special analyses, as in studies of a purely philosophical and sociological character, most authors concur in their final characterization of the products of popular culture.

The decline of the individual in the mechanized working processes of modern civilization brings about the emergence of mass culture, which replaces folk art or "high" art. A product of popular culture has none of the features of genuine art, but in all its media popular culture proves to have its own genuine characteristics: standardization, stereotypy, conservatism, mendacity, manipulated consumer goods.

There is an interdependence between what the public wants and what the powers of control enforce upon the public in order to remain in power. Most students are of the opinion that the habit of advertisement is the main motivating force in creating receptivity to popular culture and that the products themselves eventually take on the character of advertising. There is no consensus on the taste of the populace. Whereas some have confidence in the people's instinct for the good, the prevailing view seems to be that only the bad and the vulgar are the yardsticks of their aesthetic pleasure.

There is considerable agreement that all media are estranged from values and offer nothing but entertainment and distraction—that, ultimately, they expedite flight from an unbearable reality. Wherever revolutionary tendencies show a timid head, they are mitigated and cut short by a false fulfilment of wish-dreams, like wealth, adventure, passionate love, power, and sensationalism in general.

Prescriptions for improvement run the gamut from naïve proposals to offer aesthetically better merchandise, in order to create in the masses a taste for the valuable in life, to the theory that within the present setup of social power there is no hope whatsoever for improvement and that better popular culture presupposes a better society.

Finally, there is considerable speculation about the relations between the product of mass culture and real life. The radio, the movies, the newspapers, and the best sellers are, at the same time, models for the way of life of the masses and an expression of their actual way of life.

THESES ON CRITICAL THEORY AND
EMPIRICAL RESEARCH

In this section, I shall present some of the theoretical motivations which underlie contemporary philosophical speculation about mass madia. They comprise some of the ideas which the staff of the Institute of Social Research, under the leadership of Max Horkheimer, has tried to apply in a number of writings.[20]

1. The starting point is not market data. Empirical research, it is argued, is laboring under the false hypothesis that the consumers' choice is the decisive social phenomenon from which one should begin further analysis. We first ask: What are the functions of cultural communication within the total process of a society? Then we ask such specific questions as these: What passes the censorship of the socially powerful agencies? How are things produced under the dicta of formal and informal censorship?

2. We do not conceive such studies to be psychological in the narrow sense. They aim rather at finding out how the objective elements of a social whole are produced and reproduced in the mass media. Thus we would not accept the taste of the masses as a basic category but would insist on finding out how taste is fed to the consumers as a specific outgrowth of the technological, political, and economic conditions and interests of the masters in the sphere of production. We would want to investigate what "likes" or "dislikes" really mean in social terms. While it is true, for example, that people behave as if there were a large free area of selection according to taste and while they tend to vote fanatically for or against a specific presentation of popular culture, the question remains as to how such behavior is compatible with the actual elimination of free choice and the institutionalized repetition characteristic of all media. This is probably the theoretical area in which one would have to examine the replacement of taste—a concept of liberalism—by the quest for information.

3. We would question certain more or less tacit assumptions of empirical research, as, for example, the differentiation into "serious" and "nonserious" written, visual, or auditory communications. We would say that the problem of whether we are faced with serious or nonserious literature is two-dimensional. One would first have to furnish an aesthetic analysis of qualities and then investigate whether the aesthetic qualities are not subject to change under the conditions of mass reproduction. We would challenge the assumption that a higher increase in so-called "serious" programs or products automatically means "progress" in educational and social responsibility, in the understanding of art, and so on. We would say that it is erroneous to assume that one cannot decide what is right and what is wrong in aesthetic matters. A good example of the establishment of aesthetic criteria will be found in the works of Benedetto Croce, who tries to show conceretely that works of art have immanent laws which permit decisions about their "validity." It is neither necessary nor sufficient to supplement a study of the reaction of respondents by a study of the intentions of art producers in order to find out the nature and quality of the artistic products, or vice versa.

4. We are disturbed by the acceptance at face value of such concepts as "standardization." We want to know what standardization means in industry, in behavior patterns, and in popular culture. We think that the specifically psychological and anthropological character of popular culture is a key to the interpretation of the function of standardization in modern man.

5. In connection with the latter point, we are particularly interested in the phenomenon of psychological regression. We wish to know whether the consumption of popular culture really presupposes a human being with preadult traits or whether modern man has a split personality: half mutilated child and half standardized adult. We want to know the mechanisms of interdependence between the pressures of professional life and the freedom from intellectual and aesthetic tension in which popular culture seems to indulge.

6. As for the problem of the stimulus and its nature, here the connection with European philosophical heritage is particularly noticeable. Our thinking has its roots in the concept of understanding (*Verstehen*) as it was established philosophically and historically by Dilthey and sociologically by Simmel. We are inclined to think that empirical research conceives the stimulus to be as devoid of content as a color stimulus in a psychological laboratory. We hold that the stimulus in popular culture is itself a historical phenomenon and that the relation between stimulus and response is preformed and prestructured by

the historical and social fate of the stimulus as well as of the respondent.

NOTES

1. Alexis de Tocqueville, *Democracy in America* (New York: Knopf, 1945), p. 4.
2. E. J. Trechmann, trans., *The Essays of Montaigne* (New York: Oxford University Press, 1935), II, p. 291ff.
3. Blaise Pascal, *Pensées* (London and New York: Everyman's Library, 1931), p. 44.
4. *Ibid.,* pp. 39-42.
5. Coulton Waugh, *The Comics* (New York: Macmillan, 1947), p. 354.
6. James T. Farrell, *The League of Frightened Philistines* (New York: Vanguard Press, n.d.), pp. 176-77.
7. Friedrich Nietzsche, *The Will to Power,* in *Complete Works,* II (London, 1910), pp. 265-66.
8. Barbara Deming, "The Artlessness of Walt Disney," *Partisan Review* (spring 1945): 226.
9. Friedrich Nietzsche, *Human All-Too-Human: A Book for Free Spirits,* in *Complete Works,* VII, p. 227.
10. For a comprehensive theory on myth and art see Max Horkheimer and Theodor W. Adorno, *Dialektik der Aufklärung* (Amsterdam: Querido Verlag, 1947), *passim.*
11. De Tocqueville, *Democracy in America,* p. 264.
12. Joseph Goerres, *Rheinischer Merker,* July 1 and 3, 1814.
13. Helen MacGill Hughes, Introduction to *News and the Human Interest Story* (Chicago: University of Chicago Press, 1940), pp. xii-xiii.
14. *Middle-Class Culture in Elizabethan England* (Chapel Hill: University of North Carolina Press, 1935), pp. 659-69.
15. Samuel A. Stouffer et al., *The American Soldier: Adjustment during Army Life* (Princeton: Princeton University Press, 1949), p. 8.
16. J. P. Mayer, *Sociology of Film* (London: Faber & Faber, 1945), p. 273.
17. *Recent Social Trends in the United States,* I (New York and London: McGraw-Hill, 1933), p. 215.
18. Samuel A. Stouffer et al., *The American Soldier,* jacket of vols. I and II.
19. Introduction to *Made for Millions: A Critical Study of the New Media of Information and Entertainment* (London: Contact Publishers, 1947), p. xvii.
20. For example, Max Horkheimer, "Art and Mass Culture," *Studies in Philosophy and Social Science,* vol. IX (1941); T. W. Adorno, "On Popular Music," *Studies in Philosophy and Social Science,* vol. IX; Leo Lowenthal, "Biographies in Popular Magazines," *Radio Research, 1942-43,* ed. Paul F. Lazarsfeld and Frank Stanton (New York, 1944).

Chapter 2
THE DEBATE OVER ART AND POPULAR CULTURE: A SYNOPSIS

The purpose of this chapter is to single out some of the significant elements of the historical discussions which have centered around the problem of art versus entertainment, as a first step toward providing a broader base for the study of contemporary mass media, particularly television. To present a systematic inventory of this material, which extends over several centuries, would require the long-range and cooperative efforts of historians, philologists, and social scientists.[1]

Within the framework of a memorandum it is obviously necessary to make a careful selection from the voluminous and uncharted material which could be provocative for our problem. Therefore, we shall start the discussion with the development of the printing press with its potential for becoming a mass medium; but even within this period we shall have to make further selections both in terms of time periods and individuals. (This may be an appropriate point, too, to remind the reader that we are concerned here with the *discussions* which surrounded the problems of art versus popular media rather than with an historical review and analysis of the products themselves.)

Popular art as such is, of course, not a specifically modern phenomenon; it has probably existed, in one form or another, since the beginnings of stratified society. But until the modern era, this fact did not give rise to intellectual or moral controversies because within the framework of, for instance, the feudal structure, leisure-time activities were firmly regulated by church and state, with a set of rules for each class. There was no point of cultural contact between the elite and the masses, nor was there a middle class to complicate the picture or to bridge the gap. Within each domain, because the producer usually belonged to the same class as the consumer, there was considerable unity of interest, and contact or conflict between the two domains in this or any other area of life was inconceivable.

Controversy arose only after the two domains had come in contact. The exact date when that happened is difficult to determine; the process that led to the change was gradual, but there is little doubt that it was associated with broad social and technological changes which ushered in the beginnings of a middle class. The artist, traditionally dependent for his subsistence on the direct consumers of his art, no longer had to please only one rich or powerful patron; he had now to worry about the demands of an increasingly broader, more "popular" audience. The process took place in all great European nations with varying speed; by the middle of the nineteenth century there had arisen in each of them a class of writers or playwrights who were specialized in catering to the needs of these broader audiences. And it was about then that the controversies about popular culture began to rage in earnest, and the first fears about its threat to civilization were voiced. (This climatic period had been heralded by many signs during preceding centuries, and the beginnings of the controversy could probably be traced to the period of the first translations of the Latin Bible into national tongues.)

Since our purpose is not to trace the history of the great cultural change marking the modern era, but merely to single out some significant concepts which have emerged in the course of the controversies on popular forms of art and entertainment, we shall begin at a point where these problems were formulated in terms that have stayed with us. Accordingly, the first section of this chapter is devoted to Montaigne's ideas on the psychological and social function of entertainment, which are discussed in contrast to the ideas of Pascal, the great French seventeenth century philosopher.

By 1800, the changes which were merely incipient in the middle of the sixteenth century had taken place: nearly all remnants of the feudal system had been destroyed, at least in political and economic fields; industrialization and the resulting division of labor in a predominantly middle class society were well under way. Artists and intellectuals had freed themselves from the bonds of both church and state and were struggling to establish well-defined roles in this society. They experienced the growing emancipation of the middle classes as a threat, and feared that, as the middle group became more prosperous they would use philosophy and art as a kind of mass ornament, threatening the integrity of the scholar and artist which had been so newly wrested from church and state. The artist or scholar was not concerned with the salvation of the soul as were their predecessors, but with the preservation of a mission, the search for truth and beauty. The artist bent his efforts, therefore, to educating this great emerging public in the difficult task of art appreciation and, at the same time, to fighting with all his strength against the literary manipulators and imitators who corrupted the public before it could be educated. In this period, then, the artist, especially the writer, felt it his mission to establish the reading of great literature as the only permissible pastime on every level of society. From the point of view of the relations between the producers and the consumers of art, these concerns reflect an intermediary stage of development: the interests of the producers and consumers no longer coincide, but they are not felt to be completely divergent either.

Half a century later, the rift was consummated. By then the middle classes had achieved unchallenged rule in most of Europe and America, and the modern form of mass society had emerged. Mass media of communication, above all the newspapers, had established their dominance, and the literary market was flooded by products designed to attract the broadest possible public. Those writers or artists who held a lofty conception of their mission began to be and to feel isolated, and some of them met the challenge of the times by further accentuating the rift, by proclaiming that true art was above mass communication, that it was, in other words, art for art's sake, by its very nature to be understood and enjoyed only by the few.

Historians of literature, critics, and publicists of that time viewed the rise of popular literature with mixed feelings. Their reaction to it assumed three distinct forms: (1) righteous indignation, a sense of outrage, a resolve to ignore the mass products, a conception of the authors of these products as parasites, as polluters of the noble ideals of art; (2) moral worries regarding the fate of our culture: popular culture, in this context, was regarded as a phenomenon of decay, as heralding the end of our civilization; at the same time it was contrasted with "true" culture and genuine art; (3) attempts to understand the new phenomenon in sociological terms, i.e., to relate it to basic problems of politics, economics, etc., without necessarily passing judgment.

While for the sake of clarity it seemed desirable to review each of these forms in a separate chapter, it is apparent that all three types of reaction appeared more or less simultaneously, and all of them are still echoed in contemporary discussions.

Throughout the nineteenth century, the writers who viewed the new developments with alarm were seldom contradicted. While the public continued to buy bestsellers, the champions of higher culture seemed to dominate the theoretical field. However, some opposition developed also in this theoretical field, and there were writers who took up the cudgels in defense of an art for and of the people.

Of the many individuals who have made notable contributions to the discussion of popular culture, an effort has been made to select those who were not limited to a narrow area of intellectual activities. For the first period, as we have already indicated, Montaigne and Pascal were the outstanding figures, the former an essayist, lawyer, politician and civil servant in addition to being a philosopher, the latter was mathematician, theologist and spiritual leader of a religious movement. For the turn of the eighteenth and nineteenth centuries, German authors have seemed most representative as well as most eloquent: Goethe—poet, statesman, theater manager and natural scientist; Schiller—philosopher, aesthetician, professor of history as well as great creative writer; Lessing—dramatist, historian, theologian and theater critic all in one. For the latter part of the nineteenth century, we have paid particular attention to the poet, critic and school administrator, Matthew Arnold, and to Walter Bagehot, who was an outstanding public and political figure. Tocqueville's range of interest is by now also well known—diplomat, political writer, essayist; the other Frenchman in our group is Hippolyte Taine—historian, sociologist and literary critic. Taine's German contemporary, Gervinus, who is also included in this discussion, was an active liberal politician as well as historian of note and literary critic.

DIVERSION AND SALVATION IN THE SIXTEENTH AND SEVENTEENTH CENTURIES

The Need for Diversion: Montaigne

Our review begins with two literary figures who, although separated by no more than sixty years in time are, in some respects, poles apart in viewpoint: Montaigne, the founder of modern scepticism, and Pascal, the forerunner of modern religious existentialism. These two philosophers had in common, however, a quest for certainty in a world which was no longer circumscribed and governed by one church, one empire (the Roman-German), and by the almost unchanging economy of feudal society. With other intellectuals of their times, they sought a philosophy for the governing of man's spiritual and emotional life in this period of painful transition. Montaigne's concern was with how man could *adapt* himself to increasing societal pressures; Pascal's was with how man could *save his soul* in the face of the temptations to which he is subjected in periods of profound change. Both philosophers were concerned for the individual's development and security, but their differences in approach are apparent in their analyses of many problems of life, including, as we shall see, the problems of art and entertainment. These two fundamental themes, adaptation versus salvation, have persisted, as we shall see, through most discussions of popular culture down to the present day.

The traumatic nature of the realization that the standards of the Middle Ages had broken down is suggested by the extent to which Montaigne and his contemporaries felt compelled to attribute to man a universal and inherent unhappiness. Montaigne believed that a painful inner state resulting from spiritual, social and economic insecurity made it necessary for man to run away from himself. He even uses the word so often applied in interpreting the gratifications in the consumption of modern mass media—*escape:*

> A painful fancy takes possession of me; I find it shorter to change than to subdue it; if I cannot replace it by another contrary idea, I replace it at least by a different one. . . . If I cannot combat it, I run away from it. . . . By changing place, occupation, company, I escape. . . . It loses my trace and leaves me safe."[2]

But in order to be successful in the alleviation of inner pain, the escape must be into diversified materials and activities. Montaigne believed that nature has endowed man with a capacity for great variety, and that this capacity provides him with the wherewithal, if not for saving, at least for soothing his soul:

> In this way does Nature proceed . . . for Time, which she has given us for the sovereign physician of our passions, chiefly obtains its results . . . by supplying our imagination with other and still other matters.

The inner suffering attendant upon the deep moral and spiritual uncertainties of the transition from feudal to modern society, then, resulted in a need to escape into a variety of diversions. Montaigne then asks himself whether the arts, particularly the literary arts, can serve as instrumentalities for this kind of escape, and his answer is affirmative. Even though they may not believe in fictional tales, Montaigne finds that his countrymen can escape into and be carried away by "the laments of fiction; the tears of Dido and Ariadne." He believes (unlike his successors in later centuries) that these fictional emotions move the writer, the actor (and the barrister) just as they do the audience, because the writers and actors share with their audiences the need to escape from their own woes:

> (They are) . . . like those men who are hired at funerals to assist at the ceremonial of mourning, who sell their tears and grief by weight and measure; for although they are stirred by borrowed emotions . . . they are often quite carried away and affected by genuine melancholy.

In a tentative and exploratory way, Montaigne also turned his attention to the problem of the various levels of art, and, as many social philosophers after him (including our contemporaries), finds much in common between folk and high art, if not in essence in form:

> The simple peasants are honest people, and honest people are the philosophers . . . strong and clear natures, enriched with an ample store of useful knowledge. . . . The popular and purely natural poetry has a charm and artlessness in which it may compare in its principal beauty with poetry perfected by art.

He seems to imply that honesty and spontaneity have a beauty all their own, and that this beauty is to be valued nearly as much as the highest forms of art. Both are true, and therefore beautiful expressions. He goes on, then, to castigate the in-betweens, those who despise folk art but are not capable of great art—dangerous, foolish, troublesome people whose products "disturb the world." These are the producers of mediocrity, the "halfbreeds, who despise the first stage (folk art) . . . and have not been able to join the others (great artists), with their seat between two stools." Montaigne thus tentatively established standards for primitive and high art, and places what might be called the forerunners of the mass media into a kind of limbo in-between. His criterion for judgment can probably best be labelled as moral, growing out of the Renaissance ideal of the intertwining of the true and the beautiful.

The Dangers of Diversion: Pascal

One of Montaigne's greatest admirers and searching critics is Blaise Pascal, the great seventeenth-century French philosopher, who, in his most famous work, *Pensées,* often takes issue with his sixteenth century predecessor. Pascal has no quarrel with Montaigne's conviction that man needs diversion, and he too realizes that this need springs from the lack of spiritual belief and other uncertainties of the postfeudal era, "the natural poverty of our feeble and mortal condition."[3] No more than Montaigne does Pascal minimize the force of this drive: men "have a secret instinct which impels them to seek amusement and occupation abroad, and which arises from the sense of their constant unhappiness."

But whereas Montaigne justified entertainment and art (high and low, if not middle), or at least accepted it as an inevitable response to a deep-seated human need, Pascal finds this kind of escape something to be fought against. Man is impelled to continuous motion, to "noise and stir." But he should fight it, for he is driven to run away from the inner contemplations which can lead to his salvation. Far from alleviating suffering by diversion, Pascal thinks that he has "discovered that all the unhappiness of men arises from one single fact, that they cannot stay quietly in their own chamber." If they did, they "would reflect on what they are, whence they came, and whither they go"; but men are so frivolous, he fears, that "though full of a thousand reasons for weariness, the least thing such as playing billiards" is sufficient to amuse them.

Most dangerous diversion of all in Pascal's view is the theater. It absorbs all our senses and therefore has a great capacity for deceiving man into believing he has all those noble qualities he sees portrayed on the stage: "All great diversions are a threat to the Christian life, but among all those which the world has invented, none is to be feared more than the theater." In a way, Pascal's critique of entertainment (and so far as we know he includes even great art under this category), prefigures one of the most important themes in modern discussions on popular culture: the view that it is a threat to morality, contemplation, and an integrated personality, and that it results in a surrender to mere instrumentalities at the expense of the pursuit of higher goals.

The difference between Montaigne and Pascal, insofar as their ideas have a bearing on those modern discussions, may be summed up as follows: Montaigne stands for a pessimistic conception of man—the demands of human nature cannot be changed, and we must make the best of them; there is no point in denying them gratifications (illusory or real). All we can do is to try to raise somewhat the quality of the cultural products we offer man. Pascal, his inspiration and motivation deeply religious, stands for spiritual progress: the need for entertainment and escape is not ineradicable, man's nobler impulses must be mobilized against it, and heightened consciousness of our inner selves, which we can achieve only in solitude, away from the distractions of entertainment, opens the way to salvation. Pascal's language naturally lends itself to translation into the language of modern reformers and champions of social and cultural change; Montaigne's superficially resembles that of the modern box office manager—"The public wants or needs it"; actually, Montaigne's view goes deeper. He has a keen sense of the audience as participant, and his conception of the function of entertainment leaves no room for the possibility of manipulation or passivity, which later are to become serious problems.

THE ARTIST AND HIS PUBLIC

The lively disputes which played so great a role in French intellectual life between 1650 and 1750, often centered around the question whether the theater, including Racine, Molière, and Corneille, was a frivolous pursuit incompatible with the requirements of morality and religion. By 1800, the problem was obsolete. All over Europe, and especially in Germany, the threater had become an accepted institution. But partly as a result of this firm entrenchment, a new dilemma developed: What should be the relationship between playwright and audience?

Goethe

The seriousness with which this problem was viewed is attested by the fact that Goethe found it necessary to precede his great metaphysical tragedy *Faust* with a "Prelude on the Stage," which deals precisely with the questions whether and to what extent an artist should make concessions to the taste of the populace and its predilection for mere entertainment and relaxation. The "Prelude on the Stage" is presented in the form of a dialogue between two characters identified as the Manager and the Poet. The matter at issue is the character of the works to be presented to the public, and the Manager, who is interested only in box office receipts, has some definite ideas about "art." According to him, the secret of success is quite simple:—"a hash, a stew—easy to invent" will do the trick. The public, the Manager observes cynically, is stupid, and you win its favor by "sheer diffuseness":

> Only by mass you touch the mass; for any
> Will finally his bit select.

When the Poet objects that "such a trade debases," and that to produce "botching work" is inconsistent with the artist's pride and love of truth, the Manager invokes the age-old principle that the end justifies the means, and form and content must be adjusted to the audience:

> A man who some result intends
> Must use the tools that best are fitting.

The material on which the Poet works is the public, says the Manager, and the public is passive: "soft wood is given you for splitting." People come to the theater bored, exhausted, or worst of all "fresh from reading the daily papers." They come "as to a masquerade," their sole motive is curiosity, or (this refers to the ladies) to display their finery. He invites the Poet to have a look at his patrons' faces—"The half are coarse, the half are cold."

Why should you rack, poor foolish bards,
For ends like these, the gracious Muses?
I tell you, give but more—more, ever more.

This dialogue shows how the basic components of the discussions about entertainment changed from the times of Montaigne and Pascal to that of Goethe. The two French writers looked upon entertainment as a means for satisfying the need to escape from inner suffering, a need to be gratified (on a high artistic plain) according to the one, and to be denied gratification in favor of spiritual pursuits according to the other. Here in *Faust* we find the discussion divested of its religious and moral overtones, and three new elements introduced: consciousness of the manipulative factors inherent in entertainment; the role of the business intermediary between artist and public, whose criterion is success and whose goal is economic; and a sense of conflict between the needs of the true artist and the wishes of a mass audience. The Manager implies that the audience will take anything so long as there is sufficient quantity and variety, and he endeavours to convince the Poet that the audience is putty in his hands. But unlike Montaigne, the Manager does not advise the Poet to give his audiences variety because it is psychologically wholesome, but because by providing something for everyone, success is insured (if he thought more money could be earned by moral sermons, the Manager would not hesitate to exhort the Poet to write accordingly). Finally, whereas Montaigne makes no clear-cut distinction between the psychological motives of artist and audience, Goethe seems to see the artist as the spokesman for the high standards of his "trade," and the public in the passive role of consumers. Similarly, when the Poet resists the Manager's exhortations, he does not do so in the name of religious or spiritual values, but in terms of the artist's mission.

This divergence between the interests of the artist and those of the public was later to lead to complete cleavage between the two. But with Goethe, we are only at the beginning of the period which witnessed both the spread of popular newspapers and magazines and an unprecedented flowering of great literature. At this stage, the artist and his audience were still on speaking terms. It is not surprising, then, that we find Goethe, not in any systematic and sustained way, but in passages scattered throughout his writings and extending over his long lifetime, considering such problems as the character of the audience, the nature of the mass media, the problem of artistic standards, and the responsibilities of the artist.

On the Character of the Modern Audience. Goethe both echoes Pascal and foreshadows a fundamental theme in modern criticism of organized entertainment when he complains of the restlessness, the continuous desire for change, novelty and sensation which characterizes the modern audience. "The theater," he says, "like the world in general, is plagued by powerful fashions," and fashion (we might call it fad) consists in adoring something with great abandon, only to "ban it later forever."[4]

Not only the theater, but the newspapers reflect this restlessness:

> We have newspapers for all hours of the day. A clever head could still add a few more. This way everything, what everybody does, wants, writes, even what he plans, is publicly exposed. One can only enjoy oneself, or suffer, for the entertainment of others, and in the greatest rush, this is communicated from house to house, from town to town, from empire to empire and at last from continent to continent.[5]

Goethe is not disturbed because of this restless urge for novelty in itself, but rather because it prevents the kind of ripening that is essential to the creative process—that in the constant reading of newspapers about the events of yesterday, for instance, one "wastes the days and lives from hand to mouth, without creating anything."[6]

A second characteristic of the modern audience noted by Goethe is its passivity. He refers to it in the above-quoted passage from *Faust*, when he has the Manager say to the Poet that the audience "is soft wood given you for splitting." The audience wants to be given pleasure for their money, they have no genuine interest in the message of the play offered them. They "throng into the theater unprepared, they demand what they can enjoy directly. They want to see something, to wonder at something, to laugh, to cry."[7]

Another characteristic of modern mass culture singled out by Goethe is that of conformism. He hints at it in his ironical remarks on the fashionably dressed theater goers, and he anticipates Tocqueville and other social critics such as Toennies in Germany, Ward and Cooley in America, Karl Kraus in Austria, by his insight into the role of newspapers in producing conformism; the so-called free press, he says, is actually contemptuous of the public; seemingly everything is acceptable except dissenting opinion:

> *Come let us print it all*
> *And be busy everywhere;*
> *But no one should stir*
> *Who does not think like we.*[8]

On the Nature of the Mass Media. For Goethe, the art which appeals to the lower instincts of the public is not generically different from esoteric art, but merely "botching work." His characterizations of such artistically inferior products anticipate many of the elements of the modern social critic's characterization of the popular art produced for the mass media. Inferior art, he suggests, aims only at entertainment. "All pleasures, even the theater," Goethe writes in a letter to Schiller dated August 9, 1797, "are only supposed to distract, and the strong affinity of the reading public to periodicals and novels arises out of the very reason that the former always and the latter usually bring distraction into distraction." He understands well the urges of the audience, but refuses to condone those who capitalize on them by offering inferior products; "everyone who fools the public by swimming with the current can count on his success" (letter to Schiller, January 3, 1798). The works of these manipulators of popular taste are indiscriminate in their content; they reproduce the world mechanically, in all of its details, and appeal to the public's lower instincts. The lack of creativity in the common man is partly their fault.[9]

At one point in his career, Goethe planned a project with Schiller which was to involve cataloguing the distinctive characteristics of such inferior art, which they designated as dilettantism. In another letter to Schiller, dated June 22, 1799, Goethe refers to this study of dilettantism as a "project of the greatest importance":

> For the extent to which artists, entrepreneurs, sellers, buyers, and amateurs of every art are steeped in dilettantism, is something I discover to my horror only now, after we have reflected so much on the matter and given the child a name. . . . When we open the sluice gates, we will cause the most unpleasant rows, for we shall flood the whole lovely valley in which quackery has settled so happily. But since the main feature of the quack is *incorrigibility*, and since the contemporary quacks are stricken with a quite bestial arrogance, they will scream that we are spoiling their gardens, and after the waters recede, they will restore everything as it was before, like ants after a downpour. But never mind, they shall be condemned once and for all.

The result of this enterprise is a "Schema on Dilettantism" drafted by Schiller. It consists of a table of all the arts, from poetry to the dance; the usefulness and harmfulness of each are indicated in separate columns. A glance at this table reveals at once that the writer had a hard time trying to fill the "useful" column. For instance, under music, the beneficent effects include "whiling away the time," "sociability," "gallantry," whereas the corresponding "harmful squares" are filled out with phrases such as "emptiness of thought," "lack of neighborliness," "strumming." Under poetry we find in the "harmful" column such descriptions as "platitudes," "awkwardness," and "mediocrity." The *Schemata* never went beyond the draft stage, but it is clear from the context that it represents an attempt to judge what we would today call popular culture from the point of view of classical humanistic aesthetics.

On Artistic Standards. In the eighteenth century the artist produced for a relatively small, cultivated public whose needs and tastes were fairly uniform; at the beginning of the nineteenth century, a new, much larger public, which foreshadows the modern audience for the mass media, is clamoring for attention, and this fact confronts the artist with new problems, the most important of which is that of "true" standards. As Goethe remarks in *Xenien,* "Formerly there was one taste, now there are many tastes. But tell me, where are those tastes tasted?"

The problems of standards occupies a central place in modern discussions about popular culture, and it is invariably connected with the problem of the influence of public taste on the character of the mass products. We find in these discussions some of the arguments advanced by Goethe's Manager. Some tend to believe that prevalent standards originate in the dispositions and needs of the public, and seek to determine some invariable elements in the public taste, elements that reflect basic unchangeable features of human nature. Others claim that public taste is not a spontaneous but an artificial product, and that it is determined by political or economic vested interests which, via the mass media, manipulate the consumers' fantasies and frustrations for specific selfish purposes. There are also those who defend an intermediate position: standards of taste, according to them, are determined as a result of an interplay of these two sets of forces.

Goethe speaks for the artist, and his own position with regard to standards is quite clear: he represents the humanistic tradition which places responsibility for the fate of culture and individual morality in the hands of the intellectual elite. This elite betrays its mission when it plays up to the cheap instincts of the populace by producing inferior books and vulgar plays. In other words, Goethe does not ask how the writer could go about gaining the attention of a large public, but the opposite: how can the public be persuaded to undertake the intellectual effort required by true art, and what can the artist himself do to facilitate the process. Like many artists and theoreticians since the Renaissance, Goethe felt that the specific function of art, as contrasted with religion, philosophy, and the sciences, is to stimulate productive imagination. One of the implications of his criticism of cheap art as being too literal, as catering to specific emotional needs, is precisely, as we have seen, that it hinders creativity. In his essay on the Weimar Court Theater, he insists that the public "should not be treated as rabble," and that in selecting plays for performance the guiding purpose should not be catering to the public's *needs,* but encouragement of imagination and contemplation: the playgoer should be made to feel, Goethe says, "like a tourist, who does not find all the comforts of home in the strange places which he visits for his instructions and enjoyment."[10]

In his emphasis on this function of art, Goethe is in agreement with his countryman Lessing, the poet, dramatist and critic, who was also keenly interested in the development of the German theater. In his *Laocoon*[11] and *Hamburg Dramaturgie,*[12] Lessing devoted several pages to a discussion of the differences between genuine art and imitative art. He explicitly condemns artistic works that fail to leave scope for the audience's imagination. He attacks the conception (ascribed to an ancient writer) according to which painting should be silent poetry, and poetry, speaking painting. Such a conception, he observes, would paralyze the imagination of temporal relationships in the case of poetry and the imagination of spatial relationships in the case of painting. Realizing that it is more difficult for the painter and sculptor to appeal to the imagination than it is for the writer or playwright, Lessing recommends that they portray "the most fertile moment," i.e., the moment that affords an optimum of free scope for imagining what precedes and what follows the action represented in a painting or a sculpted figure. "The more we see, the more we must be able to add by thinking. The more we add by thinking, the more must we believe to see." Similarly, according to Lessing, dramatists who like Racine or Voltaire portray rigid types are inferior to the ancients and to Shakespeare who portray characters in the process of development, and enable the spectator to identify himself with them.

Needless to say, the danger discerned by Lessing and Goethe has become more acute with the advent of the more modern media.[13] A little epigram by Goethe could be applied almost verbatim to television:

> *Talking a lot of nonsense,*
> *Or even writing it,*
> *Will kill neither body nor soul,*
> *Everything will remain unchanged.*
> *But nonsense, placed before the eyes*
> *Has a magical right:*
> *Because it fetters the senses*
> *The mind remains a vassal.*[14]

Goethe believes, then, that the more a given work of art occupies the senses of the audience, the less scope is left for the imagination; in this respect, the impact of a bad book is infinitely less than the impact of a bad spectacle that appeals simultaneously to the eye, and the ear, and that reduces the spectator to almost complete passivity.[15] In sum, he is uncompromising in his standards for art and the artist; his suggestions are confined to efforts to improve the repertoire of the theater, and to raise the intellectual level of the audience. Unlike later writers such as the French novelist Gustave Flaubert, who view the rising influence of the populace with despair and expect the end of civilization, Goethe implicitly condemns the artist who withdraws to his ivory tower. He once said in a conversation that only in decadent ages do artists and poets become self-centered, while in ages of progress the creative mind is always concerned with the outer world ("Conversations with Eckerman," January 29, 1826). At no point, however, must the artist stoop to the public; he serves it best by retaining full freedom, by following only his own inner voice. In his essay on experimentation, Goethe compares the artist with the scientist, whose conclusions must be continually submitted to the public, while "the artist may be well advised to keep his work to himself till it is completed, because no one can readily help him or advise him with it."

Schiller and the Social Role of Aesthetic Experience

Throughout his discussions of the problems of the artist in relation to society, Goethe, as we have seen, maintained an olympic detachment toward immediate social and political problems. Friedrich Schiller, on the other hand, was a true son of the French Revolution, and in both his artistic and theoretical works he paid enthusiastic tribute to its political achievements. His central concern was with the development of a "moral" society, and his studies on aesthetics, as well as his analysis of the roles of art and popular culture, are all concerned with the problems to be overcome in the attainment of such a society. While a detailed, systematic analysis of Schiller's writings would be most rewarding for our purposes, we must confine ourselves here to a mere outline of his conception of the central role of artistic experience in attaining an ideal state.[16]

The Experience of Beauty as the Means to the "Good" Life. Schiller did not believe that the individual is caught in a struggle between evil and good forces within himself, but rather that man in all cases would "prefer the good because it is good," providing it does not entail trouble or exclude the agreeable. Man knows within himself what moral goodness is, and it is not innate evil forces but simply our sensuous desires for comfort and pleasure which prevent us from attaining it:

Thus in reality, all moral action seems to have no other principle than a conflict between the good and agreeable; or, that which comes to the same thing, between desire and reason; the *force* of our sensuous instincts on one side, and, on the other side the feebleness of will, the moral faculty; such, apparently, is the source of all our faults.[17]

Schiller did not believe that this conflict could or should be resolved by a victory of one of these forces over the other; if, for instance, human life were organized only on the basis of the gratification of instincts, we would achieve the state described by Hobbes which (according to Schiller) would "only make society possible by subduing nature through nature." On the other hand, he did not believe a moral state such as that of Rousseau, which orders the individual to subordinate himself to the general will, could be achieved, for such a state, though on a higher plane, would negate individual freedom. The only acceptable state would be one in which the freedom of each individual is fully preserved without destroying the freedom of others, and this state, Schiller believed, can come into being through an aesthetic experience which utilizes and reconciles the two forces in man, namely, the experience of beauty.

This experience of beauty can be enjoyed through great art and it produces, Schiller believed, both individual and social blessings. On the individual level, the perception of beauty involves and unifies man's sensuous and spiritual beings, aspects of himself which are otherwise often conflicting and unreconcilable. On the social level, genuine aesthetic experience is the only form of communication which has a unifying rather than a dividing effect (all other forms of communication grow only out of self-interest and appeal only to self-interest):

It is only the perception of beauty that makes of him an entirety, because it demands the cooperation of his two natures. All other forms of communication divide society, because they apply exclusively either to the receptivity or to the private activity of its members. . . . The aesthetic communication alone unites society, because it applies to what is common to all its members.

Today, with inferior artistic products dominating our communications, this seems an almost utopian idea. Even for Schiller the dangers threatening genuine art (which he believed to be the only source of true beauty) by the increasing demands of an industrialized society were a matter for great concern.

The Problem of Mediocre Art. Schiller recognized that as society became more mechanized, it made harsher demands on the life of the individual. These demands exhaust both mind and body, and man therefore requires rest and relaxation in his leisure-time:

> Now labour makes rest a sensible want, much more imperious than that of the moral nature; for physical nature must be satisfied before the mind can show its requirements.

Beauty, it is true,

> . . . addresses all the faculties of man and can only be appreciated if a man employs fully all his strength. He must bring to it an open sense, a broad heart, a spirit full of freshness.

Mediocre art, however, makes no such demands, he goes on. It does not quicken but merely suspends thought:

> After this, can one wonder at the success of mediocre talents . . . ? Or the bitter anger of small minds against true energetic beauty? They reckon on finding therein a congenial recreation and regret to discover that a display of strength is required to which they are unequal.

Here Schiller describes what might be called the tired businessman's conception of art, and foreshadows those more recent critics who are concerned about the extent to which mediocre artistic products lull the reader, listener or viewer into passivity. Such passivity, in turn, is conducive to the experience and appreciation of form but not of substance.

The over-development of taste (Schiller uses the word as synonymous with a sense for form) can grow out of aesthetic sensualism or from a more elevated appreciation along the lines of the formalistic theory of art (in which beauty consists only in proportion, or in the suitability of the means employed by the artist to the end he pursues). The danger here is that "good taste becomes the sole arbiter," and men merely indulge in an amusing game, becoming "indifferent to reality and finish by giving value to form and appearance only." Man realizes his highest potential only when he gives free play to all of his forces. He must not let himself become beguiled into thinking that because taste (or sense for form) has successfully replaced or suppressed his instinctual drives that he is free. "Taste," he says, "must never forget that it carries out an order emanating elsewhere."

In discussing the ever new forms offered by a developing culture, Schiller in a way anticipates the modern mass media and the danger that they will, by creating new demands for form, crowd out creative and moral thinking:

> Culture, far from giving us freedom, only develops new necessities as it
> advances; the fetters of the physical close more tightly around us so that
> the fear of loss quenches even the ardent impulse toward improvement.

While recognizing the danger, however, Schiller remains much more
optimistic than we are today. Whereas we are inclined to believe that
the experience of true art and beauty is reserved for exclusive groups,
he is still able to envisage an "aesthetic" state or a state governed by
the concept of beauty, through which all men become free:

> In the midst of the formidable realm of forces and of the sacred empire
> of laws, the aesthetic impulse . . . creates a . . . joyous realm. . . . To give
> freedom through freedom is the fundamental law of this realm.

Here, in essense, is the eighteenth and nineteenth century liberal-idealistic
concept of the potentialities of man, where political, philosophical and
aesthetic theories all converged on the potential of every man for a
spontaneous, productive and creative existence. Schiller, in short, was
aware of, but did not succomb to, the stirrings of modern scepticism
about the opportunities for individual development in a mass society
which were soon to prevail.

LITERATURE FOR THE MASSES: THE ACADEMIC REACTION

Between 1800 and 1830, a great flood of sentimental plays swept the
classics from the German stage, and the literary market was swamped
by a deluge of novels, short stories, popular biographies and almanacs,
all of them written with an eye to the mass reader. Goethe's idea of
reconciling the divergent interests of artist and public by gradually
educating the latter seemed completely utopian under the new conditions.
A new class of writers had arisen who no longer needed to be urged by
managers to produce trash, for they did this of their own accord, to
achieve popularity or simply to make a living. Those writers who were
faithful to their ideals, and who only a short time before had been looked
upon with veneration, were rapidly losing their audiences. The masses
preferred to read cheap imitations of their works, and Goethe himself
was not spared. Commenting much later upon the fate of the *Wanderjahre,*
a German historian of literature writes:

> When Goethe's *Wanderjahre* appeared, it caused only disappointment, even
> among the few who still regarded Goethe as the greatest among the great.
> . . . And a Pastor Pustkuchen of Westphalia could publish an "improved"
> version or parody of the *Wanderjahre,* which sold more copies and found

more readers than Goethe's own book. It almost seemed to the burgher who had in the meantime acquired a liberal outlook that Goethe, whom his father had worshipped as a hero, was but a glorified lackey and little more. What was almost the whole nation had twice hailed Goethe with unanimous approval, first on the publication of *Werther,* and perhaps also when the first part of *Faust* saw the light of day. Later only a minority followed him, a very small minority, and then finally the pack began to bark after him.[18]

This historian clearly relates the change of public taste to the change in the political outlook of the German burgher, who by rejecting the hero worshipped by the preceding generation, affirmed his right to follow his own inclinations instead of bowing to higher authority. The reaction of professional critics who witnessed this development, and who represented the point of view of the educated minority, seems to confirm his view.

One of these early critics, Herman Marggraff, speaks of the new writers as intruders who desecrate the lofty temple of literature, whose very presence is a threat to German culture. For one thing, the new literature aimed only at entertainment:

Literature at that time disintegrated into mere writing for entertainment— long and short novels, short stories, and short short stories. The process was almost frightening, it seriously threatened to undermine the national significance of literature. The magazines were brimming with this merely novelistic, merely entertaining type of writing. One writer always imitated another.[19]

Marggraff found another reason for condemning these writers in their obviously successful attempts to appeal to the lowest instincts of the public. He was particularly indignant when he discussed *Mimili,* a best-selling novel by Clauren, which was published in 1816. Like so many other best-sellers, this novel and its author have long since fallen into oblivion, but judging from reports by contemporary critics, its heroine, with her deep red lips, peaches-and-cream complexion, and perfect manners, deeply impressed the good German burghers. Although Mimili cannot of course compete with Amber, she had and showed enough charms to arouse the admiration of the book-buying public, if not that of austere lovers of good literature:

The reader is warned that we are now in the period in which the authors of almanacs and the late Clauren are leading the dance of literature. Mediocrity, naked, unadorned, wanton, with its paunch, wallowed on the slovenly couch of literature and on the boards of the stage. There it stretched itself and blinked its eyes, and molded, with the very soft wax of language, delicate little figures with kissable lips and velvety cheeks, with dainty calves and lovely legs that could be seen as far as the garters, for Mimili's frock was rather short; and quite a good deal of the bosom could be seen for the bodice was cut low.[20]

Marggraff also speaks with great scorn of the commercial methods used to spread this kind of literature. He referred to its publishers as "dealers in literary knicknacks," who, to make their merchandise attractive to their customers sold it in the form of almanacs that bore fanciful titles such as "Tulips, Roses, Carnations, Amaranths, or Forget-me-nots." Moreover, even as early as the 1830s, more modern methods of advertising were in vogue, which, like today's television programs, associated literary favorites with products of the dry goods or food industries.[21]

Even authentic writers, such as Tieck and Hoffmann, succumbed to the new fashion, and wrote for almanacs. Only a very small minority appreciated these writers for their notable literary qualities. Commenting on the reaction to Hoffmann, Marggraff says:

Everyone else read him for pleasure and as an aid to digestion. . . . No one suspected the sad gulf that lay between the inspired writer and his unresponsive male readers or sentimental female readers, whose sole purpose was to feel shudders running down their spines.[22]

Such laments and irate pronouncements from the champions of great art proved of no avail. A generation after Marggraff, popular literature was flourishing more than ever. Critics still viewed the development with righteous indignation, although their feelings seemed to be somewhat tempered by the realization that they could do little about it. G. G. Gervinus, whose five-volume *History of German Belles-Lettres* enjoyed a wide reputation in his time, wrote:

The manufactured goods are so inexpensive, and so indispensable for domestic use, that it is impossible to fix any barrier high enough to stop their flow once the intellectual consumption of these goods has become as widespread as it is in our country. When such products have been in circulation for a few years, they remain saleable without any basic change in their design, and are considered all the more distinguished and fashionable.[23]

In addition to the force of habit or inertia, Gervinus mentions the need for relaxation which according to him accounted for the vogue of cheap literature. He recognizes with regret that the tired businessman cannot be expected to make the necessary effort to ascend the lofty peaks of Parnassus:

> We, men, caught in the monotonous routine of business activities, need relaxation, and ultimately we should regard it as a sign of culture and of good sense that, after performing labors that dull the mind, we should seek intellectual refreshment. We do not wish to be unfair to reading done for entertainment. It is undeniable that such reading is necessary: we cannot banish from our lives the toil that makes us incapable of effort during leisure hours. However, when we realize that authentic literature declined suddenly almost before it had had time to flower, we can scarcely repress our displeasure at seeing once more confirmed a fact that we had suspected from the outset, namely, that the scaling down of literature to the demand of the masses has everywhere stood in the way of the highest achievements.

Unlike Schiller, whom Gervinus echoes here (no doubt unwittingly), he sees no way out of the dilemma. The hope that the multitude will be aesthetically educated has lost out to the conviction that great art will forever remain inaccessible to the broad public. The genuine artist must comfort himself with the thought that his work will remain immortal, while popular products remain beneath the dignity of even the literary historian:

> Those who consider the situation historically will find that this quotidian literature stands in the same relation to true creative writing as private life to public events. It is natural for the historian to disregard the former. . . . Likewise, it is natural for us to ignore these private literary colations although they outrank in size the tree of authentic literature, and to take the part of the immortal against the ephemeral. History has always been compelled to make such a choice.

Gervinus suggests still another cause for the decay of literary standards—a cause that has nothing to do with the poor taste of the public, but which stems from the very nature of artistic creation. At a certain point in its development, fine literature appears to have exhausted its supply of lofty subjects; it becomes tired and turns to more earthy matters. As Gervinus puts it:

> After treating all of the great subjects pertaining to public life, fine literature seized upon the whole range of subjects pertaining to social life in the narrower sense, and to private life. History does not concern itself with this domain: it deals only with the seeds which are planted at the proper time in the public soil of a national culture and which come to their appointed fruition. The rank weeds that grow wild in this soil are of interest

to the historian of literature only as he observes that they divert nourishing juices from the truly valuable crops.[24]

The above statement, which implicitly formulates a criterion of literary value based on subject matter, suggests that not only melodramatic trash but also naturalistic novels seem to be excluded from the well-trimmed garden of belles lettres. But the naturalistic novel reached Germany only in the 1880s, that is, after the time of Gervinus, and we cannot be sure whether he would have condemned it as a "rank weed." What seems certain, however, is that his negative reaction to popular writing is largely determined by his rigid adherence to the standards of art established by the classics. He regards these standards as fixed, eternal canons of aesthetics, and every violation is a manifestation of the coarser side of human nature, of weakness or evil, a wild growth that should be rejected. At no point does Gervinus—or for that matter any German historian of literature or the nineteenth century—attempt to analyze the relationship between popular entertainment and genuine art in objective sociological terms.[25]

The social horizon of these historians was severely limited, largely because they lived in a period when political expression was muzzled. They had no influence whatsoever in the conduct of public affairs, and saw the new development as something that was taking place within the separate domain of literature. Indeed, the very violence of their condemnation of literary trash may reflect their frustration arising from lack of outlets for social criticism. However that may be, the reaction to the rise of popular literature which they represent is by no means confined to Germany or to the nineteenth century. Historians of literature and professional critics in all countries—this class of champions of an aesthetic canon (which incidentally is rarely defined)—arose simultaneously with the class of writers for mass consumption. Their intellectual successors have continued to this day to condemn popular media, whether in the form of pulp literature or radio serials, on grounds similar to those adduced by the German critics quoted in this chapter. This would not be worth noting, perhaps, were it not that modern academic critics often propound the old truths as though they were being said for the very first time. To account for this monotony, we must infer that either the character of popular audiences has not changed, and that they are today as exposed to the temptations of vulgarity, escape, and passive enjoyment as they were a century and a half ago, or that academic criticism cannot by its very nature broaden its perspective to encompass popular media. These alternatives are of course not exclusive of each other, and they may very well both be true.

"CULTURE WORKS DIFFERENTLY"

Whereas in Germany the reaction to the tide of popular literature was largely confined to academic dismay and a sense of futility, a different attitude came to the fore in other countries, one reflecting a broader social outlook and greater political freedom. Particularly in England, critics of popular art, while rejecting it on aesthetic grounds, tended to see in it only one of many manifestations of deeper social forces.

This new attitude was formulated as early as 1800—the tide of popular writing hit England several decades before it had reached Germany—in William Wordsworth's famous preface to the second edition of his *Lyrical Ballads*. The great English poet voiced his alarm about the extent to which the "beauty and dignity" represented in true art was threatened by "frantic novels, sickly and stupid German tragedies and the deluge of idle and extravagant stories in verse." In analyzing the spread of this popular literature, he makes use of a psychological construct which by now has become familiar to us: the need of modern man for "gross and violent stimulants" tends "to blunt the discriminating powers of the mind," whereas the function of true art is to stimulate these powers. Popular literature reduces people to an attitude of passivity or, in the words of Wordsworth, to "a state of almost savage torpor." He finds these predispositions activated by social change, by "the great national events which are daily taking place, and which the increasing accumulation of intelligence hourly gratifies."[26] In the same context, Wordsworth says that his own works are a modest endeavor to "counteract the new degrading tendencies."

The few sentences quoted here contain in embryo almost all of the themes that characterize English criticism as compared with nineteenth century German criticism of popular culture: the concern about art is subordinated to the concern about culture as a whole; attention is focused on institutionalized social pressures; the threat of conformism is particularly emphasized; and an attempt is made to account for the audience's attitude not on the basis of some kind of inborn tendency to passivity, inertia or debased instincts, but as the natural result of social pressures. Finally, these critics believe that great art can counteract the bad effects of increasing industrialization.

Matthew Arnold is perhaps the most eloquent spokesman among the English critics. In contrast to Wordsworth, and reminiscent of Pascal, his concern is more with spiritual than with aesthetic values: what for Wordsworth is "beauty and dignity" is for him "spirituality and sweetness and light."[27] Where Wordsworth evokes Shakespeare and Milton, Arnold points to Lessing and Herder as writers who broaden the basis for life by diffusing "sweetness and light to make reason and the Will of God prevail." He is deeply troubled lest the rapid spread of industrialization overwhelm "culture," which for him is the "idea of perfection as an inward condition of the mind and spirit." This role of true culture, he believes, is more essential to mankind than ever before:

> This function is particularly important in our modern world of which the whole of civilization is, to a much greater degree than the civilizations of Greece and Rome, mechanical and external and tends constantly to become more so. . . . Faith in machinery . . . is our besetting danger.

Having thus juxtaposed cultural goals against concern with industrial progress, Arnold goes on to deal with specific phenomena of popular culture. Not unlike Pascal (or, for that matter, the social critics in modern "little" magazines), he deals with the games, sports and mass media as various manifestations of the same trend away from the true essence of life:

> The result of all the games and sports which occupy the passing generation of boys and young men may be the establishment of a better physical type for the future to work with. . . . Our generation of boys and young men is in the meantime sacrificed.

In the same context, he attacks the producers of literature for mass consumption:

> Plenty of people will try to give the masses, as they call them, an intellectual food prepared and adapted in the way they think proper for the actual condition of the masses. The ordinary popular literature is an example of this way of working on the masses.

Such manipulation, he believes, is incompatible with culture which "works differently." He, too, singles out the newspaper (particularly the American newspaper) for special attack, and finds its pragmatism the very opposite to culture:

> Because to enable and stir up people to read their Bible and the newspapers and to get a practical knowledge of their business does not serve the higher spiritual life of a nation so much as culture, truly conceived, serves; and the true conception of culture is . . . just what America fails in.

Walter Bagehot, in his treatise on *The English Constitution,* written in 1867, says that the English inclination toward "the outward show of life," its remoteness from "true philosophy" exposes the nation more and more to a style of superficiality and adoration of success. He is concerned lest the values of British aristocracy go completely astray under the pressure of the sorry alliance between professional politicians and professional moneymakers, and he deplores the extent to which this modern idolatry will also be reflected in the writings of the nation:

> It is not true that the reverence for rank—at least for hereditary rank—is as base as the reverence for money. As the world has gone, manner has been half hereditary in certain castes, and manner is one of the fine arts. It is a style of society; it is in the daily spoken intercourse of human beings what the art of literary expression is in their occasional written intercourse.[28]

He goes on to isolate newspaper reading as the only intellectual activity which still finds a broad audience. Just as the classical European or American sociologists (Toennies, Max Weber, Ward or Ross), he points at the newspapers as reinforcements of public opinion, deliberately subservient to specific political and business interests: "Even now a dangerous distinction is given by what is exclusively called public life. The newspapers describe daily and incessantly a certain conspicuous existence; they comment on its characters, recount its details, investigate its motives, anticipate its cause." Referring to the world of politics, he complains that the newspapers "give a precedent and a dignity to that world which they do not give to any other," whereas "the literary world, the scientific world, the philosophical world, not only are not comparable in dignity to the political world but in comparison are hardly worthy at all. The newspaper makes no mention of them and could not mention them." Bagehot, quite in line with German idealistic thinking as developed by Schiller, believes that the source of this inclination rests with the producers, not with the consumers, who, however, are eventually seduced:

> As are the papers, so are the readers; they, by irresistible sequence and association, believe that those people who constantly figure in the papers are cleverer, abler, or, at any rate, somewhat higher than other people.... English politicians ... are the actors on the scene, and it is hard for the admiring spectators not to believe that the admired actor is greater than themselves.

Bagehot is completely steeped in the traditional discussion about the irreconcilable contrasts between true culture and art, on the one hand, and popular products which lower the intellectual and moral standards of a people on the other. In his *Literary Studies,* most of which were written in the 1850s, we find an essay on the Waverly Novels (the German critics too were keenly aware of the entertainment functions of the novels of Scott) in which Bagehot, after having paid oblique praise to the successful manufacturer of novels, comments as follows:

> On the whole, and speaking roughly, these defects in the delineation which Scott has given us of human life are but two. He omits to give us a delineation of the soul. . . . We miss the consecrating power. . . . There are perhaps such things as the love affairs of immortal beings, but no one would learn it from Scott. His heroes and heroines are well dressed for this world, but not for another; there is nothing even in their love which is suitable for immortality. As has been noticed, Scott also omits any delineation of the abstract unworldly intellect. This too might not have been so severe a reproach, considering its undramatic, unanimated nature, if it had stood alone; but taken in connection with the omission which we have just spoken of, it is most important. As the union of sense and romance makes the world of Scott so characteristically agreeable—a fascinating picture of this world in the light in which we like best to dwell on it—so the deficiency in the attenuated, striving intellect, as well as in the supernatural soul, give to the "world" of Scott the cumbrousness and temporality, in short, the materialism, which is characteristic of the world.[29]

Schiller said that a literature which served only to gratify the reader's need for relaxation could not be called art. Bagehot expresses the same idea in different terms; popular literature is to him a literature that lacks moral and intellectual values. He criticizes Scott's novels on the ground that they fail to show the tension between the human soul and the real world, that they remain on the level of the sensuous and agreeable, instead of stressing immortality. Bagehot thus comes close to the point of view of Pascal: art which excludes spiritual and intellectual struggle is not art.[30]

Arnold, Bagehot, and the other critics of the times did not view esoteric artistic production on the one hand, and substitute products seeking the market or popularity on the other, as alternatives. Rather, they formulated a concept of art which made it neither exclusive nor condescending, but, at the same time, it granted no living space to the products of popular culture. What these thinkers believed was that art's and particularly literature's basic function is to bring about the universal liberation of mankind.[31]

Such a concept of art, particularly of literature, as a liberating force, goes far beyond that of the classical humanists of the late eighteenth and early nineteenth centuries whose first concern was the individual, organized society being viewed as an agglomerate of autonomous moral subjects. This newer concept came to the fore after the boundless optimism about the potentialities of the individual had begun to recede, and was rooted in the idea of superimposed social change which in turn would benefit the individual. Curiously enough, writers as different in national origin and literary style as Matthew Arnold and Leo Tolstoy expressed this newer concept in almost the same way when they elaborated on the capacity of the arts and literature to provide the basis for man's emancipation from any sort of social manipulation by conveying ideas of truth and freedom. Their texts are rich (as well as astonishingly similar) in the expression of this concept (see Appendix A for illustrative quotations).[32]

THE SOCIOLOGICAL APPROACH

For all their differences, the academic and the cultural reactions to the rise of mass culture have one important feature in common: both are essentially moralizing, both, that is, hark back to Pascal's religious condemnation of entertainment. The more modern condemnations differ from Pascal's in that they substitute art for religion, but art is here conceived as a kind of divine service to truth and beauty, essentially moral and spiritual in nature. Thus while popular art is depicted as the pursuit of relaxation or the attempt to escape reality, higher art is assumed to be a legitimate and spiritually fruitful pursuit, which ennobles the soul, and raises it to an ideal realm. The causes that induce men to engage in the inferior, nonspiritual activities and the nature of that higher art which is opposed to these activities are conceived in various ways, but in each case, explicitly or implicitly, the spokesmen for the academic and for the cultural approach formulate an injunction, a moral judgment, which amounts to a condemnation of popular art.

It is perhaps no accident that another, third attitude to the new phenomenon was for the first time formulated and applied in the country of Pascal and Montaigne. This new attitude, which we shall call the "sociological," marks, in a sense, a return to Montaigne, to his method of dispassionately studying all human phenomena, with moral judgment suspended. The French intellectual tradition of exploring each new idea to its ultimate consequences and to formulate it in its most extreme form is not alone responsible for the fact that the phenomenon of popular culture was studied in a spirit of dispassionate objectivity in France before any other country. There is also the historical circumstance that in France the political and social struggles of the nineteenth century were fought with the greatest intensity and ideological movements achieved the greatest measure of articulate expression. The numerous upheavals which France underwent after the French Revolution from the Napoleonic dictatorship to the Communist experiment of the Commune of 1871 favored the development of that ironic detachment in the face of social phenomena which is the precondition of a scientific approach.

Alexis de Tocqueville, one of the precursors of the modern social scientist, as early as 1835 analyzed the phenomenon of popular culture and its relationship to literary art in just such a detached scientific spirit. He does not ask whether popular art is good or bad, he merely states that so-called superior forms of art do not find a favorable soil in modern capitalist democracies because men "engaged either in politics or in a profession" have neither time nor mind to allow them more than "to taste occasionally and by stealth the pleasures of mind" which "are considered as a transient and necessary recreation amid the serious labors of life." Men in the American democracy, for instance, "can never acquire a sufficiently intimate knowledge of the art of literature to appreciate its more delicate beauties." Members of an industrialized society are inured "to the struggle, the crosses and the monotony of practical life." Like many sociologists of the preresearch era, he proceeds to infer that predispositions conditioned by the means of earning a living in turn give rise to the need for excitement in leisure time, in order to offset the boredom of the job. Thus he believes that modern man "requires strong emotions, startling passages, truths and errors brilliant enough to rouse them up and to plunge them at once, as if by violence, into the midst of the subject." After having rooted the psychological needs in the groundwork of the economic situation, Tocqueville describes (without, by the way, giving any concrete examples) the literature of the democratic age in terms of the satisfaction of social needs. He believes that no true art or respect for form will be possible, but that:

> Style will frequently be fantastic, incorrect, overburdened, and loose, almost always vehement and bold. Authors will aim at rapidity of execution more than at perfection of detail. Small productions will be more common than bulky books; there will be more wit than erudition, more imagination than profundity; and literary performances will bear marks of an untutored and rude vigor of thought, frequently of great variety and singular fecundity. The object of authors will be to astonish rather than to please, and to stir the passions more than to charm the taste.[33]

His conclusion is pessimistic. He believes that only mass communications will be successful in modern societies, and that they can only be products of popular culture, unrelated to valid intellectual, artistic or moral criteria. The writer, then, becomes part and parcel of a business civilization and is, in his way, just as much a manufacturer of commodities as any other businessman:

> Democracy not only infuses a taste for letters among the trading classes, but introduces a trading spirit into literature. . . . Among democratic nations a writer may flatter himself that he will obtain at a cheap rate a moderate reputation and a large fortune. For this purpose he need not be admired; it is enough that he is liked. The ever increasing crowd of readers and their continual craving for something new ensure the sale of books that nobody much esteems. In democratic times the public frequently treats authors as kings do their courtiers; they enrich and despise them. What more is needed by the venal souls who are born in courts or are worthy to live there? Democratic literature is always infested with a tribe of writers who look upon letters as a mere trade; and for some few great authors who adorn it, you may reckon thousands of idea-mongers.[34]

About two decades later, Tocqueville's countryman, Hippolyte Taine, elaborated on these concepts. The five volumes of his *History of English Literature,* shot through with observations about the relationship of the writer and his public, could be reread today as a sociological classic. The differences between pure art and popularly accepted literature are not as important to him as to his colleagues at home and abroad, and he finds fault with English criticism because it is "always moral, never psychological, bent on exactly measuring the degree of human honesty, ignorant of the mechanism of our sentiments and faculties."[35] This approach to literature comes close to being "applied science." Take, for instance, his analysis of Dickens which consists of three chapters: the first analyzes the life and character of the author, the third, the characters of his novels, while the intermediary chapter is devoted to a phenomenology of the public of Dickens. A few ironical lines from his chapter "The Public" will illustrate how he goes about describing public receptivity for popular literature:

> Plant this talent on English soil; the literary opinion of the country will direct its growth and explain its fruits. For this public opinion is its private opinion; it does not submit to it as to an external constraint, but feels it inwardly as an inner persuasion; it does not hinder, but develops it, and only repeats aloud what it said to itself in a whisper. The counsels of this public taste are somewhat like this; the more powerful because they agree with its natural inclination, and urge upon its special course: "Be moral. All your novels must be such as may be read by young girls. We are practical minds, and we would not have literature corrupt practical life. We believe in family life, and we would not have literature paint the passions which attack family life. We are Protestants, and we have preserved something of the severity of our fathers against enjoyment and passions. Amongst these, love is the worst. Beware of resembling in this respect the most illustrious of our neighbors. Love is the hero of all George Sand's novels. Married or not, she thinks it beautiful, holy, sublime in itself; and

she says so. Don't believe this; and if you do believe it, don't say it. It is a bad example. . . ."[36]

With Taine we have nearly reached the threshold of modern times. Going on to the turn of the century, we find the discussion on art and popular culture centered around two schools: that of Nietzsche and that of Karl Marx. We cannot analyze the approaches of these two schools in any detail, but what both have in common is an attitude of negativism with regard to present-day political and cultural civilization. In a way (at least within our frame of reference), Nietzsche and his school are more radical than the Marxists because of their belief that all intellectual life (including the great work of the past), is besmirched by the pragmatic utilitarianism of modern civilization. In the interests of a higher type of intellectuality and vitality, Nietzsche and his students, above all the Austrian writer, Karl Kraus, reject practically all literary products of the present, finding that their style and language reveal nothing but commercialism, immorality and untruth. Marx himself, who never more than occasionally referred to literature, was still very much steeped in humanistic tradition, differentiating between genuine artists such as Shakespeare, Goethe and Balzac who are devoted to truth, and what he would call lackey literature in the service of the interests of ruling groups.

TOWARD A CLARIFICATION OF THE DISCUSSION

In reviewing the historical background of the controversies on popular culture, we find that the field tends to have been dominated by the Pascalian condemnation of all entertainment. Because most authors we have so far considered have consistently equated popular literature with entertainment, their attitude toward popular culture is, by and large, negative. Even the representatives of what we have called the sociological approach are far from defending popular culture, which at best is considered a necessary evil. How is the other side of the controversy represented?

Because of the intellectual tradition of most critics, we probably cannot expect to discover any champions of "inferior" art as such. A theoretical defense of popular art seems to be possible only in the form of rebuttal, or in the form of questioning of the basic assumptions of the defenders of "genuine" art. For example, one might question prevalent assumptions about the function of high art; one might question the implicit assumptions stemming from Montaigne and Pascal that popular productions serve only to gratify lower needs; finally, since the condemnation of popular products has always been associated with a condemnation of the mass media as such, one might ask whether the mass media are irrevocably doomed to serve as vehicles of inferior products.

Have any of these three potential lines of defense ever been manned? When we try to answer this question, we feel the lack of historical studies most acutely. Not only is there no comprehensive work on the subject, but even those small analyses which do exist are generally unsatisfactory, unsystematic, and often superficial. In this chapter, then, even to a greater extent than in the preceding chapters, we can only hint at the kind of insights and formulations that might be developed in the light of serious historical research.

Questioning of Basic Assumptions about the Function of Art

If the Pascalian idea had been adopted in its original form, not only popular art but all art would have been condemned as distractions which block man's path to individual salvation. Many critics of popular art assume that high art fulfills a purpose other than that of entertainment or escape and belongs on an exalted plane. There are, however, social philosophers (as well as champions of popular art) who have questioned this assumption. If high art is not entertainment, what, they ask, is it? What is its content, its function, its value? No general agreement on these matters has ever been achieved, although a great many philosophies of art have been formulated.

Especially in France, where the most extreme theories of art for art's sake were developed in reaction to the rise of popular art, esoteric art was under attack throughout the nineteenth century, and many French critics regarded movements such as naturalism as a healthful return to popular art. It was certainly awkward to defend so-called art for art's sake on the ground that it performed a moralizing or educational function. In 1901, George Sorel, the French social philosopher whose *Reflections on Violence* profoundly influenced political thought in the twentieth century, wrote *La Valeur Sociale de l'Art* (The Social Value of Art), where he suggests that it would be difficult to defend great art on the grounds of its educational function:

> It would be impossible to find two persons who agree on the educational value of famous works by our contemporaries. This is also true of past works. Thus M. Brunetière [famous French literary historian and critic] even wonders whether *Bajezet* and *Rodogune* [classical tragedies by Corneille] do not contain adventures whose proper place would be in the chronicles of crime and licentiousness.

Arguing in the same book against another French critic, Guyot, who maintained that "true artistic beauty is moralizing in itself and expresses true sociability," Sorel asks ironically: "Should we then assume that there is a true beauty and a false beauty?"

Whether such arguments against high art are valid is beside the point here. No doubt, they were often based on superficial views that took too literally the pronouncements of the defenders of such art. But it is pertinent that writers such as Flaubert, who are generally regarded as champions of the esoteric and who were extreme in their rejections of popular entertainment, held views on art that by no means coincide with those of the academic critics. In his private correspondence where he expresses himself freely, Flaubert often complained about the existing cleavage between the artist and the public. He regarded modern art, including his own, as inferior to Greek art precisely because it reflected this cleavage, and he fervently hoped that some day the situation would change:

> The time for Beauty is over. Mankind may return to it, but it has no use for it as the present. . . . It is beyond the power of human thought today to foresee in what a dazzling intellectual light the works of the future will flower. Meanwhile we are in a shadowy corridor, groping in the dark. We are without a lever. . . . We all lack a basis—literati and scribblers as we are. What's the good of all this? Is our chatter the answer to any need? Between the crowd and ourselves no bond exists. Alas for the crowd; alas for us, especially. . . . But we must, regardless of material things and of mankind, which disavows us, live for our vocation, climb into our ivory tower, and dwell there along with our dreams. [From a letter to Louise Colet, April 24, 1852.]

Such views were alien to the classical age, to Goethe and Schiller, for example, who did not by any means believe that genuine art was incompatible with a function of entertainment. Schiller, for instance, in his *Letters on the Aesthetic Education of Mankind,* to which we have referred earlier in this memorandum, saw the art of the future as the manifestation of what he called the "play instinct," and spontaneity as one of its main characteristics.

The French critics of the naturalistic school, and some of its branches such as the so-called populist movement whose avowed aim was to work toward a new literature that would adequately express modern mass culture, turned against esoteric art the arguments its champions used to condemn popular art, namely, that its main function was to serve entertainment and escape. Art for art's sake, esoteric art, in short nonpopular art, was, in the eyes of those naturalistic critics a luxury, a means of escape—"the private property of a kind of caste of mandarins which jealousy defends it in order to safeguard its privileges," wrote

Henri Poulaille, a novelist who led the populist movement in the late 1920s and early 1930s. He championed an art of the people, for the people, and by the people, an art that would tell the truth, and according to him such an art had a respectable tradition, including such names as Balzac, Hugo, Zola. He condemned popular trash as the means of escape of the poor classes, and was optimistic about the possibilities of a new nonescapist art and the potentialities of the new mass media, which he believed would eventually release literature as a means of escape:

> A simple gramophone record transports us to the Hawaii Islands, to China, to Mexico. We can see on the screen, at a moment's notice, the Fiji Islands, India, Siam. The entire symphony of the world is available to our eyes, to our ears, if we just choose to look or to hear.
>
> Our literature is a thing of the past. It no longer gratifies the need of escape that summons man at every moment. At least it cannot gratify it as well as the modern mechanical discoveries.[37]

Merits of Popular Art

Here again we are confronted with a welter of opinions and arguments, which have never been systematized, and we must confine ourselves to a random sampling. A strong case for at least the historical study of popular art has been made by a renowned scholar, Louis B. Wright, who thoroughly analyzed the Elizabethan age in England. Unlike Gervinus, who refused to admit popular art to his history of literature, Wright thinks that it is an important and fruitful subject of study, and criticizes previous works on Elizabethan England on the ground that "in all that welter of books one subject has been comparatively neglected: the important matter of the average citizen's reading and thinking, his intellectual habits and cultural tastes." Later in the book he observes that study of such matters is important for our understanding of the present time: "If it is desirable to trace the pedigree of the popular culture of modern America, it is possible to find most of its ideology implicit in the middle class thought of Elizabethan England. The historian of American culture must look back to the Renaissance and read widely in the forgotten literature of tradesmen." According to Wright, and this is another important argument in favor of popular art, entertainment is not the sole function of this art: "The bourgeois reader liked to be amused, but more important than the desire for amusement was the demand for information of every conceivable sort."[38]

Other authors have pointed out the possibilities of development inherent in popular art, and even singled out some of its products as equal in value to those "major arts." In 1924, Gilbert Seldes made a strenuous and sophisticated effort to introduce the popular arts—comics, movies, vaudeville, etc.—into the Parnassus of respectable, time-honored art. Referring to comics, for example, he says:

> Krazy Kat, the daily comic strip of George Herriman is, to me, the most amusing and fantastic and satisfactory work of art produced in America today. With those who hold that a comic strip cannot be a work of art I shall not traffic. The qualities of Krazy Kat are irony and fantasy—exactly the same, it would appear, as distinguish *The Revolt of the Angels;* it is wholly beside the point to indicate a preference for the work of Anatole France, which is in the great line, in the major arts. It happens that in America irony and fantasy are practised in the major arts by only one or two men, producing high-class trash; and Mr. Herriman, working in a despised medium, without an atom of pretentiousness, is day after day producing something essentially fine. It is the result of a naive sensibility rather like that of the *douanier* Rousseau; it does not lack intelligence, because it is a thought-out, a constructed piece of work. In the second order of the world's art it is superbly first rate—and a delight![39]

This appraisal of Krazy Kat was echoed by Robert Warshow, in his essay "Krazy Kat" in the *Partisan Review* (November-December 1946), who finds that while most phenomena of "mass art forms" can be dismissed as "Lumpen Culture," "Krazy Kat is as real and important a work of art as any other." It is interesting that in neither case are any serious analyses made within the broader social and moral contexts which we have met in the earlier discussions of these problems.

Artistic Possibilities of Popular Media

As early as 1930, that is fifteen years before the television era, Henri Poulaille, the populist writer whom we quoted in another context, observed that:

> The motion pictures are in the process of destroying the old prejudice of written art, on which all literatures are based. . . . Thanks to the motion pictures, the reader of books restores his contact with objective reality, and soon we shall be able to see the effects of television, which will further continue the training of the senses that was begun by the motion pictures.[40]

More recently René Sudre, another Frenchman, has dealt with the same problem in a provocative study on the potentialities of radio, which deserves somewhat more lengthy discussion because it deals with a great number of relevant problems. It is entitled *The Eighth Art,* and it was published in 1945, when television was still in its infancy. The primary purpose of this book is to show that radio has the potentialities of a new *artistic* medium, and that it can create new artistic values.

After discussing in a dozen chapters the most diversified aspects of radio, from the physical theories of Hertz to the time allocations of news over French radio networks, he challenges those dissidents in modern civilization who condemn radio as the devil's instrument for the elimination of all values of civilization:

> No, culture is not in danger because those in command of radio are public entertainers and not educators. The tendency towards vulgarity and towards the least effort is eternal and radio is not the instrument for which this tendency has waited in order to compromise forever after the work of civilization. With each invention which contributed some pleasure or some new convenience, one has been afraid for the spirit. Photography allegedly damaged the habit of writing letters and the art of style; railroads and trips allegedly endangered meditation; sports alledgedly favored the muscles at the expense of the brain; the automobile, aviation, the cinema allegedly were schools of depravation, etc. No doubt, there was some foundation in those apprehensions and morals have gained nothing by this stunning progress of science. But the ground of human nature never has been touched. The good passions have continued to exist next to the bad. There always have been charitable souls and spirits eager to rise. Upon them civilization depends.[41]

If we analyze Sudre's statement, we find the following problems and concepts in his discussion: the problem of controls; the conflict between entertainment and education; the location of popular tastes in the interplay of entertainment institutions and human nature; the concept of mass communications as one among many elements of a social whole; the apprehension about the survival of values; the interconnection between technological progress and popular culture. In his own cultured way, Sudre illustrates the searching, insecure and not quite consistent attitude which has prevailed in discussions of popular culture through the ages and across the oceans. He begins by making radio an instrument with which to challenge traditional philosophy and psychology:

> The radio confuses the philosophers. What is it that I am not present for the speaker at the microphone while he is present for me? Does presence itself split itself up? This is a very serious psychological problem which Pierre Janet has posed when he analyzes the troubles of inner thought.

He then plunges into an ode to the listener:

> *Beatus solus!* Happy is the solitary man. Less secluded than the man of Pascal, he retreats in order to meditate about his salvation; your (radio's)

devotee lets the world enter into his chamber whenever he pleases. Without removing him from the world you favor this contemplative attitude which becomes a refuge from modern restlessness for an ever growing number of refined people. If he has a family you wisely isolate it by keeping it at home. One assembles around you protecting tubes.

This is indeed a remarkable passage. Without being aware of the controversial aspects of his statement, this French author outlines in a rudimentary form a conceptual framework for some much needed research to explore the socializing or individualizing, integrating or isolating, the family-conserving or family-destroying aspects of residential, electronic entertainment. Furthermore (perhaps unknowingly) he repeats within the context of modern entertainment institutions the concerns of the sixteenth and seventeenth century philosophers about the salutary or damaging effects of diversion. As a matter of fact, to the best of my knowledge, this is the only instance in our time where an author has echoed Pascal's worries about the potential deterioration of the individual under the impact of postmedieval, leisure-time activities.

The author's attempt at introspection on radio listening leads him to formulate two issues which are basic to the popular culture discussion: the relationship between the instruments of mass communications and traditional art forms, and the generic rights of a new medium. In a chapter titled "Radio and Civilization," he defends the radio against professional pessimists who would indict it for "unfavorable and even demoralizing effects on the intellectual habits of the average man, and in a facetious comment he argues against those who characterize radio as a "torrent of noise": "But one could say that a library is an ocean of blackened paper." And he adds: "The radio does in no way do away with our freedom of decision. To turn a button is an operation just as simple as to close a book. We are not condemned to listen continuously." He refuses the thesis (not on the basis of reserarch but of speculation on human nature) that radio drives out the reading of good books or the enjoyment of live theater. "Books of quality which constitute noble nourishment for intelligence or delicate treatment for sensibility are beyond competition."

For our purposes the specific value of Sudre's essay comes to the fore when it is scrutinized for its apparent inconsistency and arbitrariness. After having defended radio for 200 out of 202 pages in philosophical, phenomenological, psychological, technical, aesthetic terms, he turns about on the last two pages and vehemently attacks the universe of radio programs.

If there are frivolous books, pernicious books, there are also heroic books
and sublime books and this compensates. As far as radio is concerned,
one hardly notices any balance. The performance of the Ninth Symphony
or the presentation of some noble literary production does not expiate for
the disturbing stupidity, the chronic lawlessness of many radio programs.

And he goes on to propose a device for improvement which is halfway
between the tradition of a French enlightener and an American tradition-
minded social reformer:

We would wish for radio a permanent observer who would give us something
to think about every day. Actuality is an inexhaustible material for education
if one looks upon it from a moral angle. What one would need is not a
sceptic or pessimistic philosopher, but a man of good will, smiling and
nevertheless manly, who would understand everything but who would not
leave us in despair.

Of television at the time of the writing of this book, relatively little
was known. Still, the alert author throws out in a naive, involved and
partisan fashion some quick judgments on the future of television without
being quite sure that it would ever come to pass. In principle, what he
says here belies everything he has previously expounded as a raison
d'etre for a modern, technological instrument of popular culture. While
radio seems not to be the enemy of imagination, television is:

Will television give us the photographic beauty of certain cinematic productions? We must recall that true art is based on the principle of the
economy of means, namely, to suggest and not to show, not to say everything
but to leave much to the imagination.

What conclusions can be formulated in the light of this brief exploration
of our three possible lines of defense? The answer seems obvious: the
possibility for developing genuine arguments which may lead to some
conclusive answers exists, but by and large the discussion has been
unreal, in the sense that the pros and cons for the most part miss each
other, and that the concepts used in those arguments remain vague,
usually because a historical perspective is lacking. Take, for instance, the
last-mentioned argument advanced by Sudre to justify his pessimistic
view of television, and which seemingly goes back to Lessing's and
Goethe's theory on creative imagination. What Sudre fails to see is that
the concept of imagination is itself relative and determined by the historical
context. Otherwise, if he were consistent he could just as well argue
against the use of color in painting and advocate a return to the cave
drawings. In other words, the principle of artistic economy in question

is defensible only in the relative sense that good art achieves a maximum effect with minimal means, and not in the absolute sense that good art is *defined* by paucity of means. Similar confusions can be detected all along; the very concept of popular literature or art has been used in a variable sense, without regard for historical determinents, as we had occasion to hint before. And it would seem fair to say that the present discussion on popular culture and on the possibilities of the mass media will continue to turn in circles until a new and systematic effort is made to clear the field from confusions, and to make real discussion possible. We certainly cannot do that in this memorandum, but we can perhaps offer some illustrations in terms of a few substantive problems which we have come across in this review.

RECAPITULATION IN TERMS OF SELECTED PROBLEMS

It may be useful to conclude this fragmentary survey with a brief summary of a few of the specific problems which have turned up repeatedly. Again we can only be tentative, for in this memorandum we have merely passed the narrow beam of a flashlight over a vast area; nevertheless, even these few glimpses suggest that most of the problems raised by the existence of the modern mass media of communication have been with us throughout modern history, now in this guise, now in that, each time expressed in different language, and each time with a new emphasis, reflecting a given social configuration.

The Psychological Problem

The basic concepts which Montaigne was the first to introduce in order to account for the need and the function of entertainment—variety, escape, identification—can all still be found in present-day discussions. But their meanings have undergone a basic change, which to some extent can be related to the growing differentiation between the consumer and producer of artistic or quasi-artistic products serving the need of entertainment. In a modern context it is no longer possible to view these concepts as psychological attributes of the audience, spontaneously generated, for the factor of manipulation has assumed increasing importance. Today, any discussion of entertainment per se which does not take into account its close interrelationship with advertising or ideological propaganda would miss essential elements of the problem. This is not to say that spontaneity no longer exists, but rather that the relation between spontaneity and manipulation, between activity and passivity, has become problematic. The question has become further complicated through the fact that certain functions allegedly performed by entertainment have become so radically changed that one may legitimately ask whether the terms used to describe them still have any meaning. Throughout our review we have seen much discussion on the need for distraction through variety: does the mass audience of media such as radio, television, or the pulp magazines really get "variety"? Or are we confronted today with a problem that Montaigne does not seem to have suspected, that of satiation leading, possibly, to sensory and intellectual numbness on the one hand, and yet more restlessness on the other?

Whatever modern answers have been given to this or similar questions are far from satisfactory. Lack of historical perspective also seems to vitiate other concepts introduced to account for modern mass phenomena, concepts such as those of passivity or conformism. Is a modern radio listener who whistles the tune of a popular hit any more passive than a seventeenth century peasant who repeated a folk song? Is the modern reader who unconsciously adopts the editorial point of view of his newspaper more conformist than the farmer or housewife of a few centuries ago who listened to and repeated various items of village gossip?

The Moral Problem

Here, too, we have witnessed shift of emphasis and a growing complication. Pascal seems to be the spokesman for an extremist position: just as Plato banished the artists and poets from his ideal state (which incidentally has many totalitarian features), so Pascal banishes all entertainment, diversion, escape, vicarious living, and summons men to devote themselves exclusively to their salvation. At a later period, when the terms of the moral problem change, when the conflict becomes translated into aesthetic categories, and is formulated as that between genuine art and sham art, we again find that the spokesmen for true beauty condemn inferior art or corrupt taste more sharply than the lack of art or bad taste.[42]

The moral problem raised by popular culture is inseparable from the problem of values and standards, and in the modern context, aesthetic standards. (In fact it does not seem too far fetched to wonder whether the direction taken by modern art toward abstraction and esoterism may be partly due to a conscious or unconscious reaction to the nature and effects of popular art.) We have seen that Goethe and Schiller were preoccupied with the problem of standards, and Schiller's definition of true beauty as involving all of man's faculties acquires full meaning only when set against his condemnations of bad art as that which merely relaxes or diverts. The very concept of productive or creative imagination seems to have been formulated in juxtaposition to inferior art. It seems hardly necessary to point out that we have here a domain whose exploration promises to be fruitful in many respects.

Finally, increasing social pressure, and the growing importance of the manipulative factor have modified certain terms of the moral problem as posed by Pascal in the same sense as they have modified the terms of the psychological problem. For instance, some modern writers condemn the so-called escapism of modern popular culture productions not on the ground that they afford escape, but on the ground that they afford only a sham escape, that they serve only to reinforce the individual's subjection to social pressure, his conformism.

The Social Problem

Although the problems of mass communication and popular culture began to be treated from a purely sociological point of view only recently, we have seen that even Montaigne correlates his qualitative differentiations with social groups. From the middle of the nineteenth century onward the discussions of popular culture largely revolved around the opposition between the elite and the masses. Here, too, the emphasis has somewhat shifted. Schiller seeks the aesthetic state; "the establishment and structure of a true political freedom" is, in his opinion, "the most perfect of all works of art," but "to arrive at a solution even in the political problem *the road of aesthetics* must be pursued, because it is through beauty that we arrive at freedom" (emphasis provided). Wordsworth, and Arnold after him, also dreamed of a liberation of mankind through art.

Today we are certainly less ambitious: our hopes are not so great and our concerns are both more modest and practical, by and large limited, as we have seen in our small sampling of current writing on this subject, to the question of how mass media can be used as instruments for encouraging the cultural and educational development of broad segments of the population.

APPENDIX A

LITERATURE OF OTHER (NONLITERARY) MANIFESTATIONS OF POPULAR CULTURE

The role of the mass media is of course but part of an even larger perspective than the literary context in which it is here discussed. It has a history of many centuries and is probably as old as human civilization. We have only to think of the differentiation between esoteric and exoteric religious exercises in early Oriental and Occidental civilizations, of the dichotomy between high and low tragedy and comedy on the stages of ancient Greece and Rome, of the gulf between the philosophizing elites at the estates of Roman emperors and the circuses promoted by the very same elite, of the organized medieval holidays with their hierarchical performances in the cathedral and the folksy entertainments at popular fairs to which the crowd surrendered immediately after participation in the services.

To give an inkling of the diversified literature which would eventually have to be scrutinized to put the discussion of mass media into an even broader context, one might start with a review of the discussions on popular culture in the works of such encyclopedic historians or historical philosophers as Toynbee, Rostovzeff, Burckhardt, Spengler; many publications on the history of toys and games, or works on the modes of life in specific epochs (there are, for instance, any number of books on life in Paris or London in the seventeenth, eighteenth, or nineteenth centuries). The conservative critics of liberalism and its civilization in France, England and Germany during the first half of the nineteenth century would also provide rich sources. The closer one comes to the present-day scene, the richer the sources flow: all the media, printed and otherwise, popular or serious, have been the object of discussions in academic and nonacademic contexts in thousands of publications, and I am not speaking here of research in the specialized sense of the word.

In addition to nonresearch oriented media studies, one would find rich descriptions and speculations about popular culture in books describing quickly changing fads and the changes in fashions and mores between the two last wars. Just to name a few pertaining to America alone: Louis Allen's *Only Yesterday;* Philip Wylie's *Generation of Vipers;* David L. Cohen's *Love in America: An Informal Study of Morals and Manners in American Marriage;* the collection *The Pleasures of the Jazz Age,* edited by William Hodapp, or more historically oriented books, such as Arthur M. Schlesinger's *Learning How to Behave: A Historical Study of American Etiquette Books.* The classic in this field of the description of general mores is perhaps the richly illustrated book on England by Alan Bott, *Our Fathers (1870-1900): Manners and Customs of the Ancient Victorians, A Survey in Pictures and Text of Their History, Morals, Wars, Sports, Inventions and Politics.*

Another particularly interesting type of nonacademic literature in this field is represented by the critique of popular culture in the "little" magazines and in periodicals such as the *New Yorker,* where the writings of the self-styled spokesmen for intellectual and moral purity tend to become in themselves another medium of entertainment for those who, reading their critiques, become vicariously indignant, but the outlet for their indignation, thanks to these writers, is amusement. In a way, such writers, by offering such an outlet, enable their readers to become bystanders in their criticism of social practices. Such an analysis could very well be supplemented by the investigation of cartoons, some of which appear in the high-brow magazines, though more can be found in the syndicated columns of mass-oriented newspapers, making supercilious fun of the new habits of the modern mass communications public.

No review of the broader contexts of popular culture would be complete without reference to the work of the Institute of Social Research, particularly to the writings of Max Horkheimer and T. W. Adorno, who have contributed philosophical and aesthetic analyses on the field as a whole and on specific issues, particularly in the realm of popular music.[43] Finally, André Malraux's three volumes, *Psychologie de l'Art* (Psychology of Art), lately published in a revised and shortened edition under the title: *Les Voix du Silence* (The Voices of Silence), which discusses in many places the relationship between esoteric and popular sculpture and painting, would also have to be analyzed were such a broad context to be delineated.

APPENDIX B

MATTHEW ARNOLD AND LEO TOLSTOY ON THE SOCIAL ROLE OF ART

Matthew Arnold

"Plenty of people will try to indoctrinate the masses with the set of ideas and judgments constituting the creed of their own professions and party. Our religious and political organizations give an example of this way of working on the masses. I condemn neither way; but culture works differently. It does not try to teach down to the level of inferior classes; it does not try to win them for this or that sect of its own, with ready-made judgments and watchwords. It seeks to do away with classes; to make the best that has been thought and known in the world current everywhere; to make all men live in an atmosphere of sweetness and light, where they may use ideas, as it uses them itself, freely—nourished and not bound by them."[44]

Leo Tolstoy

"Art of the future, that is to say, such part of art as will be chosen from among all the art diffused among mankind, will consist, not in transmitting feelings accessible only to members of the rich classes, as is the case today, but in transmitting such feelings as embody the highest religious perception of our times. Only those productions will be considered art which transmit feelings drawing men together in brotherly union, or such universal feelings as can unite all men. Only such art will be chosen, tolerated, approved, and diffused. But art transmitting feelings flowing from antiquated, worn-out religious teaching—Church art, patriotic art, voluptuous art, transmitting feelings of superstitious fear, of pride, of vanity, of ecstatic admiration of national heroes—art exciting exclusive love of one's own people, or sensuality, will be considered bad, harmful art, and will be censured and despised by public opinion. All the rest of art, transmitting feelings accessible only to a section of people, will be considered unimportant, and will be neither blamed nor praised. And the appraisement of art in general will devolve, not, as is now the case, on a separate class of rich people, but on the whole people; so that for a work to be esteemed good, and to be approved of and diffused, it will have to satisfy the demands, not of a few people living in identical and often unnatural conditions, but it will have to satisfy the demands of all those great masses of people who are situated in the natural conditions of laborious life."[45]

NOTES

1. An ideal framework would be very broad indeed, encompassing not only relations of art and entertainment but all elements of popular culture such as manners, customs, fads, games, jokes, and sports, on which even greater masses of material exist. See Appendix A of this chapter.
2. This and the following quotations from Montaigne are from *The Essays of Montaigne,* vol. 2 (Oxford University Press, 1935).
3. These and the following excerpts from Pascal are quoted from his *Pensées* (Everyman's Library, n.d.).
4. Goethe, "Weimarisches Hoftheater," in *Sämtliche Werke* (Stuttgart-Berlin: Jubiläumsausgabe, n.d.), vol. 36.
5. Goethe, *Maxims and Reflections* (1829).
6. Ibid.
7. Goethe, "Weimarisches Hoftheater," op. cit.
8. Goethe, *Zahme Xenien, Sämtliche Werke,* vol. 4.
9. Compare this concept, for instance, with the castigations which the great American sociologist, E.A. Ross, formulated in *Social Control,* around the turn of the century: "The great agencies of Law, Public Opinion, Education, Religion and Literature speed to their utmost in order to fit ignoble and paltry natures to bear the moral strains of our civilization, and perhaps by the very success of their work cancelling the natural advantage of the noble over the base, and thereby slowing up the development of the most splendid qualities of human nature." Edward Alsworth Ross, *Social Control: A Survey of the Foundations of Order* (New York: Macmillan, 1939).
10. Goethe, "Weimarisches Hoftheater," op. cit.
11. Lessing, "The Limits of Painting and Poetry" (1766).

12. Lessing, "Collection of Theater Reviews" (1767-69).
13. To modern critics, the stultifying effects of popular art on the imaginative faculty are no longer a matter for speculation. One of these critics, Randall Jarrell, observes that "the average article in our magazines gives any subject whatsoever the same coat of easy, automatic, 'human interest.'" He contrasts the attitude of Goethe who said that "the author whom a lexicon can keep up with is worth nothing," with that of Somerset Maugham who says that "the finest compliment he ever received was a letter in which one of his readers said: 'I read your novels without having to look up a single word in the dictionary.'" And Jarrell concludes that "popular writing has left nothing to the imagination for so long now that the imagination too has begun to atrophy." Randall Jarrell, *Poetry and the Age,* no. 4, 1953.
14. *Zahme Xenien,* op. cit.
15. The American sociologist William Albig, in his extremely stimulating book, *Public Opinion* (New York, 1939), has discussed this problem by contrasting the possible effects of reading versus motion picture viewing. In his analysis of modern man's "need for more and more stereotypes," he believes that stereotypes presented in the movies "influence opinions about real persons" to a very high degree while "printed descriptions are rarely so vivid." He believes that "superficiality may be disarmingly convincing when provided in pictorial forms. In reading, even at the lowest levels, one may stop to think, or just stop at any point. In the pictures, the tempo of portrayal is mechanically controlled outside the individual. Analysis is thereby discouraged and, indeed, often frustrated. The individual is a more passive recipient than is the case in other means of communication."
16. Lest this over-simplified review unwittingly distort Schiller's breadth of vision, we should perhaps here remind the reader that he was an outstanding student of Kant and an exponent of the German idealistic philosophical school; a notable professional historian; an outstanding dramatist and poet and an intimate associate of Goethe. He has written voluminously on the problems with which we are here concerned, including such essays as: "Letters on the Aesthetic Education of Mankind"; "The Moral Utility of Aesthetic Manners"; "On the Sublime"; "On the Pathetic"; "On Grace and Dignity"; "On the Necessary Limitations in the Use of Beauty of Form"; "Reflections on the Use of the Vulgar and Low Elements in Works of Art"; "Detached Reflections on Different Questions of Aesthetics"; "On Simple and Sentimental Poetry"; "The State as a Moral Institution"; "On the Tragic Art"; "On the Cause of the Pleasure We Derive from Tragic Art"; "On the Cause of the Pleasure We Derive from Tragic Objects"; "Philosophical Letters"; "On the Connection Between the Animal and the Spiritual Nature in Man."
17. These and all subsequent quotations from Schiller are taken from *Essays Aesthetical and Philosophical,* trans. from the German (London: George Bell & Sons, 1875).
18. Eilhard Erich Pauls, *Der Beginn der buergerlichen Zeit* (The Beginnings of Middle-Class Culture) (Lübeck: Otto Quitzow Verlag, 1928).
19. Herman Marggraff, *Deutschlands jüngste Literatur-und-Kulturepoche* (Literature and Culture in Contemporary Germany) (1839), quoted in "Das Biedermeier im Spiegel seiner Zeit" (Stuttgart: Bong, 1913).
20. Ibid.

21. As Pauls later reported: "Walter Scott and Jean Paul, of course, these were the great ones who have survived. Heine jeered: 'All Berlin talks about Walter Scott, who is read and re-read. The ladies go to bed with *Waverly* and get up with Robin Hood.' There was a fabric called Amy Robsart, and a Walter Scott porridge that sold ten pennies a half gallon," *Der Beginn der Buergerlichen,* op. cit.

22. Marggraff, op. cit.

23. This and the following quotations are from G. G. Gervinus, *Geschichte der Deutschen Dichtung* (Leipzig: Engelmann, 1874), vol. 5, 5th edition.

24. Ibid.

25. Only recently have German historians begun to subject German popular literature of the nineteenth century to a more objective analysis. Of particular interest is a small study by Ruth Horovitz, in which she attempts to cast some light on the problem of manipulated taste. *Gartenlaube,* the magazine mentioned in the following quotation, was the German counterpart of our *Saturday Evening Post.* "The writers for *Gartenlaube* who at first wanted to form the taste of their readers, and who later gave expression to their readers' wishes and opinions—to an extent shown by the growing circulation of this magazine—did not come from the social and educational stratum for which they wrote primarily. They were in fact superior to their readers, both socially and culturally. Since the majority of them belonged to the bureaucratic class, they also constituted a stationary axis in the midst of general change, and served as a support and an example to the strata then in the process of disintegration and transformation." *Vom Roman des Jungen Deutschland zum Roman der Gartenlaube* (The Novel—from the Period of Young Germany to the Period of *Gartenlaube*), (Breslau, 1937).

26. Quoted from *An Oxford Anthology of English Prose* (Oxford University Press, 1937).

27. Those and the following quotations are from Matthew Arnold, *Culture and Anarchy* (Cambridge University Press, 1950), (first published in 1869).

28. This and the following quotations are from Walter Bagehot, *The English Constitution,* The World's Classics (Oxford University Press, 1944).

29. Walter Bagehot, *Literary Studies* (Everyman's Library, n.d.), vol. 2.

30. It is interesting to note that John Stuart Mill, whose social and political views are completely opposed to those of Bagehot, also condemned an art dominated by utilitarian values. In his literary essays he praises Coleridge for being "ontological, conservative, religious, concrete, historical and poetic," and attacks Bentham for being "experimental, innovative, infidel, abstract, matter of fact, and essentially prosaic."

31. The contemporary critic, Lionel Trilling, has made the observation that "in the nineteenth century, in this country as in Europe, literature underlay every activity of mind. The scientist, the philosopher, the historian, the theologian, the economist, the social theorist, and even the politician, were required to command literary abilities which would not be thought irrelevant to their respective callings." *The Liberal Imagination: Essays on Literature and Society* (New York: Doubleday, 1953), p. 99.

32. This is the extreme all-or-nothing concept of art, implying that if art be liked by the people it is likely to be no art. In the contemporary discussion of the mass media one can find a quite opposite view, one which sometimes brushes off the art Tolstoy and Arnold discussed on the grounds that it was

not for the people. Such a viewpoint is quite expressly stated, for example, in Coulton Waugh's book on the comics. He asks the question, "Sidestepping for a moment the principal facts that the strips are successful because they are popular entertainment, is any artistic and literary development possible?" His answer is *yes*. And he goes on to say:

> For in the old days the artists and writers and craftsmen were not writing at the behest of the people, but to please small powerful groups, the kings and lords and chieftains, who drew the talent of the time inward towards them and kept it circumscribed within the bounds of their castles and baronies. Much of the fine art of today remains alive only through a similar connection.

> Yet taking civilization as a whole, this ancient process is now in reverse. There is an outward movement. Pictures, entertainment, fun, are beginning to be seen as the rightful possession of all, and the comics join in and reflect this spreading democratization. And if the people's standards are at present lower than those which were set by workers around the seats of the mighty, the people's artists will have the satisfaction of knowing that they are identified with a vast and forward movement, which is giving to everyday folks their right to laugh and flourish under the sun. [Coulton Waugh, *The Comics,* Macmillan, 1947.]

33. Alexis de Tocqueville, *Democracy in America* (New York: Knopf, 1945), vol. 2, ch. 13.
34. Ibid.
35. H. A. Taine, *History of English Literature,* trans. from the French (London: Chatto & Windus, 1886), vol. IV.
36. Ibid.
37. Henri Poulaille, *Nouvel Age Littéraire* (Paris, 1930).
38. Louis B. Wright, *Middle Class Culture in Elizabethan England* (University of North Carolina Press, 1935).
39. Gilbert Seldes, *The Seven Lively Arts* (New York: Harper & Brothers, 1924).
40. Henri Poulaille, op. cit.
41. These and the following quotations are from René Sudre, *Le Huitième Art: mission de la radio* (Paris: Juillard, 1945).
42. The broader problem to be raised here is to what extent the function performed by art serves as a substitute for that formerly performed by religion. Hegel says somewhere that modern man does the equivalent of going to mass when he reads his daily newspaper at breakfast—for the newspaper makes him "feel that he is a part of a greater whole." And as we have seen, Schiller, before Hegel, believed that art was the only legitimate form of social communication, precisely because it served to restore a sense of social unity, of communion among the members of a society increasingly divided by private interests.
43. See, for instance, their joint contribution "Kulturindustrie" (Cultural Industry) in *Dialektik der Aufklaerung* (Amsterdam: Querido Verlag, 1947); and Max Horkheimer, "Art and Mass Culture" in *Studies in Philosophy and Social Science* (1941) vol. 9; or T. W. Adorno "Popular Music" (op. cit.). See also, Walter Benjamin, "L'Oeuvre d'art à l'époque de sa reproduction mecanisée"

(The Work of Art in the Era of its Mechanized Reproduction) in *Zeitschrift für Sozialforschung* (1936), vol. 5.

44. Matthew Arnold, *Culture and Anarchy* (Cambridge University Press, 1950), pp. 69, 70, 71.

45. Leo Tolstoy, *What Is Art?* (London: Walter Scott Publishing Co.), pp. 192, 193. Trans. from the original Russian manuscript.

Excursus A
NOTES ON THE THEATER AND THE SERMON

The following remarks originate in a long-range enterprise of the author to inquire into the history of the social controls of the arts in Western civilization. I have lately become interested in the ideological origins of formal and informal censorship of artistic production. There is no other artistic genre that has uninterruptedly remained the target of social criticism though the sources and scope of power of the criticizing agencies has undergone enormous metamorphosis. I am speaking about the theater, which has continued to be subjected to social and moral criticism by the professional practitioners of the sermon, as well as their self-styled imitators.

Clearly the sociological roots of this tournament change drastically over time, though the sermonizers are consistently legitimizing their position by reference to the verities of Christianity. But to say a word about the drastic sociological differences in this particular controversy on leisure-time culture: for the Church Fathers the theater competes with salvation, and for the puritanic zealots it competes with the needed internalization of work discipline in an unfolding manufacturing and trade economy.

We shall shortly refer to the rather well-researched attacks on the theater during the age of the Restoration and then give some examples of the subterraneous pamphleteering which has gone on since the middle of the eighteenth century, particularly in England and America. Some of the authors of this pamphleteering are hard to identify but they are obviously clergymen or church-going zealots of sectarian Protestant persuasion.

We begin with a reference to the book by Joseph Krutch, *Comedy and Conscience After the Restoration.* Krutch's discussion is, of course, by way of an explanation of the shift from Restoration drama to eighteenth

---

This chapter was written with the assistance of Ina Lawson.

century sentimental comedy. Although his primary interest is in tracing the development of a new genre, he also reports on the debate over the theater as a part of the process of its sociological development. He points out:

> The deep-seated distrust of the theater, which at different times finds more or less passionate expression, is in itself perpetual. It is more deep-rooted than Christianity, and arises as a logical application of the much more ancient doctrine of asceticism. As the seventeenth century controversialist was fond of pointing out, not only did the early Church Fathers thunder against the theater, but the sterner sort of Pagans, from whom surely less was to be expected than from Christians, were at best doubtful concerning it. True, Aristotle wrote a treatise on the drama, but Plato banished the players from the Republic.

Speaking of the Church Fathers, the modern sociologist should at least get the flavor of the style of one of these, as, for example, St. John Chrysostom's attack on the theater, to remain aware of the continuity of ideological positions maintained in the Christian era from the Byzantium of the fourth century to the Boston of the twentieth. In speaking of the Roman spectacles, our Church Father thunders:

> When then wilt thou be sober again, I pray thee, now that the devil is pouring out for thee so much of the strong wine of whoredom, mingling, so many cups of unchastity?
>
> As it is, all things are turned upside down. For whence are they, tell me, that plot against our marriages? Is it not from this theater? Whence are they that dig through into chambers? Is it not from that stage? Comes it not of this, when the wives are contemptible to their husbands? Of this, that the more part are adulterers? So that the subverter of all things is he that goes to the theater; it is he that brings in a grievous tyranny.

And as if he were speaking out against the predecessors of San Francisco's "topless" night-club performers, he continues:

> "What then? I pray thee, are we to overthrow all the laws?" Nay, but it is overthrowing lawlessness, if we do away with these spectacles. For hence are they that make havoc in our cities; hence, for example, are seditions and tumults. For they that are maintained by the dancers, and who sell their own voice to the belly, whose work it is to shout, and to practice every thing that is monstrous, these especially are the men that stir up the populace, that make the tumults in our cities. For youth, when it hath joined hands with idleness, and is brought up in so great evils, becomes fiercer than any wild beast. . . . Comes it not hence, when men are forced to spend without limit on that wicked choir of the devil? And lasciviousness,

whence is that, and its innumerable mischiefs? Thou seest, and it is thou who are subverting our life, by drawing men to these things, while I am recruiting it by putting them down.

To return to Krutch's analysis of the stage controversy in England, he isolates two distinct threads in the debate; one is the ascetic objection, which found its strongest bulwark in Christianity. The Stoic contempt of pleasure became ascetic doctrine in the hands of the Christians, appealing to a less rarified sentiment than did the Stoics. To give up pleasure insured the heavenly reward. This asceticism was fundamentaly opposed not only to bad plays (attacking obscenity, profanity, etc.) but to plays, as such, and to all art. As Krutch describes it, "The more one can withdraw from life, the safer he is. The wise man will, therefore, live in seclusion, and only a madman will . . . seek to increase the temptations by allowing imagination to strengthen his interest in the world."

The second distinct thread in the controversy is the moral objection, constantly in the background, and often joining with the ascetic element in "unstable union." It is Krutch's view that "the movement for the reform of indecency was confused and even hindered by the introduction of a purely ascetic element, and that those who wished to purify the stage were joined in a somewhat unstable union with those who wished to destroy it." Although it is true that Restoration commentary about the theater was less severe than it had been (partly, at least, because of the political bankruptcy of Puritanism), there still exists a body of criticism that preceded Jeremy Collier and his *Short View of the Immorality and Profaneness of the English Stage* (1698) and made him not something unexpected.

By the time Collier appeared, the ground had been well prepared. It is Krutch's contention that Collier was in the tradition of asceticism and that he did not want to reform the stage, but to destroy it. Collier's "authorities" are Aristotle, Cicero, Livy, Tacitus, Valerius Maximus, as well as Spartan legal measures that banished plays completely. Lactantius, Augustine, Ambrose, and the early Church Fathers "are ransacked for all references, weighty or trivial, against the stage or shows. Authorities are piled one upon another in an effort to damn the whole institution on the strength of traditional opposition." The truth is that Collier was essentially narrow in his views and yet achieved such prominence because he arrived at an extremely opportune moment in the history of the English stage, namely, at the height of the clash between the decadent leisure-time culture of the landed gentry and the new values and style of life of an increasingly prosperous class of manufacturers and tradesmen.

So important was Collier's book that books on the stage "became almost a recognized department of literature, and varied from ponderous and unreadable volumes . . . to modest pamphlets." Most of the works of controversy are anonymous, and the names we do have are not as arresting as that of Collier.

The seventeenth century and the first twenty-five years of the eighteenth were fertile ground in England for the controversy over the stage. Every class was addressed through the innumerable works written on this topic, and interest in the controversy cut across a large segment of English society. Krutch says that the audience was familiar with three "classic" questions: Is the theater a permissible institution? Is it its duty to teach morality? Can comedies best teach morality by administering poetic justice? Collier was received favorably by a public already predisposed toward reform, a public which awoke to the realization that Restoration comedy did not express the ideals of the age.

There were two distinct schools of opposition: there were those who spoke from positions within the establishment of Church and society, and there were those who spoke from the fringes of the establishment and as spokesmen of the dissenting, nonconformist religious groups. A particularly rewarding source for religious populist undercurrents which were trying to subvert the entertainment aspects of bourgeois leisure activities may be found in an increasing number of pamphlets which began to appear in England and America after the middle of the eighteenth century and have continued to do so almost to the present time. These writings were characterized by a spirit of dogma, a close reliance on Scriptural interpretations as touchstones for attack, and a deep sense of the continuing tradition of declamatory and exhortatory prose. We shall give a sample of this kind of material.

The anonymous author who wrote *The Stage, the High Road to Hell: Being an Essay on the Pernicious Nature of Theatrical Entertainments* (1767) addressed his work to "the Reverend Mr. Madan." Although the essay itself is not a sermon, it is written in what might be called the exhortatory style. Secular writers, as well as religious ones, who were involved in the theater debate as opponents, had as their prime model the writings of the Church Fathers. They made the Church Fathers models not only for the lines of attack but also for their manner and mode. For over a thousand years the pronouncements of the early Christian writers in this matter received as little elaboration as they did much attention. This is understandable since, for them, the Word of God was changeless through all time and was not subject to worldly fluctuations or critical accretions.

The author of the above work begins by saying that the arts are proof of the degeneracy of the human species, and thus it follows that theatrical art "must surely be allowed to be the height and summit of all corruption, since stage . . . shews a fallen creature to himself, and, by laying before him all the various abuses to which the depravity of his nature has subjected him, renders him still more prone to sin." The author is aware of the support of the theater by those who hold that the presentation of vice upon the stage increases man's distaste for it, but he argues that the stage only presents to man examples of the variety of forms which sin can take. The idea of the theater as education in morality is reversed by the writer; he regards it as education in the varieties of vice. He states further: "I think it can admit of no dispute that dramatic authors have perverted the theater, and done their utmost to increase the temptation to vice, by shewing it in an amiable light." Sin, our author points out, is not only set forth on the stage in all its varieties, but is also made to appear desirable.

As the writer warms to his topic, he turns to an examination of the participants in theatrical production. He tells his reader that playwrights are second only in debauchery to actors, who are no less than "demons in human shape." They are "debauchers," "greater pests of society than murderers"—perhaps an allusion to the Scriptural admonition that those who "kill the body" are less to be feared than those who endanger the life of the soul. No wonder, the writer argues, that acting is considered traditionally a degraded profession, as actors are no more than liars who assume a feigned character. As for English tragedy, it abounds in the most flagrant instances of immorality, "calculated to banish all principle from the minds of the young and inexperienced; to shake the foundations of morality, and introduce the most dangerous skepticism." Even Shakespeare's *Hamlet* concentrates on the theme of revenge, "contrary to the dictates of religion, which expressly forbids the revenging of one crime by the commission of another." Comic writers, he continues, are no better. Dryden is "a monster of all sorts of impurities," Vanbrugh "a man of daring impieties," both of whom ridicule the clergy in their works. Adultery and cuckolding are the constant themes of comedy and are presented in favorable terms.

The diatribe continues and builds to a climax with the description of the French theater. The French stage is the nadir of immorality, for it is in France that homosexuality is rampant in the theater. Molière, says our author, was a homosexual; French figure dancers, as well as Italian singers, are particularly prone to this unspeakable vice. The French demonstrate that the theater breeds corruption in its participants as well as in its audience. And it is recognized as such: In Paris, actors are buried in dunghills and denied the sacrament if they do not renounce the stage. Character assassination of the lowly as well as the illustrious is easily the next step. We are informed that the actor Wilkes debauched a Mrs. Rigers, a clergyman's daughter. As for the remedy the legislature should outlaw the theater and have it closed forever.

We recognize here many of the themes of the Church Fathers. The dramatization of vice increases the incidence of vice in the audience and in the participants. Playwrights and actors join in a demonic onslaught on private and social morality. The tone and style are in the tradition of the Fathers—righteous indignation and moral wrath—also the tradition to seventeenth century puritan pamphleteering. The language is powerful, strong, and direct, written from a point of unassailable virtue. The sexual particulars are, however, a departure from traditional material. Their aim seems to be to present a shock by naming names and pointing fingers, in order to remove any doubts that may linger in the reader's mind. Apparently the "homosexual playwright" is already an idea of some popular currency; the author is not breaking ground on this point but seems to be playing on already established popular tradition. He admits in the dedication that the theme of "the theater as a moral sink" will be an unpopular one, and perhaps the sexual gossip is introduced to familiarize and popularize it. Our author is not above a little sensationalism himself to make a point. The sexual gossip departs from the traditional body of material and may very well be a concession to the times.

Another eighteenth century work, *The Absolute Unlawfulness of the Stage* by William Law (1726), while it follows the general exhortatory style of the first selection, offers a more subtle presentation and is not as gross in manner. It avoids sensational disclosures, and, in a more scholarly manner, uses as its touchstone argument the Scriptural passage, "Let no corrupt communication proceed out of your mouth, but that which is good to the use and edifying."

The emphasis is on the theater as a communication center. Since corrupt communication is forbidden to individuals (and, as the author carefully explains, offends the Holy Ghost) how much more offensive is it to go to a place set apart for that very purpose? I think the use of the word "communications" is significant because the playhouse is, after all, the prime competitor of the Church as a communication center. Elaborating on this theme, he writes that corrupt communication involves the whole unit: the stage and the audience; he also includes "filthy jesting," "ribaldry, prophaneness, rant, and impurity of discourse"—the actual substance of the communication—as a sub-topic in his discussion. He adds that "vile and impure communications" can be hidden in "fine language" so that the spoken word becomes an agent of deception, and the divinely given act of communication is further defiled.

The first selection we considered discussed, as does this one, the idolatry of the theater-goer by relating plays historically to heathen worship. Once again, this writer is more subtle; to kneel before images is bad enough, he writes, but "an image is not so contrary to God as Plays are contrary to the Wisdom . . . of Scripture." It is a more serious offense to sit in the playhouse than to kneel before the voiceless golden calf. Speech is more powerful than images.

Our first writer, in the *High Road to Hell,* wrote: "I am well aware that the piece I now offer to the pubic will meet with but an unfavourable reception, as it opposes the current of their inclinations and condemns their favorite amusements. Conscience, however, forces me to speak, and endeavor to stem the torrent of corruption by a feeble, but well meant opposition."

One hundred years later the rhetoric of tradition that in the eighteenth century was out of step with this world, has been altered. In 1823 David M'Nicoll's *A Rational Enquiry Concerning the Operation of the Stage on the Morals of Society* was published and represents a new direction in the arguments against the theater: "He who fights against the theater, perhaps goes on to dogmatize, as if his own naked opinion were sufficient to give law to the public; and it is well if he does not assume a manner of illogical dictation amounting to overt acts of uncharitableness; and thus his well meant endeavours only injure the cause he means to support." This writer thus criticizes his predecessors and declares himself a "modern" stylist, freed from the religious rhetoric of opposition. Notice the phrase, "assume a manner," which gives us a description of the professional disclaimer of the old style and his deliberate "pose." Heavy-handed pronouncements hurt the cause; moral wrath and divine indignation can too easily be interpreted as "uncharitableness." Exercising a new caution, M'Nicoll represents a softening of the implacable lines of the Church Fathers.

This writer demonstrates in his essay much of the nineteenth century vogue. For example, he gives the opposition a wide berth, such as would have been unthinkable a century earlier. The psychological point of view is being introduced and the entire argumentation has a more secularized flavor. He points out that the simple pleasure of the stage is not to be denied, that reason tells us that immorality must be part of the play itself in order that it achieve some semblance of probability. What is needed to keep things in check is self-censorship: "Have such arts no bounds?" he asks. Then follows a species of nineteenth century sensitivity to "communications," but now it is more elaborate than we saw in

William Law. Wicked language or writing, says M'Nicoll, reaches the understanding; but language used by the "public actor" reaches the passions—a potent force unequalled by the printed word. "History abounds with instances of moral evil; but these are not to be compared with dramatic pictures of this kind." In this pamphlet we find already an awareness of a much more sophisticated and astute variety, of what makes the theater a powerful instrument of communication. The power of the actor upon the public stage is seen as derived from the greater size of his audience, the emotional impact of spoken words, and the sanctity and authority given to public speech by the stage and institution which are the contexts of this form of communication.

M'Nicoll attempts an elementary form of audience analysis. He departs from the view that the theater acts its evil upon innocents and entices them. Rather, his view is that contemporary society is already in a state of corruption: "That society is in a state of actual corruption is indisputable; and the argument is the same, whatever be the origin of the mischief." Therefore, he continues, the inflaming of the passions on a "huge mass of similar corruption . . . adds momentum to an avalanche." Rough estimates of the way in which popular entertainment achieves wide audiences is also taken into consideration: "The stage must conform to the taste of the people. This conformity is not denied but is freely acknowledged, and often used as an exculpation of the poet and player." M'Nicoll, while seemingly basing his argument on the scientivistic mode of reasoning of the nineteenth century, makes his essay a minor compendium of nineteenth century canons of conservative taste. The religious base is discarded almost totally; "reason" has taken its place. M'Nicoll recognizes that "The popularity of the drama leads to monstrous abuses . . . of multitudes of writers being brought into operation, who are nearly destitute of the genius and of the knowledge of mankind, which are necessary to a just conception of character." Here his discussion takes an interesting twist; his argumentation seems closely to approach the utilitarian mood. The theater is not "useful" as an outlet for the men of reason and science; on the contrary, it attracts those pseudo-creative elements in modern society who feed on the need for sensationalism and distraction of the modern audience.

On the possibility of theater reform he states: "Suppose the stage to be completely reformed, and to continue equally popular—a thing impossible in a corrupt state of society—it would then in its fundamental principles be quite another thing compared with the present theater."

And where, we may ask, are the Church Fathers? In the conclusion, M'Nicoll finally turns to them as little more than reference points. There weakened status in the theater debate is obvious as M'Nicoll spends time trying to resolve certain quibbles that have grown up around the Fathers' writings. Is it true (as the opposition says) that the Fathers, in their condemnations of the theater, were really talking only about pantomimes? And is it true that St. Chrysostom used to sleep with Aristophanes under his pillow? And if it is true, does this fact neutralize the validity of his opposition to public acting? Here we see that, deprived of traditional supports, M'Nicoll's essay deals with the Church Fathers in the context of a kind of "sociology of ideology" focussing on the relationship of a man's opinions to his behavior. He expresses some insights into the nature of popular culture which serve only to condemn the theater further, and his generalized commentary on theater mores brands them as morally culpable.

The stage is not without defenders, of course. A contemporary of M'Nicoll named Mansel published, in 1814, his *Free Thoughts upon Methodists, Actors and the Influence of the Stage*. Mansel is among the defenders of what our anonymous author of *High Road to Hell* is among the opposition: he is full of fire and energy, mincing no words, but he has modulated the old-time "wrath" into modern sarcasm and irony. He begins by examining the opposition's formidable traditions: "The Fathers have unequivocally and avowedly proclaimed their opinion violently and diametrically in opposition to the use of the stage. Most of its succeeding adversaries have followed their mode of condemnation. All its present opponents, who embellish themselves with the name of Christian, look up to the early and learned churchmen as precedents for their conduct. It behooves us, therefore, to search more strictly into this enormous . . . display of ecclesiastical vengeance." In an almost Hegelian tone, but definitely in a historicistic mood, he concedes one point—that the Church was correct in condemning the abominations that existed on the stage at the time the Fathers wrote. In addition, he calls into question "the means they adopted to check the profligacy of the thing they condemned." The historical view is joined here by a psychological perspective. As Mansel put it, St. Chrysostom "studied all the dramatic poets," and his famous, eloquent orator borrowed heavily from dramatic writers, while Tertullian had a vivid imagination of his own, to which he was prey. Tertullian, after all, did fall into heresy, and Mansel suggests that his vehemence against the stage was one way he managed to redeem himself. Mansel may be the first writer to call the writings of the Church Fathers "an overwhelming of nonsense and stupidity . . . directed against a sublime art." By insisting on relating the Fathers' views on the theater to the specific historical conditions of their times, and by showing how that condemnation did not mitigate the value of theatrical prose which even the Church Fathers utilized, Mansel seeks to discredit these early Christian writers as spokesmen for modern social values.

Mansel, good scholar that he was, substitutes Addison, Milton, and Johnson as great Christians, moral practitioners, and spiritual spokesmen whose contributions to the stage are testimony enough of its moral fiber. Historical distance worked in Mansel's favor; he could with ease point to the clay feet of the Fathers and the defects revealed in their biographies. Moreover, his defense of the stage had behind it the solid tradition of English belles lettres and the humanistic foundations of the English stage.

The few selections offered here need to be reinforced by additional data covering the history of the controversy. The period 1700 to 1900, for example, has to be studied not only in the light of the changes in the nature of the debate but also with respect to changes in the theater itself. After all, the arguments change in part because of changes in the kinds of theatrical activity, and one cannot overlook the change from Restoration to Sentimental Comedy and then to the plays Tennyson and his contemporaries were producing in mid-nineteenth century. In his context the great fluorescence in the late nineteenth and early twentieth centuries of the Realistic theater also come into play.

Chapter 3
EIGHTEENTH CENTURY ENGLAND:
A CASE STUDY

The purpose of this study is to explore in detail some of the antecedents of the popular culture issues, particularly those generated by the mass media, which we face today. Since its source materials are the works of writers and philosophers, and the background is one of social and economic change in eighteenth century England, this is a chapter of literary as well as of social history. As social scientists, we have ventured somewhat afield to explore what writers in eighteenth century England had to say about problems engendered when literary works began to be produced as marketable commodities.

The eighteenth century in England was selected as the topic for this essay not because a "mass" audience in the modern sense developed in this period—that was to come only in the next century—but because, from that time on, a writer could support himself from the sale of his works to the public. In effect what took place was a shift from private endowment (usually in the form of patronage by the aristocracy) and a limited audience to public endowment and a potentially unlimited audience. At the same time, the production, promotion, and distribution of literary works became profitable enterprises. These changes affected the content as well as the form of literature, and therefore gave rise to many aesthetic and ethical problems. Not all of these problems were new; some had their origins deep in the seventeenth or even in the sixteenth century when there existed a popular audience for the theater. But in the eighteenth century, questions of the potentialities and predispositions of the audience assumed new urgency for the writer because his audience was now the exclusive source of his livelihood.

Section one is devoted to a brief summary, for background purposes, of the new literary forms which emerged during this period. Section two discusses the reactions of the literati to the various audience-building

---

Coauthored with Marjorie Fiske.

devices, largely commercial, which quickly came to dominate the literary marketplace. Section three shows how and why the optimism with which intellectuals initially greeted the increase of writers, readers, and reading materials gradually withered away. Section four analyzes the specific criticisms which intellectuals brought to bear on the new literary products and their audiences. Finally, section five shows how they sought new standards which would be applicable in a literary democracy.

The focus is on how writers experienced and tried to work through these problems—in other words, the eighteenth century literary scene is presented as they saw it. Because the source materials comprise only small segments of the work of the writers with whom we deal, no writer emerges to his full stature. It is our hope, however, that despite such limitations this excursion into an area generally outside the purview of the social sciences, while not yet in itself a theoretical contribution, will provide some of the materials required for the development of a theory of popular culture in our own time.*

THE LITERARY MEDIA

During the first few decades of the eighteenth century, the growing industrialization and urbanization of England, together with the cheaper production of paper and improved methods for producing and distributing literary goods, made reading matter less costly and more easily accessible than it had ever been before. Those who were literate read considerably more than their counterparts in the previous century; women were proving themselves to be particularly avid readers; and literacy was becoming a professional prerequisite for the merchant and shopkeeper classes. By the last quarter of the century even remote villages hired their own schoolmasters, or at least maintained Sunday schools in which the rudiments of reading were taught. Literacy estimates are scarce and unreliable, but it seems reasonable to conclude that from 1700 to 1800 the reading public expanded from one which had included mainly the

*We are indebted to several scholars in English literature and the social sciences for valuable suggestions. The senior author's interest in sociological aspects of art stems from his lifelong associaton with Max Horkheimer and Theodor W. Adorno at the Institute of Social Research. This study was completed while the senior author was a Fellow at the Center for Advanced Study in the Behavioral Sciences. We wish to thank Edgar Rosenberg for his tireless work and incisive criticism, and the administrative and clerical staff of the Center—Mrs. Maria Paasche in particular.

aristocracy, clerics, and scholars to one which also included clerks, artisans, laborers, and farmers.

Despite the fact that new literary products were developing and that commercial competition became intense, each new form, or variation on an old form, found a ready market. In the 1790s, for example, the articulate though not always reliable bookseller Lackington estimated that the sale of books had increased fourfold in twenty years. In a glowing and much-quoted description (which, it should be added, has not gone without challenge from historians), he attributes this increase to the spread of literacy among the lowest socioeconomic groups.

> The poorer sort of farmers, and even the poor country people in general, who before that period spent their winter evenings in relating stories of witches, ghosts, hobgoblins, etc., now shorten the winter nights by hearing their sons and daughters read tales, romances, etc., and on entering their houses, you may see *Tom Jones, Roderick Random,* and other entertaining books, stuck up in their bacon-racks, etc. . . . In short, all ranks and degrees now READ.[1]

Lackington may have been unduly optimistic about the heterogeneity of the audience, but the fact remains that literary production had become more highly differentiated. Many books were designed principally for the female audience; handbooks for young girls were greatly in demand, and toward the last quarter of the century, books were written especially for children. General periodicals almost invariably had sections for the ladies and for youngsters, and in addition there were professional and trade journals for lawyers, farmers, and musicians, as well as for a variety of hobbyists.

Toward mid-century, England experienced an unprecedented spate of encyclopedias, histories, almanacs, and other compendia, some of which were compiled with more attention to sales potential than to accuracy. Eminent writers (as well as many lesser) undertook compilations of one sort or another, usually when in financial straits. Tobias Smollett, for example, wrote a popularized history which met with great success, and did so quite frankly in order to supplement his income. This was certainly not the work of a scholarly historian, and Horace Walpole chided the hungry public to which "seven thousand copies of that trash were instantly sold while at the same time the University of Oxford ventured to print but two thousand of that inimitable work, *Lord Clarendon's Life.*"[2] But Walpole had no qualms about capitalizing on the fad himself; in 1760 he discovered that "natural history is in fashion," and shortly thereafter was at work simultaneously on six different scientific volumes covering such diverse areas as botany and husbandry.[3] Since not all popular science was as sound as his, so many absurd misconceptions of half-truths were spread about that several of the more conscientious magazines ran special columns devoted to correcting them.

This section comprises a brief summary of the growth of printed products and is intended merely to sketch in a background for the ensuing discussion. Three new or practically new forms will be touched upon: the popular novel, the magazine, and the newspaper—the latter two in their modern guise seeing light for the first time at the beginning of the century. A brief review of pertinent features of the stage is also included.

Magazines

It is sometimes difficult to distinguish between the newspapers and the magazines of this period. Both were likely to be folded, two-column, single-sheet folios. At first even their contents were similar: the periodical essayists (who usually edited their own periodicals) contributed features to the newspapers; conversely, many magazines included a great deal of news, often in the form of weekly summaries.

Two major changes took place in the periodical literature: a marked decline in publications supported by political parties or religious groups—the principal types prevailing in the seventeenth century—and a notable increase in magazines supported by a paying readership and by advertising. Indeed, prototypes of nearly all periodicals familiar to us today were to be found in eighteenth century England. The first magazine of miscellany, *The Gentleman's Magazine,* including news, fiction, poetry, social items, puzzles, and advice to the lovelorn, appeared in the third decade. In mid-century, the first fiction magazine designed especially for women readers, *Records of Love for the Fair Sex,* came off the press, and at the same time theatrical journals, weekly news digests, book condensations, and book reviews began to flourish.

At the close of the seventeenth century, the question and answer column had evolved as a successful device for covering a wide variety of topics. The first magazine to adopt this format exclusively was bookseller John Dunton's *Athenian Gazette,* which catered to the public demand for "information" and at the same time promoted the bookseller's wares. Some idea of the scope of these question-and-answers—which were to compose a major feature of most of the variety magazines to follow—may be gleaned from a sampling of the *Athenian Gazette:* What is the best poem which was ever made? Why are rats, toads, ravens, etc., ominous? Was it a sin for Noah to curse his son Ham for seeing his nakedness? Which is greater, the hurt or profit that comes from love? Where is the best place to find a husband? Very often, the questions and answers took the form of letters to and from the editor. On the subject of love, the problems were not very different from those confronted by Dorothy Dix.

> *Ques.* I have by promise of marriage engaged myself to a young lady, and not long after my circumstances obliged me to travel, before which I conjured my mistress to be mindful of her contract with me; she at that time gave as great testimonies of her fidelity as I could desire but it was not long 'ere she entertained another gentleman, and so successful was my Rival, that doubtless he had married her, but being discovered the very night before it was to be put into execution, all their measures were irrecoverably broke, her Relations being bitterly averse thereto. At first knowledge thereof, I did not resolve what to do, but since (after mature consideration) I so resent her Behavior, as I believe I should be as willingly hanged as married to her, therefore I have secured a Discharge in writing, wherein we mutually and voluntarily acquit each other from all the Obligations of matrimony. *Whether my unhappy contract is not void, or how far it obliges me?*
>
> *Ans.* Void, yes; we should be very unhappy creatures, if our vows must be of force, whether the women proved constant or not, for they have their share of Fickleness as well as we; and since your Reason has had the conquest, all you have to do is to pay it such a deference as to follow its advice in a second engagement.[4]

Daniel Defoe's *Weekly Review,* an eight-column, single-sheet periodical first published in February 1704, resembled the late seventeenth century political periodical in many respects. Defoe introduced several come-on devices into his paper, however, and thus paved the way for the variety magazines of later vintage. One of his innovations was a department called "Advice from the Scandalous Club, being a weekly history of nonsense, impertinence, vice and debauchery,"[5] and while Defoe eventually developed a strong distaste for such deliberate bids for popularity, his successors in the periodical field did not share his scruples. There is considerable evidence that the *Review* profited from government subsidies, but Defoe claimed that advertisements constituted its principal means of support. As in the case of most other magazine advertising of the period, promotion of books accounted for about half of all commercially sold space.

At the peak of the success of Defoe's *Review,* Richard Steele hit upon an idea which resulted in a type of periodical unique to the eighteenth

century, *The Tatler*, to be succeeded two years later by the *Spectator**
with Joseph Addison as principal editor and contributor. The *Spectator*,
as *The Tatler* before it, was published daily in the form of single essays
on social and cultural matters. Its tone was serious, its style elegant, and
the fact that it quickly became the most popular journal of its day did
much to contribute to a spirit of optimism about the potentialities of
periodical literature.

The first journal of variety, the *Gentleman's Magazine*, was founded
in 1731 by Edward Cave, a journeyman printer, post-office official, and
one-time author of hand-written news letters. His professed objective
was:

> to give Monthly a View of all the Pieces of the Wit, Humour, or Intelligence,
> daily offer'd to the Publick in the News-Papers, (which of late are so
> multiply'd, as to render it impossible, unless a Man makes it a Business,
> to consult them all).[6]

As Cave's announcement suggests, his was at first a journal made up
largely of extracts or summaries of news and entertainment items featured
in the newspapers or in other magazines. By 1741 it had attained a
circulation of 15,000 and was solvent enough to commission original
material from an impressive array of contributors. Except for a short-
lived excursion into more serious features in the mid-nineteenth century,
it continued to flourish as a magazine of miscellany until 1907.

Imitations of the *Spectator* as of the *Gentleman's Magazine* were
numerous—altogether, in the fifty-year period beginning in 1730, eighty-
one magazines were published in London, Edinburgh, and Dublin.[7] Among
the single-essay magazines notable for their literary quality if not for
their popular appeal were the *Rambler*, published by Samuel Johnson
for two years beginning in 1750, and the *Bee*, published by Oliver
Goldsmith for a few months in 1759. Among the imitators of the
Gentleman's Magazine were several which proved to be less worthy
enterprises than their model, lifting all their material from other newspapers and magazines throughout their usually brief lives. One or two
compounded the parasitism by abstracting and summarizing periodicals
which were in themselves digests of second-hand material.

---

*One of the characters in Richardson's novel *Sir Charles Grandison* distinguishes
between the literature of the late seventeenth and that of the eighteenth century
thus: "The reading in fashion when I was young was Romances. You, my children,
have in that respect fallen into happier days. The present age is greatly obliged
to the authors of the *Spectator*."

Popular Novels

Whereas the single-essay and the miscellany periodicals represented new literary forms, the novel, though not a new genre, found a new popularity, particularly after the middle of the century.

During the first two or three decades, the best-selling works were more likely to have been reprints of seventeenth century romances than new fiction. Translations, notably from the Spanish, supplemented the meager supply of home-grown materials, and the *Arabian Nights* was published in six editions between 1708 and 1725.[8] The few new romances written during this period were dull and feeble, often nothing but poor imitations of the seventeenth century style.

The publication of Defoe's novels in the 1720s, but more particularly of Richardson's *Pamela* in 1740, marked a major change. With these first novels of the middle class the form was given the impetus which has made it a major literary medium ever since. For thirty years after *Pamela*, novels were characterized by a mixture of middle-class realism and sentimentality which the four major authors, Richardson, Fielding, Smollett, and Sterne, expressed in varying proportions. With them the eighteenth century novel reached its peak; after them came a period of imitation, repetition, and poor craftsmanship, so bleak the writers feared that this form was dying out altogether. Not so the audience, however, for whom this entertainment continued to be popular even when it consisted mainly of patch-works of several old volumes issued under catchy new titles.

Toward the latter part of the century, a revival if not of great novels, at least of more craftsmanlike work set in than had been seen in the 1720s. Harbinger of the new era had been Horace Walpole's *Castle of Otranto,* which added a fillip to the worn-out novel of sentiment by placing it in mysterious gothic settings and generously interlarding it with episodes of supernatural terror. The English public, sickened by the endless sentimentalities which had been paraded before it, eventually welcomed these innovations with enthusiasm. The fad spread, and by 1794 the Buckingham Palace librarian Thomas Mathias, author of a vigorous satire on contemporary fiction entitled *Pursuits of Literature,* was lamenting the consequences: "[Walpole's] Otranto ghosts have propagated their species with unequaled fecundity; the spawn is in every book shop."[9]

Though the most widely read—or at least most widely approved—volume for children continued to be *Pilgrim's Progress,* by the late 1780s works more amusing if not less instructive began to become available to young readers. One such volume was *Sandford and Merton.* This novel was not written only for the juvenile market, although the two heroes are youngsters: Sandford, a boy endowed with natural wisdom and common sense, and Tommy Merton, a fitful product of luxury. The story was certainly didactic, though less pointedly so than its predecessors, and suggests a philosophy of education derived from *Emile*.[10] Toward the end of the century the Penny Chap-books, small paper-bound volumes illustrated with wood-blocks, long favorites with adults, began to be issued in titles suitable for children, including nursery rhymes, fairy tales, and extracts of longer works such as *Robinson Crusoe*.

As more people joined the ranks of the literate, novel writing became an increasingly lucrative affair. During the 1790s, even a relatively unknown writer could draw a comfortable income by writing serialized novels for enthusiastic publics. The three-volume novel format was especially popular with the ladies, it was said, because one section could be conveniently perused in a single sitting at the hairdresser's.[11] Small-sized books of all kinds were much in evidence throughout the latter half-century, both consequence and reinforcement of the interest in abstracts, abridgements, and anthologies. A popular example of the latter was Isaac D'Israeli's excerpts from famous writers, *Curiosities of Literature* (1792), designed as "an experiment whether a taste for literature could not be infused into the multitudes." This small book quickly went through five editions, was revised several times over, and often imitated. The growing taste for what Dr. Johnson called "general and easy reading" seems to have been satisfied by these small and light books. He himself highly approved of the development: books, after all, should be held readily in the hand and should be easy to carry about; heavy books give a discouraging appearance of erudition and may succeed in frightening away the public altogether.[12]

Newspapers

The prototype of the modern newspaper came into its own soon after the lapse of the Licensing Act in 1695. Within a year or two the Whigs and the Tories sponsored political newspapers, and by 1700 several papers circulated about London and were delivered to the provinces three times a week when the posts went out. Many English gentlemen living abroad or in the country subscribed to "newsletters issued by confidential sources" which in tone and substance resembled today's confidential and not so confidential newsletters and "dope sheets" on politics and finance. News-letters, more often handwritten than not, had been a commonplace in the metropolis itself since the 1660s; in the eighteenth century they were more likely to deal with foreign than with domestic affairs.

At the beginning of the century the major source of news in the city continued to be the coffee house. Each class had its favorite rendezvous which, whether simple or elaborate, was invariably stocked with all periodicals available. Anyone willing to read aloud could attract a sizable audience at a moment's notice, and the news of whatever he read, whether of parliamentary debates or town gossip spread rapidly. Perhaps rightly not trusting the loyalty of their papers, the leading politicians of the day employed "runners" who went from coffee house to coffee house, dropping tidbits and guiding the conversations along whatever lines their bosses happened to be espousing at the moment. Newspapers of the first half-century were singularly short-lived. However, two tri-weekly evening papers, *The London Evening Post* (1727) and *The General Evening Post* (1733) lasted into the nineteenth century; and *The Daily Advertiser,* established in 1730 and continuing for sixty-eight years, had by far the longest life of any daily.[13]

In the course of the century, the daily newspaper became self-supporting and self-respecting: self-supporting because of the spread of literacy, self-respecting because of a successful struggle against religious and political control.[14] In 1709 eighteen newspapers were published once a week or more in London, amounting altogether to some fifty issues. By 1730 the coffee house owners complained that it was impossible to subscribe to them all. Papers grew steadily in size as well, and in the middle of the century six-page editions were the rule. Furthermore, as Dr. Johnson observed, almost every important provincial town had its local organ.[15]

The stamp tax, imposed by the Tories in 1712 in an unsuccessful effort to crush the Whig papers, provides a cue for measuring the growth of the newspaper circulation. In 1776 approximately twelve million copies were sold in the entire year. Though this amounted to only one copy per day for every 300 persons,[16] at least one member of Parliament became alarmed and complained that newspapers were treated with more respect than the spokesmen of the nation.

> The people of Great Britain are governed by a power that never was heard of as a supreme authority in any age or country before. . . . It is the government of the press. The stuff which our weekly newspapers are filled with, is received with greater reverence than Acts of Parliament, and the sentiments of one of these scribblers have more weight with the multitude than the opinion of the best politician in the kingdom.[17]

But the average reader viewed newspapers with mixed feelings. One correspondent to the *St. James Journal* for August 2, 1722, slandered *Mist's Newspaper,* a weekly, as being written only for "Porters and

Cobblers and such dirty Customers as are his greatest patrons." If we are to believe a writer in another magazine of the same period, however, Mist's paper found an audience in more exalted social spheres.

> The Two famous Universities of this Land are the grand Centers of it: Men and Horses are employed to convey it in large Quantities to *Oxford* and *Cambridge;* where, senseless as it is, it is constantly read and applauded.[18]

On the whole those who paid attention to the growing literary market were more concerned with its potentialities for the intellectual and aesthetic development of the country than with the dangers of its possible influences on public opinion. Only in the early decades of the nineteenth century, when there were some four hundred newspapers in England and Ireland, did the problem of the newspaper as a manipulative device become a major concern to the intellectual.

Changes in the Theater

At the beginning of the eighteenth century the stage had long since been an English institution, rising and falling in popularity and prestige with changes in politics and religion, but always a major arena in which a writer could present his works.

Restoration drama, with its mirroring of the manners and mores of the aristocracy, had been sufficiently uninhibited to provide reforming pastors and laymen with ample reason for attack. In fact, in the first decade of the century neo-Puritans such as Jeremy Collier and Daniel Defoe waged campaigns to have the theaters, "those Houses of Sin and Nurseries of Vice" (Defoe),[19] abolished altogether. Assaults against the English stage were nothing new, and the moralistic and theological arguments brought to bear on them changed very little between the sixth and the eighteenth centuries.[20] The charges handed down by the grand jury of Middlesex in 1703 are typical.*

> We, the Grand Jury of the County of Middlesex do present, that the Plays which are frequently acted in the play-houses in Drury-Lane and Lincoln's-Inn-Fields in this Country are full of prophane, irreverent, lewd, indecent, and immoral expressions and tend to the great displeasure of Almighty

---

*And they were by no means limited to the theater. All popular amusements were assumed to be conducive to excessive drinking, immorality, and breaches of the peace. (Vide, M. D. George, *London Life in the Eighteenth Century,* New York: Knopf, 1925, New York: Knopf, p. 287.)

God, and to the corruption of the auditory, both in their principles and their practices.[21]

As the Restoration play gave way to middle-class themes, play-going became more respectable and, with the licensing of the two patented theaters at Drury Lane and Covent Garden in 1737, the stage once more became a legitimate means of entertainment for the pious as well as the worldly—which is not to say that the zealots ceased to attack it.

Toward the middle of the century, when Garrick took over the management of the Drury Lane, the theater reached a new peak in popularity and in quality of production. In addition to the sentimental comedies of the day, Garrick brought Shakespeare back to the English public after a long period of neo-Puritan—and later neo-classical— obscurity. But despite the general excellence of their performances, both patented theaters, in order to keep their attendance high, resorted to elaborate pantomimes, "spectacular" operas, ballet operas, and a variety of sensational devices—different more in degree than in kind from those common in Shakespeare's day.

While even the clergy were now found in attendance at the theater, the actors themselves remained more or less outcast until the last quarter of the century. More than one debate in Parliament included attacks on the high salaries of actors, particularly those of Italian performers imported for the opera. In the course of one debate in 1735, a member of the House of Commons observed that

> it was astonishing to all Europe that Italian eunuchs and signoras should have set salaries equal to those of the Lords of the Treasury and Judges of England.[22]

Such complaints, however, only served to whet public curiosity about the private lives and morals of the theatrical world, a curiosity fed with increasing detail in the gossip-mongering parts of the press.

It was customary in Garrick's time to stage two performances every evening, one more or less serious and one light. While many members of the audience who attended the first performance sat through the second, it is apparent from the financial records of the major theaters that an even larger group customarily came only for the latter half of the evening. Since the curtain rose at six, it was inconvenient for working people to attend the first performance. One "Citizen" in the 1730s wrote a letter of complaint to the Lord Mayor of London in which he pointed out that only the "mechanick of pleasure" could attend the theater at such an early hour.

Gentlemen who have no employment may sleep whole days and riot whole nights. . . . Compare the life of a careful honest man . . . with your mechanick of pleasure who is to frequent the theater. . . . He must be a fine gentleman, leave his work at five at the farthest . . . that he may be drest and at the playhouse by six.[23]

Still more important was the prevailing custom of cutting the admission price in half after the first or "major" piece of the evening was over. On the one or two occasions when the theaters attempted to abolish this custom, public demonstrations and even riots quickly forced a reinstatement. The behavior of the English audience continued to be anything but passive. The noisiness of sailors and their girls and the preening of fops and dandies were ridiculed in many a prologue and epilogue and amazed more than one foreign observer.

The audience increased considerably in the course of the century. Not only did many smaller playhouses begin to flourish in the City and in the provinces, but theaters themselves were enlarged. The two patent theaters together could accommodate 14,000 persons per week in 1732, over 15,000 in 1747, and 22,000 in 1762.[24] Actual attendance, however, may have averaged considerably less than capacity.[25]

AUDIENCE BUILDING

Despite the lack of reliable literacy figures, there seems little doubt that two upsurges in reading took place among the English public during the eighteenth century. The first was in the thirties and forties, as the popular magazines and presently the novels began to flood the market. This spurt was due more to the fact that the literate were reading more material than to an increase in the numbers of people who could read. In the last two decades of the century, on the other hand, when the Bible societies, the political pamphleteers and the reformers produced reams of inexpensive literature in a concerted attempt to counteract the influence of revolutionary writers such as Tom Paine, the increased consumption was due to a growth in the reading public itself. In between, the village schoolteachers and the Sunday schools, the former in order to make a living, the latter in order to spread the Good Word, had gone about the business of teaching children of the clerical, working, and farming classes their ABC's.* Printing presses in London, according to

---

*Richard D. Altick suggests, in *The English Common Reader,* the manuscript of which he generously made available to us, that while the consumption of reading matter certainly increased steadily throughout the eighteenth century, it was only after the 1790s that the structure of the reading audience became democratic. On the whole, he feels, the seventeenth century may have had a more representative, and not necessarily a smaller, reading audience than the eighteenth.

contemporary estimates, increased from 75 in 1724 to 150-200 in 1757; the annual publication of new books quadrupled in the course of the century;[26] and the profession of letters became established as a respectable (and often very profitable) livelihood, indeed so well established that as early as 1752 Samuel Johnson labelled his the "Age of Authors."[27]

Part cause and part consequence of the increase in reading and the professionalization of the author, a number of channels for expanding the market for literary products sprang into being or took a new lease on life after the first quarter of the century, notably the circulating libraries, the bookselling and publishing trade, and the book-review periodicals. These institutions were closely related to each other as well as to the authors whose works they promoted or exploited and, as today, friction between authors and those responsible for the channels of distribution was not a rarity. Several noncommercial devices also served to promote the consumption of literary goods. Literary societies and reading groups spread throughout London and were eventually imitated in the provinces. The coffee houses in the city and in the towns continued to be centers where people gathered to read or to hear newspapers and magazines read aloud, and lingered to discuss what they had read or heard.

Some coffee houses were primarily literary resorts. Pope, for example, spent a great deal of time talking with fellow-writers in his favorite coffee house, until he found that the consumption of wine was beginning to get the better of his health. Among the more notable literary coffee clubs in the earlier part of the century was the Kit-Cat Club, which counted numerous leading writers of the period among its members and had Tonson, the outstanding book-seller of his time, as secretary. This club consisted mainly of Whigs, but it went out of its way to encourage young writers, presumably regardless of political persuasion, with financial prizes, particularly for comedies. Swift helped to found the Brothers' Club, whose members were mainly Tories, but whose interests were largely literary—and they, too, contributed to the support of promising younger writers.[28]

The bluestocking clubs, organized in mid-century by a group of literary-minded upper-class women, determined to substitute talk of letters for card games, were eventually imitated by middle-class women both in London and in the provinces. If nothing else, these groups did much to make reading (and writing) among women socially acceptable, even desirable. By the latter part of the century, informal book-discussion and book-buying clubs throve in every part of the country. How these clubs promoted the sale of books is described by Lackington in his *Memoirs:*

> A number of book-clubs are also formed in every part of England where each member subscribes a certain sum quarterly to purchase books: in

some of the clubs the books, after they have been read by all the subscribers, are sold among them to the highest bidders, and the money produced by such sale is expended in fresh purchases, by which prudent and judicious mode each member has it in his power to become possessed of the work of any particular author he may judge deserving a superior degree of attention.[29]

Although would-be purchasers in the provinces sometimes complained that the metropolitan dealers ignored their mail orders, enterprising booksellers visited the clubs in outlying districts, sent them catalogues and in other ways offered moral if not material encouragement.

The principal audience-building efforts of the book dealers (who were publishers as well) were, however, directed to commercial channels.

Circulating Libraries

The first circulating library in England was founded in 1740, the same year in which Richardson's *Pamela* was published. The establishment of one of the major institutions for accelerating the spread of reading in the middle class thus coincided with the first important novel of that class.

It was customary for the libraries to charge an annual membership fee which entitled a subscriber to access to all books and magazines carried by the particular establishment to which he belonged. By the turn of the century, approximately one thousand of these profit-making institutions were scattered throughout the country, and their customers included members of the working as well as of the middle classes. Free public libraries, however, were noticeably lacking. The library of the Royal Society accumulated only a fair collection, and the British Museum, already distinguished for its collection of original manuscripts, made a poor showing in printed books. Edward Gibbon had reason to complain that "the greatest city of the world was still destitute of a Public Library."[30]

The booksellers at first viewed the development of circulating libraries with suspicion; but they soon recognized that, far from cutting off the sale of books, these outlets promised to constitute both an important market and a major advertising medium.[31] Not only did the circulating libraries provide books for families which could not afford to buy them, but they gave readers a chance to preview a book before investing in it.[32]

The ladies took to the new institution with delight. Toward the end of the century, there is scarcely a popular novel whose heroine does not in the course of her transports or travails select a novel from her circulating library or send her maid to fetch one. By that time, the booksellers were enthusiastic. Lackington was convinced that, along with his own bookshop of course,

> Circulating libraries have also greatly contributed toward the amusement and cultivation of the sex; by far the greatest part of ladies now have a taste for books. . . . Ladies now in general read, not only novels, although many of that class are excellent productions, and tend to polish both the heart and the head; but they also read the best books in the English language, and may read the best authors in various languages; and there are some thousands of ladies who frequent my shop, and that know as well what books to choose, and are as well acquainted with works of taste and genius as any gentleman in the kingdom, notwithstanding they sneer against novel readers, etc.[33]

While some of the literati toward the later part of the century blamed the circulating libraries for whetting the apparently insatiable appetite for novels which the booksellers were eager to feed by all manner of means, and while many writers poked light fun at the institution in their own fictional works, few serious attacks on this audience-building device were forthcoming in the course of the century.*

Bookselling

The conscientious man of letters was rather less tolerant of the booksellers. Possibly his newly acquired financial dependence on the publisher and dealer occasioned some degree of nostalgia for the days of aristocratic patronage; certainly the practices of a good many booksellers provided him with good reason for intolerance.

Messrs. Tonson and Curll represent the two extremes of prestige and notoriety the bookseller could achieve in the days of Alexander Pope. Tonson, the afore-mentioned secretary of the Kit-Cat Club, left his mark on the history of the book trade as the esteemed publisher of *Paradise Lost* and numerous works by Dryden and Addison. He commanded the admiration of most of his authors, to whom he was generous in his commercial dealings and stimulating in his intellectual contacts.

Edmund Curll, one of the infamous names in the history of commerce, neither got nor deserved a modiocum of respect from the literati. Unscrupulous and clever, he displayed a kind of stupid adroitness which repeatedly landed him in jail and encouraged him, on his discharge, to resume with redoubled vigor the very activities for which he had been

---

*Coleridge was later to speak scathingly of "devotees of circulating libraries" whose reading he considered to be on a par with reading word for word "all the advertisements of a daily newspaper in a public house on a rainy day."

imprisoned. He had a special knack for exploiting the scandalous, a thriving business in his as in more recent days, and while he did publish some useful works, given the length of his publication lists, he could hardly have avoided it. He dedicated most of his energy to a search for attractive titles and intimately personal (often scurrilous) advertisements for biographies and pornographic pamphlets which were thrown together willy-nilly by hacks to whom he paid starvation wages.[34] He came in for a lot of scathing criticism in Pope's *Dunciad,* and the reasons are not far to seek. Fielding tells the following story in the *Champion* about a fraud which Curll perpetrated by misusing the name of Pope:

> But the most remarkable piece if ingenuity, if it had been done by design, was exhibited this winter, in which a poem was published with the following title-page, printed in the same manner as it is here inserted.
>
>
>
> SEVENTEEN HUNDRED THIRTY NINE
> being the sequel of
> SEVENTEEN HUNDRED THIRTY EIGHT
> WRITTEN BY MR. POPE
>
>
>
> If this had been published by any other bookseller than Mr. C—l, we should have believed that it was intended to impose the year nine on the world as a work of Mr. Pope's, who is I think avowedly the author of the year eight, but the said Mr. C—l is too well known to have any such attempt suspected, both from the nicety of his conscience and his judgment, which should not suffer him to hope that he should be able to exhibit the pop of a pistol for the fire of a cannon.[35]

By 1800 the bookselling and publishing trade was one of the major industries in the country. Needless to say, both Tonson and Curll had their share of descendants. Lackington was the most successful as well as the most articulate book dealer of the latter part of the century: he went into business in 1774; in 1779 he published his first catalogue of 12,000 titles and estimated that some 30,000 people a year made use of it. It was Lackington who first hit upon the idea of remainder sales, and by the turn of the century he was selling over 100,000 volumes a year.[36] While he conceded that he made a substantial amount of money, he also took credit for making books available to groups who might not otherwise have been able to afford them:

> When I reflect what prodigious numbers in inferior or *reduced* situations of life, have been essentially benefited, in consequence of being thus enabled to indulge their natural propensity for the acquisition of knowledge, on easy terms: nay, I could almost be vain enough to assert, that I have thereby been highly instrumental in diffusing that general desire for READING now so prevalent among the inferior orders of society.[37]

After 1780 the cost of books, already high, rose further.* Well-established publishers were making their formats ever more elaborate and costly, in part because the etiquette of the more elegant members of the feminine audience demanded ostentatious bindings. But new booksellers soon entered the lists and issued reprints, including small, modestly priced pocket editions of the classics. Another successful sales device adopted by the booksellers was the publishing of the classics, poetry, and fiction in newspaper-like serials, printed in weekly installments at sixpence each.[38] After allowing a suitable period for the reader to forget the first version, the less scrupulous booksellers did not hesitate to reissue the trashier of these works, particularly the novels, under new titles, but otherwise unchanged.

Advertising methods ranged from the spectacularly absurd to the eminently reasonable and included, in fact, most of the devices which have remained the stock-in-trade of the publisher's business to this day. There was first the matter of the title. If it was catchy, slick, and sensational, it could not go very far wrong. There were *Beauty Put to Its Shift, Adultery Atomized, Female Falsehood,* and a thousand other titles like them. Old books in new titles were not limited to the folios; the salvation of many a hard-cover work came about by the simple expedient of removing the title page, replacing it with a more vivid or salacious one, and offering the renovated product as "Second Edition, corrected and improved."[39] A particularly successful device was to endow the author (or authoress) with qualities of fame, mystery, or notoriety, and writers said to have been "banished from the realm" were promoted with special avidity. Endorsements by "men of distinction," too, were a commonplace. On the whole the booksellers maintained close and friendly relations at least with their leading writers, and only one writer seems to have found his dependence on the bookseller sufficiently restraining to endeavor to free himself. In 1765, one John Trusler founded a Literary Society intended to eliminate the middleman and to secure all profits for the author by enabling him to bring out his own works independently. This society probably helped nobody but Trusler himself who managed, at most, to sell only one of his books.[40] Until the middle of the century, a great many books continued to be financed by advance subscriptions, but these were solicited by the bookseller himself, except for an occasional penurious and unknown author who went knocking from door to door.

---

*Some indications of the comparative cost of books and other leisure activities may be found in the following figures given by H. W. Pedicord, and applicable for the mid-century decades: a seat in the first gallery at the Drury Lane 24 pence, a pot of beer 3 pence, cheapest dinner 3½ pence, a small book 36 pence.

Despite the thriving enterprises of the leading booksellers in London in the second half of the century, their influence was not particularly strong in the provinces, except indirectly through the circulating library and the itinerant pedlar. Lackington describes a journey to Edinburgh in 1787, during which he made it his business to stop at every town with the twofold objecive of keeping his finger on the pulse of his trade and picking up scarce or valuable books. His trip, on the latter count, was a notable failure: not only did he find depressingly few valuable books, but the shelves of the provincial bookshops were littered mainly with trash.[41] When he repeated his trip a few years later, he reported the situation very little changed.

Although an unscrupulous bookseller like Curll might arouse almost unanimous expressions of antagonism, the writers were rather less in agreement on the institution of book publishing itself. Both Samuel Johnson and Oliver Goldsmith, for example, were highly dependent on their publishers; but while Johnson was the nearest thing to grateful, Goldsmith—at best—viewed the situation with one auspicious and one drooping eye. Perhaps, as Krutch suggests,[42] Johnson's favorable disposition was the result of a very happy early experience he had with a bookseller who lent him enough money to keep him from starving. In any case, Johnson was not sparing of his commendations. In one of his *Idler* papers, for instance, he credits the booksellers rather than the schools with "popularising knowledge" among the common orders of England.[43]

In his early career as a writer, Johnson suffered from much keener poverty than did Goldsmith, whose main problem was that his money slipped through his fingers. Johnson's poverty was of a more spartan kind. We know how he wrote *Rasselas:* the book was dashed off in a few days to pay for his mother's funeral expenses. And Boswell reports that even when Johnson was finally paid for his *Dictionary* (first published in 1755) there was scarcely any money left after his expense in compiling it had been met. Yet he countered Boswell's commiserations with a stout defense of the bookseller, justifying the lack of profit to the author by citing the risks to which the publisher exposed himself.[44]

Goldsmith was no party to this kind of defense. In his *Enquiry into the Present State of Learning* and in two of the letters in the *Citizen of the World,* one of which is devoted entirely to the dubious practices of the bookseller, he examines the bookseller's role in a forthrightly critical spirit. In his *Enquiry* he notes at the outset that the interests of the writer and those of the publisher are diametrically opposed:

> The author, when unpatronized by the great, has naturally recourse to the bookseller. There cannot perhaps be imagined a combination more prejudicial

to taste than this. It is the interest of the one to allow as little for writing, and of the other to write as much as possible.[45]

And he directly attacks some of the more underhanded promotional techniques, particularly the device of attaching impressive status, real or invented, to the authors of books in the process of being promoted. Booksellers "seem convinced, that a book written by vulgar hands, can neither instruct nor improve; none but Kings, Chams and Mandarines can write with a probability of success."[46] But it is in Letter LI of *The Citizen of the World* that we find the most biting sarcasm. Here Goldsmith describes a bookseller's visit to the ironically ingenuous Citizen. The bookseller begins by noting the seasonal appetites of his readers: "I would no more bring out a new work in summer than I would sell pork in the dog days." He next boasts that his works are always new, and that at the end of every season the old ones are shipped off to the trunkmakers. If he should have a scarcity of new books, there is no dearth of new title pages: "I have ten new title-pages now around me which only want books to be added to make them the finest things in nature." He is quite willing to make a virtue of his lack of cultural pretensions, modestly confessing that he has no desire to lead the public; on the contrary, the public—and the lowest stratum of the public at that—leads him.[47]

The writer's plight vis-à-vis the bookseller trade is well epitomized by a tragi-comic episode reported by Thomas De Quincey in his essay on Goldsmith:

> The pauperized (or Grub Street) section of the literary body, at the date of Goldsmith's taking service amongst it, was . . . at its very lowest point of depression. . . . Smart, the prose translator of Horace and a well-built scholar, actually *let* himself out to a monthly journal on a regular lease of ninety-nine years. What could move the rapacious publisher to draw the lease for this monstrous term of years, we cannot conjecture.

"But think Reader," De Quincey continues,

> But think . . . of poor Smart two years after, upon another publisher's applying vainly to him for contributions, and angrily demanding what possible objections could be made to offers so liberal, being reduced to answer—"No objection, sir, whatever, except an unexpired term of ninety-seven years to run." The bookseller saw that he must not apply again in *that* century; and in fact Smart could no longer let himself but must be sub-let, if let at all, by the original lessee.[48]

Book Reviews

Book reviewing came into being at the end of the seventeenth century largely as a professional service. The review journals of that time were limited to scientific and philosophical works, and at first their principal purpose was to provide scholars with convenient summaries, in English, of the works of their colleagues abroad. One of the earliest of the eighteenth century reviews, the *Memoirs of Literature* (1710-1714), published by the Huguenot refugee LaRoche, served as prototype for the scholarly review. This periodical contained abstracts of English and foreign works in about equal proportions. Critical comments were rare. In 1725, reputedly with the help of a book publisher, LaRoche produced a second journal, *New Memoirs of Literature,* in which he proved to be more enterprising: this review—usually running to some seventy-five pages an issue—not only abstracted but added comment to the works selected for review. *The Literary Magazine,* first published in 1735 under the editorship of Ephraim Chambers, covered a wider range of works, though it still limited itself to the "serious." It went further in comment and biographical background than had its predecessors, but was reluctant to set itself up as judge. In the words of its editor, the responsibility of the reviewer is

> to give a faithful account of books which come into his hands. . . . When he affects the air and language of a censor or judge, he invades the undoubted right of the public, which is the only sovereign judge of the reputation of an author, and the merit of his compositions.[49]

The first book review journal to move into the field of popular literature and thus to qualify as an audience-building institution was *The Compendious Library,* a one-hundred page bi-monthly publication printed in Dublin (1751-52). Its steps in this direction, however, were both rare and gingerly. In introducing Fielding's *Amelia,* for example, the reviewer first notes that romance and novels have no place in literary journals, but in this instance he justifies the exception on the grounds that fiction which serves "the reformation of manners and the advancement of virtue" may be allowed, and goes on to remark that "This seems to be one, if not the chief, point from which Mr. Fielding's performance ought to be considered. . . ."[50]

With the founding of the *Monthly Review* by Ralph Griffith in 1749, the book review purporting to cover all releases from the presses got its start. The *Monthly,* which at first had the reputation of being hostile to state and church, soon provoked the founding of a rival journal, the *Critical Review,* published by Archibald Hamilton, edited by Tobias Smollett from 1756 to 1763, and laying claim to Tory and Church support.

Both reviews boasted eminent contributors: Goldsmith contributed twenty pieces to the *Monthly,* and Johnson as well as Smollett wrote for the *Critical.* Each journal dealt with the more important books of the month in considerable detail; in a "catalogue" appended to each issue, all other publications of the month were covered in three- or four-page reviews. The objective proclaimed by the *Critical* could be applied to the *Monthly* as well:

> To exhibit a succinct plan of every performance; to point out the most striking beauties and glaring defects; to illustrate remarks with proper quotations, and to convey those remarks in such a manner as might best conduce to the entertainment of the public.[51]

The *Critical* successfully competed with the *Monthly* until 1790, but the *Monthly* managed to survive it well into the middle of the nineteenth century. Although criticized by authors for high-handedness on some occasions, these reviews and their competitors were inclined rather more to praise than to criticize. Witness, for instance, the prospectus of the *New London Review,* a short-lived publication of the years 1799 to 1800:

> The Plan is suggested, and will be executed in the conviction, that few performances are wholly destitute of merit; that it is more useful to disclose latent excellence, than to exaggerate common faults; that the public taste suffers less from inaccurate writing than from illiberal criticism.

Criticism was to be reserved for the works of writers who went off any one of a number of beaten tracks:

> Though no arrogance will be indulged in this Publication, whatever disturbs the public harmony, insults legal authority, . . . attacks the vital springs and established functions of piety, or in any respect clashes with the sacred forms of decency, however witty, elegant, and well written, can be noticed only in terms of severe and unequivocal reprehension.[52]

The task of covering all new books as they were released became more and more unmanageable. One of the *Monthly* reviewers in 1788 complained: "The Reviewer of the modern novel is in the situation of Hercules encountering the Hydra—One head lopped off, two or three immediately spring up in its place."[53] The less conscientious journals solved the problem by a process of selection calculated to please the chief suppliers of their advertising revenue, the booksellers, who distributed review copies only to the journals in which they advertised. These books were reviewed first; time and space permitting, a reviewer might then send his "collector" around to other houses for books possibly deserving of his notice. Thus books often were reviewed months after they were released; in the case of particularly popular publications which were sold out by the time a collector arrived, no reviews appeared at all.[54]

As to the reviewers themselves, the *Monthly* and *Critical* and a number of similar journals had, in addition to eminent or well-known contributors, other conscientious ones as well. More often, however, they were poorly paid devisers of makeshift who filled up page after page with direct quotations, selected, as one report has it, after first reading the preface, closing the book, sticking a pin between the leaves at random, opening and transcribing the page so chosen, or even a few pages, and then repeating the operation. One novelist of the 1770s accused the reviewers of passing on the merits and demerits of an author on the basis of the title-page alone. A correspondent to the *Gentleman's Magazine* in 1782 accused the reviewers of praising the works of those booksellers who owned shares in their journals and running down all others. Yet another novelist accused them of taking bribes from authors, sometimes even going so far as to let them write their own reviews.[55]

Samuel Johnson, as we might expect from his more favorable attitude toward booksellers, was considerably more indulgent toward the reviewers than was Oliver Goldsmith, who devoted a substantial portion of another of his *Citizen of the World* letters to a castigation of their practices. Goldsmith links the undiscriminating nature of the book reviewer's work to the fact that he is being paid by the bookseller or, worse still, to the fact that the bookseller himself sometimes writes reviews:

> There are a set of men called answerers of books who take upon them to watch the republic of letters, and distribute reputation by the sheet . . . and to revile the moral character of the man whose writings they cannot injure. Such wretches are kept in pay by some mercenary bookseller, or more frequently, the bookseller himself takes this dirty work off their hands, as all that is required is to be very abusive and very dull.

The Chinese visitor goes on to ask his host whether this is the fate of every writer, to which the Englishman replies, "Yes . . . except he happened to be born a Mandarin. If he has much money, he may buy a reputation from your book answerers."[56]

Such was the ambiguous state of book-reviewing in the second half of the century. Only with the founding of the *Edinburgh Review* and the *Quarterly* in the early nineteenth century did the book reviewers begin to be free of publisher influence. If they kowtowed at all, it was likely to be in response to political party rather than to publishing house pressures.

STAGES OF REACTION

The acid comments of writers about the devices used to promote book sales did not herald an immediate negative reaction to the development of a literary market. Alexander Pope, to be sure, made dire prophesies about the low level to which literature was sinking; but though he was later to be looked back upon by Henry Fielding as "King Alexandre," the despotic ruler of the literary kingdom, Pope's "subjects" did not join in his protest against changes in the literary scene until much later. On the contrary, many literary figures in the first half of the century founded periodicals especially designed for the growing middle-class readership, and all of them contributed to magazines or newspapers at one point in their careers.

Their predecessors had been writing for a more homogeneous group: the nobility, the landed gentry, and scholars had composed the bulk of their readers. These readers debated about the "rules" and about good and bad writing along with the writers, just as they debated about good and bad music, architecture, and painting; but they did not distinguish between "high" and "low" art, nor did they discuss differences in aesthetic appreciation among different social segments of the audience. The growth of a broader market did not at first change the nature of these discussions. Each form was presumed to have its own special means of providing pleasure, but the accepted function of all writing remained similar to that summarized by the critic John Dennis in his discussion of "greater" and "less" poetry:

> 1. The greater Poetry is an Art by which a Poet justly and reasonably excites great Passion, that he may please and instruct. . . .
> 2. The less Poetry is an Art by which a Poet excites less Passion for the foremention'd Ends. . . .[57]

Not all of John Dennis' contemporaries in the world of letters would have agreed with him that the excitation of great passion is the *sine qua non* of great poetry, but his view that the objective of all writing is to instruct would have evoked little controversy. The writer has a social task; he must use his gift as a means of contributing to the elevation of his readers. And just as the writers' creative gifts were assumed to go hand-in-hand with high moral responsibility, so was it assumed that a public which is responsive to moral teachings must also be capable of aesthetic appreciation.

This section will describe how, as writers, readers, and literary products multiplied, such initial optimism gave way to a mood very close to pessimism.

Optimism

Very early in the century, the English public had begun to display a powerful bent for reform of manners and morals, not the least manifestation of which was its wide-spread support of organizations such as the Society for the Propagation of Christian Knowledge and the Society for the Reformation of Manners—groups with far-flung networks through which numerous pamphlets and books of a moralizing, neo-Puritan nature were distributed.[58] The ideal of the "gentleman" to which tradespeople and aristocrats alike aspired was not the exaggeratedly ornamental and rakish figure which had become the stereotype of Restoration comedy, but the virtuous Christian citizen. In such an atmosphere it was taken for granted that the new literary forms would edify and elevate; an aristocrat, such as the Earl of Shaftesbury, and Defoe, a writer who saw himself as the very conscience of the middle and lower-middle classes, could agree with the crusading Sir Richard Blackmore that the responsibility of the writer is to "cultivate the mind with instruction of virtue."[59] To be sure, early magazines and newspapers were often attacked for their political bias— the fittest punishment Pope could conjure up for one of the "low" writers he attacked in the early *Dunciad,* for example, was to have him "[end] at last in the common sink of all such writers, a Political News-paper."[60] And Addison puffed his own journal at the expense of the newspapers, which he gently chided for emphasizing "what passes in Muscovy or Poland," rather than the "knowledge of one's self."[61]

The belief that the inclination for moral uplift so apparent in the audience presupposed a capacity for aesthetic advancement was at first reinforced by the success of the single essay type of magazine, which combined elegant writing with social and cultural purpose, and which first came into its own with the launching of Steele's *Tatler* in 1709. The *Tatler's* immediate successor, the *Spectator* (1711), founded as a joint enterprise of Steele and Addison, became the most popular journal of its day. In one of the early issues, Addison announced that his publisher had just reported a daily circulation of three thousand copies for the journal, and goes on to estimate with some assurance that each copy had twenty readers (or "hearers," as the case may be).* Addison used these figures as a point of departure for a statement of objectives which is not only a succinct summary of the principle of "art as a means of instruction," but a statement of faith in the capacities of his readers:

> Since I have raised to myself so great an Audience, I shall spare no Pains to make their Instruction agreeable, and their Diversion useful. For which Reasons I shall endeavour to enliven Morality with Wit and to temper Wit with Morality. . . . It was said of *Socrates,* that he brought Philosophy down from Heaven, to inhabit among Men; and I shall be ambitious to have it said of me, that I have brought Philosophy out of Closets and Libraries, Schools and Colleges, to dwell in Clubs and Assemblies, at Tea-Tables and in Coffee-Houses.

These worlds of tea-table and coffee house were not, in Addison's view, limited to the gentry and the scholars; in his "fraternity of spectators" he sees tradesmen as well as physicians, "statesmen that are out of business" as well as Fellows of the Royal Society, and all those "blanks of society" who until now have been "altogether unfurnished with ideas till the business and conversation of the day has supplied them." Finally he envisages the whole "female world" among his readers, but particularly the "ordinary" woman whose most serious occupation is sewing and whose drudgery is cooking. While there are some women who live in a more "exalted Sphere of Knowledge and Virtue," they are all too few, and he hopes to increase their ranks "by Publishing this daily Paper, which I shall always endeavour to make an innocent if not an improving Entertainment, and by that Means at least divert the Minds of my Female Readers from greater Trifles."[62]

That most of what Addison called entertainment was indeed both morally and aesthetically "improving" is apparent to the modern reader who selects any issue of the *Spectator* at random. Between them, Addison and Steele covered the spectrum of their age from "Puritan Piety" (Addison) to "Miseries of Prostitution" (Steele). Addison informed his readers that he belonged to a club which served as a kind of "advisory committee" for the *Spectator;* in fact, his readers "have the satisfaction to find that there is no rank or degree among them who have not their

---

*Since there was no eighteenth century equivalent to a "continuing index of magazine circulation," these figures are debatable. Samuel Johnson (in *Lives of the Poets*) reckoned, on the basis of stamp tax figures, that the *Spectator* had an average sale of 1,700 daily copies. Addison's editor, Richard Hurd, and others offer average daily estimates closer to those ventured by Addison himself.

representative in this club, and that there is always somebody present who will take care of their respective interests." He describes a recent meeting of the club during which he was congratulated by some members and taken to task by others. On occasion, members of this panel try to lobby for their special interests, but Addison hastens to assure the reader that he will remain unmoved by such pressures:

> Having thus taken my Resolutions to march on boldly in the Cause of Virtue and good Sense, and to annoy their Adversaries in whatever Degree or Rank of Men they may be found: I shall be deaf for the future to all the Remonstrances that shall be made to me on this Account.[63]

Running throughout the series (the *Spectator* was published daily until December 6, 1712) is a strong admixture of literary criticism, mostly Addison's, clearly designed to establish a link between the "wit" of the elite classical tradition and the moral truths so in keeping with the ethos of the rising middle class.[64]

But that a moral reformation was inseparable from an aesthetic one became an assumption increasingly difficult to support. If it is true that the *Spectator* eventually attained a readership of twenty or thirty thousand, perhaps there came a point in eighteenth century England when the literary development of many persons hung in the balance, attracted to the refinements of an Addison who did not write down to his readers, and not yet seduced by the sensational or sentimental devices to be utilized by his successors. If so, it was for a relatively short period, and subsequent events have blurred the evidence. Historians of literature credit the essayists with high literary achievement, but suggest that they were victims of self-delusion if they believed that the moral concerns of their readers were in any way associated with a capacity for—or interest in—aesthetic growth. What Addison and the other essayists hoped for was a rapprochement between English classicism and middle-class morality; what they paved the way for was compromise.[65]

Before the middle of the century the public was beginning to make its preferences abundantly clear. Defoe's *Robinson Crusoe,* which was mainly read as an adventure story, became an instantaneous bestseller seven years after the last copy of the *Spectator* was printed, and it went through numerous editions and translations during the next thirty years. In 1750, *The Oeconomy of Human Life** was published, went through

---

*The authorship is disputed—some historians credit Dodsley, others Chesterfield, with the work.

twenty-one editions in the eighteenth century (several more than that in the nineteenth) and was translated into six languages. This book, distinguished for its commonplaceness of thought, achieved unprecedented popularity and has been characterized as testimony to "the insatiable appetite of the eighteenth century for moral platitude."[66] In the same year in which the *Spectator* was founded, Shaftesbury had written, "Thus are the arts and virtues mutually friends,"[67] but that the mid-century audience thought differently is further attested by the fate of one of the *Spectator*'s more eminent imitators, *The Rambler*. This bi-weekly periodical was founded by Dr. Johnson in the same year in which *The Oeconomy* achieved its spectacular success. Like the *Spectator* four decades earlier, *The Rambler* aimed at intellectual and aesthetic as well as moral refinements. But except for one issue written by Samuel Richardson (Number 97) the peak circulation of *The Rambler* was 500, or one-sixth of the circulation claimed for the *Spectator* after its tenth day of publication.[68]

Opportunity and Opportunism

While the hundred imitations of the *Spectator* published between 1712 and 1750 were remarkably short-lived, the *Gentleman's Magazine,* some fifty pages of news and entertainment features, went into five editions at its first issue in 1731. Twenty years or so later Johnson wrote of it as one of the most lucrative publications (it then had a circulation of 15,000), and its manager at the end of the century, John Nichols, reported it as still a highly successful enterprise.[69]

With the public expressing its interests by buying certain kinds of literary products and by not buying others, the publisher, bookseller, and writer with a knack for gauging public opinion could become, if not wealthy, certainly most comfortable. There were five thousand people subsisting by writing, printing, publishing, and marketing papers in the London of 1722,[70] and those who earned a living in the literary market by the middle of the century would probably have to be reckoned in the tens of thousands. It was no longer necessary to be a "man of letters" or a university graduate to be a professional writer. Housewives and bookkeepers who wanted to make a few extra pounds now wrote novels, as did country clergymen who had formerly dabbled in botany or archeology. Few of these writers felt any need to defend either their works or their profits, and few apparently were concerned about literary standards.

No longer were elegant and polished "wits" and intellectuals endeavoring to search out truth, beauty, and reason for themselves and a few readers much like themselves. Instead middle-class novelists such as

Richardson and Fielding were writing for their social peers. They, and Smollett and Sterne after them, may have been concerned with truth and reason, at least insofar as these values were related to morality, but they were little concerned with beauty. Their world, as Leslie Stephen put it, had become that of "the middle-class John Bull. . . . The generation which listens to Wesley must have also a secular literature, which, whether sentimental as with Richardson or representing common sense with Fielding, must at any rate correspond to solid substantial matter-of-fact motives, intelligible to the ordinary Briton of the time."[71] Fielding himself, satirist though he often was, offered a summation of this solemn atmosphere. Denouncing those writers who merely amuse or shock, he made it clear that he was even not "afraid to mention Rabelais, and Aristophanes himself," among those who have ridiculed the only means to moral health and wisdom: "sobriety, modesty, decency, virtue and religion." He then went on to state a precept which was adhered to—with varying degrees of sincerity—by most writers of his age:

> In the exercise of the mind, as well as in the exercise of the body, diversion is a secondary consideration, and designed only to make that agreeable, which is at the same time useful, to such noble purposes as health and wisdom.[72]

Indeed, so ingrained were these moral precepts that the majority of mid-century writers quite uncalculatingly fulfilled the reader's need to be convinced that he was being improved while being amused, diverted, or horrified. Adults told themselves that novel reading was instructive for young people, and the upper classes were persuaded that reading or play-going was uplifting for the lower. The actor, writer, and producer Garrick, in his *Bon Ton,* lightly ridiculed such rationalizations in a conversation between master and servant:

> *Sir John:* Why, what did I promise you?
> *Davy:* That I should take sixpen'oth at one of the theaters tonight, and a shilling place at the other to-morrow.
> *Sir John:* Well, well, so I did. Is it a moral piece, Davy?
> *Davy:* Oh! Yes, and written by a clergyman; it is called the "Rival Cannanites; or the Tragedy of Braggadocia."
> *Sir John:* Be a good lad, and I won't be worse than my word; there's money for you.[73]

A few writers, particularly lady novelists writing for the education of young girls, seem to have found it unnecessary to follow the caveat "to amuse," with apparently no great loss in sales. Parents of the innocents saw to it that they kept such books as Mrs. Chapone's *Letters on the Improvement of the Mind*—consisting of 200 pages of solid advice on religion, the Bible, the affections, the temper, and politeness—constantly by their sides. According to the moralizing novelist Hannah More, Mrs. Chapone's work "forms the rising age," and another contemporary, Samuel Hoole, has the heroine in his *Aurelia* envisage an ideal woman as one whose dressing table features Mrs. Chapone's volume:

> On the plain toilet, with no trophies gay
> Chapone's *instructive volume open lay.*[74]

At the other extreme were the sensational novelists who loaded their works with sex and sadism, inserting, as a kind of afterthought, a warning line or two, pointing out to the reader that his, or more frequently her, fate will be a ghastly one if he or she slips from the path of virtue. Under the guise of "satiric indignation," revelations of vice and licentiousness in high and low places were exploited in novels, on the stage, and in the magazines as well as in the press—some true, some offered under the pretext of being true.* Almost any device "enabled authors to pass in satiric review various classes and professions in corrupt society."[75] Charles Johnstone (1719–1800) suggested—with disarming candor in view of the fact that he himself was the author of *Chrysal*, one of the more notorious of these exposés—the extent to which the moralizing note was merely an excuse for feeding the appetite for prurient detail:

> There cannot be a stronger argument against the charge of degeneracy in moral virtue and religion brought against the present age, than the avidity with which all works exposing the breaches of them by the unerring proof of facts, are read by all people.[76]

In his preface to the first edition of the *Dunciad* (1728) Pope had made it clear through the words of a fictitious commentator on his work

---

*An idea of the topics covered is conveyed by the titles of a few of these novels:
Love-Letters between a Nobleman and his Sister.
The Unnatural Mother; or Innocent Love Persecuted; being the history of the fatal consequences that attended the . . . passion of a gentleman . . . and a young Lady.
The Cruel Mistress; being the genuine trial of E. B. and her daughter for the murder of Jane Buttersworth, their servantmaid, etc.
The Fatal Connexion, Colonel Digby and Miss Stanley.

("Martinus Scriblerus") that he was disturbed both by the pedants and fops of the literary world and by the sheer numbers of authors who cropped out all over the country once paper became cheap and plentiful in supply:

> He [our Poet] lived in those days, when (after providence had permitted the Invention of Printing as a scourge for the Sins of the learned) Paper also became so cheap, and printers so numerous, that a deluge of authors cover'd the land: . . . our author . . . did conceive it an endeavour well worthy an honest satyrist, to dissuade the dull and punish the malicious, *the only way that was left*. In that public-spirited view he laid the plan of this Poem. . . .[77]

Thus Pope, in the early third of the century of the Enlightenment, served as the conscience of conservatism. In challenging the idea of technical progress as a good in itself, he anticipated the coming debate about the defensive position of the creative individual in a mass society. His was not an article of faith but an article of doubt, and toward the end of the first edition he issues a strong warning not to underestimate these changes and the people who were capitalizing on them:

> Do not, gentle reader, rest too secure in thy contempt of the Instruments for such a revolution in learning, or despite such weak agents as have been described in our poem, but remember what the *Dutch* stories somewhere relate, that a great part of their Provinces was once overflow'd, by a small opening made in one of their dykes by a single *Water-Rat*.

He concludes the poem with a prophecy:

> *Art after Art goes out, and all is Night. . . .*
> *Thy hand great Dulness! lets the curtain fall,*
> *And universal Darkness covers all.*[78]

Fourteen years later, in the preface to *The New Dunciad* (1742), Pope writes that he is setting out "to declare the *Completion* of the *Prophecies* mention'd at the end of the former [Book]."[79] By that time his fellow authors had begun to wonder whether the first edition, outlet for injured professional pride though it may have been, did not also have some of the character of a true prediction.

Rising Dismay

After the middle of the century the writer faced two problems which had not previously struck him as matters for concern. Was the expanding audience for literary products (now beginning to reach into the lower classes as well)* in fact capable of, or interested in, being "improved" either aesthetically *or* morally by means of the written and spoken word which it was consuming in ever greater volume? And what was this new state of affairs—in which he depended for his livelihood upon pleasing this broad public instead of one or two aristocratic or political patrons—doing to the integrity of the artist?

The writers who became most disturbed by these problems were not members of the aristocracy who might have been expected to look with some distaste on the cultural encroachments of the *nouveaux riches* and the tradespeople. Nor were they embittered men who had failed to achieve recognition. They were those writers, mainly of middle-class origin, who had supported themselves by producing serious works for the very public about which they were now becoming sceptical. The *Spectator*, the *Tatler*, and most of their imitators had tried to show these new readers what constituted good taste—in morals, manners, music, architecture, furniture, and landscape gardening as well as in literature. For thirty or more years, the best had been made available to all who could read. Those who had offered it, Garrick, Goldsmith, Johnson, and Fielding and others, began to echo Pope's early and not very exalted opinion of public taste. He had worried about fashions in taste, "snob appeal," and the fickleness of the public:

> *Some ne'er advance a Judgment of their own*
> *But catch the spreading notion of the Town.*
>
> *Some judge of authors' names, not works, and then*
> *Nor praise nor blame the writings, but the men.*
>
> *Some praise at morning what they blame at night;*
> *But always think the last opinion right.*[80]

Now Fielding found the bulk of mankind "clearly void of any degree of taste" and suggested that the common denominator of the audience of his day was very low indeed:

---

*It is almost impossible to pinpoint the moment when the reading public began to include a significant number of the working classes, but most literary historians put it roughly around 1760-70. Tompkins, for example, in *The Popular Novel in England: 1770-1800,* reports that novel-reading had replaced story-telling in the farmhouses, and that in town "the milliner's apprentice, who turns up in contemporary satire with the regularity of Macaulay's schoolboy, spared twopence at the library for a volume of *The Fatal Compliance* or *Anecdotes of a Convent*."

It is a quality in which they advance very little beyond a state of infancy. The first thing a child is fond of in a book is a picture; the second is a story; and the third is a jest. Here, then, is the true Pons Asinorum, which few readers ever get over.[81]

And from a less detached viewpoint a Mr. Jackson, who wrote essays but was primarily a designer and painter of wallpaper in Battersea, berated the level of public taste in a piece on engraving and printing:

> Persons who should prefer the gaudy and unmeaning Papers (so generally met with) . . . would prefer a Fan to a picture of *Raphael* . . . It seems also, as if there was a great Reason to suspect wherever one sees such preposterous Furniture, that the Taste in Literature of the Person who directed it was very deficient, and that it would prefer *Tom D'Urfy* [writer of scurrilous ballads and melodrama in the first quarter of the 18th century] to *Shakespeare*, Sir *Richard Blackmore* to *Milton* . . . an Anagrammatist to *Virgil*. . . .[82]

He concludes, of course, with a commercial "snob appeal": the reader of his essay could demonstrate his sensitive taste in literature and on all other counts by buying Mr. Jackson's "classical" wallpaper.

Doubts about the capacities of their audience forced writers in turn to face the problem of the effects of a broadening market on the writer himself. Pope, himself an author living from the sale of his works, despite his general pessimism about the quality of much contemporary writing, was convinced that the literary genius would eventually win public support, and, conversely, that the writer who did not live well must also be dull. "To prove them *poor*," wrote an anonymous contributor to *Mist's Journal* in 1728, Pope "asserts that they are *dull;* and to prove them *dull* he asserts they are *poor*."[83] His successors were not so sure; Johnson, Fielding, and Goldsmith were writing works that were certainly not "dull" in Pope's meaning of the word for an audience which made it increasingly clear that it was not capable of awarding the good writers with more popularity than the bad. How, they asked, does the author's conviction that his readers are both fickle and debased in their taste affect his integrity and creativity, and how does the book and periodical publishers' insistence on quantity affect the level of the writer's work?

For Oliver Goldsmith, who contributed to at least ten periodicals and was responsible for innumerable compilations and translations which he undertook in order to supplement the income derived from his other works, these were not academic questions. He debated them with all the fervor of a man who feels his professional reputation at stake. Consciously or otherwise, the writer is influenced by the preferences of his audience; it may mean, as Goldsmith said, in his early essay *Upon Taste,* that

> genius, instead of growing like a vigorous tree, extending its branches on every side . . . resembles a stunted yew, tortured into some wretched form, projecting no shade, displaying no flower, diffusing no fragrance, yielding no fruit, and affording *nothing but a barren conceit for the amusement of the idle spectator.*[84] [italics supplied.]

In the course of his prolific years to come, Goldsmith reflected often upon the ethical and artistic conflicts of the writer dependent on popular preferences and answered his own question whether genius must now produce only "barren conceit" alternately yes and no. His first original work, *Enquiry into the Present State of Polite Learning in Europe* (1759), explored the dilemma in which the writer for a growing market found himself. In this book, and in his *Citizen of the World* letters written during the next few years, he managed to place himself squarely on both horns of the dilemma.

For example, on the question of financial dependence on a paying audience, he wrote in Chapter VIII of the *Enquiry:*

> A long habit of writing for bread thus turns the ambition of every author at last into avarice. . . . He despairs of applause and turn to profit. . . . Thus the man who, under the protection of the great, might have done honor to humanity, when only patronized by the bookseller, becomes a thing little superior to the fellow who works at the press.[85]

A few years later (in the meantime he had published his short-lived periodical *The Bee,* written a life of Voltaire as hack-work for the booksellers, and received a much-needed advance of 60 pounds, presumably with the help of Samuel Johnson, on the *Vicar of Wakefield*) he wrote a paean of thanks that the patronage of the public had replaced the "protection of the great." The writer comes into his own as the crucial shift from Patron to Public is completed:

> At present the few poets of England no longer depend on the Great for subsistence, they have now no other patrons but the public, and *the public, collectively considered, is a good and generous master.* . . . A writer of real merit now may easily be rich if his heart be set only on fortune: and for those who have no merit, it is but fit that such should remain in merited obscurity. [Italics supplied]

Not only will he reap his due rewards; for the first time, he can now be self-respecting and independent:

He may now refuse an invitation to dinner, without fearing to incur his patron's displeasure, or to starve by remaining at home. He may now venture to appear in company with just such clothes as other men generally wear, and talk even to princes, with all the conscious superiority of wisdom. Though he cannot boast of fortune here, yet he can bravely assert the dignity of independence.[86]

Or again, in the *Enquiry,* he had written that the author who turns to the bookseller because he can no longer find patronage gets paid for quantity and not for quality; that "in these circumstances the author bids adieu to fame, writes for bread . . ." with "phlegmatic apathy."[87] In the ninety-third *Citizen of the World* letter, on the other hand, he pointed out that "almost all of the excellent productions . . . that have appeared here [in England] were purely the offspring of necessity" and went on to recommend fasting for the sharpening of genius: "Believe me, my friend, hunger has a most amazing faculty of sharpening the genius; and he who with a full belly, can think like a hero, after a course of fasting, shall rise to the sublimity of a demi-god."[88]

Johnson, usually less torn by conflicts between writer and market, raised similar questions. Who is to judge the merit of an author, he asked at about the same time that Goldsmith voiced concern about the fate of the literary genius, and how is he to find his way to recognition in all this "miscellany"? In discussing this problem, Johnson first described some of the needs and predispositions of a "mass" audience:

He that endeavours after fame by writing, solicits the regard of a multitude fluctuating in pleasures, or immersed in business, without time for intellectual amusements; he appeals to judges, prepossessed by passions, or corrupted by prejudices, which preclude their approbation of any new performance. Some are too indolent to read any thing, till its reputation is established; others too envious to promote that fame which gives them pain by its increase.

He then went on to develop a catalogue of audience reaction:

What is new is opposed, because most are unwilling to be taught; and what is known is rejected, because it is not sufficiently considered, that men more frequently require to be reminded than informed. The learned are afraid to declare their opinion early, lest they should put their reputation in hazard; the ignorant always imagine themselves giving some proof of delicacy, when they refuse to be pleased.

If an author achieves recognition, he concludes, it will certainly not be attributable to the discernment of his readers:

And he that finds his way to reputation through all these obstructions, must acknowledge that he is indebted to other causes beside his industry, his learning, or his wit.[89]

Such an audience cannot serve as judge; the writer therefore has to examine the literary scene himself. He must look at the works which are being purchased at so great a rate, and he must try to determine why the public had not soared upward on the two wings of morality and beauty as Addison had hoped they would, and as Pope, for all his self-assurance about the recognition of his own works, had feared they would not.

INDICTMENT

In asking themselves what effect the growing market for printed goods was having on the moral, intellectual, and aesthetic development of the individual and upon the country as a whole, English literati probably became the first group consciously to face the problem of popular culture in modern society. In examining the scene about him, the eighteenth century critic was not so much concerned with the new format in which literature was being produced, such as popular magazines, newspapers, cheap editions or reprints of books; this concern was to develop later, when these new literary shapes had become firmly entrenched features of modern society. He tended, rather, to focus upon changes in content which resulted from the fact that many writers were deliberately catering to the lower levels of taste in the growing audience. The very term "popular writer," in the derogatory sense, came into usage for the first time in this period. Oliver Goldsmith, for example, used it in the *Enquiry* when he expressed fear that "affectation in some popular writer" would lead "others to vicious imitation."[90] While Pope did not actually use the word "popular" in his *Dunciad,* he believed that the drive for popularity accounted for the low level to which many writers of his time had sunk.[91]

Marked changes in the content of the drama and the novel took place in the first half of the century, changes which amounted to a whole-hearted espousal of character-types of the emerging middle class. The genre which replaced Restoration drama, sentimental or "weeping" comedy, centered around the professional and domestic problems of middle-class characters. The hero of these "realistic" dramas was likely to be an everyday sort of person who was a model of virtue, and the villain an everyday sort of person with familiar and commonplace vices. These changes may have contributed to the respectability of the theater but, according to at least one well-qualified observer, they also made it considerably less amusing. Fielding wrote: "In banishing humour from the stage, which was tantamount to banishing human nature, the dramatist made the stage as dull as the drawing-room."[92] This shift from socially elevated characters to city merchants and apprentices in private life—a shift epitomized by the domestic tragedies of George Lillo in the 1730s— brought about a notable change in the experience of the audience: it was now possible for the ordinary theater-goer to identify with the heroes and heroines on the stage. Restoration dramatists had created half-real people and completely unreal situations; in the new dramas of middle-class life, realism and believability were paramount goals.[93] This possibility for identification and imitation was the basis for many moral (as contrasted with aesthetic) anxieties which began to harass the intellectuals of the mid-century as they attempted to assess and to come to terms with the new literary phenomena.

It was the novel which stimulated most of the uneasiness about the consequences of identification with fictional characters. Many more novels were written in a year than there were plays produced, and for many it must have been easier to read novels than to attend the theater. A small book, to be sure, cost about three times as much as a seat in the upper gallery at one of the licensed theaters; but books could be borrowed from friends and from circulating libraries, and they could be read and re-read at the convenience of the reader. Not only was the novel a convenient form of recreation, but its length and considerably less rigorous construction made it more suitable to the limning of the details and nuances of middle-class life. In general, its contents differed from the romance of the seventeenth and early eighteenth centuries in much the same way as sentimenal comedy differed from the Restoration drama. Realism of character and situation was, as Samuel Johnson pointed out in his *Rambler* essay, "The Modern Form of Romance," the distinguishing feature of the new fiction:

> The works of fiction, with which the present generation seems more particularly delighted, are such as exhibit life in its true state, diversified only by accidents that daily happen in the world, and influenced by passions and qualities which are really to be found in conversing with mankind.

Johnson goes on to demonstrate how this stress on realism creates a new problem for the writer. He can no longer rely on his book-learning alone, secure in the knowledge that he is better informed than most of his readers. He must become an astute observer of the world of people around him. Should he make a mistake, every "common reader" will know it, because "our present writers" are "engaged in portraits, of which every one knows the original, and can detect any deviation from exactness of resemblance."[94]

Dangerous Realism

Restoration comedy had mirrored the foibles of the aristocracy with a light touch, with considerable humor, and with no small amount of caricature. The playgoer or reader may well have been amused by the wit and elegance of these clever writings, but he would have been hard put to identify with its highly stylized characters. And the heroic romance of the same period, as Johnson remarked, had discouraged identification by resorting to machines and other convenient but far-fetched expedients such as "giants to snatch a lady away from the nuptial rites" and "knights to bring her back from captivity."[95]

While Samuel Johnson was not alone in his concern, his analysis of the problems raised by the new stress on realism is so pertinent that his essay on the modern novel warrants closer analysis. He asks the question whether, in his eagerness to portray reality, the contemporary novelist might not so closely interweave the reprehensible with the exemplary qualities of a character that the reader will become as favorably disposed to evil as to virtue:

> Many writers, for the sake of following nature, so mingle good and bad qualities in their principal personages, that they are both equally conspicuous; and as we accompany them through their adventures with delight, and are led by degrees to interest ourselves in their favor, we lose the abhorrence of their faults, because they do not hinder our pleasure, or, perhaps, regard them with some kindness for being united with so much merit.

In exploring this dilemma he points out that there have been, in the course of history, some "splendidly wicked" men whose crimes were never viewed as "perfectly detestable" because their often agreeable personalities cast a pleasing aura about them. He protests against true-to-life portrayal of such characters because they are "the great corrupters of the world, and their resemblance ought no more to be preserved than the art of murdering without pain."

For all his scorn of the *deus ex machina,* Johnson looked back with a tinge of regret upon the highly unrealistic romances which he had read in his youth:

> In the romances formerly written, every transaction and sentiment was so remote from all that passes among men, that the reader was in very little danger of making any applications to himself; the virtues and crimes were equally beyond his sphere of activity; and he amused himself with heroes

and with traitors, deliverers and persecutors, as with beings of another species . . . who had neither faults nor excellences in common with himself.

He then formulates the processes of identification and imitation encouraged by the new realistic fiction.

But when an adventurer is levelled with the rest of the world, and acts in such scenes of the universal drama as may be the lot of any other man, young spectators fix their eyes upon him with closer attention, and hope, by observing his behaviour and success, to regulate their own practices, when they shall be engaged in the like part.

While such processes could have unhappy consequences, Johnson believed that identification with fictional characters might be put to constructive use and realistic stories made a boon to the educator: "These familiar histories may perhaps be made of greater use than the solemnities of professed morality, and convey the knowledge of vice and virtue with more efficacy than axioms and definitions." Perhaps, Johnson concluded (with notably greater emphasis on effects than on artistic integrity), the author should manipulate reality a bit. Virtue should be judiciously exalted, and vice, while not to be eliminated altogether, should always be portrayed in a way which leaves the reader with a feeling of repulsion:

In narratives, where historical veracity has no place, I cannot discover why there should not be exhibited the most perfect idea of virtue . . . the highest and surest that humanity can reach . . . which . . . may, by conquering some calamities and enduring others, teach us what we may hope and what we can perform. Vice, for vice is necessary to be shown, should always disgust.

As though he were formulating a self-regulatory code for novel-writers, he concludes with a plea for what amounts to "all-white or all-black" character portrayals:*

Nor should the graces of gayety, or the dignity of courage, be so united with it [vice] as to reconcile it to the mind: wherever it appears, it should

---

*Johnson's criticism of Shakespeare was based largely on the grounds that he did not do any judicious weighing of good against evil in his characterizations. In the preface to his edition of Shakespeare, he writes that on the contrary, Shakespeare "carries his persons indifferently through right and wrong, and at the close dismisses them without further care, and leaves their examples to operate by chance. This fault the barbarity of his age cannot extenuate; for it is always a writer's duty to make the world better . . ."

raise hatred by the malignity of its practices, and contempt by the meanness of its stratagems; for while it is supported by either parts or spirits, it will be seldom heartily abhorred. . . . There are thousands of readers . . . willing to be thought wicked, if they may be allowed to be wits.[96]

Johnson was not alone in his complaints about the abuses of realism. Lady Mary Wortley Montagu, a writer of charming letters though not a professional critic, touched upon the matter in a private correspondence. Referring to the realism of the character portrayals in Richardson's *Clarissa* and *Pamela,* she singled them out as the "two books that will do more general mischief than the works of Lord Rochester."[97] And Oliver Goldsmith went even further than Johnson in recommending that novels be especially adapted to youth. In an essay on education, he expressed concern about the effects of true-to-life characterizations and advocated that

> there be some men of wit employed to compose books that might equally interest the passions of our youth . . . to be explicit as possible, the old story of Whittington, were his cat left out, might be more serviceable to the tender mind than either Tom Jones, Joseph Andrews or an hundred others.

Instead of suggesting that professional writers adapt their works to the educational needs of youth, Goldsmith proposed that schoolmasters be put to work composing novels:

> Were our schoolmasters, if any of them have sense enough to draw up such a work, thus employed, it would be much more serviceable to their pupils, than all the grammars and dictionaries they may publish these ten years.[98]

While both Johnson and Goldsmith drew fairly clear distinctions between mature and immature readers (that is, their worries about the effects of realism were largely confined to youth), they did not draw hard and fast lines between various levels of fiction. Moral problems, they felt, were posed by all realistic fiction, whether the work of a genius or of a hack.

Few writers maintained consistent viewpoints on questions of realism. Henry Mackenzie, for example, the author of what has become a proverbially sentimental novel, *The Man of Feeling,* followed this "all-white" product a few years later with *The Man of the World* in which the hero was from a quite different color of cloth. A contemporary reviewer of the second novel scolded Mackenzie for not sufficiently punishing his wayward hero, a reformed seducer, who "should either have been sent

to the devil, or his reformation should have been in consequence of a
long and bitter repentance."[99] Mackenzie himself either changed his mind
or kept his various writing selves distinctly separate: ten years after *The
Man of Feeling* he wrote disparagingly, in his *Lounger,* of the

> mingled virtue and vice which is to be found in some of the best of our
> novels. Instances will readily occur to every reader, where the hero of the
> performance has violated, in one page, the most sacred laws of society, to
> whom, by the mere turning of the leaf, we are to be reconciled, whom we
> are to be made to love and admire, for the beauty of some humane, or
> the brilliancy of some heroic action.[100]

Dr. Johnson, on the other hand, while he had on one occasion
recommended that characters be thoroughly good or thoroughly evil, on
another endorsed realism, though it necessarily involved the picturing
of wickedness. In his *Lives of the Poets,* published nearly thirty years
after the *Rambler* essay on fiction, he insists that the writer, while
occasionally justified in gratifying the audience by making things pleasant,
is bound also to show life as it really is.*[101]

True-to-life portrayals could easily become boring, and writers resorted
to many devices for sustaining interest in the ordinary people and
situations portrayed in their novels and plays. Two methods for insuring
audience appeal were full descriptions of tender sentiments and, at the
other extreme, detailed spellings-out of scenes of aggression, violence, or
horror. Very often, in the manner of the Hollywood motion picture, these
two sets of attractions were combined in the same production, always
making sure that the sensitive hero was the victim and not the perpetrator
of aggression.

These devices for offsetting boredom confronted the creative writer
with a number of additional problems.

First, does not the realistic portrayal of *crime and violence,* of which
the English audience was considered to be inordinately fond, both reflect
and encourage sadism in the audience?

Second, when everyday characters are made less boring by a generous
endowment of *sentimentality,* are not the heads of the readers filled with
romantic notions which will stand them in no good stead as they go

---

*This does not mean a victory of realism over moralism in Dr. Johnson's approach
to literature. As René Wellek points out, in his *History of Modern Criticism,* the
two strands—together with an element of abstractionism—were closely interwoven
in all of Johnson's criticism, but "more frequently the moralist is dominant, to
the exclusion and even detriment of the critic (V. I, p. 83)."

about the business of making a living (or marrying a man) in the workaday world? Worse still, may they not use identification with the unreal world of emotion as a means of escape from the exigencies of everyday life?

Third, perhaps again because of the very familiarity of these realistic characters and situations, the audience began to attach increasing importance to *novelty and variety* as values in themselves. How, asked the writer, can we keep this desire for sensationalism from even further debasing the taste of the public?

Fourth, with an avalanche of mass-produced material which makes few demands on the reader and not many more on the writer, is there not a very real danger that the world of letters may be entering a period of *mediocrity?*

Crime and Violence

Though the modern media have more graphic, and more ubiquitous, representational device at their disposal than did those of the eighteenth century, descriptions of sadism and brutality did not spring full-blown from the comic book or the television set. As a matter of fact, some of the "horror" novels which enjoyed popularity in the last three decades of the century make those "comic" books of sex and sadism which are sold from under the counter today look pallid by comparison.

The genre called "Gothic" romance, foreshadowed by Walpole's *Castle of Otranto* (1764), reached its peak a quarter of a century later in M. G. Lewis' *The Monk,* a romance built almost entirely around scenes of sadism, sensuality, and fright.* Lewis's work rapidly went through a number of editions and set a new standard for brutality which was to be imitated in most of the English Gothic novels to come. But while these horror tales stirred up small furors at the time of publication, the peak of popular as well as intellectual reaction was not reached until after 1800.

The debate over "crime and violence" in the drama, however, was waged with vigor throughout the eighteenth century. Concern about the murders and tortures which had long been commonplace on the stage had formed part of the objections to the theater raised by the neo-Puritans. But in general neither they nor their successors differentiated

---

*Mrs. Radcliffe's *The Mysteries of Udolpho* was perhaps the outstanding novel of suspense of the period; in contrast to M. G. Lewis, Mrs. Radcliffe explained away the supernatural by rational means, and relied on curiosity rather than fear as the main appeal of her work.

between profanity and lewdness on the one hand and criminal or brutal behavior on the other. Furthermore, when Defoe and others referred to the stage as a "nursery of crime," they were as much distressed about the behavior of the audience and about the "corrupting" environs of the theater as they were about what took place on the stage. Among less moralistic critics, aggression and violence on the stage were the main objects of concern. Even Addison, who was rather tolerant of the excesses of the opera and stage, raised the issue:

> But among all our Methods of moving Pity or Terror, there is none so absurd and barbarous, and what more exposes us to the Contempt and Ridicule of our Neighbours, than that dreadful butchering of one another which is so very frequent upon the *English* stage.

He sympathizes with French critics who had pointed to the sight of "Men stabbed, poisoned, racked or impaled" on the English stage as "the Sign of a cruel Temper" in the English national character. Addison goes on to decry the favorite climax of the stage tragedies of his day, wherein every prop for murder and torture is used in a grand free-for-all of mass slaughter:

> It is indeed very odd, to see our Stage strewed with Carcasses in the last Scene of a Tragedy; and to observe in the Ward-robe of the Play-house several Daggers, Poinciards, Wheels, Bowls for Poison and many other Instruments of Death.[102]

But in spite of such disdain, the English audience's love of blood and violence continued to be fed. In the mid-thirties, Henry Fielding published his skit, *Pasquin,* which ridiculed several of the dramatic excesses of the day, not least the addiction to slaughter and poison. Twenty years later, Oliver Goldsmith observed that "death and tenderness are leading passions of every modern buskined hero; this moment they embrace, and the next stab, mixing daggers and kisses in every period."[103] And David Hume, in his treatise *Of Tragedy,* excoriated such realistic portrayals of horror because they interfere with the main objectives of tragedy:

> An action, represented in tragedy, may be too bloody and atrocious. . . . Such is that action represented in the *Ambitious Stepmother,* where a venerable old man, raised to the heights of fury and despair, rushes against a pillar, and striking his head upon it, besmears it all over with mingled brains and gore. The *English* theatre abounds too much with such images.[104]

Unlike present-day discussion of this topic, no eighteenth century critic seems to have condoned fictional or dramatic portrayals of "crime and violence," and reference to the Aristotelian concept of catharsis is in this connection (though not in connection with suffering from other causes) conspicuously absent.

Sentimentality

Goldsmith, in his *Essay on the Theatre,* reports the reaction of "a friend" to the unembroidered presentation of middle-class city-types and their practical problems. The friend left the theater in the middle of a play about a moneylender remarking, "It is indifferent to me whether he be turned out of his counting house on Fish Street Hill, since he will have enough left to open shop in St. Giles's. . . ."[105] While the drama tried to counteract such boredom with violence and other "special attractions," the novelists, for their part, had their own devices. Richardson had set the tone: portrayals of the plights and successes of the middle and lower middle classes could be invested with considerable appeal by the inclusion of detailed descriptions of their affairs of the heart. Goldsmith's *Vicar of Wakefield* is generally considered to be an outstanding work of this genre and Mackenzie's *The Man of Feeling* represents the extreme of the novel which combined the ordinary and the realistic in character and setting with detailed descriptions and exaltations of sentiment.*

In "the novel of sentiment" and the "novel of sensibility" (which differed from each other more in degree than in kind) the emotions were more important than behavior, and rationality in either thought or behavior was relegated to crude and insensitive souls. Forgiveness and repentance were the pinnacles of human feeling, and the reasons for actions which led to forgiveness or repentance were as irrelevant as the murder which opens the modern mystery story. It was the detailed and lengthy portrayals of emotions that gave rise to the first discussions about the dangers of escapism.

Because of the improbable nature of the seventeenth and early eighteenth century romance, and perhaps also because it had been read by

---

*The prevailingly sentimental tone of the novels of this period has been attributed in part to the fact that there was a great influx of women novelists who wrote for the largely female novel-reading public. Certainly contemporary satire on such lady novelists was not lacking: Tobias Smollett, among others, went out of his way, in *Humphrey Clinker,* to point out that the failure of one of his characters as a novelist was excusable because the ladies had the field of "spirit, delicacy, and knowledge of the human heart" all to themselves.

fewer people than was the novel of sentiment, few before the middle of the century had been concerned about the effect of fiction on the reader. Addison, to be sure, had poked mild fun at a gentlewoman who consumed many of these fanciful tales and eventually undertook to while away her time by re-doing her estate to resemble a romantic grotto,[106] but he was neither indignant nor alarmed about the social consequences of such indulgence.

The stress on sentimental bliss in the novels of the second half of the century gave rise to the more socially significant kind of concern. Over-indulgence in fiction has two serious consequences: it keeps the reader from useful endeavours and fills his head with romantic dreams, which will be impossible to attain in real life. Oliver Goldsmith, despite *The Vicar of Wakefield,* often warned against the dangers of living in the transported world of sentiment. In a letter to his brother about his nephew's education, he even advised the father to prohibit novel reading altogether. Such romantic pictures of the world are snares and delusions to youth: "They teach the young mind to sigh after beauty and happiness which never existed; to despite the little good which fortune has mixed in their cup, by expecting more than she gave."[107] The reading of sentimental novels, in short, is not practical. But the pastime is perhaps more dangerous for the young girl than for the young man, because she who is fed on sentiment and sensibility will be hard pressed to love a man whose daily life is filled with the routine demands of earning a living for wife and family. Furthermore, as William Cowper noted with some indignation, the young lady is likely to become so over-stimulated by the reading of such "sentimental frippery and dream," of "sniv'ling and driv'ling folly," that no mere insertion of a warning will "quench the fire."[108]

The middle-class character had best be equipped with middle-aged sentiments, for too great a concern with tender feelings ill-equips a youth for bourgeois life. Richardson's Charlotte Grandison argue that "a mild, sedate convenience is better than a stark staring mad passion. . . . Who ever hears of darts, flames, Cupids . . . and such like nonesense in matrimony? Passion is transitory."[109]

But such warnings did not stem the tide of sentimental literature which provided readers with escape from the humdrum of everyday life. The middle class may have wanted to see itself in a mirror but it wanted to see its materialistic self dressed up and made more appealing with delicate sensibilities.

Novelty and Variety

Concern about man's search for distraction did not come into being with the dawn of the eighteenth century and the development of saleable literary goods. Montaigne, and later Pascal, had debated the issue in the sixteenth and seventeenth centuries.* But it was Voltaire's *Essay on Taste,* published in 1757, which alerted writers and scholars to the implications of the problem in a society rapidly becoming inundated with all kinds of written entertainment.

Voltaire, examining the general cultural scene of his times, found that

> the publick, fond of novelty, applauds their invention; but this applause is soon succeeded by satiety and disgust. A new set of artists start up, invent new methods to please a capricious taste, and depart still further from nature. . . . Overwhelmed with new inventions, which succeed and efface each other with incredible rapidity, they scarcely know where they are . . .[110]

Looking at the growing market for literary product and at the manifest inclinations of the audience which was purchasing them, the English men of letters found ample proof that Voltaire's concern was justified.

David Garrick faced the public demand for novelty in his three-fold capacity as dramatist, actor, and theater manager. In the course of his thirty-year career he found it increasingly necessary to water down his artistic standards with "propping-up" devices and double feature billings which would supply "the many various objects that amuse these busy curious times."[111] Dr. Johnson devoted one of his *Idler* essays to "terrific" diction—a mannerism of obscurity adopted by some writers to add a note of novelty to the commonplace. In explaining the motivation behind this device (which he dubs the "bugbear" style), Johnson says that the demand to see "common things in an uncommon manner" is characteristic of the times. The kinds of devices which popular writers resort to are those on the order of telling time by algebra, drinking tea by stratagem, in short "to quit the beaten track only because it is known, and to take a new path, however crooked or rough, because the straight was found out before."

In another *Idler* essay he speaks of "the multiplication of books," particularly of compilations, and notes that they serve no real purpose but merely "distract choice." He concludes, however, that such writers do little harm in the long run because they are merely symptoms of a short-lived fad.[112]

It was the magazines which most conspicuously catered to the demand for variety, but oddly enough, these popular "miscellanies," whose number increased rapidly as the century wore on, were not attacked with any

---

*See Chapters 1 and 2 of this volume.

consistency by the serious writers.* Oliver Goldsmith, however, did devote one of his essays to some good-natured raillery of the magazines. He compares his lot as an essayist who can write upon only one subject at a time with those more "fortunate" magazine writers who can write upon several and thus avoid the risk of boring their readers. The magazine which he describes resembles the *Gentleman's Magazine* or some similar eighteenth century original of *Reader's Digest:*

> If a magazine be dull upon the Spanish war, he soon has us up again with the Ghost in Cock Lane; if the reader begins to doze upon that, he is quickly roused by an Eastern tale: tales prepare us for poetry, and poetry for the meteorological history of the weather. It is the life and soul of a magazine never to be long dull upon one subject; and the reader, like the sailor's horse, has at least the comfortable refreshment of having the spur often changed.

Ironically complaining that he sees no reason why the magazine writers should "carry off all the rewards of genius," Goldsmith goes on to outline a plan for changing the format of his own essays, making them a magazine in miniature in which he proposes to "hop from subject to subject." He also gives notice that, if properly encouraged, he will decorate his magazine with pictures. The journal is to be called the *Infernal Magazine* and, unlike others of the same genre, it will live up to its advertised promise to astonish society. Obeisances are then made to the prospective audience in the usual style of eighteenth century prospectuses, and Goldsmith assures his readers-to-be that the magazine is to be run by gentlemen of distinction (and means) who will perform this public service not for personal gain but purely for their own amusement.[113]

Nuances of feeling and sentiment offered one way to add appeal to the pedestrian characters and situations which dominated the popular writings of the time. Exotic settings provided another. The opening up of the Far East to British trade had resulted in what was perhaps one of the most sweeping fads England has ever experienced. Music, fabrics, dress styles, furniture, architecture, gardening, and painting—nothing escaped the great demand for the Oriental. The "nabob" who disappeared into China for a year or two and came home with his pockets full of gold became, for a time, a hero. Writers made short shrift of turning the situation to their own advantage. Nabobs were adulated on the stage

---

*It is possible that the intellectuals were inclined to consider the magazine beneath their notice, just as they seem to have left criticism of the popular novels of the latter part of the century to "middlebrow" writers.

where they often proved to be a great dramatic convenience, and essays, letters, and novels took the ordinary Englishman into extraordinary surroundings, replete with elaborate trappings and a heavy veil of mystery (it need hardly be added that the adventurer usually followed tradition and remained an Englishman for all that). In these tales of Oriental adventure, the "wisdom of the East" was often exalted, as in William Whitehead's prologue to Arthur Murphy's version of Voltaire's *L'Orphelin de la Chine* (1759)—"and boldly bears Confucius' morals to Britannia's ears. Accept th'imported boon."[114]

A few chauvinistic voices were heard saying, in effect, "What does the Orient offer that England cannot match or better?" But by and large the fashion for the Oriental, which was as popular among royalty as among shopgirls, was not considered as dangerous to the reader as was indulgence in the sentimental. Furthermore, it was good for trade and perhaps, with its tales of hard-won riches, even provided additional incentives, if any were needed, for concentrating on the practical (and remunerative) aspects of life.

For the most part, the world of letters confined itself to pointing to the Chinese fad as one more proof of the public's insatiable need for novelty and variety. The jaded European, as Goldsmith remarked with considerably more detachment than he had shown in his remarks about the novel of sentiment, "has, of late, had recourse even to China, in order to diversify the amusements of the day."[115] He himself, not without some apology, used the Oriental touch as a device for strengthening the appeal of his commentary on various aspects of contemporary life, as his *Citizen of the World*—"letters from a Chinese philosopher residing in London to his friends in the East"—testifies. In his introduction to these letters, he first complains about the fickleness of the audience and the indiscriminate way in which praise is lavished on the "mob" of popular writers, and then reports a dream in which

> the success of such numbers [of authors] at last began to operate on me. If these, cried I, meet with favour and safety, some luck may, perhaps, for once attend the unfortunate. I am resolved to make a new adventure.

He then comments that, while thus far the "frippery and fireworks of China" have merely served to "vitiate" the public taste, he will "try how far they can help to improve our understanding."[116]

Goldsmith and his fellow writers were less tolerant of the far reaches to which the public's desire for novelty had led in the opera and drama. The seventeenth century theater had catered to a rather more heterogeneous audience than had the printed works of the time. To sustain the interest of people with diverse tastes it had made use of a variety of audience appeals. The "spectacular" or "sensational" devices to which eighteenth century dramatists and theater managers resorted were, therefore, not essentially different in kind from those used in the days of Addison (or, for that matter, in the Elizabethan period). Addison had, in fact, devoted more than one issue of the *Spectator* to the abuses of the operatic stage, though his remonstrances were mild in comparison with those Pope was to write in twenty years and those of Goldsmith and Fielding forty years later. Addison found many of the popular attention-getting devices quite legitimate—his plea was merely for a more judicious application. Thunder and lightning, bells and ghosts, all have their "proper season" and, used with restraint, are to be applauded. The same is true of the much-maligned handkerchief, the "principal machine" for the "moving of pity": it should not be eliminated, but its flutterings should have some connection with the words of the actor.[117] About one minor attraction, however, he was not quite so tolerant. In another issue of the *Spectator* he writes that it is customary to impress the audience with the lofty character of the hero by the lofty height of the plumes on his head, as though "a great Man and a tall Man" were the same thing. Not only is this an affront to the audience, but most embarrassing for the actor because, "notwithstanding any Anxieties which he pretends for his Mistress, his Country or his Friends, one may see by his Actions that his greatest Care and Concern is to keep the Plume of Feathers from falling off his Head."[118]

Addison's sharpest sarcasm was reserved for the indiscriminate mixing of the representational with the real. In ridiculing the release of live birds from a cage on the stage of the opera house, he objected not that they were put there in the first place but that their songs emanated all too obviously from man-blown instruments hidden behind the scenery. Apparently intending to frighten stage-managers into their senses, he concludes with a description of where such absurdities might lead:

> I found . . . that there were great Designs on Foot for the Improvement of the Opera; that it had been proposed to break down a part of the Wall, and to surprize the Audience with a Party of an hundred Horse, and that there was actually a Project of bringing the *New-River* into the House, to be employed in Jetteaus and Waterworks.[119]

Had Addison lived on to the middle of the century, he would have found that instead of giving the stage-managers pause, he may have put new ideas into their heads, for audio-visual claptrap became more than ever the order of the day as the stage and opera had more strenuously to compete with magazines and novels for public attention.

Eloquent satirizers were not lacking as the abuses multiplied. Pope certainly did not overlook the stage as he lampooned the world of letters of his time:

> The play stands still; damn action and discourse,
> Back fly the scenes, and enter foot and horse;
> Pageants on pageants, in long order drawn,
> Peers, heralds, bishops, ermine, gold, and lawn.[120]

But again it remained for Goldsmith to conduct the most thoroughgoing analysis, this one in his *The Chinese Goes to See a Play.* First he points out that daggers and kisses are mixed in every scene. He then goes on to report an entr'acte episode which took place right after the curtain fell on just such a mixture of love and sadism:

> My attention was engrossed by a new object; a man came in balancing a straw upon his nose, and the audience were clapping their hand in all the raptures of applause. To what purpose, cried I, does this unmeaning figure make his appearance; is he a part of the plot?

Analyzing the nature of the appeal of this vaudeville-like performance, Goldsmith postulates an ironic theory about its projective potentialities. Such a trick has something in it for everyone:

> Unmeaning, do you call him, replied my friend. . . . This is one of the most important characters of the whole play; nothing pleases the people more than the seeing a straw balanced; there is a great deal of meaning in the straw; there is something suited to every apprehension in the sight; and a fellow possessed of talents like these is sure of making his fortune.

Between the third and fourth acts, the "Chinese" is surprised to see a child of six appear, "learning to dance" on the stage. At the end of the fourth act the heroine fell into a fit, whereupon the

> fifth act began, and a busy piece it was. Scenes shifting, trumpets sounding, mobs hallooing, carpets spreading, guards bustling from one door to another; gods, daemons, daggers, racks and ratsbane. But whether the king was killed, or the queen was drowned, or the son was poisoned, I have absolutely forgotten.[121]

Another *Citizen of the World* letter is devoted to a description of the seasonal opening of the two licensed theaters, the Drury Lane and Covent Garden. Goldsmith first remarks on the competition between the two houses in which

> the generals of either army have . . . several reinforcements to lend occasional assistance. If they produce a pair of diamond buckles at one house, we have a pair of eyebrows that can match them at the other. . . . If we can bring more children on the stage, they can bring more guards in red clothes, who strut and shoulder their swords to the astonishment of every spectator.

He ridicules the idea that the audience—despite the virtuous platitudes of the times—can possibly derive any instruction from such performances, and reports that, "what with trumpets, hallooing behind the stage and bawling upon it," he himself always gets dizzy long before the performance is over. Calling the situation what it largely was—a money-making proposition—Goldsmith expresses surprise that the play-writing trade has not set up an apprentice system, since there would seem to be nothing easier than to write for the English stage:

> The author, when well acquainted with the value of thunder and lightning; when versed in all the mystery of scene-shifting and trap-doors; when skilled in the proper periods to introduce a wire-walker or a waterfall; . . . he knows all that can give a modern audience pleasure.

And—as in the case of the *Infernal Magazine*—he continues his essay with some ironic advice to the author who wishes to achieve popularity. First, he should never expect the actor to adjust to the requirements of a drama; it is the author's responsibility to appraise the particular abilities of each actor, and to write his play around their respective talents for expressing fear, pain or surprise. Such moans and groans and exclamations are the surest way to win the applause of the audience. There is, in fact, no other way to win an audience. The author will find his consolation in the knowledge that once having acquired such skills, he needs no other talents, and the playgoer can relax in the certainty that once in the theater he can "dismiss from the mind all the fatigue of thinking."[122]

To this facetious advice to the dramatist can be added a number of other examples. In his *Essay on the Theater* written two decades after the *Citizen of the World* Goldsmith formulates the problem of the "paying" audience in terms so modern that they might well be taken for a mid-twentieth century discussion of the motion picture. He begins with a criticism of sentimental comedy and suggests that such plays are largely popular because the dramatists go out of their way to cater to the public demand for novelty. He then acts as his own antagonist, saying that after all the theater is "formed to amuse mankind, and that it matters little, if this end be answered, by what means it is obtained." Whatever pleases the audience is good, "success . . . is a mark of [its] merit." Assuming his own role once more, he then raises the question—since become very familiar, but no more answered in our time than his— what would happen if the audience were provided with *good* drama?[123]

But the English audience continued to enjoy the various devices hit upon for its excitement and amusement. The grotesque effect of the "intermingling of daggers and kisses" is reported by a German visitor to a British play, in which the leading lady was so moved by her tragic situation that she was incapacitated for the rest of the performance

> and had to be carried off the stage unconscious. And the audience, too, unable to endure the strain, departed, so that the piece had to be finished without the leading lady, before a handful of unusually hard-boiled spectators.[124]

However powerful the appeal of the tragic emotions, it was for lavish displays that the eighteenth century audience reserved its most unbounded enthusiasm. During Garrick's management of the Drury Lane, four lush pantomimes and Garrick's own "spectacular" *The Jubilee* all ran considerably longer than any serious drama produced in the same period. After a very brief initial run, most of the genuine works of art, as Garrick regretfully remarked even of his Shakespeare productions, had to be "propped up" by the addition of well-advertised and ever "new" baubles such as parades, masquerades, and dances.[125]

It was this demand for novelty from the reading and playgoing audiences which made it possible for almost any writer to have his day of popularity, provided only he could convince his public that he was giving them something they had never experienced before. Pope attempted to discourage the opportunists who cared to this propensity by deriding them with names and titles, but he had the advantage of perusing the scene fairly early in the century when one book could contain them all. His successors, unable to cope with the deluge case by case, were of necessity considerably less specific.

Mediocrity

The idea of cyclical movements in the arts and sciences is to be found in almost any age. In eighteenth century England, this concept, together with the idea that his own period was one of decline, seems first to have been formulated by David Hume in the essay on *The Rise and Progress of the Arts and Sciences* (1742). He states that when the "arts and sciences come to perfection in any state . . . they naturally, or rather necessarily, decline . . . and seldom or never revive in that nation. . . ."[126] A few years later, somewhat less dogmatically, Voltaire echoed Hume from across the Channel: "The taste of a nation may degenerate and become extremely depraved; and it almost always happens that the period of its perfection is the forerunner of its decline."[127]

Neither Hume nor Voltaire seem to have related their ideas about a decline directly to the growing audience and the popular literature with which it was being fed, though Hume did say that the public's desire for novelty "leads men wide of simplicity and nature, and fills their writings with affectation and conceit."[128] But other writers of the mid-century did connect their fears with the new tyranny of public demand and the new spate of popular works. Among the first protagonists of this concept, we find Pope and Swift complaining about the lack of literary qualifications of writers in general; we find less eminent authors complaining about hack novelists and their methods of production; and we find readers as well as writers complaining about the literary un-worthiness of the new crop of fictional characters emerging in eighteenth century literature. Finally, we find a group of philosophers and writers seriously disturbed about the fact that, with the increase in literacy, anyone and everyone can become a literary critic, that incompetents are now passing judgment, and that literary standards may, as a result, be shattered altogether.*

Some time before the publication of the first edition of *The Dunciad* (1729), Pope wrote to Swift that it was the "little" writers of the world who made him angry, the "party writers, dull poets, and wild criticks."

> My spleen is at the little rogues of it; it would vex one more to be knocked on the head with a piss-pot than by a thunderbolt. . . . But to be squirted

---

*Thomas Carlyle, in reviewing English literature of the eighteenth century in his *Lectures on the History of Literature* (1838), regretted the quackery resulting from the selling of literary goods and reflected that it would bring about great confusion among "all men."

". . . an observer sees the quack established; he sees truth trodden down to the earth everywhere around him; in his own office he sees quackery at work, and that part of it which is done by quackery is done better than all the rest; till at last he, too, concludes in favor of this order of things and gets himself enrolled among this miserable set, eager after profit, and of no belief except the belief always held among such persons, that *Money will buy money's worth*, and that *Pleasure is pleasant*. But woe to that land and its people if, for what they do, they expect payment at all times! It is bitter to see. . . . All men will suffer from it with confusion in the very heart of them."

to death, as poor Wycherly [the eminent Restoration comic playwright had died in 1716] said to me on his death-bed, by apothecaries' apprentices, by the understrappers of under-secretaries to secretaries who were no secretaries—this would provoke as dull a dog as Philips* himself.[129]

The objective of the book was, in his own words, to "dissuade the dull and punish the malicious" authors of his day. The poem consists of direct and often highly personal attacks not only on those writers whom Pope considered to be second-rate, but on the booksellers, book-puffers, and book-reviewers who by promoting such writers were assuaging the public hunger for information and novelty. The heroine, or better, the *bête noire* of the *Dunciad* is the Goddess of Dullness, a "laborious, heavy, busy, bold and blind" deity who seems to be coming into her own in the eighteenth century world of letters. In addition to her coterie of writers and hacks, she is surrounded by a public whom Pope categorizes as Tasteless Admirers, Flatterers of Dunces, Indolent Persons and Minute Philosophers. Early in the poem the Goddess requests the Dunces to instruct a group of young students who enter the scene. The consequence of their teaching is that the youths taste the cup "which causes total oblivion of all Obligations, divine, civil, moral or rational" and are thus rendered unfit to play a constructive role in life.[130] In other words, the future of civilized society has become endangered because the students, who are the hope of that society, are being corrupted by dull, stupid, uncreative reading material produced by incompetents.[131]

The second edition of *The Dunciad* (1743) was considerably less personal and at the same time broader in scope than the first, going beyond the realm of literature proper to address itself to the theater, the opera, and even to education and politics. The two editions together compose the major broadside against particular writers; and the popular "little rogues" of literature whom Pope attacked have, as one of his recent editors has pointed out, all vindicated his judgment by sinking into oblivion.[132]

The fear of a decline centered on both the novel and the drama. In the case of the novel, the peaks attained by Richardson and Fielding, and later by Sterne and Smollett, were infinitely higher than anything achieved in the subsequent two or three decades of the century. Their works, in retrospect, were seen not as a starting point of a new era in the novel, but as its culmination. It was the serious-minded journalists rather than the few great literary figures of the latter half of the century

---

*Presumably John Philips, 1631-1706, a nephew of Milton, employed largely as translator and hack-writer.

who trained their sights on the cruder novelists.* To take one instance, *The Sylph,* a short-lived single-essay periodical published late in the century, devoted an issue to a lively parody of the way in which the popular novels were being slapped together: the trick is to spread the words mechanically across the page, shuffle them about to form sentences, and

> according to the arrangement and collection of them [they] become *narrations, speeches, sentiments, descriptions, etc.* and when *a very great quantity of them* . . . are wedged together after a particular form and manner, they are denominated a NOVEL.[133]

Another magazine writer recommended, in the manner of Swift, that engines be adopted to make the novel-writing process easier, and contributors to several other respected journals of the latter half of the century made frequent quips about the plagiarisms, repetitions, and patchwork that often went into what was released as a novel. With such a multitude turning out novels, grumbled one, all themes have been used up; the novel has had its day:

> The manufacture of novels has been so long established, that in general they have arrived at mediocrity. . . . We are indeed so sickened with this worn-out species of composition, that we have lost all relish for it.[134]

The deterioration in the English drama after 1740 has been attributed in part to the sheer accident that no great dramatist developed in this period; but the fact that audiences represented a broader social background and were at the same time artistically less interested than audiences of the first half of the century also deserves consideration.[135] Furthermore, as we have already remarked, middle-class realism tended to be more boring on the stage than in print. Another reason ventured for the decline in the drama was that the physical alterations made in order to accommodate larger audiences required adaptations by playwright and actor which militated against "good theater." The lighting was dim, the acoustics poor, and the exaggeration required to overcome these deficiencies lent a farcical note to the tragic and comic alike.

---

*In twentieth century terminology we might say that this is a typical example of the middlebrows criticizing the lowbrows. Highbrows, as we have seen, did not differentiate, at least not until the end of the century when Jane Austen's parodies of the novel of terror might be viewed as the highbrow singling out the middlebrow.

But for many artists it was the multiplication of "judges and critics" which seems to have been most portentous of a decline in the literary world. As the ability to read spread to all ranks of society, it seemed that anyone could become an arbiter of standards; "in short," as one periodical essayist remarked, "fiddlers, players, singers, dancers and mechanics themselves are all the sons and daughters of taste."[136] Oliver Goldsmith, in his *Enquiry*, which he prefaced with the remark that he takes the decay of genius in his age for granted, placed much of the blame squarely on the multiplying number of critics or would-be critics.[137]

What rankled most seems not to have been the professionals but the amateurs in the audience. Writers had long had the field of literary standards to themselves, and the only threat to their self-imposed criteria was the necessity of now and then composing a paean of praise to a wealthy patron, when they were fortunate enough to have one. In the final analysis, this concern about the voices of the people amounted to a rallying behind Goldsmith in his pessimistic mood—"when only patronized by the bookseller the writer becomes a thing little superior to the fellow who works at the press"—rather than behind his optimistic formulation: "the public, collectively considered, is a good and generous master." Not only was "everyone" becoming articulate in the expression of literary judgments; worse still, there were so many levels of audience opinion that it seemed to the artists that their tastes were irreconcilable.

From all sides came the complaint. Fielding wrote:

> *How is it possible at once to please*
> *Tastes so directly opposite as these?*[138]

And Garrick addressed the several levels of his audience as follows:

> *What shall we do your different tastes to hit?*
> *You relish satire (to the pit) you ragouts of wit (to the boxes)*
> *Your taste is humour and high-season's joke. (First Gallery)*
> *You call for hornpipe and for hearts of oak. (Second Gallery)*[139]

The critic Warburton sympathized with the fate of the dramatists who

are often used like ladies of pleasure: they are received with rapture and enthusiasm by the public on their first appearance, but on farther acquaintance are received very coolly, though they have indeed by this time greatly improved themselves in the *art of pleasing*.[140]

Cibber, speaking in his role of stage manager, was first to point out a new way of looking at the audience, one which was eventually to effect a compromise between the standards of the artist and the divers tastes of the new public. In one of his *Two Dissertations on the Theatres,* he speaks of the phrase "the Town" which was commonly used to designate the audience. Ask an author or an actor (individually) whom he has in mind when he uses this phrase, predicts Cibber, and he will tell you that he means the "judging few"—but if you ask him to specify these judging few you will see that each will point to his respective friends, to "those who approve, and cry up their several Performances." Ask a theatrical manager and he will also refer to those opinions of the "Town" which are most agreeable to him and which echo what he wants most to hear. Actually, Cibber continues, the matter is not so simple. It is necessary to distinguish several levels of influence within the audience. Regardless of walk of life, it is those people who are interested in and who, in their respective circles, give encouragement to the theater who constitute the true "opinion leaders."

> I think, the Town may be supposed to include all Degrees of Persons, from the highest Nobleman, to the lowly Artisan, etc., who, in their different Stations, are Encouragers of dramatic performances: Thus all persons, who pay for their places, whether Noble, Gentle, or Simple, who fill the Boxes, Pit and Galleries in a theatrical Sence, form the Town.[141]

In a way, Cibber's remarks might be construed as a plea for democracy in art. Many more gifted artists, in the face of the dilemma posed by the growing middle- and lower-class audience, were to attempt to find theoretical grounds for supporting this pluralistic viewpoint. But the task was difficult, and there were class as well as aesthetic barriers to be faced.

In the early half of the century, the middle class struggled successfully to assert its values and interests against those prevailing among the aristocracy. The increasing industrialization and the new importance attaching to the role of the worker in the latter half of the century, however, brought about a shift in focus: the middle class now began to suspect that its most dangerous enemies were below instead of above it. And while class lines in the world of letters were not sharply etched, neither were they altogether obscured.

During the latter half of the century the social status of fictional characters became an object of some concern. In the 1770s this form of snobbism was sufficiently recognized that the name *tapino-phoby* was coined for it. In 1773 the cleric-novelist Richard Graves used the term in his book *The Spiritual Quixote;* just after introducing a cobbler into his story, he interrupted the narrative with a warning to

> such readers, as are possessed with modern tapino-phoby, or dread of everything that is low either in writing or in conversation. If he is of the opinion that every representation of nature, that does not relate to the great world, is to be exploded as contemptible stuff; he will certainly repent of having read thus far; and I would exhort him, by all means, to return in peace to his card-assembly or to his chocolate house and pursue so low a subject no further.[142]

Tapino-phoby seems to have affected the literary elite as well. G. Sprague Allen, to whom we owe the above quotation, notes that the classicists— and here he names Goldsmith and Johnson among others—resented that such characters as Lillo's apprentice George Barnwell or Richardson's servant-girl Pamela should have serious attention paid to them in literature.[143] And the Buckingham Palace librarian, Thomas Mathias, in his vigorous (and very popular) satire on contemporary authors saw, among other evils accruing from the reading of novels, the possibility that young people might not only become morally corrupted thereby, but democratic as well:

> Mrs. Charlotte Smith, Mrs. Inchbald, Mrs. Mary Robinson, Mrs. etc., though all of them are very ingenious ladies, yet they are too frequently *whining* or *whisking* in novels, till our girls' heads turn wild with impossible adventures, and are now and then tainted with democracy, and sometimes with infidelity and loose principles.[144]

As the charity schools and the Sunday schools went about fulfilling their missions of increasing the literacy rate among the workers and farmers, the problem of who should read soon became even more controversial than the problem of whom should be written about. In this case the anxiety seems not to have originated with the literati*— insofar as it can be located at all, it seems, rather, to have originated with the nonintellectuals of the middle class. The issues they raised were not aesthetic; they did not fear that literature might become debased in order to meet the tastes and capacities of a working-class audience. The problem was one of economic self-interest: if workers developed a strong

---

*Samuel Johnson, for one, asked by an affluent acquaintance whether his workers would become less industrious if they were to attend school and learn how to read, answered with an unequivocal "No, Sir."

predilection for reading, might they not acquire a distaste for manual work along with it?

The gist of the argument against workers reading was that the poor will remain tractable and useful only so long as they are kept in "some degree of ignorance." The Bible, perhaps, might be permitted, but any other type of reading is more than likely to make workers dissatisfied with the "manual labor" which is "destined to occupy their lives."[145] Correctives proposed ranged from putting a complete stop to the teaching of reading to children of the lower classes to censoring their reading so that only religious works would be accessible to them. A letter-to-the-editor in the *Gentleman's Magazine* proposed a rather modern-sounding method of censorship: a citizens' book-reviewing board should be established which would draw up approved reading lists for youth, workers, and other "lower orders." This committee, made up of "worthy persons," would peruse the novel output annually, print their lists in "a monthly publication" and point out "such as were of an improper tendency with candour, and recommending those of merit."[146]

It was in this atmosphere of aesthetic and class concerns that the debate about "taste" took place—what is it, who has it, how can it be acquired?

THE DEFENSE

In the seventeenth and early eighteenth centuries the slowly expanding upper-middle class, composed of men of business and men of property, had tended to identify with the aesthetic tastes and aspirations of the aristocracy. There was no need for writers to adjust to the professed interests of this new audience because it was indistinguishable from the reading public which had existed before. The problems of the literati had not so much to do with who was to judge literature as with the role of literature in relation to other intellectual pursuits, the limits of the genres, and the place of the poet in the wide scheme of things. Questions might be raised whether the poet excelled the philosopher in his function as teacher (this in the sixteenth century); or about the comparative status of writer and scientist (this in the seventeenth century); or whether the classical rules were the only yardsticks to be legitimately applied in judging a work of literature (this in the early eighteenth).

By the middle of the century a middle class, not only consisting of wealthy businessmen and landowners, but of shopkeepers, clerks, apprentices, and farmers was becoming increasingly affluent, literate, and ambitious. Its literary interests were not necessarily identical with those of the upper classes, its educational background was certainly more primitive and, at the same time, its cultural pretensions were distinctly noticeable. It was, in short, an age when

> *all men may procure*
> *The title of a connoisseur;*
> *When noble and ignoble herd*
> *Are govern'd by a single word;*
> *Though, like the royal German dames,*
> *It bears an hundred Christian names;*
> *As genius, fancy, judgment, gout,*
> *Whim, caprice, je-ne-sais-quoi, vertu;*
> *Which appellations all describe*
> Taste, *and the modern tasteful tribe.*[147]

Or, in the even more pessimistic words of Oliver Goldsmith:

> Without assigning causes for this universal presumption [of taste], we shall proceed to observe, that . . . this folly is productive of manifold evils to the commuity. . . . Hence, the youth of both sexes are debauched to diversion, and seduced from much more profitable occupations into idle endeavours after literary fame; and a superficial, false taste, founded on ignorance and conceit, takes possession of the public.[148]

As a result, a reorientation in aesthetic discussions began to take place. The change was dramatic and unprecedented in the history of letters; its essence was a shift from neo-classical objectivism with its stress on the rational analysis of literary works to concern with the experience of the public.

The new audience did not, by and large, have a classical education, and it placed more emphasis on feelings than on reason. Furthermore, middle-class realism did not allow for pleasure in purely intellectual pursuits. The problem was to get ahead, to improve oneself with practical information—a bent that was to reach a climax in the nineteenth century craze for the statistical and instantly utilitarian, for the kind of guides and manuals on every activity under the sun which Matthew Arnold found so distressing and which he was to dismiss with the lofty phrase "culture works differently." In such a situation the lines between art and life, between literature and persuasion, between the aesthetic and the emotional experience became easily blurred and often indistinguishable.[149] After the middle of the century the position of the critic is therefore by no means unequivocal. He may speak about the qualities of a book, the intellectual and emotional processes involved in producing it, the critical process of evaluating it—but whatever approach he takes, concern with the experience of the reader or of different types of readers is rarely absent.[150] In short, once the profession of letters depended for support entirely upon the interest, good-will and purchasing habits of a broad public, it began to pay serious attention to the way in which this public experienced literary products and to raise questions about its role in the formulation of literary standards. The task was to distinguish, for the writer and for the public on which he was dependent, between the wheat of art and the chaff of trash.

Most mid-eighteenth century writers were themselves part of the bourgeoisie which came into its own in the course of the industrial revolution. Its empiricist spirit informed their approach to literary problems; and the ways in which they endeavored to cope with the demands of an increasingly diversified public were as pluralistic as the tastes of that public itself—ranging from Oliver Goldsmith's belief that the "universal presumption" to taste would have a "debauching" effect to Edmund Burke's faith in the idea of democracy in literary standards. By the middle of the century almost every writer of note could point to at least one essay—and often a volume—on the subject of taste.

This section will indicate briefly how the man of letters formulated the problem, how he searched for literary standards which would take the taste of "all men" into account; how this search led, at one extreme, to elite concepts and, at the other extreme, to the idea of diversity. Finally, we shall see how the concept of diversity in taste and judgment harbingered a change in the critic's role.

The Discussion about Taste

In the debate about the validity of the classical rules, the issues had been rational and sharply defined: Should the writer adhere to the dramatic unities? Should he imitate the early Greek and Roman models or was he free to express his indivduality in his own fashion? As the century progressed, individualizing, as it were, psychological aspects of a democratic society gradually came to take precedence over rationalist absolutes. Analyses of "wit" and "judgment," terms which were applied to the interplay of the sophisticated intellect with images and ideas, gave way to analyses of such concepts as "imagination," "enthusiasm," and finally "genius." "Genius," in turn, became synonymous with originality. Where the poet had in former times functioned as a high artificer, he emerged, toward the latter part of the century, as an inspired instrument of the poetic furor, working by seizure rather than by thought. The earlier set of critical categories had placed a premium on objectivity, reason, and knowledge; the new categories focussed on subjective qualities of emotion and spontaneous creativity.

Addison, though he wrote in the early part of the century when the discussion about the rules still flourished, had pioneered in the analysis of imaginative writing. He spoke of "imagination" not in abstract aesthetic terms but in terms of the appeal of imaginative works for the reader, using concepts related to everyday human experience. He addressed himself to all those "middle-station" people whom he conceived to be fit audience for the *Spectator*. His essays on imagination, indeed, predicated a great many categories which have appeared in most subsequent discussions of popular culture, including *variety, diversion,* the appeal of *facts,* and the emotional *gratifications* involved in hearing or reading about torture and other forms of horror.[151]

A later, less pedagogic and at the same time less optimistic approach than that of Addison was to differentiate among the various segments of the public in matters of literary judgment. Goldsmith, in examining the theater audience, observed that those who could afford seats in the pits at the Drury lane and Covent Garden were ostentatiously eager to "show their taste," but "not one in a hundred," he felt, was qualified to do so.[152] And in less class-conscious but similarly statistical terms the critic Joseph Warton discriminated between two levels of the audience, one which could appreciate the works of genius, another sensitized only to commonplace products. Warton was rather more liberal in his estimate than Goldsmith: "For one person who can adequately relish, and enjoy a work of imagination, twenty are to be found who can taste and judge of observations on familiar life and the manners of the age."[153]

In short, to the bewildering problem for the writer as to the kinds of standards which were to take the place of the now discredited classical rules, was added the cultural ambition of a public whose judgments often seemed "false" to him. The task for the writer, then, was to search out some means by which to reconcile these various tastes with his own artistic integrity.

Not the least conspicuous feature of mid-eighteenth century thought was a faith in the perfectibility of human nature which seemed to go hand in hand with faith in material progress. Is it not possible, several writers began to ask, that it is merely lack of proper education which keeps the audience from developing into true connoisseurs?

Turning once more to Oliver Goldsmith, we find him questioning whether "natural" good taste was not being corrupted by the numerous examples of "false" taste which prove singularly attractive to the "unwary mind and young imagination."[154] And this suggests, despite his disparaging remarks about the actual competence of the theater audience, that

Goldsmith gave some credence to a concept of "innate" standards of judgment which, if they could be corrupted, could also be improved. Fielding, while he agreed that "natural taste" could so be corrupted, expressed even more aptly than Goldsmith the characteristic faith in progress when he described how the "small seeds of taste" which are present in practically all men can be fructified by training and education. Fielding goes on to say that he will "probably . . . in a future paper endeavour to lay down some rules by which all men may acquire some degree of taste."[155] That this paper was not written serves as one commentary on the obstacles met in attempting to seek out and describe those bases of judgment which all men were presumed to hold in common.

The Search for Common Standards

Three paths were followed in the search for common principles: (1) recourse to a feeling of "inner conviction" that there must be such principles; (2) attempts to prove their existence by deriving them from certain tests; and (3) efforts to deduce them by determining how they work. At no point, however, did any analyst of taste get so far as to describe or define what those principles might in fact be.

1. The first of the three approaches—the argument of inner conviction—started early in the century and sought validation by pointing to "simple" people who manifested clear judgment and true taste. Anticipating the admiration later to be accorded the "natural" man, the "noble savage," and the "unspoilt child," the *Tatler,* for example, had presented a young woman "who had that natural sense which makes her a better judge than a thousand critics," and the *Guardian* pointed to a foot soldier as the "politest man in a British audience, from the force of nature, untainted with the singularities of an ill-applied education."[156] Later, in a philosophical vein, Hume and Burke (the latter in his early aesthetic writings) based their concepts of taste common to all men on their own inner conviction that universal standards of judgment exist. Burke, in his *Essay on Taste,* first defined his subject as "that faculty or those faculties of the mind, which are effected with, or which form a judgment of, the works of imagination and the elegant arts." The objective of his inquiry is

> to find whether there are any principles, on which the imagination is affected, so common to all, so grounded and certain, as to supply the means of reasoning satisfactorily about them. And such principles of taste I fancy there are. . . .[157]

As we shall presently see, however, though Burke continued his essay by discussing the human faculties involved in the acquisition of taste he neither isolated any particular principles, nor did he demonstrate that "common" human faculties underlie them. Hume similarly postulated the universality of taste. All people whose "organs" are sound have a "considerable uniformity of sentiment" and from this uniformity "we may thence derive an idea of the perfect and universal beauty."[158] But Hume, too, failed to specify common aesthetic principles.

Even those who clung strongly to the idea of uniformity in taste in the abstract could not avoid the evidence of considerable disagreement when it came to judging a given work. Failing to define the common principles they sought, they could at least describe, and attempt to explain away, those tastes which were so deviant that they could not be considered manifestations of the assumed principle. Burke, who was echoed almost word for word by the Scottish literary critic Hugh Blair a few years later, resorted to the analogy of sensory taste in discussing these deviants. He pointed out that a man might be found who could not distinguish between milk and vinegar or who called both tobacco and vinegar sweet, milk bitter, and sugar sour. Such a man, said Burke, cannot be considered a person of taste, nor can he even be called a man of wrong taste. He is, quite simply, "absolutely mad":

> When it is said, taste cannot be disputed, it can only mean that no one can strictly answer what pleasure or pain some particular man may find from the taste of some particular thing . . . but we may dispute, and with sufficient clearness too, concerning the things which are naturally pleasing or disagreeable to the sense.*[159]

It remained for Lord Kames to draw most unequivocally upon inner conviction as "proof" of the existence of a common set of artistic standards. When he attempted to demonstrate his belief, however, he moved far from the concept of universality.

Like most critics and philosophers who tried to reduce the multiplicity of tastes in the eighteenth century audience to some common denominator, Kames began by asserting that there is a "universal conviction" in the sphere of morality and went on to state that, "This conviction of common nature or standard . . . accounts not less clearly for the conception we have of a right and a wrong taste in the fine arts." Kames disposed of

---

*Blair, in his *Lectures on Rhetoric,* writes: "If any one should maintain that sugar was bitter and tobacco was sweet, no reasoning could avail to prove it. The taste of such a person would infallibly be held to be diseased, merely because it differed so widely from the taste of the species to which he belongs." [3 vols., Basle, 1801, V. 1, 35]

the extreme exceptions in the same way as Burke: "The individual who dislikes objects which most people like or who conversely likes objects which most other people dislike" is "a monster." His principal argument for the existence of uniform taste is the fact that works of art are acknowledged as such: "We are formed . . . with an uniformity of taste. . . . If uniformity of taste did not prevail, the fine arts could never have made any figure." A "conviction of a common standard," he concludes, is therefore "part of our nature."[160]

2. Further validation of the inner conviction theory was sometimes sought by the application of certain "tests." Cultural products exist; those which have a universal appeal and which have stood the test of time can be accepted as proof of the existence of common standards. Addison had anticipated the universality test: the fact that he, a cultivated English gentleman, could enjoy the folk songs of all countries in which he traveled demonstrated that whatever is enjoyed by "a multitude" must have been judged by a universal standard: "Human Nature is the same in all reasonable Creatures; and whatever falls in with it, will meet with Admirers amongst Readers of all Qualities and Conditions."[161] Joshua Reynolds in his *Discourses* picked up this argument—all questions of taste can be settled by an appeal to the "sense" which all mankind has in common. He, too, avoided the question of what standards, principles, or criteria compose this common sense. What he does say is that the better acquainted a writer is with the works of various periods and of various countries, the more likely is it that he will be able to derive these unspecified—but uniform—standards. To the test of universality Reynolds then added the test of permanence. "What has pleased, and continues to please, is likely to please again: hence are derived the rules of art."[162] If one accepts these two proofs of the existence of common artistic standards, as most mid-century writers evidently did accept them, it follows, as Hugh Blair put it in his *Lectures on Rhetoric,* that it is to the concurrence of the majority that one must look for standards of taste:

> That which men concur the most in admiring must be held to be beautiful. His taste must be esteemed just and true, which coincides with the general sentiments of men. In this standard we must rest . . . the common feelings of men carry the same authority, and have a title to regulate the taste of every individual.[163]

Thus did the writers of the mid-eighteenth century pay their respects to their new patrons, the great audience. But the discussion did not end on a note of faith in a common denominator.

3. The works of Lord Kames, particularly his *Elements of Criticism,* illustrate the entanglement in which those who attempted to describe the workings of common principles found themselves.[164] He begins by equating the now familiar terms—common nature, common sense, common standards—with good taste. By and large, Kames observes, every man is aware that such common standards exist. Like Burke and Blair, he condemns the taste of the individual whose judgment deviates: "We justly condemn every taste that swerves from what is thus ascertained by the common standard." At the same time he postulates the mysterious "we" (which also appears in Burke's remarks on taste) endowed with the right to condemn.

The crucial question becomes, then, who constitutes this "we," and here, despite his use of the term "common" standards, Kames begins to differentiate. In the sphere of moral judgments he feels that one may rely on "everyone's" standards. When it comes to judgment in literature and the arts it will hardly do to "collect votes indifferently." In the aesthetic domain "a wary choice" must be made. His preliminary assumption of a "universal conviction" notwithstanding, Kames goes on specifically to exclude the greater part of mankind from the right to contribute to the "common" standard. "Particularly"—and here Kames establishes rigid class lines in what seems to have started as a democratic premise—"particularly all those who depend for food on bodily labor are totally devoid of taste." They can share in the formulation of moral principles and they must comply with them, but they can have no voice in the worlds of art and literature.* But Kames is not content to stop with the elimination of workers; there are others to be disenfranchised in cultural matters. At the other extreme are the rich and opulent who delight in conspicuous consumption, who are "voluptuous" both morally and aesthetically, and these, too, are disqualified. Since the manifest objective of this upper crust is simply to "amaze and humble all beholders," they can have no understanding of the "faint and delicate emotions of the fine arts." All that remains are those individuals who maintain a strict separation from the lower orders but who at the same time are free from envy or imitation of the members of the aristocratic remnants

---

*This is a far cry from the unqualified remarks of Addison earlier in the century, before the middle classes were making their tastes clearly felt through purchases of literary products. Prior to his statement that "Human Nature is the same in all reasonable Creatures," Addison had said: ". . . it is impossible that any thing should be universally tasted or approved by a Multitude, tho' they are only the Rabble of a Nation, which hath not in it some peculiar Aptness to please and gratifie the Mind of Man." (*Spectator,* No. 70.)

of the Restoration period and their obsolete style of life. Furthermore, within this group, which by now is defined as the middle class, only those can become judges who have "good natural taste . . . improved by education, reflection and experience." In other words, only the intellectual elite are qualified to evaluate cultural products—a clear instance of the intellectual defining his social role as the mentor and cultural leader of the new middle-class order.

Having narrowed those capable of aesthetic judgment to a chosen few, Kames then doubles on his tracks and once more assures his reader that the "good" and "bad" qualities in cultural products are clearly discernible and that "mankind" is able to distinguish between them. His elite theory becomes democratic once more by means of postponement: you have only to wait until the standards now formulated and applied by the select few will be recognized as universal by all mankind. And that time, Kames is confident, is bound to come.

For David Hume it remained to summarize most succinctly the contradictory position which was maintained by those who sought universal criteria for the judging of art. Hume stated that the principles of taste are universal "and nearly if not entirely the same in all men;" but he concluded this very sentence with the observation that "few are qualified to give judgment on any work of art, or establish their own sentiment as the standard of beauty."[165]

Kames, Hume, and Blair are foremost among the critics who, beginning with the idea—or the hope—that sandards for the judging of literary and other cultural products are held in common by all men, arrived at a conclusion almost the very opposite: the "all" spelled out to read a select few. Other writers and critics who looked for a common, egalitarian principle with as little success escaped from the dilemma by formulating concepts which may be subsumed under the rubric "the idea of diversity."

From University to Diversity

To recapitulate briefly, we have traced three phases in the discussion about the new public and the literary goods produced for it. First, a period of hope during which the men of letters waited for the aesthetic proclivities of this public to catch up with their moral inclinations. Second, a period of "opportunity and opportunism," when new writers and new products developed at a rapid rate, and the literati adopted a policy of watchful waiting. Third, a period of dismay among the intellectuals during which both audience and media were severely strictured. The controversy over "taste" might be said to constitute a fourth period. This discussion, as we have seen, was conducted as though the participants hoped that the manifold differences in taste, and the obviously low level of taste in some segments of the audience, were more apparent than real, and that they would eventually find underlying standards on which both artist and audience could agree. But the exploration came to nothing more than to a more or less general agreement: those literary and artistic accomplishments which hold up through space and time are "good," be they folk ballads or Greek sculpture, and the fact that some such achievements do so hold up indicates that common standards of judgment do exist. These assertions were of little practical avail in resolving the conflict between the integrity of the artist and the inclinations of the public which paid the piper. What did emerge from the exploration, however, was a widespread conviction that the experience of this public had to be taken into account in any discussions of literary standards.

As the search for common standards waned, such psychological and descriptive concepts as perception, individual differences, national differences, and "comparative" or "historical" views became increasingly conspicuous in the words of the critics, who paid increasing attention to the need for enjoyment, pleasure, amusement, and recreation. The emphasis, in short, was placed more and more on the analysis of the audience experience, as though in the hope that a study of reader gratifications would lead inductively to new knowledge about the nature of "common" standards.

To what extent this shift in emphasis resulted from the writer's dependence on his audience and to what extent it reflected the absence of powerful literary figures is a moot question. Fielding expounded a "great man" theory in an almost sociological vein. In a *Covent Garden Journal* article on the "Commonwealth of Literature," he traced the general state of literature through a variety of phases: first, an "ecclesiastical" democracy; then a period of absolutism coexistent with the political absolutism in the age of Henry VIII; next, an era of literary aristocracy, headed first by Shakespeare, Ben Jonson, and Beaumont and Fletcher, next by Dryden, and finally by Pope, whom Fielding always sees as literary autocrat. But in his own period, Fielding sees a decline in literary leadership; "after the demise of King Alexandre the literary state relapsed again into a democracy, or rather into downright anarchy."[166]

While the stress on the effects of literary works on their readers became dominant, not all of the writers, philosophers, and literary critics involved in the discussion of standards were in agreement as to whether the experience of the audience should be looked upon as the only valid basis for literary criteria. Kames and Blair began their search for standards with the assumption that beauty lies in the eye of the beholder. Hume and Burke, on the other hand, began with the assumption that beauty is a quality residing in the object itself.[167] But it is characteristic of the descriptive approach which came into being at this time that even those who began with a premise of objective standards moved from the application of general principles such as reason, truth, and nature toward the development of long and detailed compendia of the attributes of literary works. Such itemizations may be found, for example, in Burke's *On the Sublime and Beautiful,* in which he isolates and describes literary qualities such as smoothness, sweetness, variety, smallness, color, aggregate words, abstract words, everyday words, and the like.[168] These compendia, in turn, served as a point of departure for an impressionistic analysis of reader experience.

In general, three early approaches to the problem of effects can be distinguished. The first we might call relative; the second psychological; the third descriptive. Needless to say, then as now these categories overlapped conspicuously.

Relative concepts had some history in the world of letters before the participants in the taste controversy got hold of them. The *Tatler,* as early as 1710, had suggested that the way of life and the peculiarities of a writer or a reader serve to some extent to condition their respective tastes.[169] This concept of "relativity" (which is in reality a qualified endorsement of diversity in taste) finds a good deal of application in the works of Addison and the later writers who explored such questions as the relationship between exposure and taste. The idea of relativity also became manifest in a new approach to the study of literature itself. Pope, for example, in the preface to his controversial edition of Shakespeare, had stressed the importance of historical, climatic, and national factors in the conditioning of ideas as to what constitutes good or bad literature.[170] But it was Johnson who, in his *Lives,* set the stage for the comparative historical study of literature as well as, incidentally, for exact textual study.[171] The comparative study of literature, in short, went hand in hand with the comparative approach to the study of the *impact* of literary works.

There was a strong relationship between such comparative or relative approaches and the psychological theories and hypotheses which were being aired at the same time. The expression "association of ideas" seems to have become a favorite one in the analysis of audience experience, and there was general agreement that a great variety of such associations could be expected when a widely assorted group of people were exposed to the same work. Pleasure in literary experience thus was more and more conceived as a matter of individual sentiment, not necessarily connected with objective standards of beauty or reason. Whatever a given individual with his own perceptive mechanisms found agreeable was also acceptable.[172] Even Johnson, despite his firmer adherence to rational principles, insisted that these were subordinate to individual response. If such principles are to be applied, he felt, they must be applied with caution, and he goes on to speak of "the cant of those who judge by principles rather than perception."[173]

At the other extreme of the descriptive approach we find those who brushed rules aside altogether, and justified their doing so on the grounds that the audience reacts impulsively in the process of reading and does not have time, even though it might have the capacity, to apply them. *The Monthly Review,* for one, supported Lord Kames' attack on the rules on these very grounds, and paraphrased him with approval: "For when the mind is affected or disgusted, the affection or aversion takes place, as it were, by impulse and gives no time for the formal application of given principles to influence the judgment."[174]

The long-range effect of this new attention to audience experience was to legitimize emotional gratifications. While it is clear that an endorsement of emotion has persisted to the present time, it is by no means apparent to what extent the shift from the application of rational standards to the analysis of emotional response was the result of the need to take into account a new mass audience and a new group of literary products. What is clear, as a recent historian has put it, is that "examination of the mechanism of the mind by more philosophical thinkers like Hume resulted in the analysis of reason into imagination and belief, of common sense into intuition. The basis of classical art was shattered by these blows . . . and uncertainty paved the way for the emphasis on emotion as the most important factor in life and art."[175]

Recognition of this kind of gratification was comparatively unknown in the early decades of the century, when any literary or other cultural product had to subordinate (or pretend to subordinate) pleasure to moral uplift. For the first time in the century we find terms such as "relaxation" and "amusement" used without apology:

> Such is the nature of man, that his powers and faculties are soon blunted by exercise. . . . During his waking hours, amusement by intervals is requisite to unbend his mind from serious occupation. The imagination . . . contributes more than any other cause to recruit the mind and restore its vigor, by amusing us with gay and ludicrous images; and when relaxation is necessary, such amusement is much relished.[176]

This acknowledgment has no didactic overtones. It was as if a sense of defeatism in the search for a common aesthetic perception in the audience were accompanied by a sense of release from the obligation to assist in its moral reformation. Hume, for example, discusses how man seeks to escape from the pressures which weary him when he is alone with his thoughts: "To get rid of this painful situation, it [the mind] seeks every amusement and pursuit; business, gaming, shows, executions; whatever will rouse the passions, and take its attention from itself." He proceeds to list the kinds of passion that may be aroused by such means and remarks that whether they be agreeable or disagreeable, happy or sad, confused or orderly, they are still preferable to "the insipid languor" of a man thrown back upon his own inner resources. He points to the gambling room to validate his thesis; wherever the most exciting play is going on, most members of the company may be found, even though that table may not have the best players. To identify with people who are experiencing the passions of loss or gain is to relieve oppression: "It makes the time pass the easier with them, and is some relief to that oppression, under which men commonly labour, when left entirely to their own thoughts and meditations."[177] Archibald Alison, a critic writing later in the century, analyzed the various "qualities of mind" which can be evoked by reading. He even distinguished between passive and active gratifications:

> The qualities of mind which are capable of producing emotion, are either its active or its passive qualities; either its *powers* and capacities, as beneficence, wisdom, fortitude, invention, fancy, etc., or its *feelings and affections,* as love, joy, hope, gratitude, purity, fidelity, innocence, etc.[178]

As in many analyses of audience experience undertaken after the middle of the century, one is struck by Alison's pragmatism, which is in such strong contrast to the moralizing tone uppermost in the middle of the century. It was this almost scientific approach to the experience of the audience which paved the way for a new conception of the critic's role.

The Critic as Mediator

Dissatisfaction with the kinds of rigid and pedantic literary criticism which had prevailed in the early part of the century had been brewing for some time. Swift already had attacked such pedantry; his *Battle of the Books* overflows with denunciations of the "malignant deity, called Criticism." The mixture of bookishness and glibness in these critics was of no benefit other than to give "the coffee house wits some basis for literary pretensions."[179] Pope, who needed no inspiration from Swift on the subject (although he apparently got a great deal of it), similarly attacked the destructiveness, or at best the futility, of those who lived by petty and often meaningless attacks on the writing of others. Nothing is sacred to these critics; on any subject "they'll talk you dead/ For Fools rush in where Angels fear to tread."[180] Later Goldsmith, in discussing German writings, echoed the disdain of his eminent predecessors for this type of critical hairsplitting:

> Their assiduity is unparalleled; . . . they write through volumes while they do not think through a page. Never fatigued themselves, they think the reader can never be weary; so they drone on, saying all that can be said on the subject, not selecting what may be advanced to the purpose.[181]

Again it was Addison who presaged a new concept, this time of the critic's role. He was to be creative and constructive: in a word, a "revealer of beauties." Beginning with Addison's influential pieces on *Paradise Lost* in the *Spectator,* almost every important author had at least one book-length criticism written about his work entitled *The Beauties of. . . .*[182] This concept of a revelatory function for the critic implied that he was to assume a role of responsibility in relation to the general public as well as to his fellow writers and intellectuals, and most of the writers and critics of the mid-century followed suit. It was the critic's function, as Johnson put it, to help men "to enjoy life or to endure it."[183] At the same time, it was characteristic of the mid-century writers—in their optimistic mood—to view the critic's contribution as a means of raising the aesthetic level of the public. In this light the critic has an educational role. Goldsmith sees him—and he is speaking of the "man of taste" as contrasted with the scholar or compiler—as "placed in a middle station, between the world and the cell, between learning and common sense."

But perhaps the most far-reaching change which took place in the concept of the critic was that a two-way function was premised for him. Not only was he to reveal the beauties of literary works to the general public by means of which, in Goldsmith's terms, "even the philosopher may acquire popular applause"; he must also interpret the public back to the writer. In brief, the critic not only "teaches the vulgar on what part of a character to lay the emphasis of praise," he must also show "the scholar where to point his application so as to deserve it." Goldsmith believed that the absence of such critical mediators explained why wealth rather than true literary fame was the goal of so many writes. The result, he feared, might be that nothing would be remembered of the literary works of his time.[184]

We have observed that Goldsmith, in his endeavor to come to grips with the dilemma of the writer, represented a variety of sometimes conflicting views. We have seen, however, that it was likely to be Goldsmith in his optimistic rather than in his pessimistic vein who set the tone for what was to come. So, too, his view of the "ideal" critic, of his function as one of mediation between the audience and the writer, was to prevail. Critics, writers, and philosophers, such as Johnson, Burke, Hume, Reynolds, Kames, and the Wartons, all adopted his premise as they began to analyze the experience of the reader.

A critic must try to understand what goes on in the mind of the readers. In Johnson's words he must "improve opinion into knowledge, and . . . distinguish those means of pleasing which depend upon known causes." Johnson then outlines what we might today look upon as a scientific, descriptive approach to the study of media experience, pointing out that "literary criticism, which has . . . hitherto known only the anarchy of ignorance, the caprices of fancy and the tyranny of prescription . . . can now be placed under the dominion of science."[185] Joseph Wood Krutch points to him as the formulator of the concept that the critic "derives his right from the rights of the general public of which he is a part—not from the fact that he *is* a critic. He will generally agree with the public's considered judgment because literature is to be judged, not in the light of learning . . . but in accordance with the same common sense which guides us as we go about the business of life."[186] It was this orientation to audience experience which opened up an entirely new dimension in the debate over art and popular culture. In spite of their conflicts and contradictions, the mid-eighteenth century English writers paved the way for the nineteenth century critics and philosophers who were to formulate the metaphysics of cultural democracy. They were the first to recognize the importance, in an increasingly industrialized and mobile society, of relaxation, amusement, and escape from the pressures of work, whether the individual be a tired businessman or a manual worker, and in so doing were far more detached than were their counterparts across the Channel. While Hume, for one, analyzed the psychological factors involved in "distraction" or amusement, Schiller and Goethe were to take a moral position: the public may need distractions, but unless they find a less passive way to achieve it, culture will surely degenerate.

NOTES

1. A. S. Collins, *The Profession of Letters: Study of the Relation of Author to Patron, Publisher, and Public, 1780 to 1932* (London, Routledge, 1920), 83.
2. A. S. Collins, "The Growth of the Reading Public During the Eighteenth Century," *Review of English Studies,* Vol. II (1926), 429.
3. William Lecky, *History of England in the Eighteenth Century* (New York, Appleton, 1888), 560 ff.
4. Walter Graham, *English Literary Periodicals* (New York, Nelson, 1930), 35.

5. Ibid., 59.
6. George Sherburn, *The Restoration and the Eighteenth Century,* Pt. III of *A Literary History of England,* Ed. Albert C. Baugh (New York, Appleton-Century-Crofts, 1948), 1053.
7. Collins, "The Growth of the Reading Public," 289-90.
8. Ibid., 291.
9. Collins, *The Profession of Letters,* 96.
10. Ernest A. Baker, *The History of the English Novel* (10 vols., London, Witherby, 1934), V, 252-53.
11. Collins, *The Profession of Letters,* 98.
12. Ibid., 65.
13. Sherburn, 1052.
14. W. T. Laprade, *Public Opinion and Politics in Eighteenth Century England* (New York, Macmillan, 1936), 13-14.
15. Samuel Johnson, *The Idler,* No. 30. *The British Essayists,* Ed. A. Chalmers (38 vols., Boston, Little, Brown, 1856), XXVII, 104.
16. A. Aspinall, *Politics and the Press* (London, Home and Vanthal, 1949), 6-7.
17. Lecky, I, 561-62.
18. Alexander Pope, *The Dunciad (A),* Ed. James Sutherland (London, Methuen, 1953), 448. (Vol. V of the Twickenham edition, general editor John Butt.)
19. Daniel Defoe, *The Review,* Aug. 30, 1709. *Defoe's Review in 22 Facsimile Books* (New York, Columbia Univ. Press, 1938), VI, Bk. 15, 253-54.
20. Arthur Y. Trace, "The Continuity of Opposition to the Theater in England from Gosson to Collier" (unpublished dissertation, Stanford University, 1955), 11.
21. H. W. Pedicord, *The Theatrical Public in the Time of Garrick* (New York, King's Crown, 1954), 41.
22. Lecky, I, 586.
23. M. D. George, *London Life in the Eighteenth Century* (New York, Knopf, 1925), 14-15.
24. Pedicord, 14-15.
25. Ibid., 16.
26. Ian Watt, *The Rise of the Novel* (London, Chatto and Windus, 1957), 37.
27. *Adventurer,* No. 115. *British Essayists,* XXI, 137-38.
28. Leslie Stephen, *English Literature and Society in the Eighteenth Century* (London, Duckworth, 1904), 37-38.
29. James Lackington, *Memoirs of the Forty-Five First Years of the Life of James Lackington, Written by Himself* (London, 1803), 250.
30. Lecky, I, 165.
31. Collins, *Profession of Letters,* Ch. I, (v), *passim.*
32. Lackington, 225.
33. Ibid., 259.
34. Ralph Straus, *The Unspeakable Curll* (New York, McBride, 1928).
35. Ibid., 49-64.
36. Lackington, 224.
37. Collins, 63-64.
38. Ibid., 58.
39. J.M.S. Tompkins, *The Popular Novel in England: 1770-1800* (London, Constable, 1932), 7.

40. Tompkins, 10.
41. Lackington, 286.
42. Joseph Wood Krutch, *Samuel Johnson* (New York, Holt, 1944), 35.
43. Collins, "Growth of the Reading Public," 429.
44. James Boswell, *Life of Samuel Johnson* (London, Oxford Press, 1953), 217.
45. Oliver Goldsmith, *An Inquiry into the Present State of Polite Learning in Europe* (1759). *The Works of Oliver Goldsmith,* Ed. Peter Cunningham (4 vols., New York, Haprer, 1881), II, 56-57.
46. Oliver Goldsmith, *The Citizen of the World,* Letter XCIII (London, Everyman, 1934), 255.
47. Ibid., Letter LI, 142.
48. Thomas De Quincey, "Oliver Goldsmith." *The Eighteenth Century in Scholarship and Literature* (Boston, 1877), 335.
49. Graham, 204-205.
50. Ibid., 208.
51. Ibid., 213.
52. Ibid., 224-25
53. Tompkins, 15.
54. Ibid.
55. Ibid., 15-16.
56. Goldsmith, *Citizen of the World,* Letter XIII, 34.
57. John Dennis, *The Grounds of Criticism in Poetry, Critical Works of John Dennis,* Ed. Edward Niles Hooker (2 vols., Baltimore, Johns Hopkins Press, 1943), I, 338.
58. Sherburn, 826.
59. J.W.H. Atkins, *English Literary Criticism: 17th and 18th Centuries* (London, Methuen, 1951), 102.
60. Pope, *Dunciad,* 165 n.
61. Joseph Addison, *The Spectator,* No. 10 (4 vols., London, Everyman, 1950), I, 32.
62. Addison, *Spectator,* No. 10, I, 31-33.
63. Ibid., No. 34, I, 104.
64. Ibid., No. 63, I, 196.
65. Emile Legouis and Louis Cazamian, *A History of English Literature* (New York, Macmillan, 1933), 738.
66. B. Sprague Allen, *Tides in English Taste* (2 vols., Cambridge, Mass., Harvard Univ. Press, 1937), II, 36-37.
67. Allen, I, 87.
68. Graham, 120.
69. Ibid., 152 ff.
70. Laprade, 249.
71. Stephen, 219.
72. Henry Fielding, *The Covent Garden Journal,* No. 10. *The Works of Henry Fielding,* Ed. James P. Browne (10 vols., London, Bickers, 1903), X, 26.
73. Pedicord, 31.
74. Chauncey B. Tinker, *The Salon and English Letters* (New York, Macmillan, 1915), 177-79.
75. Sherburn, 1031.
76. Tompkins, 47.
77. Pope, *Dunciad,* 49-50.

78. Ibid., 192 n.
79. Ian Jack, *Augustan Satire, 1660-1750* (Oxford, Clarendon Press, 1952), 119.
80. Pope, *Essay on Criticism, The Best of Pope,* Ed. George Sherburn (New York, Ronald Press, 1940), 64-65.
81. Fielding, X, 28.
82. Allen, I, 243-44.
83. James Sutherland, "Introduction," *Dunciad,* xlviii.
84. Allen, II, 189.
85. Goldsmith, *Inquiry into the Present State, Works,* II, 57.
86. Goldsmith, *Citizen of the World,* Letter LXXXIV, 234.
87. Goldsmith, *Inquiry into the Present State,* loc. cit.
88. Goldsmith, *Citizen of the World,* Letter XCIII, 256.
89. Johnson, *The Rambler,* No. 2. *British Essayists,* XVI, 76.
90. Goldsmith, *Inquiry into the Present State, Works,* II, 47 ff.
91. Pope, *Dunciad* (B), 272-73.
92. Baker, IV, 15.
93. F. W. Bateson, *English Comic Drama: 1700-1750* (Oxford, Clarendon Press, 1929), 8.
94. Johnson, *The Rambler,* No. 4, *British Essayists,* XVI, 82-83.
95. Ibid.
96. Johnson, *The Rambler,* No. 4, 84-88.
97. Mary Wortley Montague, *Complete Works,* Ed. Lord Wharncliffe (2 vols., Paris, 1837), II, 100-105.
98. Goldsmith, *The Bee,* No. 6. In: *Citizen of the World,* 399.
99. Tompkins, 74.
100. Henry Mackenzie, *The Lounger,* No. 20, *British Essayists,* XXX, 124.
101. Johnson, *Lives of the English Poets,* II, 135.
102. Addison, *Spectator,* No. 44, I, 133.
103. Goldsmith, *Citizen of the World,* Letter XXI, 56.
104. David Hume, *Of Tragedy, Four Dissertations* (London, 1757), 198-99.
105. Goldsmith, *A Comparison between Sentimental and Laughing Comedy, Works,* III, 380.
106. Addison, *Spectator,* No. 37, I, 112.
107. Francis Gallaway, *Reason, Rule, and Revolt in English Classicism* (New York, Scribner's, 1940), 115.
108. William Cowper, *The Progress of Error, Poetical Works of William Cowper,* Ed. H. S. Milford (London, Oxford Univ. Press, 1934), 24.
109. Richardson, *The Novels of Samuel Richardson* (20 vols., London, 1902), XIX, 15-16.
110. Jean Marie Arouet Voltaire, *Essay on Taste;* Alexandre Gerard, *An Essay on Taste; With Three Dissertations on the Same Subject by Mr. de Voltaire, Mr. d'Alembert, and Mr. de Montesquieu* (London, 1759), 220.
111. David Garrick, "Prologue," *The Farmer's Return from London, Poetical Works of David Garrick* (2 vols., London, 1785), I, 186-88.
112. Johnson, *The Idler,* No. 36 and No. 85, *British Essayists,* XXVII, 124, 297-98.
113. Goldsmith, *Specimen of a Magazine in Miniature. The Miscellaneous Works of Oliver Goldsmith,* Ed. David Masson (London, Macmillan, 1925), 288.
114. Allen, II, 25-26.
115. Ibid.

116. Goldsmith, "Editor's Preface," *Citizen of the World*, 4.
117. Addison, *Spectator*, No. 44, I, 133.
118. Ibid., No. 42, I, 127.
119. Ibid., No. 5, I, 18.
120. Pope, *First Epistle to the Second Book of Horace*, *The Best of Pope*, 236-37.
121. Goldsmith, *Citizen of the World*, Letter XXI, 56-57.
122. Ibid., Letter LXXIX, 219-20.
123. Goldsmith, *A Comparison between Sentimental and Laughing Comedy*, loc. cit.
124. John A. Kelly, *German Visitors to the English Theaters in the Eighteenth Century* (Princeton, Univ. Press, 1936), 55.
125. Pedicord, 135-39.
126. David Hume, *The Rise and Progress of the Arts and Sciences, Philosophical Works* (4 vols., London, Tait, 1826), III, 152.
127. Voltaire, loc. cit.
128. Hume, *Of Simplicity and Refinement in Writing, Philosophical Works*, III, 223.
129. Sutherland, "Introduction," *Dunciad*, x-xi.
130. Pope, *Dunciad* (B), 337-38.
131. Pope, *First Epistle to . . . Horace, The Best of Pope*, 233.
132. Sutherland, xlii.
133. *The Sylph*, No. 19, qu. J. T. Taylor, *Early Opposition to the English Novel: The Popular Reaction from 1760 to 1830* (New York, King's Crown, 1943), 43.
134. Tompkins, 5.
135. Bateson, 145.
136. Allen, I, 110.
137. Goldsmith, *Inquiry into the Present State, Works*, II, 58.
138. Fielding, "Prologue," *The Universal Gallant*, Works, III, 165.
139. Garrick, "Epilogue to Arthur Murray's *All in the Wrong*," *Poetical Works*, I, 173-74.
140. Pedicord, 119.
141. Theophilus Cibber, *Two Dissertations on the Theatres* (London, 1756), 5.
142. Allen, I, 269.
143. Ibid., I, 255.
144. Collins, *Profession of Letters*, 96-97.
145. Taylor, 101 ff.
146. Ibid., 97.
147. Robert Lloyd (satirist, poet, member of Trinity College) writing in *The Connoisseur*, No. 135, qu. Gallaway, 277.
148. Goldsmith, *Taste, Miscellaneous Works*, 313.
149. René Wellek, *A History of Modern Criticism* (2 vols. to date, London, Cape, 1955), I, 26.
150. Sherburn, 997.
151. Addison, *Spectator*, Nos. 411, 412, 416; III, 276-82, 290-93.
152. Goldsmith, *Citizen of the World*, Letter XXI, 55.
153. Joseph Warton, *An Essay on the Genius and Writing of Pope* (1756). In: H. A. Needham, *Taste and Criticism in the Eighteenth Century* (London, Harrap, 1952), 113.

154. Goldsmith, *Taste,* 314-15.
155. Fielding, *Covent Garden Journal,* No. 10, *Works,* X, 29.
156. Addison, *Tatler,,* No. 165; *Guardian,* No. 19. *British Essayists,* III, 319; XIII, 162.
157. Edmund Burke, *Essay on Taste, Harvard Classics* (50 vols., New York, Collier, 1909), XXIV, 13.
158. Hume, *On Taste, Four Dissertations,* 215.
159. Burke, XXIV, 14-15.
160. Henry Home, Lord Kames, *Elements of Criticism* (3 vols., Edinburgh, Kincaid and Bell, 1762), III, 358-65.
161. Addison, *Spectator,* No. 70, I, 215.
162. Gallaway, 53.
163. Hugh Blair, *Lectures on Rhetoric* (3 vols., Basle, J. Decker, 1801), I, 34-35.
164. Kames, passim.
165. Hume, *On Taste,* 228.
166. Fielding, *Covent Garden Journal,* No. 23, *Works,* X, 41-47.
167. Needham, "Introduction," 38.
168. Burke, *On the Sublime and Beautiful, Harvard Classics,* XXIV, 108 ff.
169. Richard Steele, *Tatler,* No. 173, *British Essayists,* III, 356-60.
170. Needham, 36.
171. Ibid., 52.
172. Gallaway, 347.
173. Sherburn, 1001.
174. Edward Niles Hooker, "The Reviewers and the New Criticism, 1754-70," *Philological Quarterly,* Vol. XIII (1934), 197.
175. Gallaway, 345.
176. Kames, I, 337.
177. Hume, *Of Tragedy, Four Dissertations,* 186-87.
178. Archibald Alison, *On Taste* (1790), qu. Needham, 181.
179. Atkins, 173-75.
180. Pope, *Essay on Criticism, The Best of Pope,* 71.
181. Goldsmith, *Inquiry into the Present State, Works,* II, 31.
182. Sherburn, 841-42.
183. Atkins, 312.
184. Goldsmith, *Inquiry into the Present State, Works,* II, 47.
185. Johnson, *The Rambler,* No. 92, *British Essayists,* XVII, 182.
186. Krutch, 497.

Excursus B
THE DEBATE ON CULTURAL STANDARDS IN NINETEENTH CENTURY ENGLAND

It has lately become fashionable in sociological circles to make culture a topic for investigation. Yet, one of the difficulties of making sociology of culture a viable area is that it requires a commitment to historical orientation—a source of popular infatuation on the continent and of reactions of boredom and impatience in our country. Nevertheless, sociologists have made great strides toward overcoming parochial compartmentalization in discovering increasingly that many of our colleagues in literary history and criticism have spoken good sociological prose all along, by placing literature as a cultural phenomenon in a social context. Raymond Williams in England as well as Henry Nash Smith, Lionel Trilling, and Ian Watt in this country are some outstanding examples.

One of the most promising sociological approaches to contemporary culture is to study intellectuals as a professional class—in particular, as the administrators of prevailing cultural symbolic systems. Four British magazines from the nineteenth century have been examined—*The Quarterly Review* and *Blackwood's Edinburgh Magazine,* one Whig journal, *The Edinburgh Review,* and *The Westminster Review,* the organ of the philosophical radicals. These reflect the passionate and partisan concern of first-rate and middle-rate writers with the fate of cultural institutions and mores in the prevailing middle-class climate of industrialization and urbanization. One of the most striking features of the contributions in these magazines is their use of a kind of primordial sociological approach in close proximity with literary and aesthetic concerns. Juvenile delinquency and crime rate statistics, urban developments and styles of family life, technological advances and educational institutions are just a few of the complexes around which arguments are built.

The task is to analyze intellectual statements made in a clearly defined medium, i.e., widely distributed magazines featuring mostly book reviews, whose contributors include almost all significant "name" writers of the era as well as other reputable writers. What is the general social climate, and what are the specific social circumstances operating in the intellectual and cultural universe which induce people to write on certain subjects in certain ways? Our chances for drawing valid sociological inferences from these intellectual productions as indicators of a social context are heightened by the fact that we deal primarily with a cumulative body of writing, accepted for a given magazine which, in turn, had *editorial* intentions reflected in the selection of contributions, and *marketing* intentions with regard to sustaining a sufficient circulation.

These intellectual productions are looked upon in the context of social change, i.e., increasing industrialization; new forms of transportation and communication; urbanization; the industries of "culture" (newspapers, publishing, theatres, adult education, etc.). It is expected that these changes are reflected typically in the magazine material. Ideologically, the sum total of this literature reproduces the inconsistencies, antagonisms, and contradictory value judgments concomitant with the drastic changes between 1800 and 1900 in industry and commerce, in political as well as educational institutions, and sociological analysis tries to interpret these "derived" social data of literary source material as symbolic expressions of underlying social trends and counter-trends.

The problem of cultural standards certainly did not start with the nineteenth century, but emerged with the beginning of middle-class civilization. Its theoretical roots might be identified with Montaigne and Pascal, and pragmatic questions on standards of taste and aesthetic quality developed with the magazines of Addison and Steele. The debate over culture in nineteenth century England is a continuation, on a grander scale, of problems and issues that found expression in the previous century. All facets of national life came in for their share of appraisal, and often in a spirit of painful re-examination.

The debate over art and popular culture as it unfolds in these magazines voices several concerns that may be briefly sketched as follows:

1. What is the effect of the dissemination of popular culture—i.e., mass-produced culture for large masses of people—on the audience? Is it lowering the moral taste of the nation? Is it catering to a corrupt and degenerate taste, or is it harmless entertainment for the enslaved workingman? Is popular culture responsible for the increasing crime rate? Does it reflect the failure of the program for universal education, a failure on the part of England's educators to create a literate and discriminating audience that can uphold and better the standards of the past? Does it herald a decline in the moral fibre and intellectual quality of the nation?

2. What is the relationship between popular culture and the social conditions in which the lower classes find themselves? Is the quality and large consumption of popular literature, for example, a reflection of the impact of industrial technology on the working man, in that leisure time becomes devoted to entertainment that has taken on an escapist dimension?
3. What is the effect of popular culture on the serious artist? What hidden pressures does the situation produce? The increasing economic disadvantage of the serious artist, in the face of the commodity value of popular culture, becomes a touchy issue. Is it possible that the serious artist, forced to compete with his less talented and certainly more greedy brothers, will become hasty and enter the market-place with something less than he is capable of?
4. What is the relationship between popular culture and contemporary criticism? Can it be said that the critics, who exist primarily for the middle and upper classes, have not fulfilled their responsibility in view of their lack of contact or effect on the proliferation of popular culture? Is it a matter of literature or sociology? Art or science? What should be the role of the critic?
5. Is it a question of economics? What can one say about an economic system that allows wealth to be conferred on mediocrity, while the best goes begging? (The Tory view was that democratic capitalism was a decaying system, and that patronage was the answer.)

For purposes of our discussion, we can say that the nineteenth century was unique, if only for the reason that the professional writer and artist now faced, for the first time, a mass audience, in the modern sense of the term. A consideration of the literary picture brings us immediately to the center of the whirlpool, where the serious writer and the hack, both creatures spawned out of the new social status conferred on the writer, confront each other. Conditions had changed since the eighteenth century: with the decline of the patronage system, these two professionals had to shift their dependency from the privileged classes to reliance on the much more treacherous economic jungle in which distribution and sale of their works to a large and uncharted audience constituted the basis for their livelihood. This shift in the economic base of the professional writer was, of course, given tremendous impetus by the explosion of technologically based industry, coupled with the new power of the middle class as benefactors of culture and arbiters of taste, and the interest of the newly literate lower classes. These two groups combined to provide an audience of great proportions. Allied closely to the picture of the changing social composition of the audience was the development which to the nineteenth century was part of the new creed of progress, the new "culture for the Million" as it is called again and again—that is, the dissemination of "useful" information and knowledge through the innumerable government and private agencies set up for that purpose. The development began early, and by the 1830s England was afflicted by a plague of reading clubs, societies, workingmens' improvement committees, and all kinds of publishing guides, aids, hints, handbooks, digests. These provided for a new accessibility of a wide range of cultural phenomena, now made available to the middle and lower classes.

The reaction was not long in coming. This dispersal, or diffusion, of culture results, so said the conservative critics, in the inevitable watering down of cultural products; the new audience, while equipped with rudimentary abilities and aesthetic sensibilities, can not by any stretch of the imagination bring to cultural exchanges anything resembling a high or sophisticated level of taste. As a result of this diffusion, mediocrity in cultural products becomes the hallmark of success, and the audience— half-educated, poorly trained, but hungry to assert its right to contribute and participate in the cultural life of its country—confers on the second-rate artist and on the hack the kind of success which an age of patronage would have deemed impossible.

The serious artist, thus surrounded by such an uncongenial milieu, was seen by the conservative group to be at a great disadvantage. Forced into competition with those whose audiences ranged in the millions, he had to tighten his belt or to capitulate to the clamoring market for immediate gain. The decline of the drama, and the increasing loss of interest in poetry was cited as proof of the poor state of belles lettres. The growing breach between "highbrow" and "lowbrow" writers was signalled as the lamentable beginning of the exclusiveness of serious works, and their alienation from everyday life. One critic, in paraphrasing the scholar Courthope (with whom we shall deal presently in more detail) writes:

> The modern poet is a recluse, not a man of the world, dealing with private rather than common experiences. He withdraws from companionship into solitude, from action to reflection. In the practice of his art he becomes a law to himself instead of conforming to the standards which have been sanctioned by antiquity. . . . The charge thus stated against modern poetry is not without truth.[1]

While the lowered standards of popular taste created special social and economic pressures on the artist and called into question the utilitarian approach that had dominated England's educational systems, conservative and liberal critics alike pointed out that the plight of the artist was aggravated by the emphasis placed on such media as the ephemeral quarterlies, newspapers, penny weeklies, etc.

Here then is the marvel of the present time . . . in which unparalleled talent of every description is constantly devoted to the prosecution of literature; but in which the *new works* given forth from the press are, with very few exceptions, frivolous or ephemeral, and the whole serious talents of the nation are turned into perishable channels of the daily, weekly, monthly or the quarterly press. . . . Such a state of things . . . is alarming and prejudicial, . . . [and] may, if it continues unbated, produce . . . in the end, danger or ruin to the national fortunes.[2]

The rush and pressure characteristic of this type of literary work was found to be antagonistic to the contemplation and seclusion needed for higher orders of creative work. Reviewing Hood's poems, a critic writes:

The constantly recurring demands of Periodical Literature are fatal to all deliberation of view—to all care, or study, or delection of materials. . . . The tale of bricks must be furnished by the appointed day, let the straw be found where it will. . . . How can one—educated under such influences— be expected to deal with composition of the month as he would with works destined for eternity?[3]

The *Edinburgh Review,* for one, complained further of the plethora of amateur writers, drawn from many social levels, all intensely competitive, who were rapidly "using up" plots and situations so that the serious writer had to search, or was hard put to discover fresh material. More important, yet closely allied to this problem of the paucity of invention and the short-lived sheets was the concern of the critics to discover from historical example the social conditions necessary for the creation of great works. It was an accepted dictum that creativity cannot be hurried, that it must advance at its own pace, that the creator cannot be harried by deadlines, or be pressed in economic competition with writers of pot-boilers and fly-by-night productions. Creativity was understood to be a highly individual matter, at the very opposite end from the formula of quick success. The underlying question was whether the nineteenth century, with its heavy materialistic emphasis, could provide a nourishing milieu for the development of greatness.

The generalizations of some critics went beyond the literary frame of reference and contain some of the more piercing appraisals of the period. The critics lamented the disappearance of individual robustness, character, and with these, the possibility of intellectual greatness. A society whose creed of progress is based on the advance of science and technology has changed the national character. Nineteenth century man has become tame and enfeebled; industrialization has created a social uniformity and a lack of living models from which the poet or dramatist could choose:

> The delineations of the poet have been copies of copies, or arbitrary creations of fancy, only because the poet has no longer had frequent opportunities of studying from living models. . . . The aids and appliances which are now multiplied around men, enfeeble them. . . . Industrialism . . . is a sedative to the passions. A certian social uniformity ensues. . . . Men are thus, as it were cast in a mould.[4]

All this sounds familiar enough to our ears. As mass-produced "art"— and street literature in particular—exerted an increasing impact on the English social scene, concern was registered over the precise nature of this impact. How to define and measure it? How to evaluate it? Critics found the "penny trash of the streets" to be an agent of moral degeneracy. A typical description of the effects of street literature reads:

> Yet this is the intolerable stuff that finds tens of thousands of juvenile readers, gilds the byways of crime, and helps to fill our reformatories with precocious gaolbirds of the worst class. Of the worst class, as being not only reft of all moral sense, and vitiated in mind, taste, and affection, but possessed of cunning intelligence how to turn their knowledge to the vilest uses.[5]

A direct relation between penny trash and the high crime rate of the metropolitan areas seemed obvious. More sophisticated opinions held that while reading about crime did not make a criminal, popular literature at the very least made violence and passion attractive; the moral ending neutralized nothing. The composition of the audience itself was often loosely assumed under the rubric "the lower classes," or "the million." Audience breakdowns were only slightly more specific. The writer just quoted saw an audience composed chiefly of women, "shop-girls, maid servants, and other such half-educated and weakly inflammable young persons." Richard Altick, author of the by-now-classic *The English Common Reader,* points out that in comparison to the public of Dickens and Thackeray,

> these publics were eclipsed by the "unknown public" Wilkie Collins had described in *Household Words* in August 1858: readers—three million of them, he estimated—who seldom if ever bought a book, but who formed an insatiable market for cheap weeklies of a quality distinctly below that of Dickens. To most observers, the low literary and intellectual level of these fiction papers, read by servants, unskilled workers, shop assistants, and their families, more than neutralized whatever optimistic conclusions could be reached after contemplating *Cornhill's* success.[6]

The attachment of the three million to vulgarizations, sensationalism, and mediocrity defied the canons of progress.

Some found this audience, pounded on by technology, utilitarian notions of happiness, and half-baked philanthropic ideas, to be an expression of the failure of universal education. The huge audience, fed on pap from hucksters' pens, spelled the end of what had been the early hope of educators, legislators, and philanthropists for an educated and literate public, participating on a large scale in the fruits of cultural exchange. By the 1860s the enormous rise of popular literature as a commodity generated a bitter and long-lasting discussion on the shortcomings of universal education, and its failure to devleop, along with literacy, a discriminating standard of response to what is beautiful and good in the world. Others saw in popular literature less of a threat to the moral fibre and standards of taste of the nation than an example of the understandable need to escape from the pressures of the industrial age. Robbed of any experience of individuality, their senses deadened by the insistence of their betters on the dissemination of "useful information," the masses could be excused if they found in popular culture the "fancy" which was not provided elsewhere. They turned to it, innocently, for relief, and the fact that relief was found in the form of sensational vulgarity and pseudo-morality was certainly the responsibility not of the audience but of the producers and disseminators. The Janus-faced effect of widespread industrialization was noted as responsible for creating a kind of intellectual vacuum that had inevitably been exploited by commercial interests, and by the intellectual posturings of the writers of literary trash. That the masses were content with their trash was simply because, according to *Contemporary Review,* "there is nothing better, of the very cheap kind within their reach."[7] Even more conservative voices were heard that were outright pessimistic about anything being accomplished. The contributors to the *Quarterly Review* particularly held that correlation between popularity and quality can only become more inverse. For them the shift of the pace-setters from the manor house to women's reading clubs means the end of a progressively healthy cultural life. Taste is the product of leisure time, of an enlightened and appreciative wealthy segment of society. A high standard of cultural achievement is inevitably coupled with exclusiveness of cultural appeal; diffusion ends in mediocrity.

While the now-familiar "but we give the public what it wants" was a steady defense of the book trade, most critics refused to accept such a stand. Suggestions made for alleviating the situation included plans to flood the market with cheap editions of the classics, and to stress the great responsibility of the purveyors of popular productions. Empson, a well-known critic, spoke vaguely about the duty of the publishers and hawkers of the trade to "give good taste their casting vote."[8] While legal measures and government control were considered at times, such ideals did not make much headway. Rather, a laissez-faire attitude seemed to come to the fore. As the critic Spedding writes in the *Edinburgh Review,* with the disarming candor of bourgeois class-consciousness:

> The economy of the world requires characters and talents adapted to various offices, low as well as high; and it is vain to deny that the lower offices will be most readily undertaken and most efficiently discharged by minds which are defective in some of the higher attributes. . . . We must have spies as well as soldiers, hangmen and informers as well as magistrates and law-givers, advocates as well as judges, antiquaries as well as historians, critics as well as poets, pullers down as well as builders up. . . . There will still be more than enough of coarse grain and tortuous growth, whose abilities will be well enough adapted to the narrower spheres, whose aspirations will not rise higher, and who will rally, in performing these necessary works, be cultivating their talents to the best advantage. Being there, the only question is how they shall be dealt with; whether they shall be acknowledged, as good after their kind, or cast out as unworthy of our better company; . . . For ourselves we have no hesitation in preferring the humaner alternative. . . . There is in every man and in everything a germ of good, which, if judiciously educed and fostered, may be made gradually to prevail over the surrounding bad, and convert it more and more into its own likeness.[9]

Twenty years later, in 1859 and 1860 when, as Altick points out, the term "the million" ceased to be an hyperbole, a climax in the debate over popular culture had been reached in these journals. The early flush of optimism created by the new educational suffrage had faded, and problems had now become large and starkly defined. Those attendant on the maintenance of high cultural productivity in the face of the broadening cultural base had not been resolved. The history of nineteenth century literary criticism, which so deeply involves this matter, is a complex affair of which we shall touch only a part. Aside from the writers-turned-critic (Wordsworth, Coleridge, Hazlitt, De Quincey, Scott), the professional critics as they appear in the four journals addressed themselves to a very large audience and were looked upon as influential moulders of the opinion of their readership. The expansion of the book review into a loose critical essay allowed freedom to develop ideas, and indeed the review became a kind of forum in which "all the second speeches in the national debate were made."[10] Central was the notion, borrowed from Marx, that literature is a mirror of social and economic conditions, and this was reinforced by Darwinian ideas of culture as an evolutionary process. The old questions, "Is it normal? Does it amuse?" gave way to something like, "Is it an accurate reflection of our world?

What does it tell us about our society?" Popular literature, so critics reasoned, is immoral because it distorts reality and falsifies truth. But it is also an accurate reflection of a set of new social truths which cannot be ignored. Popular literature cannot be considered in the same light as artistic creations; it is a symptom of a new social epoch—if not of a social disease. The English reviewer of M. Nisard's book *Histories des Livres Populaires* writes about popular literature:

> This, no doubt, is one of the great social problems of the age, hardly, if at all, inferior in interest to that of primary education itself; because it involves the success of that self-education, which bears even more directly on the practical formation of character of the individual, and the determination, for good or for evil, at the outset, of the moral principles which whether unfelt or openly avowed, are destined to be his guide of action throughout life. It is plain that the arbitrary enactments of a government, or the remedial measures of a commission can but reach the externals: they deal with the symptoms rather than with the disease.[11]

By the end of the century, popular literature was the province of both social scientist and critic, combined in the person of the literary critic who struggled to provide a rationale in the wake of extensive social change.

The range of critical attitudes was large. At one extreme were the elitists with little faith in the ability of the masses ever to provide an appreciative audience for serious works. Critical decisions and cultural dictates have to be made at the top, in the most educated strata of society, and eventually filter downward. At the other extreme were the intellectual "radicals" who placed great faith in the critical taste of the masses. They said that historically, the uneducated are slow-moving, deliberate, conservative, retainers of the best of the culture. One has only to consider the fame of Voltaire or Racine, to be convinced:

> Although the less critical multitude is generally slow in acquiring correctness of taste, it is also the last to abandon the cause of good taste, when once acquired, and to follow the more mercurial leaders of fashion into corrupt extravagance. . . . Racine and Voltaire still continue to be, or were until very lately, the delight of the French populace, though the "intellectual classes" had gone wandering after the idolatries of the romantic school.[12]

In a similar vein, it was contended that the diffusion of culture, far from being a levelling agent or the harbinger of mediocrity and uniformity, provided a variety and multiplicity on the intellectual and spiritual level, a stimulus to all creative work and to novelists in particular:

Civilization, which tends to make the actions of men uniform, only multiplies varieties in their opinions and their minds. . . . There is far more food for the philosophy of fiction in the stir and ferment, . . . the working reason, the excited imagination that belong to this era of rapid and visible transition, than in the times of "belted knights and barons bold," when the wisest sage had fewer thoughts than a very ordinary mortal can boast of now.[13]

This attempt to rationalize and to answer the gloomy prophets of culture is the beginning of that uneasy alliance between science, industrialization and art that became, at the end of the century, standardized into an expression of confidence.

Let us pause here a moment and restate the primary interest of this study, that is, to explore whether and to what extent the concerns of the nineteenth century intellectuals were propaedeutic to the concerns of the contemporary intellectual scene. As radically as the underpinnings of the social order have been changing, the problems not yet resolved and probably unresolvable are the accommodation of past values to new social exigencies; further, the creation of new cultural values systems, and above all, the problem of how to deal with the values and mores emerging partly spontaneously, partly manipulatively, among the broad strata of industrialized populations. To state this problem merely in terms of the conflict between culture and mass culture would lead to sermonizing. To state it, however, in terms of the efforts of the intellectuals as a class to reconcile themselves to this obvious dichotomy is a genuine task— sociological or otherwise. The analysis of our material shows that the attempt at reconciliation or synthesis did not succeed—just as it has not succeeded today. Yet the detailed spelling out of this failure would in itself be a contribution to a more sophisticated restatement of today's intellectual positions.

An article which appeared in the *Quarterly Review* in 1874, written by William J. Courthope (the author of a *History of English Poetry,* a book still used), provides ample demonstration of this point.[14] It is not without irony that a modern literary historian raps Courthope's knuckles because of an alleged foray by this author into sociology. Our modern critic believes that this book on English poetry is "in usefulness marred by a too strict adherence to the thesis that there is a close connection between literary fashions, tastes and values, and contemporary social and political opinions and conditions."[15]

Yet the article is an important and, in a way, a very pretentious one which attempts to "review" three books of Matthew Arnold, a book by Symonds and one of Pater's, and for good measure, to reevaluate two of Carlyle's classical writings. It centers around an analysis of the concept of culture itself. The position of Courthope is one of ambiguity—in itself paradigmatic for the intellectual kibitzer who almost, but not quite, identifies with a cause. This kind of partisanship without commitment anticipates the mid-twentieth century intellectual rather than characterizes the nineteenth century literati.

Courthope contrasts Matthew Arnold's thought with liberal and Jacobinian philosophy of culture, and he does it in such a way that his sympathies seem to lie with what he described as the liberal position. His critique of Arnold is directed against "self-culture," against the refinement of the personality in isolation from the main stream of national mores. He finds the same snobbish cultural isolationism in Carlyle. Sarcastically, he calls Carlyle "the Professor," who in raising literature to the place erstwhile occupied by religion joins "the tendency of artists, men of science, poets and professions of polite letters in general, to form themselves into a priesthood for propagating a religion of ideas." He contrasts Carlyle's elitism with the position of the rather radical Frederick Harrison who, by the way, was the high priest of Auguste Comte in England and who ridiculed what he called "the very silliest cant of the day . . . the cant about Culture." According to Harrison, culture is a very restricted area of concern which might have a function in the scholarship of literary criticism, but "as applied to politics it means simply a turn for small fault-finding, love of selfish ease, and indecision in action." And he wraps it all up in the classical statement: "the man of culture in politics is one of the poorest creatures alive."

A closer reading shows that Courthope's somewhat uneasy and not quite committed juxtaposition of opposing evaluations of culture is indicative of a much more crucial ideological attitude of the intellectual toward the culture dilemmas of modern society. One might say that it is projection when he pronounces Matthew Arnold's famous self-image as "wandering between two worlds, one dead, the other powerless to be born . . . [as] important." This is exactly the situation of the highly sensitized intellectual facing two aspects of alienation: a cultural heritage which has seemingly become estranged from the temper of the times, and, on the other hand, a cultural products market courting the fickle idiosyncracies and psychological needs of the populace which is willing to pay a price if the merchandise is right. Courthope reflects this dilemma of double alienation: he cannot accept the Carlyle-Arnold-Pater position, this "irresponsible priesthood" which artificially enforces an estrangement from social responsibility. Yet he also cannot accept "the logical consequences of the law of supply and demand in literature." He quotes with disgust an article in the London *Times* which stated in positive terms the credo of market-oriented mass culture: "If one novel in ten, or one poem in a thousand, be worth reading at all, it is as much as we can reasonably expect to find. It is certain, however, that the rest supply a want which is really felt, and give undoubted pleasure to a large class of readers. If the object of literature is to give pleasure, and to divert the mind from the unpleasant realities of life, *it is impossible to refuse some praise* to the performance which does this, for however brief a period."

Courthope rejects a social philosophy which makes public opinion not only a criterion of success but also the criterion of historical judgment which has to be accepted. He notes that "national taste is decaying" and in Tocquevillian phraseology, he "revolts against this vulgar and cynical despotism" of public opinion. Sarcastically, he comments on the *Times'* editorial: "If the object of literature be what is defined by that great journal, . . . we cannot rightly refuse our praise to the art of the procurers or the trade of the opium-monger." Yet Courthope does not find himself about to resolve the dilemma by either standing aloof as the uncompromising critic or rising to the stance of the fighting revolutionary; rather, he dissipates his argument by vaguely arguing the possibility of genuine cultural activity through "consideration of the instincts, the traditions, the character of the society to which we belong."

The article is a veritable inventory of contrasting topics and themes of the cultural debate. There is awareness of a thoroughgoing change from the aristocratic to the middle-class style of life; there is insight into the differential cultural demands made in a highly stratified middle-class society; there is knowledge about the differences of cultural values reinforced by taste as an objective criterion of excellence and the demands of the market; there is, at least germinally, a fine delineation of the two social antagonists—the elitist and the populist, as it were—in the codification of what culture does and should mean; and finally there is acted out, though with many ambiguities and uncertainties, the role of the intellectual who feels no obligation to say either an absolute yes or an absolute no to the world in which he finds himself.

The debate over cultural standards in the nineteenth century was a continuation of issues already current in the eighteenth. But while the earlier century ended on a note of disillusionment,[16] the nineteenth century found its rationale. The combination of England's emergence as an imperialist power, and the tremendous advance in standards of living made this possible. In the final quarter of the century the writings in the quarterly journals take on an academic dryness; the earlier tone of immediacy and involvement is gone. The triumph of science supported an optimism that dared challenge the premises of the critique of cultural standards. Thus, in 1896 the *Edinburgh Review* reviewer can say: "If it be true that the moral and material welfare of the masses of the nation can only be obtained by making it more difficult for the man of intellect to make his mark on the age, [then] the interests of the many, must, we fear, prevail over the requirements of the few; and we must content ourselves as best we can with securing the greatest happiness of the greatest number." On this sour note of uneasy trust in the age of Science and Multitudes, the century ends.

NOTES

1. *Edinburgh Review*, No. CCCXXXIV (April 1886), pp. 467–68.
2. *Blackwood's Edinburgh Magazine*, LI (January 1842), pp. 107 ff.
3. *Edinburgh Review*, No. CLXVIII (April 1846), p. 383.
4. *Edinburgh Review*, No. CLXXX (April 1849), p. 360.
5. *Edinburgh Review*, No. CLXV (January 1887), p. 50.
6. Richard Altick, "The Literature of an Imminent Democracy," in *1859: Entering an Age of Crises* (Bloomington: Indiana University Press, 1959), p. 222. *Cornhill Magazine* was a successful example of "thoughtful middle-class journalism."
7. *Contemporary Review*, XIV (June 1870), p. 459.
8. *Edinburgh Review*, No. CXXXII (July 1837), p. 204.
9. *Edinburgh Review*, No. CXXXVIII (January 1839), p. 435.
10. Michael Wolff, "Victorian Reviewers and Cultural Responsibility," in *1859: Entering an Age of Crises* (Bloomington: Indiana University Press, 1959), p. 270.
11. *Edinburgh Review*, No. CCXVII (January 1858), p. 246.
12. *Edinburgh Review*, No. CXXXII (July 1837), p. 151.
13. *Edinburgh Review*, No. CXXXVI (July 1838), p. 356-57.
14. *Quarterly Review*, No. 274 (October 1874), pp. 404 ff.
15. Samuel C. Chew, "The Nineteenth Century and After," in A. E. Baugh, ed., *A Literary History of England* (New York: Appleton-Century-Crofts, 1948), p. 1603.
16. Cf. Chapter 3 of this volume.

Chapter 4
THE RECEPTION OF DOSTOEVSKI IN PRE–WORLD WAR I GERMANY

The plan of this study was conceived during the last year of the Weimar Republic, and it was during this period that the research data were collected.[1] The study itself was written "in exile" after Hitler had come to power. I make these remarks advisedly in order to warn the reader that the motivation for this piece of work was not so much scholarly interest per se but a political or, if you will, moral concern. Working as a sociologist in a German academic context, I became appalled at the increasing political and moral apathy of Germany's lower middle and middle classes beginning in the twenties—an apathy, if not callousness, which was hidden under the veneer of "cultural" pretensions. I was curious to find out whether a method of scientific access could be developed with which to study this constellation of political and moral decay and cultural magniloquence.

Had I known at the time about advanced methods of opinion research and projective psychology, I would perhaps have never designed this study, for it attempts to accomplish the same ends as these methodologies in a primordial fashion. It assumes that the works of a writer serve as projective devices for the display, through widely published commentaries, of hidden traits and tendencies typical for broad strata of a population. In other words, it studies readers' reactions indirectly through the medium of printed material which is inferred to represent typical group reactions.

The "sample" of this opinion study is very representative as far as it goes. Due to the generous assistance I had as a member of the Institute of Social Research at the University of Frankfurt, I was able to peruse nearly all books, all magazine articles, and even all major newspaper articles ever written on Dostoevski for the time period under investigation. The results of my research, which originally appeared in German, are here presented in a somewhat abridged form.

During the last two decades of the nineteenth century and the first two decades of the twentieth century, no other modern author received as much literary and critical attention in Germany as Dostoevski. There have been other writers, of course, who have had greater influence or who have achieved more editions, and the curve of the literary preoccupation with Dostoevski shows considerable fluctuation. But not a single year has elapsed since the end of the eighties without some significant addition to the Dostoevski literature. Nor is this literature restricted to the field of aesthetic criticism. Many political, religious, scientific, and philosophic discussions have appeared along with literary essays and critiques. Examination of the complete German bibliography on Dostoevski (approximately 800 items)[2] reveals an unusual number of important names from literary, religious, and philosophic life, distributed among the most diverse schools (only Goethe is comparable in this respect). The same applies to the diffusion of the Dostoevski literature among periodicals and newspapers. Political organs ranging from the conservative through the National-Liberal to the political left, literary periodicals in the strict sense, even scholarly journals devoted to philosophy, law, and medicine have published discussions of Dostoevski.

Such temporal continuity and social diversity suggest certain problems. Are there some particular features which condition this intensity and breadth of interest? Are there specific elements in Dostoevski's works which appeal to a particular social configuration in all its diversity and change?

This paper is not a study of Dostoevski. Certain ideological peculiarities of the German middle- and lower-middle-class reading public clearly do not apply to Dostoevski at all. In fact, the amount of attention which he has received cannot by any means be explained by reference to the content, composition, or language of his novels, by their subject matter or aesthetic qualities alone. The complete answer must lie in fields other than those which the literary historian ordinarily discusses.

THE UBIQUITOUS MYTH

Studying the written reaction to Dostoevski in all of its multiplicity, one is struck by the fact that the same broad categories of interpretation have been retained throughout. The emphasis varies here and there, to be sure, for the taste for particular works changes in time. Certain aspects, such as the religious significance of the man and his work, for example, did not become important until later. If one looks hard enough, diametrically opposed statements can be found within these categories on many specific points. One conservative critic, for example, stresses the nationalism of Dostoevski,[3] whereas a liberal critic tending toward naturalism emphasizes his humanism.[4] But the common viewpoints are far more apparent than any such differences. Whether examining the commentary of the 1890s or of the 1930s, there are the same typical judgments: Dostoevski is a special kind of psychologist, he preaches the love of man in his own way, he tends to reconcile contradictions among the most divergent theoretical and practical spheres of life, his work expresses the soul of his people, and the like. Our problem is to show the extent to which these judgments contain basic elements of the ideology of the social groups which form the hard core of his readership.

The reception given to Dostoevski, the evaluation of the categories developed in the course of that reception, is positive with a few unimportant exceptions. Dostoevski is acclaimed. One might even say that his popularity is less a matter of literary criticism than of willing and pious adoration. It is significant that there is scarcely one adequate scholarly account of his life and work by a German literary historian, and the few comprehensive treatments which do exist betray their opinionated character by their very design.[5]

From the beginning, Dostoevski is surrounded with an aura of myth. Qualities are added to his personality and works, qualities which transcend verifiable reality and have a super-historical character, and a certain indestructible unity is posited between his life and novels. They are devoid of any connection with the social process, but at the same time they are assumed to make social life meaningful against all historical theory and against every conception of social law.

An examination of mythical speculations in the commentaries on Dostoevski quickly reveals a staggering number of closely related formulations concerning the symbolic nature of the author and his works: "close to primordial conditions,"[6] a nature "full of the Devil and full of God,"[7] a saint on the road "from Nazareth to Golgotha,"[8] a "bottomless pit,"[9] "epileptic genius,"[10] one who weaves death with life,[11] "reason with madness,"[12] chaos with form.[13] Certain common ideas underlie this chaotic abundance.

First, the realm of real being appears in Dostoevski's work, that realm which stands outside mere contingency in human life. With him we approach "the mystical mothers";[14] he "projects for the most part into the new third realm of the human race";[15] "we always carry the abyss with us."[16]

Second, Dostoevski's life has a symbolic meaning. It is not molded by manifold experiences; the latter are themselves only stations in an "existence significantly conceived according to a sinister plan,"[17] stations on his "dark road."[18] "Mysterious forces, which apparently unseen, rule all the earthly destinies of Dostoevski," brought him to prison.[19] Through illness Dostoevski "was thrust into the darkest abysses of unhappiness and could taste the highest transports of ecstasy."[20] And "He was an epileptic. What does this mean? . . . That he felt a mysterious power within him, the demon, for a brief moment elevating him suddenly, sublimely prostrating him cruelly for days."[21] His death, too, took place under an unearthly sign: "He died like Beethoven in the sacred uproar of the elements, in a storm."[22] If one surveys the development of his personality, one sees that "it grows and is formed from the dark animalic and elementary roots to the highest consummation, and rises to the highest, most radiant peaks of spirituality."[23] Furthermore: "It often seems as if an invisible power presents just that man who is sensitive and receptive above all others with the most terrible of human destinies, so that a man may at length, out of his own experience, show his fellow men how a man of his type can be injured, humiliated, and tortured to death, and nevertheless remain a man. Such mysterious designs guide the destiny of Dostoevski."[24]

Such arbitrariness in the choice of mythical figures, which we meet in Christian and in pagan, in metaphysical and in sentimental form, places public life and the whole of social existence in a context which transcends criticism and dissatisfaction. The enjoyment of works of art casts a veil over reality. Apart from the gratification of the fancy which is achieved by "understanding" the deeper meaning of human life and events in general, one is transported into a sphere in which everyone can experience sublime pleasures. The mechanism which creates ideology also transmutes the lack of a social theory into a profuse wealth of images and fantasies. We shall see again and again that the ideology of the middle class tends to transfigure reality by substituting for it the inner world of the psyche. World history thus becomes private myth.

If myth as super- and prehistoricity serves to bolster the middle class in its relationship to the upper stratum, so also can the life of Dostoevski be interpreted to establish a line of demarcation from the lower classes. The same characteristically private aspect is inherent in the disposition of the life plan of the individual, of the meaning which rules his fate. The glorification of Dostoevski's terrible suffering, his imprisonment, illness, and poverty, in short, every situation to which the propertyless strata are exposed, is in the last analysis an exaltation of passivity. It is absurd to struggle against suffering inflicted by powers which elude every earthly, scientific, or social-reformist effort, and men upon whom such suffering has been imposed acquire a luster of special dignity. Such mechanisms console the middle classes for their own troubles by pointing to still greater ones. By giving full approval to the greater distress and suffering of the lower classes, they also alleviate their anxieties about potential threats from below to middle-class existence.

A third mythical factor is represented by the "meeting of opposites." Through the whole history of the reception there runs the motif that Dostoevski the man, the intrinsic quality of his works, the essence of his most important characters, in short, the whole compass of his life and creation, are characterized by a union of factors generally perceived as contradictory. Great pains are taken to show this union of opposites in the most diverse spheres. *Contradictions in Weltanschauung:* Dostoevski is "a conservative writer, yet also a naturalist."[25] The action in the *Brothers Karamazov* encompasses "heaven and hell";[26] "great saintliness and great wickedness" appear in Stavrogin;[27] Dostoevski "is a nihilist and orthodox."[28] *Intellectual contradictions:* we find the author "attaining the highest peak of reason and falling to the lowest depths of the abyss of mysteries."[29] Dostoevski often "undermines his logically constructed world of ideas in order to dash them down to an unfathomable depth."[30] *Moral contrasts:* "The saint and the sinner . . . are never opposites for him."[31] His countenance bears witness to "diseased passions and endless compassion";[32] the religious fanatic is steeped in guilt and the prostitute is pure.[33] *Contrasts of character:* "We must solve the apparent contradictions . . . in the greatness of his genius and of his heart, and look upon them in the same way as we look upon the contradictions in nature."[34] He "was an epileptic, a man in whom extremes of dullness and lucidity coalesced."[35] His countenance is "half the face of a Russian peasant, half that of a criminal."[36] Finally, there are contradictions which cannot be subsumed under fixed categories: "Every person . . . is only a bit of his immeasurable, indistinct personality . . . the sharply outlined details, the naturalistic element which we think we perceive are blurred. . . . It is the abyss in which mists brew . . . abyss and level ground are the same."[37] "We hesitate to use the formalistic hackneyed word 'harmony' of an author who permits the experience of all manner of blessedness and deviltry with cold-bloodedness."[38] His world is "full of heights and depths, narrow places and spacious extents, abysses and prospects."[39] "Chaos constantly takes on form . . . but at once the form grows soft and melts away."[40]

This mythological element illustrates a central factor in the construction of every ideology, namely, the glorification of existing social contradictions. This is the essence of the mechanism. All other factors are more or less subsidiary and may grow out of the sociopsychological peculiarity of the groups concerned, they may receive their emphasis from the historical situation involved, or they may be determined by material or cultural traditions. But the one constant is the glorification and embellishment of social contradictions.

In the first type of myth, the realm of real being, concrete reality is removed from sight. In the second, the role of the individual within the social process is isolated and overestimated; but in the third, the meeting of opposites goes straight to the social contradictions themselves. The ideological mechanism is developed in such a way that the antagonistic character of a given social order is denied more or less indirectly; an image of harmony within established order is created. The meeting of opposites assumes a unique position within the context of such ideological mechanisms. It does not deny the existence of contradictions in the most diverse spheres of culture and life; yet it justifies the contradictions metaphysically.

The following sentence could stand as a motto for this essay: "Political and social problems were transformed for him [Dostoevski] into problems of soul and faith."[41] Anti-intellectualism could hardly be manifested in more pregnant fashion. It is not a question of carrying out an idea, of admitting a sentiment, of respecting an ethical or political position as the only possible one, but of attributing equal validity to the antithetical idea, to a contrary sentiment, to a completely different position. It is never a question of anything very precise or certain; the diversity of life, its alleged depth and inexhaustibility, gives it its peculiar attraction. This expresses the fantasy life of social groups who cannot derive pleasure from a rational analysis of the external world. By reading fiction, however, they can enjoy the apparent diversity of life and resolve its social contradictions irrationally.

Finally, the national or folk myth assumes the most varied forms in the Dostoevski reception. "His literature is Asia . . . and even the impossible is entirely possible for him. . . . In the last analysis Russian mysticism is . . . yearning and fulfillment at the same time."[42] Or it is simply announced that "theory and life are one and the same to the Russian."[43] The historian Heinrich Friedjung makes a particularly open confession of his acceptance of this national mythology when he refers to Dostoevski's creed of the Russian soul: "If one applies the rules of logic to the religious and political views of Dostoevski, they crumble into contradictions. Here, too, the elementary is more powerful than the mere rational."[44] This statement recalls another typical element of the national myth, the ever-repeated assurance that Dostoevski is "one of the greatest manifestations of the Russian folk spirit,"[45] that "in him . . . the Russian soul has found its most powerful and at the same time most intimate expression,"[46] that "in Dostoevski we learn to understand the Russian and through him the Russian people."[47]

Closer inquiry into the nature of this Russian nation leaves us in somewhat of a quandary. We learn of the "Russian soul which splits its thirst for God into earthly pleasure and negating reverie."[48] We are told that there is no other nation "which is so religious in every stratum as the Russian,"[49] that the soul of the Russian manifests "itself more directly, more impetuously, more unreservedly than ours."[50] Apart from such vague and intangible characterizations, however, we must be satisfied with the knowledge that Dostoevski and his work offer us "a solution of the problem of Russia,"[51] that he "depicts with particular purity the essence of the Russian people, wondrously rich in strength and weakness, riddles and contradictions,"[52] in short, that he leads us into the "secret of the national existence."[53]

The most important documentation of this national mythology is to be found in the writings of Moeller van den Bruck, who edited the most widely circulated German editions of Dostoevski's works. Forerunner of German National Socialism, his comments represent a classical example of the social interpretation of the national myths of today. At the beginning of his introduction to *The Possessed,* van den Bruck speaks of the Russian soul, for which "man himself is a dark yearning after intuition and knowledge."[54] In contrast to the German, the "born carrier of ideas" who can often enough "return as Plato or Kant," the Slavs are "born heralds of faith." "If some day evening comes to Western humanity and the German is at rest, only a Slavic mother could again bear Buddha or Jesus out of the Eastern world."[55] The Russian *Weltanschauung* was transformed into great literary art for the first time in Dostoevski. "The expression of Russian madness, of the tragedy in Slavdom, the incarnation of all its mystical internalizations and hectic tension,"[56] he gave Russia its proper mythology of the soul. Russian life is determined by the "overly particularistic, constantly decentralizing racial developments," and on the other hand by the Russian national character—dreamy, sentimental, and resigned to fate, not active and determined. This internalized Russian nature finds expression everywhere, "even when it is unfolded in mad, and even atrocious, deeds."

Dostoevski, van den Bruck continues, was one of the very few novelists of the nineteenth century to say something new, more than Balzac, Flaubert, Zola, or de Maupassant. Only Goethe is comparable. Goethe "imbedded realism further in the spiritual and eternal by giving it a foundation of nature and the rising natural science."[57] Dostoevski went still further and, as "a complete naturalist, showed how modern life too has its mysticism and fantasies." He apprehended life "in its inner demonism . . . with its new beauties and ugliness, its new moralities and immoralities . . . and, instead of degrading naturalism into a mere copy, he again resolved it into a vision."[58] *The Possessed* reveals the demonism in the Russian conception of state and history, which, in view of degenerate social conditions, feverishly drives Russian youth to politics.

The year 1906, in which this introduction to *The Possessed* appeared, marked a definite stage in growth of monopoly, industrial and political, and the essay itself is a symptom of this ideology. If giant economic and political structures were to be accepted by the people, the ideal of competition among men through the development of reason and will had to be replaced by veneration of nonrational ideals removed from the forum of critical verification. It is one of the inherent contradictions of modern society that the growing dominance of rational planning in the economic and political structures should be accompanied by increasing suppression of rational and critical elements in the social consciousness.

Van den Bruck's essay on Dostoevski prepared the way for the development of a false legend about the nineteenth century. This is particularly clear in his over-simplification of the concept of naturalism. He extends it into a visionary, artistic conception of the world, a distortion which has been widely perpetuated, often with the help of references to the widely circulated introduction to *The Possessed*.[59] Van den Bruck denies the relationship of Dostoevski to the great tradition of European, and particularly French, realism and naturalism, and postulates an untenable connection with Goethe. Dostoevski is thus torn out of the real context of the human qualities which the nineteenth century developed, in a succession of artistic figures from Balzac to Zola, all of whom Moeller van den Bruck summarily dismisses. Realism and naturalism in the novel, which acknowledged the necessity for taking an unequivocal stand on the social conflicts, was one of the most important achievements of the nineteenth century. The artistic products of this naturalism, precisely because they strive to reflect real life, constitute an appeal for change.

But for Moeller van den Bruck the decisive element to be gleaned from the traditions and products of the nineteenth century appear under the vague title of "national mythologies." It is no longer history when he asserts that Dostoevski "encompasses in a thousand new answers not only the whole of Russia, but also the whole Slavdom in all its various nationalities, castes, and types, from the simple *mujik* to the Petersburg aristocrat, from the nihilist to the bureaucrat, from the criminal to the saint."[60] There is not the slightest scientific or even rational ground for asserting that the German is a "born carrier of ideas" (even though Plato is reckoned among the Germans), that the Slavic soul can, in its dark, yearning fashion, create a Buddha or a Jesus, or that the Russian national character is dreamy, sentimental, and submissive to fate rather than active and determined. More recently, such ideologies flourished in the powerful ideologies of totalitarian cultures.

The concept of the mythical, especially the myth of the community, comprises the most essential feature of the Dostoevski reception in Germany. But the material also affords concrete expression for several other basic factors of the social consciousness of the middle class. We shall first examine a factor which may be called *passivity*. This stance reflects the growing impotence of the middle class, and it is expressed in the glorification of the concept of duty and suffering, in the renunciation of any moral action which might be directed against social abuses. Here one comes much closer to social praxis than in the mythical, and the fact that important elements are most noticeable by their absence should not be cause for wonder. Specifically, it is the sphere of activity, and especially moral and political activity, which is missing or, at best, devaluated.

Dostoevski is used as an intellectual weapon against efforts to reorganize society. When his political doctrines are discussed, a malicious or uneasy voice is frequently heard applauding the opponent of revolutions and revolutionaries, the man who warned against political upheavals which bring distress, illness, and unnaturalness in their train. Political action is either condemned as a sin against the universal duty to submit, or transformed into mere inner exaltation, which is declared to be the essence of man. Dostoevski is a prophet of darkness, it is repeatedly said, who "foresaw the nihilist assassinations."[61] It was after the Revolution of 1905 and after the publication of the German translation of *The Possessed* in 1906, that his "baleful prophecy" revealed the future of Russia most strikingly.[62] "Many scenes from *The Possessed* are conceived as prophetic as if they were written during the revolution and today."[63] The point is repeatedly made that he "stood up so passionately and relentlessly against socialism."[64] Or: "Socialist Utopias were not only foreign to his nature, but directly counter to it. What inspired him . . . to the strongest loathing for socialism . . . was the moral materialism of this doctrine."[65]

It might be argued that one must not expect an activist approach from the apostle of love and compassion for mankind. Nearly all the literary critiques of Dostoevski do, in fact, revolve about the theme of love and compassion—in elegant formulations such as the "surpassing calm, through which only a sort of deeply secret sorrow vibrates, an endless compassion,"[66] or in painfully popular statements, such as "his heart trembles with sympathy, compassion."[67] Or censoriously, "His predilection for the oppressed and the depraved gradually assumes the morbid form of . . . 'Russian compassion,' that compassion which excludes

all upright, honest working men, and extends only to prostitutes, murderers, drunkards, and similar blossoms on the tree of mankind."[68]

This statement may be crude, but it underscores the fact that in
Dostoevski's work love remains a weak disposition of the soul. We have
here a situation similar to the meeting of opposites. The demand for
love and compassion could mean a realization of the existence of social
contradictions and the need for change; it could lead to the recognition
of the value of justice. But the idea of action cannot enter into the
consciousness of persons in a relatively impotent social stratum, any
more than they can accept a principle of justice which destroys their
solidarity with the upper class and points to their common interests with
the masses.

It has often been said that Dostoevski had no inner relation to politics,
that he was really no political theorist.[69] But how rarely has it been
pointed out that the demand for social justice is never proclaimed in
his political writings.[70] The irrelevance of this category, a category which
finds powerful expression in the outstanding works of European naturalism, that is to say in the most advanced artistic camp, is a clear sign
of the reactionary attitude of Dostoevski, and it is still more characteristic
of social groups which approve this silence.

UBIQUITOUS PSYCHOLOGY

The most frequent of all attributes of Dostoevski, acknowledged in
his reception in Germany before World War I at least, is that of
psychologist. The "most learned psychologists" could "take lessons from
him."[71] He was a "most subtle psychologist,"[72] and "all the psychological
skill of the world" pales before Raskolnikov.[73] *The Possessed* penetrates
with "overwhelming genius into all the depths of the human soul and
its demonism."[74] There are three answers to the question of the precise
nature of these extraordinary psychological accomplishments:

1. Dostoevski brings new, hitherto secret and dark psychological facts
   to light. He knows "the most secret psychic movements of the human
   soul."[75] He has an extraordinary talent for revealing "unperceived
   stirrings of the soul."[76] He "divines . . . all the unconscious, atavistic,
   and brute forces which stir the dark depths of faltering souls."[77]
2. Dostoevski is a specialist on diseases of the soul, an incomparable
   "master of pathological psychology."[78] Some of his works are all
   "psychological pathology."[79] A theologian claims that Dostoevski has
   "depicted the gradual outbreak of a mental illness more accurately"
   than any other novelist.[80] The same sentiment is expressed by a

specialist: "a better expert in the sick psyche, a greater psycho-pathologist, than Dostoevski" has probably never existed among novelists.[81]

3. Dostoevski provides a "unique psychology of crime."[82] Once again we find a specialist saying that in "Dostoevski's works we possess quite a complete, faithful description of diseased mental states and criminal types."[83]

The extent to which Dostoevski may actually have enriched psycho-logical knowledge is a separate question. Like all great novelists, he is passionately interested in psychological problems, and many of his characterizations are masterpieces even when considered against the more highly developed knowledge of today. What is important is that Dostoevski as psychologist reinforces the interest of the middle class in psychological problems. This interest has its own significant history. Before the middle-class revolutions in France and Germany, when there were sharp cleavages between the economic mechanism and the forms of political domination and between the intellectual maturity of the bourgeoisie and the feudal cultural apparatus, the protest of the bourgeoisie was expressed in literature as a fiery profession of faith in great passions and the importance of the independent life of the soul. This glorification of passion is, for example, clearly manifest in Goethe's *Werther.* It was a progressive attitude toward life, yet it was incapable of adequate social concretization. The security of feudal economy and its regulated market had disappeared, and a well-developed psychology was a necessary presupposition for a liberal economic system. One must know one's business partner; one must know with whom one is dealing. The producer, now opposed by other producers, merchants, and consumers, must know them, must be fully acquainted with their psychology, in order to calculate their possible reactions to himself and his enterprise. This is one of the social origins of the important role played by conversation and discussion in the modern novel and drama. Conversation is one indication of the psychological knowledge which competing individuals in a modern society possess. He who is rationally superior, more adroit, and more dexterous because of his knowledge of the ways in which his conversational partners react, has at his command one of the necessary conditions of economic success.

What was true in the period of middle-class absolutism is being repeated, to a certain extent, in a later phase of German society. Broad strata are again turning to the inner life for satisfaction, particularly in Germany, where liberalism never really gained control because of the merger between the feudal political power and the industrial bourgeoisie. It is an ideological consolation for the middle classes to indulge in psychological "discoveries" (a pleasure limited to the inner life) in precisely the same way as they enjoy the splendor of the German empire and, more recently, the Third Reich—as a satisfaction of imagination.

Pleasure in psychology fits this picture. The restriction of pleasure to one's own inner life acquires luster the more one loses oneself in an orgy of psychological interpretations. In this connection, the enjoyment of psychopathology and criminal psychology has an ideological significance of still another sort. The middle class cannot question the existing social organization as a whole, but must accept and approve it. This system, therefore, is "healthy." Crime and disease are overheads which are inevitable in the operation of the organism, but they are the exceptions of a temporary or peripheral nature which prove the rule, that is, the benign state of the whole.

The study of the reception of works of fiction thus becomes important from a new point of view. It contributes to the study of those factors which, over and above the mere power apparatus, exercise a socially conservative and retarding function through their psychological power. Desires do not disappear entirely, but they must be diverted, and art may help to transform the instincts. The effects of such conversion, the satisfaction of the fancy which the work of art gives, remain enclosed within the sphere of the inner life.

The German commentary on the writings of Dostoevski identifies the following psychological factors:

1. As a psychologist, Dostoevski proceeds "with the cold-bloodedness of an anatomist."[84] The so-called psychology of Dostoevski reminds one of a mighty laboratory with the finest, most precise tools and machines for the measurement, investigation, and testing of the human soul."[85] This "anatomization of human souls"[86] is "almost gruesome"[87] and "exceedingly cruel."[88] No "corner of the soul"[89] escapes him.

2. From the beginning, attention was directed to the "naked realism and naturalism,"[90] the scrupulous fidelity with which Dostoevski portrays the most "depraved characters" and the "most ghastly scenes."[91] His genius gives him insight into the "cesspools of mankind."[92] There is something tawdry about society in all his books. "They contain nothing but usurers, liars, double-crossers, grovelling upstarts, bloated fools, drunkards, and gamblers."[93] In his "repulsive images of dissolute fancy," and in his "splendidly realistic portrayal of national types of criminal and moral monsters,"[94] Dostoevski always "sees the soul naked before him in its anxiety and its agitation."[95]

3. An early critic remarks that *Crime and Punishment* lays "an incubus on the breast" of the reader by its "portrayal of a soul burdened with guilt,"[96] and this motif of being "breathlessly" clutched by "wild visions"[97] has been maintained throughout. The precise formulations vary, so that one writer states "that a cruel delight permits Dostoevski to torture his reader,"[98] another confesses "a very peculiar desire to creep on all fours" after reading Dostoevski,[99] still another experiences "genuine Gothic humility,"[100] and to a fourth it signifies that "the horrible possibility of the fall often lives in our dreams. This abyss is Dostoevski."[101] Through all these variations, however, one thing always remains true of Dostoevski and his success—the atmosphere "oppresses the heart and racks the brain."[102]

The picture of the cruel, torturing anatomist, with a predilection for the unclean and the forbidden, appeals to impulses which take pleasure in hurting and tormenting. It also reveals a peculiar contradiction in the reception. The mythical spell cast over the world, the emphasis upon its enigmatic character and upon the "irrationality of the human soul which no knowledge and no culture can set straight,"[103] cannot be reconciled with the picture of the anatomist who seeks clarity in the darkest corners. This contradiction symbolizes the contradictory social situation under discussion. The tendencies which transcend reality by making it the symbol of a higher meaning oppose the tendencies which create a sense of imagined power by permitting the experience of aggressions which have no real significance. This contradiction expresses the interrelation of the feelings of resignation and rage.

The social basis of the hymn of overflowing love and endless compassion in Dostoevski now becomes clear. These emotions are not associated with any desire to transform reality, but remain mere inner experiences. Men love or feel compassion, but no consequences are drawn. Such feelings neither remedy a deficiency, nor demand a remedy. Ideal nobility of the soul becomes the reflection of social impotence. It contributes to the satisfaction of the fancy of social groups who have been driven to the wall by reality. Love and compassion are mere social illusions in this context.

Our discussion of the mechanisms of psychological mediation is not complete. We have merely shown how certain impulses and needs are transformed and achieve satisfaction in fancy. These elements of the Dostoevski reception, however, and especially the combination of anatomist and painter of the impure meet with the restraints raised by the Freudian censor. Their nature is such that they are threatened with complete repression by the requirements of morality and conscience. In the make-up of the individual, prohibitions against the satisfaction of impulses may lead to neurosis. This neurosis can be quite typical for specific social strata, and to that extent, it is meaningless to speak of illness. A large section of the middle class has just such neuroses. But the art form of the novel, its social position, is, as it were, the reward for getting around the restraints of the censor. The formal elements in fiction corrupt the conscience, and, in the garb of fancy, permit the satisfaction of impulses which would be unthinkable outside the protective covering of aesthetic value.

Other psychological factors are also at work in the Dostoevski reception to permit the vicarious enjoyment of censored impulses.[104] Sadism acquires still greater luster if it is supposed to contribute to the fulfillment of worthwhile human impulses. If it is crime, prostitution, and the perversions associated with them that present an opportunity to practice love and compassion, then they have been legitimized. The difficulty still remains, however, that, despite all rationalization, novels afford a vicarious enjoyment of the unclean and the repugnant. The final justification for speaking of such things at all lies in the fact that the common, unclean, and loathsome are assigned to declassed outsiders. In this way, pleasure in degradation can be satisfied in the fancy, and this satisfaction and glorification appears in the sphere of politics today. In the political ideologies which are widely accepted by the lower-middle class, great emphasis is laid on dragging the dirty linen of one's opponent into the light so that its "stench" may no longer defile the air of a particular social circle. These opponents are characterized as unclean criminal elements, as riff-raff who shun the light of day.

UBIQUITOUS RECEPTION

Our discussion of the reception of Dostoevski into the ideology of the middle classes requires at least a reference to the reception by other groups. We shall illustrate the Dostoevski reception outside the middle classes by examining the attitudes of three critics of Dostoevski: (1) Rollard, contributor to a widely circulated middle-class family journal;[105] (2) the anonymous author of a postscript to the *Brothers Karamazov*,[106] employed by a rather progressive bourgeois publishing house; (3) Zabel,[107] contributor to one of the leading bourgeois political journals (which was working for a unification of all conservative and right-liberal forces),[108] a member of the upper bourgeoisie by his whole demeanor and social consciousness (in 1914 he still designated himself as National-Liberal).[109]

The culture represented by Rollard remains within the framework of simple family life when he restricts himself to the observation that Dostoevski "was the most faithful portrayer of his contemporaries and of the present conditions of his fatherland"; and that "a thorough study of Dostoevski might perhaps be more appropriate for shedding light on Russian conditions . . . which is in many respects quite unlike the conditions of the rest of Europe." Rollard speaks of Russia almost as if it were a wild tribe.

The anonymous author of the postscript to the *Brothers Karamazov* has a more enlightened and highly developed interest. He links the book to the pan-Slavic movement, and even adduces it for an understanding of the *Dreikaiserbund*. Though he regrets that Dostoevski left us in doubt "about the main lines which he had in view for the future organization of the nation," he believes that after the assassination of Alexander II "ideas made headway among the Slavophiles to which Dostoevski, the most illustrious of all the pan-Slavists and Slavophiles, gave living expression in his *Brothers Karamazov*." This political approach reflects a social conviction that learning can bring profit.

Zabel's approach to Dostoevski as a source of knowledge is still more ingenious and adequate. He ranks Dostoevski as "a highly significant phenomenon in modern literature and a completely indispensable tool for judging the Russian mind." The "recent terrorist movement has shown us how youth takes recourse to assassination." In *Crime and Punishment,* written in 1867, "Dostoevski introduces us to the beginnings of this movement," and provides "an important document for the history of our time" which "must arouse the interest of every cultured person." Here the attitude shows decided partisanship. A spokesman for the upper classes discovers a friend, so to speak, whose "life force and originality" can be praised, whose characters "are properly crammed full of real life." Even Zabel's stylistic tools (like this particular expression, "crammed full"), his emphasis upon the "living element," and his recognition of the "extraordinary force of his fancy and his power of description," of his grasp "of the complete life of man," of his "fully matured artistic nature," lead to a completely different social atmosphere. It is ruled by the possibility of great enjoyment, not limited by the need for regression into more primitive, purely illusory psychic pleasures, nor by weak and irresolute efforts to struggle upward, as expressed in the perpetual accumulation of knowledge. Zabel is the first German who gives the impression that he has read Dostoevski very carefully. And it is precisely this attentiveness, with its feeling for nuances, with its accurate understanding of what can be accepted and what must be rejected, in short, an attitude which, unlike the great mass of the reception, is without psychic inhibitions and which grasps and judges things as they are, that is characteristic of the social consciousness of the ruling strata. Zabel finds conditions in his own country entirely sound, and though he shares with the rest of the critics the stock phrases about Dostoevski's "endless sympathy for the oppressed and demonic hatred of the oppressors," the conditions which arouse these feelings in Dostoevski are for him historically and nationally determined. He refers to the "horrible cruelty of Russian justice," to the "pan-Slavis bias, the provoking insistence upon Russian manner and custom." It is noteworthy that not a single reference can be found in Zabel's essay to the whole sphere of mythical ideology.

This example of reception by the upper class finds its counterpart at the other extreme, in proletarian circles. At first, the literary spokesmen of the proletariat remained quite faithful to the conventional bourgeois picture. Rosus, for example, in his article in the *Neue Zeit* for 1884, has a purely didactic approach and uses the traditional literary categories. Apart from his remark that Dostoevski portrayed the Russian Socialists and Communists as mere "babblers and numbskulls," Rosus repeats the stock phrases, "cold-bloodedness of the anatomist," "case history of disease," "naked realism." The theoretical understanding of proletarian writers had to reach a higher level before they could formulate a clear and correct statement of the Dostoevski problem.

When we turn to Korn's essay in the *Neue Zeit* for 1908,[110] we find that all ideological character has vanished. From a proletarian position, Korn gives a better class analysis of Dostoevski than Zabel, with his upper bourgeois attitude. He calls *The Possessed* a "reactionary poisoner" (with all due recognition of "Dostoevski the novelist and *Weltanschauung*-visionary"). It is absurd to look to this work of Dostoevski for an understanding of the Russian Revolution of 1905, since there was no "revolutionary, i.e., class conscious proletariat" in the book (nor did such a proletariat exist in Russia at that time), but only "declassed nobility and petty bourgeoisie, a rabble between the classes." Korn perceives the deeper ideology-forming factors in this novel, and he notes "the paradox, bewildering at first sight, that an ideology, which in its original form may have been an accurate reflection of the economic and political situation of Russia in the '50s and '60s, is experiencing a rebirth in monopoly capitalist Germany of the twentieth century." He realizes how little Dostoevski's novel contributes to a real knowledge of historical and social relationships, how little the treatment reflects even the prerevolutionary social conditions, and how its atmosphere is "pure intellectual and ethical chaos." It is precisely those blurred tones in the development, motivation, and style of the book which give it its ideological value for the bourgeois German public: "What the literary spokesmen of our bourgeoisie have recently proclaimed as a discovery, namely, that it is not man's consciousness but his subconscious which is important, that everything worthwhile in the soul begins where the mind ends and the depths open up—that was, in fact, the programmatic psychology, the *Weltanschauung* of Dostoevski fifty years before." It must be remembered that Korn is not attacking the scientific activities of psychoanalysis, which was itself subject to the unanimous opposition of the official scientific world; he is attacking the anti-intellectual currents which appear in the myth of the demonism of the soul, in the enchantment of personalization of reality.

In the post–World War I reception of Dostoevski we find the same ideological factors as before the war, with even more abundant documentation. Immediately after the war, the myth of the inner life was predominant because of the general breakdown of social organization in Germany and, more specifically, because of the final dispossession of the middle class. More recently, however, the national myth has come to the fore as a model for the growing heroic-racial ideology. The radical tendencies of Dostoevski, though badly distorted in his writings, exercised a measure of influence upon the young German intellectuals immediately after the war, but this was an influence for socio-political radicalization only where other more powerful forces had already set in. The great mass of these intellectuals were confined to middle-class conceptions, and Dostoevski could perform a particular ideological service for them. Since he was labelled a product of the Russian nature and since the study of his works was supposed to give a clear insight into that nature, it followed that the key to the understanding of Bolshevism had also been found. Dostoevski can be put to extensive use in providing an imaginary solution whereby such middle-class groups can avoid a real analysis of the problem of transforming the social system, by satisfying anal-sadistic drives in the fancy and, at the same time, condemning them with the help of rationalizations buried in Dostoevski's writings.

The post–World War I phase of the reception points in two directions: (1) Dostoevski was placed in the intellectual context of Kierkegaard, Karl Barth, and the whole of dialectical theology. Indifference to earthly things, glorification of the individual, his inner world, and his relation to God, thus acquire extraordinary importance. This view is bound up with a social consciousness which hopes for nothing more from the present; it belongs to the circle of resigned strata. (2) The other tendency represents the politically dominant groups. It endorsed the national element in Dostoevski, but with limits imposed by the prevailing German ideology of Dostoevski's "racial" inadequacy.

NOTES

1. Comprehensive documentation is limited to the period ending 1918.
2. Good but incomplete bibliographical references are to be found in Theoderich Kampmann, *Dostojewski in Deutschland* (Münster: 1931, first published in 1930 as a dissertation).
3. Franz Sandvoss, "F. M. Dostojewski," *Preussische Jahrbuecher*, XCII (1899), pp. 330-41.
4. Hermann Conradi, "F. M. Dostojewski," *Die Gesellschaft*, V (1889), pp. 520-30.
5. See, for example, the chapter headings in R. Guardini, *Der Mensch und der Glaube; Versuche uber die religiöse Existenz in Dostojewskis grossen Romanen* (Leipzig: 1933): "The People and Its Way to Holiness," "Silence and the Great Acceptance," "Ecclesiastics," "The Cherub," "Revolt," "God-lessness," "A Symbol of Christ." Cf. titles like "Faith as the Will to Spirit," "The Experience of Real Being for Man: in His Relation to the Whole Egoless Thou: to God," in K. Nötzel, *Das Leben Dostojewskis* (Leipzig: 1925).
6. K. Weiss, review of several of Dostoevski's novels, *Hochland*, VI (1908), p. 364.
7. O. J. Bierbaum, "Dostojewski," *Die Zukunft*, XVIII (1909), p. 186.
8. O. Kaus, "Dostojewskis Briefe," *Die weissen Blätter*, I (1913/14), p. 1353.
9. L. Beer, "Quo vadis," *Die Nation*, XVIII (1900/01), p. 793; and K. H. Strobl, "Dostojewski, Russland und die Revolution," *Die Gegenwart*, XXXVI (1907), p. 87.
10. Georg Brandes, *Dostojewski, ein Essay* (Berlin: 1889), p. 3; cf. Strobl, op. cit. and Bierbaum, op. cit.
11. H. Coralnik, *Das Russenbuch* (Strassburg: 1914), p. 20.
12. W. Scholz, "Dostojewski," *Westermanns Monatshefte*, XXXIII (1888/89), p. 766.
13. Hermann Bahr in Bahr, D. Mereschkowski, and O. J. Bierbaum, *Dostojewski: 3 Essays* (München, 1914), p. 15.
14. Bierbaum, op. cit., p. 197.
15. Leo Berg, *Der Übermensch in der modernen Literatur* (Leipzig: 1898), p. 111.
16. Strobl, op. cit.
17. O. Stossl, "Die Briefe von Dostojewski," *Der neue Merkur*, I (1914), p. 499.
18. Adolf Stern, *Geschichte der neuen Literatur* (Leipzig: 1885), VII, p. 550.
19. Mereschkowski, *Tolstoi und Dostojewski als Mensch und als Künstler* (Leipzig: 1903), p. 39.
20. Frieda Freiin von Bülow, "Dostojewski in Deutschland," *Das Literarische Echo*, IX (1906), p. 204.
21. Bierbaum, op. cit.
22. Stefan Zweig, "Dostojewski, Die Tragödie seines Lebens," *Der Merker*, V (1914), p. 106.
23. Mereschkowski, op. cit., p. 222.
24. K. Nötzel, "Dostojewski," *März*, V (1911), p. 301.
25. Stern, *Geschichte der neuen Literatur*, VII, p. 550.
26. M. Necker, "Dostojewski," *Die Grenzboten*, XLIV (1885), p. 349.

27. Mereschkowski, *Tolstoi und Dostojewski*, p. 92.
28. Strobl, *Die Gegenwart*, XXXVI, p. 87.
29. R. Saitschik, *Die Weltanschauung Dostojewskis und Tolstois* (Halle: 1901), p. 9.
30. Ibid., p. 2.
31. Coralnik, *Das Russenbuch*, p. 20.
32. Brandes, *Dostojewski, ein Essay*, p. 3.
33. Kurt Eisner, "Raskolnikov," *Sozialistische Monatshefte*, V (1901), p. 52.
34. N. Hoffmann, *Dostojewski, eine biographische Studie* (Berlin: 1899), p. 2.
35. F. Servaes, "Dostojewski," *Die Zukunft*, XXXI (1900), p. 258.
36. Brandes, op. cit.
37. Strobl, op. cit.
38. Weiss, *Hochland*, VI, p. 364.
39. Bierbaum, *Die Zukunft*, XVIII, p. 196.
40. Bahr, *Dostojewski: 3 Essays*, p. 15.
41. Hoffmann, op. cit.
42. Strobl, *Die Gegenwart*, XXXVI, p. 87.
43. Joseph Müller, *Dostojewski—ein Charakterbild* (München, 1903), p. 183.
44. Heinrich Friedjung, *Das Zeitalter des Imperialismus* (Berlin: 1922), III, p. 142.
45. Joseph Melnik, introduction to A. S. Wolynski, *Buch vom grossen Zorn* (Frankfurt: 1905), p. v.
46. Theodor Heuss, "Dostojewskis Revolutionsroman," *Die Hilfe*, XII (1906), p. 9.
47. M. Schian, "Dostojewski," *Die christliche Welt*, XXVI (1912), p. 205.
48. Hoffmann, *Dostojewski*, p. 425.
49. Müller, op. cit.
50. Bülow, *Das Literarische Echo*, IX, p. 204.
51. Weiss, *Hochland*, VI, p. 364.
52. Bülow, op. cit.
53. Melnik, op. cit.
54. Moeller van den Bruck, introduction to Dostoevski, *The Possessed*, Piper-Verlag edition (München: 1906), reprinted in *Die Zukunft*, XIV (1906), p. 66; we shall cite the article in *Die Zukunft*.
55. Moeller van den Bruck, *Die Zukunft*, loc. cit.
56. Ibid.
57. Ibid., p. 68.
58. Ibid.
59. Thus Heuss, *Die Hilfe*, XII, p. 9, speaks of the "spiritual character" of Dostoevski's naturalism. Strobl, *Die Gegenwart*, XXXVI, p. 87, says that naturalism is transformed into mysticism in Dostoevski: "The naturalistic . . . becomes phantomlike as soon as we seek to focus our eyes upon it."
60. Moeller van den Bruck, op. cit.
61. A. von Reinholdt, *Geschichte der russischen Literatur* (Leipzig: 1886), p. 695.
62. L. Brehm, "Dostojewskis 'Dämonen,'" *Der Deutsche*, V (1906), p. 342.
63. Weiss, *Hochland*, VI, p. 364.
64. Müller, *Dostojewski*, p. 131.
65. Mereschkowski, *Dostojewski: 3 Essays*, p. 33.
66. Conradi, *Die Gesellschaft*, p. 528.

67. Brehm, op. cit., p. 346.

68. C. Busse, *Geschichte der Weltliteratur* (Bielfeld and Leipzig: 1913), II, p. 595.

69. Cf. Thomas Mann, *Betrachtungen eines Unpolitischen* (Berlin: 1920), pp. 532-44.

70. In the *Politische Schriften* (München: 1917), the word "just" occurs only once, if I am not mistaken—and then in a quotation from Tolstoi (cf. pp. 232 and 234). Belief in "the solidarity of men" also appears but once—and then it is a matter of establishing that "peace brutalizes much more than war" (pp. 415-16). A plea for "active love" is also made—but when it is put into concrete form, it never rises above the level of vague exhortations: "Be but straightforward and sincere" (p. 247).

71. E. Brausewetter, "Der Idiot," *Die Gegenwart,* XXXVI (1889), p. 73.

72. O. Hauser, *Der Roman des Auslands seit 1800* (Leipzig: 1913), p. 165.

73. Emil Lucka, "Das Problem Raskolnikows," *Das Literarische Echo,* XVI (1913/14), p. 1099.

74. Johann Schlaf, in *Buchbesprechungen des Piper-Verlags* (1914)—appendix to Bahr, Mereschkowski, and Bierbaum, *Dostojewski: 3 Essays.*

75. P. von Wiskowatow, *Geschichte der russischen Literatur* (Dorpat and Fellin: 1881), p. 44.

76. Stern, *Geschichte der neuen Literatur,* p. 550.

77. E. Hennequin, "Dostojewski," *Die Gesellschaft,* XVI (1900), p. 337.

78. W. Henckel, "Dostojewski," *Das Magazin für die Literatur,* LI (1882), p. 78.

79. G. Malkowski, "Der Hahnrei," *Die Gegenwart,* XXXIII (1888), p. 408.

80. J. Leipoldt, *Vom Jesusbild der Gegenwart* (Leipzig: 1913), p. 339.

81. F. Münzer, "Dostojewski als Psychopathologe," *Berliner Klinische Wochenschrift,* XXVII (1914), p. 1943.

82. Necker, *Die Grenzboten,* XLIV, p. 344.

83. W. von Tschish, "Die Verbrechertypen in Dostojewskis Schriften," *Die Umschau,* V (1901), p. 961. Cf. J. Stern, "Über den Wert der dichterischen Behandlung des Verbrechens für die Strafrechtswissenschaft," *Zeitschrift für die gesamte Strafrechtswissenschaft,* XXVI (1906), p. 163.

84. Rosus, "Ein russischer Roman," *Die neue Zeit,* II (1884), pp. 2-12.

85. Mereschkowski, *Tolstoi und Dostojewski,* p. 236.

86. Scholz, *Westermanns Monatshefte,* XXXIII, p. 766.

87. Saitschik, *Die Weltanschauung,* p. 9.

88. Bülow, *Das Literarische Echo,* IX, p. 204.

89. Münzer, *Berliner Klinische Wochenschrift,* XXVII, p. 1945.

90. For example, J. J. Honegger, *Russische Literatur und Kultur* (Leipzig: 1880), p. 146. Rosus, op. cit., p. 2.

91. *Magazin für die Literatur des Auslands,* XXXVI (1867), p. 317.

92. Brandes, *Dostojewski,* p. 7.

93. Brausewetter, *Die Gegenwart,* XXXVI, p. 73.

94. Reinholdt, *Geschichte der russischen Literatur,* p. 693.

95. R. M. Meyer, "Das russische Dreigestirn," *Oesterreichische Rundschau,* XVI (1908), p. 39.

96. Henckel, *Das Magazin,* LI, p. 73.

97. Brausewetter, op. cit., p. 72.

98. A. Garbell, "Ein Dostojewski-Gedenktag," *Das Magazin,* LXV (1898), p. 183.
99. Max Harden, *Literature and Theater* (Berlin: 1896), p. 80.
100. Nötzel, *März,* V, p. 309. Cf. Bierbaum, *Dostojewski: 3 Essays,* p. 192.
101. Strobl, *Die Gegenwart.*
102. G. Malkowsky, "Die Besessenen," *Die Gegenwart,* XXXIII (1888), p. 42.
103. Hoffmann, *Dostojewski,* p. 398.
104. See Freud, "Mourning and Melancholia," *Collected Papers,* trans. supervised by Joan Riviere (London: 1924-25), IV, pp. 152-70.
105. G. Rollard, "Dostojewskis Roman 'Raskolnikow,' "*Das Magazin für die Literatur,* LI (1882), pp. 291-92.
106. "Dostojewski," in *Brüder Karamazov* (Leipzig: Grunow-Verlag, 1884), IV, 328-31.
107. E. Zabel, "F. M. Dostojewski," *Die Gegenwart,* XXV (1884), p. 307 ff. reprinted, characteristically enough, in the extreme upper bourgeois *Deutsche Rundschau,* LIX (1889), pp. 361-91. For a discussion of the social role of the latter journal, see *Zeitschrift für Sozialforschung,* II (1933), pp. 59-62.
108. Cf. Erich Leupold, *Die Aussenpolitik in den bedeutendsten politischen Zeitschriften Deutschlands 1890-1909* (Leipzig: 1933), especially pp. 9-10.
109. *Wer ist's?* (Berlin: 1914), p. 1900; note the list of his extensive travels.
110. E. Korn, book review of *Die Dämonen,* in *Die neue Zeit,* XXVI, (1907/08), I, pp. 503-4.

Chapter 5
THE BIOGRAPHICAL FASHION

I

The biography (we are here excluding scholarly works of history), which in the period after World War I rapidly took its place alongside the traditional species of fiction as an article for literary mass consumption, reminds us of the interior in large department stores. There, in the rambling basements, heaps of merchandise have been gathered from all sections of the establishment. These goods have become outdated and now whether they were originally offered for sale on the overcrowded notion counters or in the lofty silence of the luxury-furniture halls, are being indiscriminately remaindered for relatively little money. In these basements we find everything; the only common principle is the necessity for fast sales. The biography is the bargain basement of all fashionable cultural goods; they are all a bit shop-worn, they no longer quite fulfill their original purpose, and it is no longer particularly important whether there is relatively much or little of one or the other item.

With almost statistical accuracy, the same material has been collected and displayed in about the same package. To be sure, from the outside it looks quite different. The biographies are presented as if in the intellectual realm they represent that which the exclusive and specialty stores represent in the realm of consumer goods. This comparison designates the social atmosphere in which the popular biography belongs: one of apparent wealth. It lays claim to the philosopher's stone, as it were, for all contingencies of history or life situations, but it turns out that the motley mixture of generalizations and recipes is actually an expression of utter bewilderment.

Since 1918, the political biography has become the classical literature of the German middle-brow. To be sure, it is not restricted to German language, nor did it make its first appearance after World War I—Nietzsche, years before, spoke of "our time so accustomed to the biographical contamination."[1] The best-selling German biographical writers were able to record great successes outside of the boundaries of their country and

189

language, and the French and English tongues made many contributions of their own during the twenties and thirties. But nowhere did the social role of this literature become so visible as in the German material.

An analysis of the popular biography is first of all an analysis of its reading public, and as such it comprises a critique of late European liberalism. Arbitrariness and contradiction have destroyed any claim to theory; ultimately this literature is a caricature of theory. During the ascendancy of the middle classes, when the educational novel characterizes narrative literature, the individual vacillated between his own potentials and the demands of his environment. The author drew material, which represented the substance of each individual destiny, from imagination; in only rare exceptions were data used for surface decoration and coloration. But, while imaginative, the educational novel was at the same time exact, because, as a product of poetic imagination, social and psychological reality were mirrored as they were observed within the social stratum of the author and his public. *Wilhelm Meister, Illusions Perdues, David Copperfield, Education Sentimentale, Der Gruene Heinrich, Anna Karenina*— these novels not only evoked the readers' experience of *déjà vu*, but confirmed the salvation of the individual by demonstrating the burdens and good fortunes of an invented individual existence in such a way as to permit the reader to experience them for himself. In these works of art, specific individuals, consistent within themselves and living within a concrete world, are represented as a complex of subjects closely connected with the fate of living and reading contemporaries. This is "reality" conceived as historians have conceived it since the Enlightenment, and in this sense there exists a direct relation between scientific and literary realism and the theory of society: one formulates the concern about the individual, the other tries to sketch the conditions for his happiness.

The biography is both a continuation and an inversion of the novel. Documentation in the middle-class novel had the function of background— raw material as it were. Quite otherwise in the popular biography: there documentation, the pompous display of fixed dates, events, names, letters, etc., serves in lieu of social conditions. The individual who is fettered by these paraphernalia is reduced to a typographical element which winds itself through the narrative as a convenient device for arranging material. Whatever the biographies proclaim about their heroes, they are heroes no longer. They have no fate, they are merely variables of the historic process.

II

History and time have become reified in biography—as in a kind of petrified anthropology.

Consider, e.g., "The stronger will of history is indifferent to the innermost will of individuals, often involving persons and powers, despite themselves, in her murderous game" (34/p. 117),[2] or else: "the sublime breaths of history sometimes determine the rhythm of a period at times even contrary to the will of the genius that animates it" (20/p. 424), or history, "the sterness of the goddesses, unmoved and with an incorruptible glance" looks over "the depths of the times and . . . with an iron hand, without a smile or compassion" brings "events into being" (29/p. 147), or history, "possibly the most terrible and most depriving sea journey, . . . the eternal chronicle of human sufferings" (33/p. 373), "almost always justifies the victor and not the vanquished" (33/p. 217), when she "in the ultimate sense is based on force"; or, history acts "neither morally nor immorally" (28/p. 270); "one comes to term with her," so decrees the biographer personifying world-reason which, however, does not deter him from occasionally calling history also "the supreme judge of human actions" (34/p. 476). At times history even permits herself to choose "from the million-masses of humanity a single person in order to demonstrate plastically with him a dispute of *Weltanschauungen*" (28/p. 134).

In statements of this kind history acquires the traits of an overpowering robot, who, however, hardly seems to be the result of human production, but with considerable stamping and with incomprehensible arbitrariness drives mankind before it.

To be sure, compared with the imagination of film producers and technocratic dreamers, this robot is rather paltry. The enumeration of its qualities is its appropriate interpretation: This is a cliché-robot—even with regard to concrete things.

For instance, concerning Erasmus, "Instinctively time chose correctly," in him: "time saw the symbol of calm but unceasingly operating reason" (37/p. 98); during his life: "the times forced him into the tumult to the right and to the left" (37/p. 20), and in the end: "but don't deceive yourself, old man, your true time is over . . ." (37/p. 165). Needless to say, the period-cliché and the century-cliché are used extensively. The Middle Ages, "a gloomier period" (34/p. 34), were "a cruel and violent age" (34/p. 510); when they are over, we have "a turn of the century which becomes a turn of the times" (37/p. 32). There is the "great and contradictory nineteenth century" (4/p. 10), with "the people of the nineteenth century" (4/p. 22), which "does not love its youth" (29/p. 25); and it is said of the seventeenth century: "the curious century, whose child she [Christine of Sweden] was in good and ill, died with her" (25/p. 410).

The serious European historians of ideas had neither place nor time for such pomp. These intellectuals wanted to be educators, to delve into the past to better understand the present, in which definite tasks had to be done—even if it was only the task of equipping new philologists or historians with sharper tools. True, historiography was exposed to the wrath of Nietzsche, who often tortured himself with the idea that mankind was actually doomed, that "one can recognize the basically evil nature of every human being in the fact that none of them can bear to be scrutinized carefully and closely."[3] An historical fatalism, which had taken hold of European middle classes long before the authoritarian state practiced it, led him to remark that none "who today consider themselves 'good,'" are able to tolerate "a biography."[4] He thus evaluated in advance present-day biographers who magically produce a historical sphere, about which they profess to know everything. They assure us that "history" or "the century" does this or that or has this or that quality, and the historical person appears as a mere product. With this device the popular biography—although in a distorted form—mirrors reality: the literati and the consumers of their products were becoming subjected to the "rigid rhythm of world history," the pitiless Zeitgeist, and the general expressed in these high-sounding phrases destroys the particular of individuality. In the biographies this is glossed over; although the mirror into which the reader looks hangs crookedly, he nevertheless finds reflected there something of his own historical substance. The qualities of "history" are here described somewhat in the way the person of the authoritarian "leader" and the co-ruling elite would have to be characterized: pitiless, indifferent, only intent on success; equipped with the will and the necessary apparatus to pronounce and execute decisions affecting the overwhelming majority. Such historical philosophy betrays a social attitude toward life—which at all times acknowledges its subjugation to the highest power in command. The rules of this power, so to say the drill book of history, are contained in innumerable generalizing assertions with which biographical literature abounds.

III

The biographer is the supplier of sociology for the mass consumption. What is happening here is a caricature of that inductive method which attempts to develop from empirical observations reliable rules of the game of human life across the ages. The political sociology of the biographers is the "sunken cultural heritage" of social research concerned with laws. A cue for this sociology is the little word "always," a favorite in Stefan Zweig's vocabulary, which bestows upon accidental data the dignity of the normative. Whatever was, was always that way, is that way, and so it will remain—this is the wisdom of all generalizing methods and of their popular offspring as well.

The favorite themes of popular biography are politics, power, and the leader. The new point from which the political power-apparatus and its mechanisms are discussed is that of the spectator who cannot do anything about them and who contents himself with observation. These biographers behave as if actually the whole matter was of no concern to them, as if in their wildest dreams it would not occur to them that they themselves had a stake in the matter.

In recompense they offer the general consolation: "one who has committed himself to politics is no longer a free agent and must obey other laws than the holy ones of his nature" (34/p. 42). A philistine impotence hides behind the at times grandiose, at times cynical, words, that politics ruin the character. Politics "has always been a science of contradiction. It is forever in conflict with simple, natural sensible solutions" (34/p. 28). It has been reified like the concept of history: "The individual man or woman simply does not exist for history; they amount to nothing when compared with tangible and practical values in the great game of world affairs" (34/p. 25). Whoever is in touch with politics, touches a dubious realm: "As always with politicians he made a compromise with God" (3/p. 253). From such types one cannot expect anything else but actions in accordance with not very lofty standards; we experience "The eternal and always recurrent spectacle . . . that politicians always become cowards as soon as they sense that the wind is turning" (35/p. 493). It is a pitiful trade: for instance, "the cleverest thing that a shrewd politician can do—he vanishes" (34/p. 146).

Behind the jaundiced view of politics hides the psychological corollary of infatuation with success, consciously decried: to study the politician requires a preoccupation with the phenomenology of power.

The reflection concerning the Russo-Napoleonic treaty is intelligible from the perspective of empathy with power: "It is plain that when two men are dividing the world between them, they will in the long run come to blows" (20/p. 271). "It is an eternal fate of mankind that its most memorable actions are almost always spattered with blood and that the greatest success comes to the toughest" (33/p. 318); but power is such a convincing phenomenon that it demands recognition.

The same social repression mechanism, which constructs reifications out of concepts such as history, time, and politics so that they are no longer recognizable as categories of social relationships, also affects the concept of power. Thus we read: "Power promises, even when it is silent and does not promise anything" (22/p. 23); ". . . a power can persevere, but not reveal" (3/p. 175).

The language is equally eloquent when it deals with the favorite topic of the individual in relation to society. For here is the opportunity to speak about the universal laws of the leader.

Impartiality is self-evident: "Mussolini is a man of the most refined politeness, like all genuine dictators" (19/p. 35). It is really not a simple business: "It is part of the tragedy of all despots that they fear the independent man even after they have rendered him politically powerless and speechless" (28/p. 273). This is particularly true of the revolutionary leaders, including religious fanatics: "This is one of the secrets of almost all revolutions and the tragic fate of their leaders: none of them likes blood, but they are nevertheless forced to spill it" (32/p. 61).

Regarding the relationship of society to a dictatorship, there are certain rules for the prehistory, for the beginning, for the climax, and for the decline.

Before: "Every world renewal, every complete recultivation first experiments with the moderate reformers instead of with the rabid revolutionaries" (37/p. 98 f.). A little later: "All dictatorships start with an idea" (28/p. 65). When it really arrives: "Always in the beginning of a dictatorship . . . the resistance has a certain impetus" (28/p. 49). Later on: "After the restless victory, dictators can always give humanity its due and more readily permit free speech after their power has been secured" (28/p. 239). But in the end: "Never can humanity or a part of it, a single group, tolerate the dictatorship of a single person for very long without hating him" (32/p. 96); "dictatorships represent in the over-all plan of humanity only corrections of short duration" (28/p. 327).

Here in this spiritual department store we find a Machiavellian sociology of politics and, in the next moment, a utopian conception of history. It is particularly characteristic for the social function of these biographers that they combine both of these concepts. From the sixteenth to the nineteenth century, materialistic or idealistic as well as optimistic or pessimistic interpretations of the course of history were clearly related to the goals of different social groups. But in the lukewarm and tired-out political and moral climate, in which the biographies thrive, everything goes: one puts up with the pessimistic perspective partly by exorcising it with magic and by categorizing it, as if the knowledge of its eternal recurrent formulas would make it harmless to the individual involved, or by playing the role of the cynical observer, who really is not affected. Optimism is created by the assurance that in the end the good will win. We encounter this pluralism of viewpoints time and again; it belongs to an attitude which takes nothing seriously, last of all the intellect. Its ultimate wisdom is relativism.

As far as we encounter the optimistic philosophy, it runs on many tracks. One of its versions is a "theory" of two different human types: the bad one, the politician—the good one, the moralist. "Regardless of what one calls the poles of this constant tension . . . their names express basically an ultimate innermost and personal decision, as to what is more appropriate for each individual—the human or the political, the Ethos or the Logos, the individuality or the collectivity. This inexorable demarcation between freedom and authority no people, no period, and no thinking man can escape" (28/p. 14). A sidetrack is created by the idea that perhaps after all there might be such a thing as a conciliation between the "political" and the "moral" attitude. Emil Ludwig, who specializes in Goethe-mottoes and in *realpolitisch* common sense, must be cited foremost in this connection. Here we read: "In the long run one can rule as little with the will for power without the idea of the times, as with the ideas without the will for power" (16/p. 335).

However, the overriding theme of the biographers' political sociology, when they speak about the social fate of morality, is that after all the good will always be victorious. This is recited in such a stereotype and pathetic manner that it is reminiscent of the moralizing consolation verses in certain popular tunes, namely, that it cannot go on much longer in this way and that eventually things will improve. In the light of what actually has happened it is brutally funny to be told by Ludwig that "one can read the logic in a destiny [we are dealing with Masaryk] whereby an honest man reaps what he sows" (15/p. 15). However, particularly Zweig has yet a richer list. As if it were a song entitled "Reason" we hear: "Sometimes when the others rage drunkenly, reason must be silent and lose her voice. But her time will come, it always returns" (37/p. 25). "All fanaticism directed against reason aims necessarily into the void" (27/p. 410).

Just as the moral philosophical systems, which can turn into a critical weapon against the existing, are characteristic for progressive tendencies of liberalistic thinking, so is the contention that truth and freedom always come out on top characteristic for the retreat from the sphere of action.

"Toscana defended the eternal feeling of freedom. This ideal of freedom survives the existence of all powers at large. One day of freedom topples pyramids of slavery, which seem to rise into the sky for all eternity. Freedom always returns, caresses humanity, shows it its dignity, God in her bosom, and tests the swords" (23/p. 341); or quite monumentally: "Truth always wins again. . . . Truth in the end always wins! Only those who know this are immune against the apparent eternally victorious infamy" (8/p. 326).

IV

Finally, the relationship between nature and history belongs in the general section of this pseudosystem of a social philosophy. It is treated in the spirit of a bad monism. It corresponds to the malaise, the ruin of initiative, which characterized the condition of the broadest strata of the middle class, particularly in Central Europe, during the period just before Fascism. The history of the middle classes started as the history of accelerated conquest of extra-human nature in the service of man, but mastery over nature became increasingly harnessed into the service of mastery over man, of his subjugation and destruction. I have pointed out elsewhere that important trends in literature around the turn of the century, particularly the concept of nature, reflected the resignation of the ruled confronted with a technical apparatus from which the population at large became increasingly alienated.[5] When biographical literature at times speaks of the alleged identity of natural and historical laws and at times uses natural phenomena for cliché-like comparisons with human life, it creates thereby an atmosphere of a tired-out pantheism.

This literature takes on almost mystical traits in which anything and everything merges into a great gray sameness. This is the mystique of relativism, which is shared by victims and masters alike.[6] To the latter it is the appropriate expression for the conservation of power at any price; the former confess almost masochistically how little they still value their own thoughts or the application of their minds to serious intentions. This is the place where the ideological origin of modern biography reveals itself. It hails from that *Lebensphilosophie* (philosophy of life) which, with its radical rejection of the severe rules of philosophical system, and its equally decisive opposition to any criticism of political economy, helped to prepare for the brutal vitalism of authoritarian practice in a typical manner. At times it hides behind assurances that what the biographers deal with are ultimates—a rhetoric of make-believe grandeur and magnanimity which in truth hides their own uncertainty. As in speaking about the everlasting stream of life, eternally in motion and yet always the same, one chatters about the original, the eternal, and the ultimate. We hear of "the eternal man" (30/p. 377), of "the eternal march of mankind toward the eternal goal" (6/p. 26), of "the arch-eternal man issued from the mortal body of cultural man" (31/p. 148), of freedom and justice, "the two archetypal forces" (36/p. 254), "the archetypal instincts of the human instinct world" (37/p. 18).

But there are also expressions which are taken yet directly from the relativistic thought-and-language-style of the *Lebensphilosophie*. "Man is a ceaseless wanderer" (6/p. 24); for man "in the last analysis the highest goal is limitless abundance of life" (29/p. 70). This irrationalism glorifies sentiment at the cost of thinking, and hence also at the cost of morality. It is downright senseless "to sit in moral judgment upon an individual [Mary Stuart] who happens to be a prey to an overwhelming passion" (34/p. 223). The stream of life at times is also called destiny: "But it is the tendency of destiny to mold the life particularly of the great into tragic forms. It tests its powers on the strongest, steeply it pitches the paradox of events against their strength, interweaves their lifespan with mysterious allegories, obstructs their paths, in order to confirm them in the right action. However, it plays with them an exalted game: because experience is always profit" (36/p. 11). The rhetoric about the game is revealing. It belongs to the relativistic aesthetization of history. It too is a disguise of impotence, of the enforced role of the spectator. Emil Ludwig revealed it most naively: "When the destinies of intrepid people begin to become confused the beauty of their aspect doubles" (10/p. 245).

The biographers ventured forth to conquer the kingdom of highest wisdom. They did not tarry for trifles—they aimed for the imperium of the intellect in which the riddles of history, time, nature, politics, morals, of life as such are solved. They returned with an herb and bottle collection. They feel as at home in the sphere of highest abstraction as the positivist in the realm of so-called facts. With them generalities supplant facts; they hurry from observation to observation, gathering the most divergent generalizing statements from the well-known pastures of philosophy and the social sciences. Out of these phony facts, which neither reflect empirical reality nor sketch its theoretical picture, a veil is woven which transforms history into a mythology of no significance. Quite the opposite is true of the school of Stefan George: in its esoteric cult of heroes and prophets there comes to the fore a moment of social rootedness: the dedication to an objective canon of aesthetic and moral taste. This school produced luxurious "culture" articles of such a kind that it was acceptable to an elite of social status or philosophical stature. It still fed on the great heritage of middle-class ideology and was directed to and fighting for stated goals, and could not be deterred from its original intent; it made its drive in the face of alternatives and knew when to open and when to close a door. On the other hand, modern biography is indiscriminate because it is perplexed. As numerous as are its myths of universality, as casual are its delvings into the reservoir of past human lives. As if anyone and everyone, generals, poets, chiefs of police, rulers, composers, inventors, and religious founders, were good enough to justify a consistency of the individual in which one no longer believes. History and its contents become the occasion for world historical chatter; its banner is a relativism which takes nothing seriously and which no longer is taken seriously.

V

Paradoxically, this relativistic mentality of the biographers is also present when they turn from perplexing generalities about the individual as merely a variable of the pace of "history" to his specificity and uniqueness. According to Hegel, the work of reason consisted in encasing the phenomena of nature and man in adequate concepts by searching for precise and "determined negation," i.e., the unequivocal designation of a phenomenon by excluding all the moments which are neither generically nor genuinely attached to it. The biographers, however, whose overt business is the exact portrayal of the essence and activity of a given human being, pervert Hegel's conceptual model into a muddy stew where nothing and nobody is conceived in terms of specific characteristics. True, at first sight the biographers seem to pay the greatest honor to their subjects, and, alongside the speculation about the general as the truly powerful, we find at the same time the praise of the individual. Alongside a conviction of the radical determinism by cosmic-hisorical laws and sociological rules, stands, in smooth and unobtrusive irrecon-cilability the hymn of individuality. But closer inspection reveals that the categories within which individual uniqueness is described are closely related to universal phrases which negate the autonomous nature of man. The hymn to the individual is a mere pretence, and reflects a convulsive attempt to conjure up a wish dream of the individual's autonomy and steadfastness. But this realm of freedom is deceptive, for the biographer handles the person in the same way that he handles events and objects, and under his fingers the individual is inflated into an artificial colossus. One browses through the index of a mail-order house which depends on a large turnover. Everything is the best and the most expensive, the opportunity of a lifetime. People are described as "unique" in terms of sameness, and everybody is marked by a pricetag and a sales plug making such outrageous claims that no single person in reality shows any specificity because the distinction of uniqueness is conferred on all.

The outstanding quality of the "personality" merchandise (which turns out to be a mass article) is plugged by an indiscriminate use of the superlative. Here are some examples:

Index of Superlatives

Barthou: "the most significant statesman of Europe" (5/p. 16).

Bismarck: "the two strongest German politicians of that epoch" (i.e., Bismarck and Lassalle) (9/p. 268).

Burckhardt: his "Greek cultural history, the most profound that we have on the Greeks" (12/p. 16 f.).

Calvin: "the darkest messenger of God in Europe" (4/p. 11).

Caesar: "the most sagacious Roman" (10/p. 49).

Cleopatra: "the shrewdest woman of her epoch" (10/p. 250).

Cosimo di Medici: "the mightiest man in civilian, nonmilitary dress; the world's wealthiest banker" (23/p. 7).

Francis Drake: "one of the most ingenious of Magellan's heirs and successors" (33/p. 217).

Elizabeth of England: "this most remarkable of all women" (34/p. 457).

Erasmus: "the first—and really the only—German reformer" (37/p. 20).

Fouché: "the intellectual kind of all of this most remarkable of political beings" (32/p. 332); "the most perfect Machiavellian of modern times" (32/p. 10); "psychologically the most interesting person of his century" (32/p. 10); "the most accomplished intriguer of the political stage" (32/p. 29); "most unreliable character and most reliable diplomat" (32/p. 254).

Lloyd George: "most cunning, agile, and marvelous of contemporary statesmen" (13/p. 180).

Hindenburg: "most celebrated German soldier of the last epoch" (16/p. 9).

John Knox: "perhaps the most accomplished example of the religious fanatics" (34/p. 83).

Lenin: "the most sincere, yet at the same time the coldest fanatic of our epoch" (14/p. 96).

Leonardo da Vinci: "in abundance of faces, Leonardo remains unique" (14/p. 596).

Leopold of Belgium: "the only personality of first rank among all the crowned heads of Europe" (2/p. 215).

Ludendorff: "during the war the most interesting figure and the most dangerous" (16/p. 196).

Luther: "of all ingenious men perhaps the most fanatical—the most indocile, unpliable, and discordant" (37/p. 190).

Magellan: "history's greatest seafarer" (33/p. 297); "the greatest deed of seafaring of all time" (33/p. 330).

Mary Stuart: her deed, "perhaps the most perfect example of the crime of passion" (34/p. 259); "perhaps no woman who would have been sketched in such an irregular form" (34/p. 7).

Marie Antoinette: "one of the most beautiful" tragedies "of this undesired heroism" (35/p. 9).

Masaryk: "the great European man" (15/p. 8).

Mussolini: "in conversation the most natural man in the world" (19/p. 37).

Napoleon: "this foremost field commander of his time" (20/p. 171); "concerned for the smallest matters, because he wants the great" (20/p. 48); "the burning European youth finds no greater model of warning than he, whom, of all western men, created and suffered the greatest shocks" (20/p. 676).

Nietzsche: "the brightest genius of the intellect" (29/p. 243).

Plutarch: "the most modern of all portrait painters" (14/p. 11).

Rathenau: "as a critic of the times, after Nietzsche almost without competition"; of "the noblest taste" (14/p. 140).

Romain Rolland: "he will always be tied by his relation to the most powerful" (36/p. 28).

Stanley: "the clearest, most sensible example of a hero" (2/p. 95); "he accomplished the boldest and most successful reporting" (2/p. 85).

Freiherr vom Stein: "a German, the best whom the nation has produced in its fall and deliverance" (20/p. 403).

Talleyrand: "perfection of this life as the greatest achievement possible to man" (3/p. 347).

Tolstoi: "the most powerful . . . the mightiest of the Russian land" (30/p. 232); "the most human of all men" (30/p. 234); "the nineteenth century knows no counterpart of similar primeval vitality" (30/p. 242).

The index of greatness is at the same time an index of monads. Alienation hides behind a specificity which is no longer to be surpassed. The reification of man has been broken down into a roster of qualities on which this commodity, man, is being measured, and each then represents a particular kind of merchandise. What one happens to have in stock is offered as the incomparable. It is a travesty of the development of mankind.

This whole realm of the superlative is a wish dream of the free economy. For each one it is important to reach the summit of the pyramid; only when all competitors have been removed from the field has the highest imaginable goal for an individual existence been reached. The individualism of the superlative conveys the true social meaning of this view: individualism rests on the exclusiveness of possession of a quality.

The myths of earlier humanity express the dichotomy of the natural and the historical; the cliché-like myths which the biographers report of their darlings make of each man his own myth.

Relativism is only seldom the manifest belief of this literature—but it is always present in a latent form. It is presented as an arbitrary interchange between the general and the individual, thus making clear the function of relativism in late European liberalism: a cloak for the helplessness of the vanquished on the eve of the age of the "Leaders." The pace of world history, as well as the mythical shading of oversized individuals, do not join into one theory of man and his destiny. This biographical jungle amounts to an ideology of weariness and weakness; it is an ideology of tired epigoni who lost their way.

BIBLIOGRAPHY

1. Heinrich Bauer. *Oliver Cromwell.* München/Berlin. 1937.
2. Ludwig Bauer. *Leopold der Ungeliebte.* Amsterdam. 1934.
3. Franz Blei. *Talleyrand.* Berlin. 1932.
4. Martin Gumpert. *Dunant.* New York/Toronto. 1938.
5. Wilhelm Herzog. *Barthou.* Zürich. 1938.
6. Hermann Kesser. *Beethoven der Europäer.* Zürich. 1937.
7. Hermann Kesten, *Ferdinand und Isabella.* Amsterdam. 1936.
8. Erich Kuttner. *Hans von Marées.* Zürich. 1937.
9. Emil Ludwig. *Bismarck.* Berlin. 1927.
10. _____ . *Cleopatra.* Amsterdam. 1935.
11. _____ . *Der Nil.* Amsterdam. 1935.
12. _____ . *Die Kunst der Biographie.* Paris. 1936.
13. _____ . *Führer Europas.* Amsterdam. 1935.
14. _____ . *Genie und Charakter.* Berlin. 1925.
15. _____ . *Gespräche mit Masaryk.* Amsterdam. 1935.
16. _____ . *Hindenburg.* Amsterdam. 1935.
17. _____ . *Kunst und Schicksal.* Berlin. 1927.
18. _____ . *Lincoln.* Berlin. 1930.
19. _____ . *Mussolinis Gespräche.* Berlin/Wien/Leipzig. 1932.
20. _____ . *Napoleon.* Berlin. 1926.
21. Klaus Mann. *Symphonie Pathétique.* Amsterdam. 1935.
22. Valeriu Marcu. *Das grosse Kommando Scharnhorsts.* Leipzig. 1928.
23. _____ . *Machiavelli.* Amsterdam. 1937.

24. Walter von Molo. *Eugenio von Savoy.* Berlin. 1936.
25. Alfred Neumann. *Königin Christine von Schweden.* Amsterdam. 1936.
26. Franz Werfel. *Verdi.* Berlin/Wein/Leipzig. 1924.
27. Stefan Zweig. *Begegnung mit Menschen, Büchern. Städten.* Wien/Leipzig/ Zürich. 1937.
28. _____. *Castello gegen Calvin.* Wien/Leipzig/Zürich. 1936.
29. _____. *Der Kampf mit dem Dämon.* Leipzig. 1925.
30. _____. *Drei Dichter ihres Lebens.* Leipzig. 1928.
31. _____. *Joseph Fouché.* Leipzig. 1929.
32. _____. *Drei Meister.* Leipzig. 1920.
33. _____. *Magellan.* Wien/Leipzig/Zürich. 1935.
34. _____. *Maria Stuart.* Wien/Leipzig/Zürich. 1935.
35. _____. *Marie Antoinette.* Leipzig. 1932.
36. _____. *Romain Rolland.* Frankfurt a. M. 1921.
37. _____. *Triumph und Tragik des Erasmus von Rotterdam.* Wien. 1935.

NOTES

1. Nietzsche, *Werke,* second section, vol. 10, *Die Philosophie im tragischen Zeitalter der Griechen* (Fragment, Spring, 1873; Stuttgart, 1922), p. 26.
2. The numbers in parentheses refer to the biographies quoted; they are listed at the end of this chapter.
3. Nietzsche, loc. cit., note 1.
4. Nietzsche, *The Genealogy of Morals,* Anchor Books, p. 275.
5. See Leo Lowenthal, "Knut Hamsun," in his: *Literature and the Image of Man* (Beacon, 1957), pp. 190 ff. To be included in Volume 2 of *Communication in Society* (Transaction, forthcoming).
6. See Max Horkheimer, "Der neueste Angriff an die Metaphysik," *Zeitschrift fuer Sozialforschung,* vol. VI (1937), p. 33.

Chapter 6
THE TRIUMPH OF MASS IDOLS

RISE OF BIOGRAPHY AS A POPULAR LITERARY TYPE

The following essay is concerned with the content analysis of biographies, a literary topic which has inundated the book market for the last three decades, and has for some time been a regular feature of popular magazines. Surprisingly enough, not very much attention has been paid to this phenomenon, none whatever to biographies appearing in magazines, and little to those published in book form.[1]

It started before the first World War, but the main onrush came shortly afterwards. The popular biography was one of the most conspicuous newcomers in the realm of print since the introduction of the short story. The circulation of books by Emil Ludwig,[2] André Maurois, Lytton Strachey, Stefan Zweig, etc., reached a figure in the millions, and with each new publication, the number of languages into which they were translated grew. Even if it were only a passing literary fad, one would still have to explain why this fashion has had such longevity and is more and more becoming a regular feature in the most diversified media of publications.

Who's Who, once known as a title of a specialized dictionary for editors and advertisers, has nowadays become the outspoken or implied question in innumerable popular contexts. The interest in individuals has become a kind of mass gossip. The majority of weeklies and monthlies, and many dailies too, publish at least one life story or a fragment of one in each issue; theater programs present abridged biographies of all the actors; the more sophisticated periodicals, such as *The New Republic* or *Harper's,* offer short accounts of the main intellectual achievements of their contributors; and a glance into the popular corners of the book trade, including drug store counters, will invariably fall on biographies. All this forces the conclusion that there must be a social need seeking gratification by this type of literature.

One way to find out would be to study the readers' reactions, to explore by means of various interviewing techniques what they are

TABLE 6.1

Distribution of Biographies According to Professions in *Saturday Evening Post* and *Collier's* for Selected Years between 1901 and 1941

	1901-14 (5 sample yrs.)		1922-30 (6 sample yrs.)		1930-34 (4 years)		1940-41 (1 year)	
	No.	%	No.	%	No.	%	No.	%
Political life	81	46	112	28	95	31	31	25
Business and professional	49	28	72	18	42	14	25	20
Entertainment	47	26	211	54	169	55	69	55
Total number	177	100	395	100	306	100	125	100
Yearly average of biographies	36		66		77		125	

looking for, what they think about the biographical jungle. But it seems to be rather premature to collect and to evaluate such solicited response until more is known about the content structure itself.

As an experiment in content analysis, a year's publication of *The Saturday Evening Post (SEP)* and of *Collier's* for the period from April 1940 to March 1941 was covered.[3] It is regrettable that a complete investigation could not be made for the most recent material, but samples taken at random from magazines under investigation showed that no basic change in the selection or content structure has occurred since this country's entry into the war.[4]

BIOGRAPHERS' IDOLS

Before entering into a discussion of our material we shall briefly look into the fate of the biographical feature during the past decades.

Production—Yesterday

Biographical sections have not always been a standing feature in these periodicals. If we turn back the pages we find distinct differences in the number of articles as well as in the selection of people treated.

Table 6.1 gives a survey of the professional distribution of "heroes" in biographies between 1901 and 1941.[5]

The table indicates clearly a tremendous increase in biographies as time goes on. The average figure of biographies in 1941 is almost four times as high as at the beginning of the century. The biography has nowadays become a regular weekly feature. Just to illustrate how relatively small the number of biographies was forty years ago: in fifty-two issues

TABLE 6.2
Proportion of Biographies of Entertainers from the Realm of Serious Arts[a] in
SEP and *Collier's* for Selected Years between 1901 and 1941
(In percent of total biographies of entertainers in each period)

Period	Proportion entertainers from serious arts	Total no. entertainers
1901-1914 (5 sample yrs.)	77	47
1922-1930 (6 sample yrs.)	38	211
1930-1934 (4 yrs.)	29	169
1940-1941 (1 yr.)	9	69

[a]This group includes literature, fine arts, music, dance, theater.

of the *SEP* of 1901-2 we find altogether twenty-one biographies as compared with not less than fifty-seven in 1940-41. The smallness of the earlier figure in comparison to the present day is emphasized by the fact that nonfictional contributions at that time far outnumbered the fictional material. A fair average of distribution in the past would be about three fictional and eight nonfictional contributions; today we never find more than twice as many nonfictional as fictional contributions and in the majority of cases even fewer.

We put the subjects of the biographies in three groups: the spheres of political life, of business and professions, and of entertainment (the latter in the broadest sense of the word). Looking at our table we find for the time before World War I very high interest in political figures and an almost equal distribution of business and professional men, on the one hand, and of entertainers on the other. This picture changes completely after the war. The figures from political life have been cut by 40 percent; the business and professional men have lost 30 percent of their personnel while the entertainers have gained 50 percent. This numerical relation seems to be rather constant from 1922 up to the present day. If we reformulate our professional distribution by leaving out the figures from political life we see even more clearly the considerable decrease of people from the serious and important professions and a corresponding increase in entertainers. The social impact of this change comes to the fore strikingly if we analyze the composition of the entertainers. This can be seen from Table 6.2.

While at the beginning of the century three quarters of the entertainers were serious artists and writers, we find that this class of people is reduced by half twenty years later and tends to disappear almost completely at present.

As an instance of the selection of biographies typical of the first decade of the century, it is notable that out of the twenty-one biographies of the *SEP* 1901-2, eleven came from the political sphere, seven from business and the professions, and three from entertainment and sport. The people in the political group are numerically prominent until before Election Day in the various years: candidates for high office, i.e., the president or senators; the secretary of the treasury; an eminent state governor. In the business world, we are introduced to J. P. Morgan, the banker; his partner, George W. Perkins; James J. Hill, the railroad president. In the professions, we find one of the pioneers in aviation; the inventor of the torpedo; a famous Black educator; an immigrant scientist. Among the entertainers there is an opera singer, Emma Calvé; a poet, Eugene Field; a popular fiction writer, F. Marion Crawford.

If we look at such a selection of people we find that it represents a fair cross-section of socially important occupations. Still, in 1922 the picture is more similar to the professional distribution quoted above than to the one which is characteristic of the present-day magazines. If we take, for example, *Collier's* of 1922 we find in a total of 20 biographies only two entertainers, but eight business and professional men and ten politicians. Leaving out the latter ones, we find among others: Clarence C. Little, the progressive president of the University of Maine; Leonard P. Ayres, the very outspoken vice-president of the Cleveland Trust Company; director-general of the United States Railroad Administration, James C. Davis; president of the New York Central Railroad, A. H. Smith; and the city planner, John Nolen. From the entertainment field, we have a short résumé of the stage comedian, Joe Cook (incidentally, by Franklin P. Adams), and an autobiographical sketch by Charlie Chaplin.

We might say that a large proportion of the heroes in both samples are idols of production, that they stem from the productive life, from industry, business, and natural sciences. There is not a single hero from the world of sports and the few artists and entertainers either do not belong to the sphere of cheap or mass entertainment or represent a serious attitude toward their art as in the case of Chaplin.[6] The first quarter of the century cherishes biography in terms of an open-minded liberal society which really wants to know something about its own leading figures on the decisive social, commercial, and cultural fronts. Even in the late twenties, when jazz composers and the sports people are admitted to the inner circle of biographical heroes, their biographies are written almost exclusively to supplement the reader's knowledge of the technical requirements and accomplishments of their respective fields.[7]

These people, then, are treated as an embellishment of the national scene, not yet as something that in itself represents a special phenomenon which demands almost undivided attention.

We should like to quote from two stories which seem to be characteristic of this past epoch. In a sketch of Theodore Roosevelt, the following comment is made in connection with the assassination of McKinley: "We, who give such chances of success to all that it is possible for a young man to go as a laborer into the steel business and before he has reached his mature prime become, through his own industry and talent, the president of a vast steel association—we, who make this possible as no country has ever made it possible, have been stabbed in the back by anarchy."[8]

This unbroken confidence in the opportunities open to every individual serves as the *leitmotiv* of the biographies. To a very great extent they are to be looked upon as examples of success which can be imitated. These life stories are really intended to be educational models. They are written—at least ideologically—for someone who the next day may try to emulate the man whom he has just envied.

A biography seems to be the means by which an average person is able to reconcile his interest in the important trends of history and in the personal lives of other people. In the past, and especially before World War I, the popular biography lived in an optimistic atmosphere where understanding of historical processes and interest in successful people seemed to integrate pleasantly into one harmonious endeavor: "We know now that the men of trade and commerce and finance are the real builders of freedom, science, and art—and we watch them and study them accordingly. . . . Of course, Mr. Perkins is a 'self-made man.' Who that has ever made a career was not?"[9] This may be taken as a classical formulation for a period of "rugged individualism" in which there is neither the time nor the desire to stimulate a closer interest in the organizers and organization of leisure time, but which is characterized by eagerness and confidence that the social ladder may be scaled on a mass basis.[10]

Consumption—Today

When we turn to our present day sample we face an assortment of people which is both qualitatively and quantitatively removed from the standards of the past.

Only two decades ago people from the realm of entertainment played a very negligible role in the biographical material. They form now, numerically, the first group. While we have not found a single figure from the world of sports in our earlier samples given above, we find them now close to the top of favorite selections. The proportion of people from political life and from business and professions, both representing the "serious side," has declined from 74 to 45 percent of the total.

Let us examine the group of people representing nonpolitical aspects of life: 69 are from the world of entertainment and sport; 25 from that which we called before the "serious side." Almost half of the 25 belong to some kind of communications professions: there are ten newspapermen and radio commentators. Of the remaining 15 business and professional people, there are a pair of munitions traders, Athanasiades (118)[11] and Juan March (134); Dr. Brinkley (3), a quack doctor; and Mr. Angas (20), judged by many as a dubious financial expert; Pittsburgh Phil (23), a horse race gambler in the "grand style"; Mrs. D'Arcy Grant (25), a woman sailor, and Jo Carstairs (54), the owner of an island resort; the Varian brothers (52), inventors of gadgets, and Mr. Taylor (167), an inventor of fool-proof sports devices; Howard Johnson (37), a roadside restaurant genius; Jinx Falkenburg (137), at that time a professional model; and finally, Dr. Peabody (29), a retired rector of a swanky society prep school.

The "serious" people are not so serious after all. In fact there are only nine who might be looked upon as rather important or characteristic figures of the industrial, commercial, or professional activities, and six of these are newspapermen or radio commentators.

We called the heroes of the past "idols of production": we feel entitled to call the present day magazine heroes "idols of consumption." Indeed, almost every one of them is directly, or indirectly, related to the sphere of leisure time: either he does not belong to vocations which serve society's basic needs (e.g., the heroes of the world of entertainment and sport), or he amounts, more or less, to a caricature of a socially productive agent. If we add to the group of the 69 people from the entertainment and sports world the ten newspaper and radio men, the professional model, the inventor of sports devices, the quack doctor, the horse race gambler, the inventors of gadgets, the owner of the island resort, and the restaurant chain owner, we see 87 to all 94 nonpolitical heroes directly active in the consumers' world.

Of the eight figures who cannot exactly be classified as connected with consumption, not more than three—namely, the automobile producer, Sloan; the engineer and industrialist, Stout; and the airline czar, Smith—are important or characteristic functionaries in the world of production. The two armament magnates, the female freight boat skipper, the prep school head, and the doubtful market prophet remind us of the standardized protagonists in mystery novels and related fictional merchandise: people with a more or less normal and typical personal and vocational

TABLE 6.3
The Heroes and Their Spheres

	Number of stories	Percent
Sphere of production	3	2
Sphere of consumption	91	73
Entertainers and sports figures	69	55
Newspaper and radio figures	10	8
Agents of consumers' goods	5	4
Topics of light fiction	7	6
Sphere of politics	31	25
Total	125	100

background who would bore us to death if we did not discover that behind the "average" front lurks a "human interest" situation.

By substituting such a classification according to spheres of activity for the cruder one according to professions, we are now prepared to present the vocational stratifications of our heroes in a new form. It is shown in Table 6.3 for the *SEP* and *Collier's* of 1940-1941.

If a student in some very distant future should use popular magazines of 1941 as a source of information as to what figures the American public looked to in the first stages of the greatest crisis since the birth of the Union, he would come to a grotesque result. While the industrial and professional endeavors are geared to a maximum of speed and efficiency, the idols of the masses are not, as they were in the past, the leading names in the battle of production, but the headliners of the movies, the ball parks, and the night clubs. While we found that around 1900 and even around 1920 the vocational distribution of magazine heroes was a rather accurate reflection of the nation's living trends, we observe that today the hero-selection corresponds to needs quite different from those of genuine information. They seem to lead to a dream world of the masses who no longer are capable or willing to conceive of biographies primarily as a means of orientation and education. They receive information not about the agents and methods of social production but about the agents and methods of social and individual consumption. During the leisure in which they read, they read almost exclusively about people who are directly, or indirectly, providing for the reader's leisure time. The vocational set-up of the dramatis personae is organized as if the social production process were either completely exterminated or tacitly understood, and needed no further interpretation. Instead, the leisure-time period seems to be the new social riddle on which extensive reading and studying has to be done.[12]

The human incorporation of all the social agencies taking care of society as a unity of consumers represents a literary type which is turned out as a standardized article, marketed by a tremendous business, and consumed by another mass institution, the nation's magazine-reading public. Thus biography lives as a mass element among the other elements of mass literature.

Our discovery of a common professional physiognomy in all of these portraits encouraged us to guess that what is true of the selection of people will also be true of the selection of what is said about these people. This hypothesis has been quite justified, as we propose to demonstrate in the following pages. Our content analysis not only revealed impressive regularities in the occurrence, omission, and treatment of certain topics, but also showed that these regularities may be interpreted in terms of the very same category of consumption which was the key to the selection of the biographical subjects. Consumption is a thread running through every aspect of these stories. The characteristics which we have observed in the literary style of the author, in his presentation of personal relations, of professions and personalities, can all be integrated around the concept of the consumer.

For classification of the stories' contents, we decided on a four-fold scheme. First there are what one might call the sociological aspects of the man: his relations to other people, the pattern of his daily life, his relation to the world in which he lives. Second, his psychology: what the nature of his development has been and the structure of his personality. Third, his history: what his encounter with the world has been like— the object world which he has mastered or failed to master. Fourth, the evaluation of these data which the author more or less consciously conveys by his choice of language. Granted that this scheme is somewhat arbitrary, we think that our division of subject matter has resulted in a fairly efficient worksheet, especially when we consider the backward state of content analysis of this type.

As we studied our stories,[13] we looked almost in vain for such vital subjects as the man's relations to politics or to social problems in general. Our category of sociology reduces itself to the *private lives* of the heroes. Similarly, our category of psychology was found to contain mainly a static image of a human being to whom a number of things happen, culminating in a success which seems to be none of his doing. This whole section becomes merged with our category of history which is primarily concerned with success data, too, and then takes on the character of a catalogue of "just facts." When we survey the material on how authors evaluate their subjects, what stands out most clearly is the biographers' preoccupation with justifying their hero by means of un-discriminating *superlatives* while still interpreting him in terms which bring him as close as possible to the level of the average man.

PRIVATE LIVES

The reader may have noticed in public conveyances a poster called "Private Lives" depicting the peculiarities of more or less famous people in the world of science, sports, business, and politics. The title of this feature is a fitting symbol for all our biographies. It would be an over-statement, but not too far from the truth, to say that these stories are exclusively reports on the heroes' private lives. While it once was rather contemptible to give much room to the private affairs and habits of public figures this topic is now the focus of interest. The reason for viewing this as an overstatement is in a way surprising: we learn something, although not very much, about the man's professional career and its requirements, but we are kept very uninformed about important segments of his private life.

Inheritance and Parents—Friends and Teachers

The personal relations of our heroes, on which we are enlightened, are, as a whole, limited to two groups, the parents and the friends. Both groups are taken in a specific sense: the parents comprising other older relations or forebears of former generations, the friends being more or less limited to people who were valuable in the hero's career. In more than half of the stories the father or the mother or the general family background is at least mentioned. Clark Gable's "stubborn determination" seems derived from his "Pennsylvania Dutch ancestors" (6); the very efficient State Department official, Mrs. Shipley, is the "daughter of a Methodist minister" (8); Senator Taft is a "middle-of-the-roader like his father" besides being "an aristocrat by birth and training" (101). We are let in a little bit on the family situation of Brenda Joyce because "somewhere there was a break-up between mamma and papa" (110). The general pattern of the parental home, however, is more on the Joan Carroll side, where we find the "young, quietly dignified mother . . . the successful engineer father . . . a star scout brother six years her senior" (143); we hear in a very sympathetic way about the old Fadimans, "the father a struggling Russian immigrant and pharamacist, the mother a nurse" (47); we learn a good deal about ancestors as in the case of Clark Gable cited above. Of the Secretary of Labor, Frances Perkins, we are told that her "forebears had settled all over New England between 1630-

1680" (22); the female freighter skipper, D'Arcy Grant, has "an ancestral mixture of strong-headed swashbuckling Irish and pioneer Americans" (25); Raymond Gram Swing is the "heir of a severe New England tradition" (42); the Varian brothers have "Celtic blood" (52); in the woman matador, Conchita Cintron, we find "Spanish, Connecticut Irish, and Chilean elements" (116).

The curious fact here is not that the authors mention parentage, but that they have so much to say about it and so little to say about other human relations. It is a good deal as if the author wants to impress on the reader that his hero, to a very considerable extent, must be understood in terms of his biological and regional inheritance. It is a kind of primitive Darwinian concept of social facts: the tendency to place the burden of explanation and of responsibility on the shoulders of the past generations. The individual himself appears as a mere product of his past.

The element of passivity is also found in the second most frequently mentioned group of personal relationships: friends and teachers. Let us look again into some of the material. We hear that the woman diplomat, Mrs. Harriman, was made "Minister to Norway because of her many powerful and loyal friends" (14); of the friendship between the hard-hit restaurateur, Johnson, and his wealthy doctor-friend (37); the movie actress, Brenda Marshall, was somehow saved in her career "by the friendship of a script girl" (161); Senator Byrnes got a good start because "a disillusioned old Charlestonian . . . showed him the ropes" (18); while Miss Perkins is "'protected' by her personal secretary . . . [who] worships her" (22).

There is very rarely an episode which shows our heroes as active partners of friendship. In most cases their friends are their helpers. Very often they are teachers who later on become friends. Perhaps it is stretching a point to say that a vulgarian Darwinism is supplemented at this point by a vulgarian distortion of the "milieu" theory: the hero is a product of ancestry and friendship. But even if this may be somewhat exaggerated, it nevertheless helps to clarify the point, namely, that the hero appears in his human relationships as the one who takes, not as the one who gives.

We can supplement this statement by going back to our remark that decisive human relationships, and even those which are decisive for private lives, are missing. The whole sphere of the relations with the opposite sex is almost entirely missing. This is indeed a very strange phenomenon. We should assume that the predilection for such people as actors and actresses from stage and screen, night club entertainers, etc., would be tied up with a special curiosity in such people's love affairs, but this is not the case at all. The realm of love, passion, even marriage, seem worth mentioning only in terms of vital statistics. It is quite a lot to be informed that Dorothy Thompson "got tangled up in love"; very soon Lewis "asked point blank whether she would marry him" (9); Senator Byrnes "married the charming wife who still watches over him" (18); the industrial tycoon, Sloan, remarks, "Mrs. Sloan and I were married that summer . . . she was of Roxbury, Mass." (24); Mrs. Peabody married the Rector "at the close of the school's first year" (29). We are told about Raymond Gram Swing only that he was married twice (42); as far as Lyons', the baseball player's bachelor, situation goes we hear that he "almost married his campus sweetheart" (53); while his colleague, Rizzuto, is "not even going steady" (57). In the high life of politics we are glad to know that Ambassador Lothian "gets on well with women" (115); and that Thomas Dewey is "a man's man, but women go for him" (117); we are briefly informed that Chris Martin "married, raised a family" (121); and that "one girl was sufficiently impressed to marry" Michael Todd, a producer, at the tender age of 17 (131).

These statements of fact, in a matter of fact way, as, for instance, the mention of a marriage or a divorce, are all that we hear of that side of human relations which we were used to look upon as the most important ones. If we again imagine that these popular biographies should at a very distant historical moment serve as the sole source of information, the historian of the future would almost be forced to the conclusion that in our times the institution of marriage, and most certainly the phenomena of sexual passions, had become a very negligible factor. It seems that the fifth-rate role to which these phenomena are relegated fits very well with the emphasis on parentage and friendship. Love and passion require generosity, a display of productive mental and emotional forces which are neither primarily explained nor restrained by inheritance and advice.

A rather amusing observation: we found that the eyes of the hero were mentioned in almost one-third of the stories. It is quite surprising that of all possible physiognomic and bodily features just this one should be so very popular. We take delight in the baseball umpire Bill Klem's "bright blue eyes," in his "even supernaturally good eyes" (104); or in the "modest brown eyes" of General Weygand (107). Miss Cintron, the matador, is "blue-eyed" (116); the night club singer, Moffett, has "very bright blue eyes" (119).

We are not quite certain how to explain our biographers' bodily preferences. The eyes are commonly spoken of as "the windows of the soul." Perhaps it gratifies the more inarticulate reader if the authors let him try to understand the heroes in the same language in which he believes he understands his neighbor's soul. It is just another example of a cliché served up in lieu of a genuine attempt at psychological insight.

Home and Social Life: Hobbies and Food Preferences

The heroes, as we have seen, stem predominantly from the sphere of consumption and organized leisure time. It is fascinating to see how in the course of the presentation the producers and agents of consumer goods change into their own customers. Personal habits, from smoking to poker playing, from stamp collecting to cocktail parties, are faithfully noted in between 30 and 40 percent of all stories under investigation. In fact, as soon as it comes to habits, pleasures and distractions after and outside of working hours, the magazine biographer turns out to be just a snoopy reporter.

The politicians seem to be an especially ascetic lot—Taft "doesn't smoke" (101); neither does General Weygand (107); the former British ambassador, Lothian, "hasn't taken a drink in 25 years" (115). There is also the movie actor, Chris Martin, who "doesn't smoke cigars or cigarettes" (121); the German Field Marshal Milch whose "big black Brazilian cigars are his favored addiction" (146). To quote some of the favorite habits or dishes of the crowd: Dorothy Thompson is all out for "making Viennese dishes" while her "pet hates . . . are bungled broth and clumsily buttered tea bread" (9). We are invited to rejoice in Art Fletcher's "excellent digestion" (7). We hope that Major Angas is equally fortunate, for: "Eating well is his secondary career"; he is "perpetually hungry" (20). The circus magnate, North, also seems to have a highly developed sense for food and what goes with it: "His cud-cutters for a three-pound steak are a Martini, a Manhattan, and a beer, in that invariable order, tamped down with a hatful of radishes" (26).

As for the innocent hobbies of our heroes: Art Fletcher likes "the early evening movies" and also "to drive about the country" (7); Senator Byrnes finds recreation in "telling of the long saltily humorous anecdotes which all Southerners love" (18). The pitcher, Paige, is "an expert dancer and singer" (19); Westbrook Pegler "plays poker" (28); and his special pet foe, Mayor Hague, also "likes gambling" (36); his colleague, the London *Times* correspondent, Sir Willmott Lewis, also "plays poker" (49), while Swing takes to badminton (42). More on the serious side is Greer Garson who "reads a great deal and studies the theater every minute she is free" (113). The hobby of golf unites Senator Taft (101), the Fascist Muti (114), the "Blondie" cartoonist Chic Young (165), the baseball player Lyons (53), and Ambassador Lothian (115).

We are furthermore told who likes to be "the life of the party," and who does not; and also how the daily routine in the apartment or private house is fixed. The Fletchers, for instance, "retire early and rise early" (7); while Hank Greenberg "lives modestly with his parents" but also "likes night clubs, bright lights, and pretty girls" (56). We hear of the actress Stickney's charming "town house" (145), of the "fifteen rooms and five baths and the private elevator to the street" of political Boss Flynn (138); of the way in which the Ballet Director Balanchine is "snugly installed in an elaborate Long Island home, and a sleek New York apartment" (152).

As to social gatherings: Nancy Hamilton's parties "aren't glittering at all, but they are fun" (103). The newspaperman, Silliman Evans, "has introduced the Texas-size of large scale outdoor entertainment" (39); while his colleague, Clifton Fadiman, has "very little social life, seldom goes to dinner parties" (47). His habits seem related to those of the private island queen, Jo Carstairs: ". . . A few friends of long standing make up one of the world's shortest guest lists" (54).

And so it goes, through over 200 quotations, changing a study in social relations into consumers' research. It is neither a world of "doers" nor a world of "doing" for which the biographical curiosity of a mass public is evoked. The whole trend goes toward acceptance: the biological and educational heritage; the helpful friends and teachers, the physical protection of the house, and the physiological one of eating and drinking; the security of social standing and prestige, through social entertaining; the complete resting of mind and work-wise energy through the gamut of hobbies. Here we come very close to decisive trends to which the modern individual seems subjected. He appears no longer as a center of outwardly bound energies and actions; as an inexhaustible reservoir of initiative and enterprise; no longer as an integral unity on whose work and efficiency might depend not only his kin's future and happiness, but at the same time, mankind's progress in general. Instead of the "givers" we are faced with the "takers." These new heroes represent a craving for having and taking things for granted. They seem to stand for a phantasmagoria of worldwide social security; for an attitude which asks for no more than to be served with the things needed for reproduction and recreation; for an attitude which has lost any primary interest in how to invent, shape or apply the tools leading to such purposes of mass satisfaction.

We cannot avoid getting something of a distorted picture of society if we look at it exclusively through the personal lives of a few individuals. But in the past an effort was made to show the link between the hero and the nation's recent history. As one of those earlier biographers put it: "Each era, conscious of the mighty works that could be wrought, conscious that we are all under sentence of speedy death, eagerly seeks out the younger man, the obscure man. It has need of all powers and all talents. Especially of the talents for creating, organizing, and directing."[14]

Today the emphasis is on the routine functions of nourishment and leisure time and not on "the talents for creating, organizing, and directing." The real battlefield of history recedes from view or becomes a stock backdrop while society disintegrates into an amorphous crowd of consumers. Greer Garson and Mahatma Gandhi meet on common ground: the one "likes potatoes and stew and never tires of a breakfast of porridge and haddock" (113); the other's "evening meal is simple—a few dates, a little rice, goat's milk" (124); Hitler and Chris Martin "don't smoke" (121).

JUST FACTS

Phillips's comments quoted above may serve as a transition from the sociology of our heroes to their psychology. With its emphasis on the independence and leadership awaiting the exercise of personal initiative, it expresses the ideal character type of private capitalism.

There are at least two elements in this quotation, the presence of which characterizes the psychological concept of former biographies, and the absence of which is very meaningful for the present situation: development and solitude.

"The young, obscure man" has something of the heritage, however trivial in this case, of the personality as it was conceived during the rise of the middle class culture: the individual as a totality of potentialities, mental, moral, and emotional, which have to be developed in a given social framework. Development, as the essence of human life, was connected with the idea that the individual has to find himself in the soliloquy of the mind. Human existence seemed to be made up of the loneliness of the creature and of his emergence into the outer world by displaying his own gifts. Our quotation is one of the late forms of this concept: the self-developing and fighting individual with all the chances in the world for creation and conquest.

Souls without History

In an essay on present-day man, Max Horkheimer states: "Development has ceased to exist."[15] His remarks on the immediate transition from childhood to adult life, his observation that "the child is grown up as soon as he can walk, and the grown-up in principle always remains the same,"[16] sound as if they were a comment on our biographical heroes. Among our quotations we have a collection of passages which try to tie up the childhood of the hero with his later life. Almost every second story brings some report on the road from childhood to maturity. Does this not seem to contradict our general remark, is this not a variation of the classical concept of the emerging personality? Before answering, let us examine a few representative passages: At the age of twelve "wrestling . . . was the answer to my problem," says the wrestler Allman (13). The king of horse race betting, Pittsburgh Phil, "began betting when he was fourteen—on his own game chickens" (23). Of the inventor Stout, it is remarked: "Wherever his family lived, he would rig up a crude shop and try to make things" (41). At twelve, the future actor Ezra Stone, ran a kid's radio program "directing the actors and paying them off at the end of the week" (108). For the Ringling-Barnum head J. R. North: "a real circus was his toy" (26). The future film star Greer Garson, "wanted to be an actress from the time she could walk" (113). The night club singer Hildegarde's parents "weren't surprised when Hildegarde . .

aged eighteen months, hummed a whole aria of an opera they had carried her to" (135).

Childhood appears neither as prehistory and key to the character of an individual nor as a stage of transition to the growth and formation of the abundant diversity of an adult. Childhood is nothing but a midget edition, a predated publication of a man's profession and career. A man is an actor, a doctor, a dancer, an entrepreneur, and he always was. He was not born the tender and unknown potentiality of a human life, of an intellectual, mental, emotional creativeness, effective for himself and for society, rather he came into the world and stayed in it, rubber stamped with and for a certain function. The individual has become a trademark.

In more than a third of the stories an attempt at a "theory of success" seems to be made but no magic formula is offered which an average individual might follow for his own good. The bulk of the answers consists of more or less trivial suggestions that the key may be found in "instinct" or other vague qualities. The golf player Bobby Jones "must have been born with the deep love for the game" (11). As to the Senator: "Leadership is Byrnes' real genius" (18). Pittsburgh Phil was "a good horse player by instinct" (23). The businessman Durand N. Briscoe "seemed to have an instinct for promotion and speculation" (24). The achievements of the football coach Kendrigan are a mystery even to him: "How he did it he never figured" (50). The airline tycoon Cyrus R. Smith may count on "an unerring gambler's instinct" (51). This key formula of instinct is supplemented by a collection of almost tautological truisms: The Fascist Muti "loves his danger highly spiced" (114). The sociable ambassador Lothian "likes newspapermen" (115). Howard Johnson knows what makes a restaurant successful: "A man that is properly supervised never goes haywire" (37). And as far as Clark Gable's success is concerned (and this could be applied to all the 125) "The answer . . . is personality" (6).

We venture to interpret this pseudopsychology of success as another aspect of the timeless and passive image of modern man. Just as childhood is an abbreviation of the adult's professional career, so is the explanation of this career nothing but an abstract, rather inarticulate, reiteration that a career is a career and a success is a success.

The psychological atmosphere breathes behaviorism on a very primitive level. Childhood as well as that vague realm of instincts represent, so to speak, the biological background from which a variety of human qualities emerge. It is a psychology which shows no need of asking why and, precisely in the same sense in which we tried to show it for sociology, testifies to the transformation from the worship of a spontaneous personality to the adoration of an existence shaped and molded by outside forces. These people live in a limbo of children and victims. The way leads to what we are inclined to call "a command psychology" because people are not concieved as the responsible agents of their fate in all phases of their lives, but as the bearers of certain useful or not so useful character traits which are pasted on them like decorations or stigmas of shame.

There are a few traits which seem to have some bearing on a man's ability to manipulate his environment. We mean the columnist who is a "spotlight stealer" (9); the playwright and actress who never overlooks "good spots for herself" (103); the producer who is "his own ballyhoo artist" (131). We mean the baseball manager who is "chemically opposed to being on the sucker end of a ball game" (2); the smart night club star who sees "no point in disclosing that King Gustav's favorite singer had been born over her father's delicatessen store" (135); the actress who has real "talent for meeting people" (103); the person who shows up "at the right place at the right time" (109); who is a "great man in flying, handshaking and backslapping trips" (21).

The majority of such attitudes are likely to evoke a slyly understanding smile on the part of the observer and reader. These are the "sure-fire" tricks on the road to success, a little doubtful, but not too bad; these are the equipment of the shrewd man and the smart woman. But these psychological gadgets exhaust the list of qualities pertaining to creative and productive abilities. They generate an atmosphere of pseudocreativeness in an attempt to convince us that a man has contributed his personal, individual share to the general cause of progress. "Something new has been added," insists the advertisement, but beware of inquiring too closely into the nature of the novelty. Thus, the good-natured statements of a certain lack of meticulous innocence on the road to success become for the sociological interpreter a sad revelation of a lack of originality in productive strength.

This is brought out even more clearly when we turn to the presentation of the actual history of success. Here success is not even attributed to some happy instinct—it merely happens. Success has lost the seductive charm which once seemed to be a promise and a prize for everybody who was strong, clever, flexible, sober enough to try. It has become a rigid matter on which we look with awe or envy as we look at the priceless pictures in our galleries or the fabulous palaces of the rich. The success of our heroes of consumption is in itself goods of consumption. It does not serve as an instigator for more activity, it is introduced as something we have to accept just like the food and drink and the parties; it is nourishment for curiosity and entertainment.

The mythology of success in the biographies consists of two elements, hardship and breaks. The troubles and difficulties with which the road to success is paved are discussed in the form of stereotypes. Over and over again we hear that the going is rough and hard. The baseball umpire goes "the long, rough road up to that night of triumph" (104); the lightweight champion "came up the hard way" (123); a senator knew in his youth the "long hours of hard work" (149); and the ballet director "worked hard" (152). In identical words we hear that the baseball manager (2) and the great film star (6) "came up the hard way." The "hard way" it was for Dorothy Thompson (9) and for Billy Rose (43). We are reminded of official military communiqués, reporting a defeat or stalemate in a matter-of-fact tone, rather than descriptions of life processes.

The same applies to the reverse side of hardship: to the so-called breaks. All our stories refer to successes and it is fair enough that somehow we must be informed when and how the failures stopped. Here the tendency to commute life data into facts to be accepted rather than understood becomes intensified. Usually, the beginning of the peak is merely stated as an event: A high civil servant was "fortunate in her first assignment" (8); a cartoonist merely gets a "telegram offering him a job on the paper" which later leads to his fame (34); a columnist "bursts into certain popularity" (42); an actor "got a break" (112); another "got the job and it turned out well" (121); for a middleweight champion "the turning point of his career had arrived" (142). If any explanation is offered at all, we are told that the turn occurred in some freakish way: the night club singer gets started by "a king's whim" (135); Clark Gable's appointment as a timekeeper with a telephone company appears as the turning point in his career (6); a baseball player goes on a fishing trip, loses his old job and thereby gets another one which leads to his success (133a).

These episodes of repetition and freakishness seem to demonstrate that there is no longer a social pattern for the way up. Success has become an accidental and irrational event. The dangers of competition were tied up with the idea of definite chances and there was a sound balance between ambition and possibilities. Appropriately enough, our heroes are almost without ambition, a tacit admission that those dangers of the past have been replaced by the cruelties of the present. It is cruel, indeed, that the ridiculous game of chance should open the doors to success for a handful, while all the others who were not present when it happened are failures. The "facts" of a career are a reflection of the lack of spontaneity. Behind the amusing, fortuitous episode lurks a terrible truth.[17] Hardships and breaks are standard articles for the reader. They are just a better brand of what everyone uses. The outstanding has become the proved specimen of the average. By impressing on the reading masses the idols of our civilization, any criticism or even reasoning about the validity of such standards is suppressed. As a social scientist the biographer represents a pitiless, almost sadistic trend in science, for he demonstrates the recurring nature of such phenomena as hardships and breaks, but he does not attempt to reveal the laws of such recurrence. For him knowledge is not the source of power but merely the key to adjustment.

Catalogue of Adjustment

When we turn to a study of the approval and disapproval which our authors attach to the various character traits they describe, we find a striking and simple pattern.

In tone the catalogue of these traits, like the mythology of success, resembles a digest of military orders of the day: brusque laudations and reprimands. There is no room for nuances or ambiguity. In content it is on a very simple level and the criterion of approval or disapproval is also very simple. The yardstick is social adjustment. Once we realize the subconscious and conscious opinions of present-day society on what an adjusted person should and should not be, we are thoroughly familiar with the evaluation of character traits and their owners. The yardstick has three scales: behavior toward material tasks; behavior toward fellow men; and behavior in relation to one's own emotions. The one who is efficient scores in the first sphere; the one who is sociable, in the second; the one who is always restrained, in the third.

In a separate study of all passages mentioning character traits, we found that of a total of 76 quotations referring to a hero's commendable behavior toward "things to be done," not fewer than 70, or over 90 percent, mentioned competence, efficiency, and energy; the remaining six referred to ambition. The majority read: "very capable" (154); "no sacrifice of time, effort, or my own convenience was too great" (24); "an inordinately hard worker" (48); "was never fired for inefficiency" (167); "thorough and accurate" (16); "being idle is her idea of complete torture" (140).

Out of a total of 48 quotations mentioning commendable behavior in relation to people, all 48 quote "cooperation," "sociability," and "good sportsmanship." There is a constant repetition of such adjectives as "cooperative," "generous," and "sociable." A baseball manager is "easy to meet, sociable, unsparing in his time with interviewers" (27). The "sociable" Chief of the Passport Division (8); the Secretary of Labor, "a delightful hostess" (22); the Republican candidate for the presidency with his "liking for and interest in people" (133); the matador, "genial, friendly, hospitable" (116); a smart actress, "amiable and friendly" (140)— they all belong to one big happy family which knows no limits in being pleasant and agreeable to each other. Like Don James, the barker for sideshows, they all seem to have "hearts so huge and overflowing" (127).

The number of quotations pertaining to disapproved character traits is very small, but conspicuous among them are criticisms of the unrestrained expression of emotion. It is virtually horrible that one of our baseball heroes "is no man for a jest when losing a game" (53); that a movie actress "cannot bear to be teased" (105); or that our Secretary of Labor's "public relations are unfortunate" (22). Unrestrained behavior traits like being "irritable and harsh" (32), "swift, often furious testiness" (117), being "unbalanced" (56), or even possessing a "somewhat difficult personality" (117) are really most unpleasant. Such faults can be tolerated only if they are exceptional—like the man who "for once got his feelings beyond control" (23).

The catalogue of normalcy leaves no room for individuality. This catalogue levels human behavior by the rejection of emotional eruptions; the bad marks given to the poor "joiners" and the temperamental people; the complete lack of creative and passionate behavior among the commendable qualities. The absence of love and passion in our catalogue of human relations finds its counterpart in this catalogue of human qualities. It is a world of dependency. The social implications of such atmosphere seem to be considerable because in their social status the majority of our heroes are either their "own boss" or they have climbed to such a high step in the social ladder that whole worlds separate them from the average employee. Yet the few "big ones" do not differ basically from the many little ones. They demonstrate, taken as a group, not the exception, but the typical cross-section of the socio-psychological condition of modern society.

The foregoing examples from our catalogue of character traits should make clear why we emphasize the double feature of the absence of development and solitude. The average man is never alone and never wants to be alone. His social and his psychological birth is the community, the masses. His human destiny seems to be a life of continuous adjustment: adjustment to the world through efficiency and industriousness; and adjustment to people by exhibiting amiable and sociable qualities and by repressing all other traits. There is no religious or philosophical framework according to which the character traits are classified and evaluated. The concepts of good and bad, of kindness and sin, of truth and falsehood, of sacrifice and selfishness, of love and hate are not the beacons which illuminate our human landscape. The character image on which an affirmative judgment is passed in the biographies is that of a well-trained employee from a well-disciplined lower-middle-class family. Our people could occupy an imaginary world of technocracy; everybody seems to reflect a rigid code of flexible qualities: the rigid and mechanized set-up of a variety of useful mechanical institutions. Behind the polished mask of training and adjustment lurks the concept of a human robot who, without having done anything himself, moves just such parts and in just such directions as the makers wished him to do.

Formerly it was only the sick who needed handling because it was known that their symptoms were similar to many others. Now everyone is reduced to the same dependency. The pride of being an individual with his own very personal ways and interests becomes the stigma of abnormality. Interest in the consumption of others is an expression of lack of interest in genuine consumption. The detailed character description is dominated by the same acceptance and passivity which came to the foreground in the concept of souls without development.

LANGUAGE

Superlatives

Our analysis would not be complete without some discussion of our stories' language which has several characteristic features. The most obvious one is the superlative.[18] Once we are made aware of this stylistic device, it cannot be overlooked. The heroes themselves, their accomplishments and experiences, their friends and acquaintances, are characterized as unique beings and events. The superlative gives a good conscience to the biographer—by applying a rhetorical gadget he achieves the transformation of the average into the extraordinary. Mr. Muti is "the toughest Fascist of them all" (114); Dr. Brinkley is the "best advertised doctor in the United States" (3); our hero is the "luckiest man in the movies today" (121); another is "not only the greatest, but the first real showman in the Ringling family" (26). There is a general who is "one of the best mathematicians this side of Einstein" (107). There is a columnist with "one of the strangest of courtships" (9); another statesman with "the world's most exciting job" (144). There are also the downward-pointed superlatives. Some sportsman was once "the loudest and by all odds the most abusive of the lot" (2); a newspaper man is "one of the most consistently resentful men in the country" (28); another person is "one of the unhappiest women that ever lived" (154).

As if the biographer had to convince himself and his public that he is really selling an excellent human specimen, he sometimes is not satisfied with the ratio of one superlative per sentence but has to pack a lot of them into a single passage. Pittsburgh Phil is "the most famous and the most feared horse player in America" (23). The German Labor Front is "the best led, most enlightened and most powerful labor organization in Europe" (21). The producer, Lorentz, "demands the best writing, the best music and the best technical equipment available" (126). The baseball manager, Clark Griffith, "was the most colorful star on the most colorful team in baseball" (2). Tilden is ". . . the greatest tennis player in the world and the greatest guy in the world" (111).

This wholesale distribution of highest ratings defeats its own purpose. Everything is presented as something unique, unheard of, outstanding. Thus nothing is unique, unheard of, outstanding. Totality of the superlative means totality of the mediocre. It levels the presentation of human life to the presentation of merchandise. The most vivacious girl corresponds to the best tooth paste, the highest endurance in sportsmanship corresponds to the most efficient vitamins; the unique performance of the politician corresponds to the unsurpassed efficiency of the automobile. There is a preestablished harmony between the objects of mass production in the advertising columns and the objects of biography in the editorial comment. The language of promotion has replaced the language of evaluation. Only the price tag is missing.

The superlative pushes the reader between two extremes. He is graciously invited to become conversant with people who are paragons of human accomplishment. He may be proud that to a great extent these wonderful people do nothing but entertain him. He has, at least in his leisure time, the best crowd at his fingertips. But there is no road left to him for an identification with the great, or for an attempt to emulate their success. Thus the superlative, like the story of success itself, brings out the absence of those educational features and other optimistic implications which were characteristic of biographies during the era of liberalism. What on first sight seems to be the rather harmless atmosphere of entertainment and consumption is, on closer examination, revealed as a reign of psychic terror, where the masses have to realize the pettiness and insignificance of their everyday life. The already weakened consciousness of being an individual is struck another heavy blow by the pseudoindividualizing forces of the superlative. Advertisement and terror, invitation to entertainment and summons to humility form their unity in the world of superlatives. The biographer performs the functions of a side show barker for living attractions and of a preacher of human insignificance.

High and Low Language

The use of the superlative is reinforced by frequent references to an assortment of mythical and historical associations, in order, it would seem, to confer pseudosanctity and pseudosafety to the futile affairs of modern mass culture. Clark Gable does not just make a career—he lives the "Gable saga" (6), and the movie actress, Joyce, experiences at least a "little saga" (110). "Historic" is the word for Ilka Chase (140) as well as for Hildegarde (135). What happens to the softball player Novikoff is "fabulous" (158); the fate of the actress Morison is "history" (162); of the movie producer Wallis (166) as well as of the baseball player Allen (45) "a miracle"; the baseball manager Griffith experiences "baseball destiny," he accomplishes "a historic piece of strategy" (2). Greek mythology is a favorite; Clark Gable lives in "Olympian regions" (6); the passport administrator Shipley (8) as well as the gadget inventor Taylor (167) have an "Herculean task"; the producer Todd is called an "Archon" (131) and James Taylor "Orpheus" (167). Of course Christianity and the Middle Ages have to help Dorothy Thompson "like a knight with a righteous sword" (9); the Nazi Ley is the "Jacob of German labor" with "labor itself the Esau" (21). Vice-President Wallace is "Joseph, a dreamer of dreams" (38); Casals is a "good Samaritan" (106). There are no limits. Ruth Hussey sometimes "looked a bit like a Buddha" (151); the showman Rose like a "priest of Osiris" (43). And so it goes on with myths, legends, sagas, destinies, miracles.[19] And yet, in the same breath which bestows the blessings of venerable symbols on our heroes, they and we are brought together on the easy level of slang and colloquial speech. McCutcheon, the cartoonist, might be called the "king" of his island possession, but we hear that "kingship is a safe investment" (1); Fletcher, who made history, is also "the soul—or the heel—of honesty" (7); Swing, called "an apostle," has also "radio's best bedside manner" (42). When Taft's father was president, the "crown of Roosevelt I fitted him like a five and ten toupee" (101). There is a boxer who finds it "good business to be brave" (12); there is "gossip—a dime a gross" (23); there is talk of a "personal blitzkrieg" (29); of "votes enough to elect a bee to a beehive" (109); of the "moguls of celluloid" (137); of "that genius business" (152). The historizing hymns of praise and transfiguration correspond to movie "palaces" and the sport "stadiums." It is a colossal façade, a "make-believe ballroom," as one radio station announces its swing program. Behind the façade of language there rules, just as behind the architectural outside make-up, a versatility of techniques, gadgets and tricks, for which nothing is too expensive or too cheap to serve the purpose of entertaining or being entertained.

These substitutes and successors of creative production require a language which substitutes for elucidating, revealing, stimulating words, a linguistic confusion that strives to produce the illusion of rooted tradition and all-around alertness. Thus this new literary phenomenon complies with the highest artistic criteria: inner, necessary, inseparable connection between form and content, between expression and the expressed—in short, a linguistic creation which will not permit an anatomic clear-cut separation between words and their intentions! These biographies as a literary species are "true."

Especially for You

In an unpublished analysis of songs T. W. Adorno interprets the pseudodirectness with which every one of the millions of girls for whose consumption the hit is manufactured, seems to be addressed. The pseudoindividualization of the heroes corresponds to the pseudoindividualization of the readers. Although the selection of heroes and what is reported about them are as thoroughly standardized as the language of these reports, there is the superlative functioning as the specifying agent for the chosen hero and there is also, as crown and conclusion, the direct speech as the bearer of a personal message to the reader. Affably or condescendingly, everyone is personally invited to attend the spectacle of an outstanding life. Individual meets individual; the biographer takes care of the introduction.

Coach Fletcher and his wife "can be reached only by telegram provided you know the address" (7). Should you happen to be a Brenda Joyce fan: "If you come at the right time, you will see her second-hand car" (110). Watching our election campaign: "If Hull and Mr. Taft are the candidates, your emotion will not be fired, nor will your sleep be disturbed by them" (109). For those interested in film stars: "Let's sit down with Bill Powell and listen to his story" (112); "perhaps, girls, you would like to know how Clark Gable got that way" (6). Reporting McCutcheon's acquisition of an island, the author teases the reader: "So, you want to be a king" (1). For the car owner: "You can't help seeing Johnson's restaurants if you drive along main highways" (37). There is the London *Times* representative Sir Willmott Lewis: "Meet him on Pennsylvania Avenue. He will stop and talk to you as if you were a five hundred audience" (49). Umpire Klem "knows the multitudinous rules of baseball better than you know the alphabet" (104). Let there be no mistake: the night club singer Moffett "went to the very best schools, my dear" (119). But let's not neglect her colleague Hildegarde: "If you haven't heard her or seen her, don't stand there—go, do something about it" (135). Casals's biographer is a little less imperative: "Meet the blond bowman from Spain" (106). Dependability is the word for Miss Fitzgerald: ". . . you can bank on her for the truth" (105).

The direct apostrophe is similar in function to the superlative: it creates elation and humiliation. The reader, besides being admitted to the intimate details of the hero's habits in eating, spending, playing, has the peasure of personal contact. There is nothing of the measured distance and veneration which a reader in the classics in biography had to observe before the statesman of the past, or the poet or the scientist. The aristocracy of a gallery of isolated bearers of unusual achievements seems to be replaced by a democratic meeting which requires no special honors and genuflection before the great.

But the ease of admission is not devoid of menacing features. The "you" means not only the friendly gesture of introduction but also the admonishing, calling voice of a superior agency, proclaiming that one has to observe, has to comply. The language of directness betrays the total coverage planned by all modern institutions of mass communication. "especially for you" means all of you.

THE READER

Magazine biographies have undergone a process of expansion as well as of atrophy. They have become a standard institution in magazines which count their audience by the millions. It is significant that during the present emergency the *Saturday Evening Post* and *Collier's* have been able to double their sales price without incurring any serious setback in circulation. But the scope of this expanding world of biographies has been narrowed down to the highly specialized field of entertainment. If we ask again what social need they serve, we might find the answer in this combination of quantitative increase and qualitative deterioration.

An hypothesis on the pseudoeducational and pseudoscientific function of the popular biography can be formulated as follows: the task of the social scientist is, in very broad terms, the clarification of the hidden processes and inter-connections of social phenomena. The average reader who, like an earnest and independent student, is not satisfied with a mere conglomeration of facts or concepts, but wants to know what it is all about, seems to gain insight from these biographies, and an understanding of the human or social secret of the historical process. But this is only a trick, because these individuals whose lives he studies are neither characteristic of this process, nor are they presented in such a way that they appear in the full light of it. A rather satisfactory understanding of the reader is possible if we look upon the biography as an agent of make-believe adult education. A certain social prestige, the roots of which are planted during one's school days, constantly drives one toward higher values in life, and specifically, toward more complete knowledge. But these biographies corrupt the educational conscience by delivering goods which bear an educational trademark but which are not the genuine article.

The important role of familiarity in all phenomena of mass culture cannot be sufficiently emphasized. People derive a great deal of satisfaction from the continual repetition of familiar patterns. There are but a very limited number of plots and problems which are repeated over and over again in successful movies and short stories; even the so-called exciting moments in sports events are to a great extent very much alike. Everyone knows that he will hear more or less the same type of story and the same type of music as soon as he turns on the radio. But there has never been any rebellion against this fact; there has never been a psychologist who could have said that boredom characterized the faces of the masses when they participate in the routine pleasures. Perhaps, since the average working day follows a routine which often does not show any change during a lifetime, the routine and repetition characteristics of leisure-time activities serve as a kind of justification and glorification of the working day. They appear in the guise of beauty and pleasure when they rule not only during the average day, but also in the average late afternoon and evening. In our biographies, the horizon is not extended to the realm of the unknown, but is instead painted with the figures of the known. We have already seen the movie actor performing on the screen and we have seen the cartoons of the competent newspaperman; we have heard what the radio commentator has to say and have noted the talents of boxers and baseball players. The biographies repeat what we have always known.

André Maurois has made a wrong prophecy: "We shall come once more into periods of social and religious certainty in which few intimate biographies will be written and *panegyrics* will take their place. Subsequently we shall again reach a period of doubt and despair in which biographies will reappear as a source of confidence and reassurance."[20] The reader who obviously cherishes the duplication of being entertained with the life stories of his entertainers, must have an irrepressible urge to get something in his mind which he can really hold fast and fully understand. It has been said of reading interests that: "In general, so long as the things of fundamental importance are not presenting one with problems, one scarcely attends to them in any way."[21] This remark has an ironical connotation for our biographies, for it can hardly be said that "things of importance" are not presenting us with problems today. Yet they are scarcely attended to unless we would admit that our heroes' parents, their likes and dislikes in eating and playing and, in the majority of cases, even their professions are important data during the initial stages of this war. But the distance between what an average individual may do and the forces and powers that determine his life and death has become so unbridgeable that identification with normalcy, even with Philistine boredom becomes a readily grasped empire of refuge and escape. It is some comfort for the little man who has become expelled from the Horatio Alger dream, who despairs of penetrating the thicket of grand strategy in politics and business, to see his heroes as a lot of guys who like or dislike highballs, cigarettes, tomato juice, golf and social gatherings—just like himself. He knows how to converse in the sphere of consumption and here he can make no mistakes. By narrowing his focus of attention, he can experience the gratification of being confirmed in his own pleasures and discomforts by participating in the pleasures and discomforts of the great. The large confusing issues in the political and economic realm and the antagonisms and controversies in the social realm—all these are submerged in the experience of being at one with the lofty and great in the sphere of consumption.

APPENDIX

DIFFERENCES BETWEEN THE *SATURDAY EVENING POST* AND *COLLIER'S*

Table 6.4 shows a considerable difference between *Saturday Evening Post* and *Collier's* in the occupational distribution of heroes. There are far more "serious" people and far fewer entertainers in the *Saturday Evening Post*. This corresponds to a difference in the audiences of the two magazines.[22] Surveys have shown that

TABLE 6.4
Distribution of Biographical Subjects by Occupation in the
Saturday Evening Post **and** *Collier's*
April 1940-April 1941

Occupations of subjects	*Saturday Evening Post* No.	*Saturday Evening Post* %	*Collier's* No.	*Collier's* %
Politics	16	28	15	22
Business and professions	20	35	5	7
Entertainment, sports	20	37	49	71
Total	56	100	69	100

the average *Saturday Evening Post* reader is older, wealthier, and more attached to his home and more interested in social and economic problems than the average reader of *Collier's*.

However, the difference between the two magazines becomes negligible (see Table 6.5) when we reclassify the heroes according to the spheres of politics, production, and consumption. For our purpose this is a more meaningful classification. As the two magazines are rather alike under this classification we felt justified in treating them together in the main text.

TABLE 6.5
Comparison of *Saturday Evening Post* **and** *Collier's* **Heroes**
According to General Spheres of Activity

Spheres	*Saturday Evening Post* 1940-1941 No.	*Saturday Evening Post* 1940-1941 %	*Collier's* 1940-1941 No.	*Collier's* 1940-1941 %
Politics	16	28	15	22
Production	3	5	—	—
Consumption	37	67	54	78
Total	56	100	69	100

Below is the list of the biographies from *Saturday Evening Post* and *Collier's* appearing in the issues between April 1940 and April 1941.

LIST OF BIOGRAPHIES USED

Saturday Evening Post

Date	"Hero"	Profession	No.
4-6-40	John T. McCutcheon	Cartoonist	1
4-13, 20-40	Clark Griffith	Baseball manager	2
4-20-40	John R. Brinkley	Physician	3
5-4-40	Robert Taft	Senator	4

5-4-40	Jack Johnson	Boxer	5
5-4-40	Clark Gable	Movie actor	6
5-11-40	Art Fletcher	Baseball coach	7
5-11-40	Mrs. Shipley	Chief, Passport Division, State Department	8
5-18, 24-40	Dorothy Thompson	Columnist	9
5-25-40	Richard A. Ballinger	Former Secretary of Interior	10
6-8-40	Bobby Jones	Golfer	11
6-22-40	Bob Donovan et al.	Boxers	12
6-22-40	Bob Allman	Wrestler	13
6-22-40	Daisy Harriman	Ambassador	14
7-6-40	Oché Toné	Slovenian immigrant	15
7-13-40	Ullstein Corp.	Publishing house	16
7-20-40	Hitler	Fuehrer of Third Reich	17
7-20-40	Jimmy Byrnes	Senator	18
7-27-40	Satchel Paige	Baseball pitcher	19
7-27-40	Angas	Investment counselor	20
7-27-40	Dr. Robert Ley	Head of the German Labor Front	21
7-27-40	Frances Perkins	Secretary of Labor	22
8-3, 10, 17-40	Pittsburgh Phil	Professional gambler (horses)	23
8-17, 24-40 9-14, 21, 28-40	Alfred P. Sloan, Jr.	Businessman	24
8-17-40	D'Arcy Grant	Woman sailor	25
8-24-40	John Ringling North	President of Ringling-Barnum & Bailey shows	26
9-14-40	Bill McKechnie	Baseball manager	27
9-14-40	Westbrook Pegler	Columnist	28
9-14-40	Endicott Peabody	Rector of Groton	29
10-5, 12, 19, 26-40 11-9, 16, 30-40	Will Rogers	Actor	31
10-12-40	James C. Petrillo	Pres. Am. Fed. Musicians	32
10-12-40	Louis McHenry Howe	Presidential secretary	33
10-19-40	Jay Norwood Darling	Cartoonist	34
10-19-40	Sidney Hillman	Labor leader	35
10-26-40	Frank Hague	Mayor of Jersey City	36
11-2-40	Howard Johnson	Owner of a restaurant chain	37
11-2-40	Henry Wallace	Vice-President	38
11-23-40	Silliman Evans	Newspaperman	39
11-30-40	Jesse H. Jones	Secretary of Commerce	40
12-7-40	William B. Stout	Inventor	41
12-14-40	Raymond Gram Swing	Radio commentator	42
12-21-40	Billy Rose	Showman	43
12-28-40	Charles A. Lindbergh	Aviator, etc.	44
12-28-40	Bobby Allen	Basketball player	45
1-4-41	Mrs. E. K. Hoyt and Toto	A gorilla	46
1-11-41	Clifton Fadiman	Book and radio critic	47
1-18-41	Sam Rayburn	Speaker, House of Representatives	48
1-25-41	Sir Willmott Lewis	London *Times* Emissary to U.S.	49
2-1-41	J. H. Kendrigan	Football coach	50
2-1-41	Cyrus R. Smith	Pres. Amer. Airlines	51
2-8-41	Varian Brothers	Inventors	52
2-15-41	Theodore A. Lyons	Baseball player	53

2-22-41	Jo Carstairs	Island proprietress	54
3-8, 15-41	Preston Sturges	Movie writer and director	55
3-15-41	Hank Greenberg	Baseball player	56
3-22-41	Phil Rizzuto	Baseball player	57

Collier's

4-6-40	Robert A. Taft	Senator	101
4-13-40	Mme. Chao Wu-Tang	Chinese Partisan Chief	102
4-13-40	Nancy Hamilton	Playwright, actress	103
4-13-40	Bill Klem	Baseball umpire	104
4-20-40	Geraldine Fitzgerald	Movie actress	105
4-20-40	Pablo Casals	Cellist	106
4-27-40	General Weygand	General	107
4-27-40	Ezra Stone	Stage, radio and screen actor	108
5-4-40	Cordell Hull	Secretary of State	109
5-4-40	Brenda Joyce	Movie actress	110
5-4-40	Bill Tilden	Tennis champion	111
5-11-40	William Powell	Movie actor	112
5-18-40	Greer Garson	Movie actress	113
5-25-40	Ettore Muti	Fascist politician	114
5-25-40	Philip Kerr, Marquess of Lothian	British Ambassador	115
5-25-40	Conchita Cintron	Woman matador	116
6-8-40	Thomas Dewey	Politician	117
6-8-40	Athanasiades	Munitions merchant	118
6-15-40	Adelaide Moffett	Night club entertainer	119
6-22-40	Dutch Leonard	Baseball player	120
6-22-40	Chris Martin	Movie actor	121
6-29-40	Gene Tierney	Movie actress	122
7-20-40	Lew Jenkins	Lightweight champion	123
7-20-40	Mahatma Gandhi	Indian political leader	124
7-27-40	Jean Arthur	Movie actress	125
8-3-40	Pare Lorentz	Movie producer	126
8-10-40	Don James	Sideshow barker	127
8-24-40	Larry Adler	Harmonica player	128
8-31-40	Ernest Bevin	British Minister of Labor	129
9-7-40	Helen Bernhard	Tennis player	130
9-7-40	Mike Todd	Producer—show business	131
9-14-40	Ingrid Bergman	Movie actress	132
9-21-40	Wendell Willkie	Politician	133
9-28-40	Walters and Derringer	Baseball players	133a
10-5-40	Juan March	Industrialist	134
10-5-40	Hildegarde	Night club singer	135
10-12-40	Jack Grain	Football player	136
10-12-40	Jinx Falkenburg	Advertising model	137
10-12-40	Eddie Flynn	Democratic National Chairman	138
10-19-40	John Latouche	Writer	139
10-26-40	Ilka Chase	Actress: movie, radio, film	140
11-2-40	Winston Churchill	British Prime Minister	141
11-2-40	Ken Overlin	Middleweight champion	142
11-9-40	Joan Carroll	Child movie actress	143
11-9-40	Lord Woolton	Britain's Minister of Food	144
11-16-40	Dorothy Stickney	Actress—theater	145
11-30-40	Field Marshal Erhard Milch	Organizer of German air force	146

11-30-40	Barbara Ham	Musical writer—college girl	147
12-7-40	Martha Scott	Movie actress	148
12-7-40	Joseph H. Ball	Senator	149
12-14-40	"Schnitz"	Producer—jitterbug leader	150
12-21-40	Ruth Hussey	Movie actress	151
12-28-40	George Balanchine	Ballet director	152
1-4-41	Billy Soose	Boxing champion	153
1-4-41	Carol and Magda Lupescu	Ex-King of Roumania and paramour	154
1-4-41	Annie Laurie Williams	Hollywood literary agent	155
1-11-41	Katherine Dunham	Dancer	156
1-18-41	Dorothy Comingore	Actress: theater and films	157
1-25-41	Lou Novikoff	Softball player	158
2-1-41	Zivic Brothers	Boxers	159
2-8-41	Three Young actresses in "Charley's Aunt"	Actresses	160
2-15-41	Brenda Marshall	Movie actress	161
2-24-41	Patricia Morison	Movie actress	162
3-1-41	Marilyn Shaw	National ski champion	163
3-15-41	Cliff Thompson	Hockey coach	164
3-15-41	Chic Young	Comic strip cartoonist	165
3-15-41	Hal Wallis	Movie producer	166
3-29-41	James Taylor	Inventor of gadgets	167
3-29-41	Bob Riskin	Scenario writer	168

NOTES

1. Cf. Edward H. O'Neill, *A History of American Biography* (University of Pennsylvania Press, 1935). His remarks on pp. 179 ff. on the period since 1919 as the "most prolific one in American history for biographical writing," are quoted by Helen McGill Hughes, *News and the Human Interest Story* (University of Chicago Press, 1940, pp. 285 f.). The book by William S. Gray and Ruth Munroe, *The Reading Interests and Habits of Adults* (New York: Macmillan, 1930), which analyzes readers' figures for books and magazines, does not even introduce the category of biographies in its tables on the contents of magazines, and applies it only once for books in a sample analysis of readers in Hyde Park, Chicago. The only comment the authors have to offer is: "There is some tendency to prefer biographies and poetry, especially in moderate doses to other types of reading except fiction" (p. 154). Finally, I want to quote as a witness in this case of scientific negligence, Donald A. Stouffer, *The Art of Biography in Eighteenth Century England* (Princeton University Press, 1941), who in his excellent and very thorough study says: "Biography as a branch of literature has been too long neglected" (p. 3).
2. Up to the spring of 1939, 3.1 million copies of his books were sold: 1.2 million in Germany, 1.1 million in the U.S., 0.8 million elsewhere. (Cf. Emil Ludwig, *Traduction des Œuvres* [Moscia, 1939], p. 2.)
3. It should not be inferred that the results as presented here are without much change applicable to all other magazines which present general and diversified

topics. From a few selections taken from less widely circulated and more expensive magazines, ranging from *The New Yorker* to the dollar-a-copy *Fortune,* it seems very likely that the biographies presented there differ in their average content structure and therefore in their social and psychological implications from these lower-priced popular periodicals. The difference in contents corresponds to a difference in readership.

4. Cf. note 12 of this chapter.
5. For the collection of data prior to 1940 the writer is indebted to Miss Miriam Wexner.
6. We have omitted from our discussion and our figures a number of very short biographical features which amounted to little more than anecdotes. These were published fairly regularly by the *SEP* until the late 1920s under the headings "Unknown Captains of Industry," "Wall Street Men," sometimes called "Bulls and Bears," "Who's Who and Why," "Workingman's Wife," "Literary Folk."
7. See, for instance, the *SEP,* September 19, 1925, where the auto-racer Barney Oldsfield tells a reporter details of his racing experiences and of the mechanics of racing and automobiles; September 26, 1925, in which the vaudeville actress, Elsie Janis, comments on her imitation acts and also gives details of her techniques. The same holds true for the biography of the band leader Sousa in the *SEP,* October 31, 1925, and of the radio announcer Graham McNamee, May 1, 1926; after a few remarks about his own life and career, McNamee goes on to discuss the technical aspects of radio and his experiences in radio with famous people.
8. *Saturday Evening Post,* October 12, 1901.
9. *Saturday Evening Post,* June 28, 1902.
10. Here and there we find a casual remark on the function of biographies as models for individual imitation. Cf., for instance, Mandel Sherman, "Book Selection and Self Therapy," in *The Practice of Book Selection,* ed. Louis R. Wilson, University of Chicago Press, 1939, p. 172. "In 1890 a book appeared entitled *Acres of Diamonds,* by Russell H. Conwell. This book dealt especially with the problems of attaining success in life. The author attempted to encourage the reader by giving examples of the struggles and triumphs of noted successful men and women. This pattern of encouraging the reader by citing examples of great men has continued, and in recent years a number of books have appeared in which most of the content dealt with case histories of noted individuals. Some psychologists have suggested that interest in autobiographies and biographies has arisen in part from the attempts of the readers to compare their own lives with those about whom they read, and thus to seek encouragement from the evidence of the struggles of successful people." Helen McGill Hughes in her suggestive study, *News and the Human Interest Story,* has not avoided the tendency to settle the problem of biographies by rather simplified psychological formulae. By quoting generously O'Neill, Bernarr MacFadden, and André Maurois, she points to the differences of the more commemorative and eulogistic elements in earlier biographies and the "anxious groping for certainty of people who live in times of rapid change," which is supposed to be connected with the present interest in biography (see especially p. 285).

11. The figures in parentheses refer to the bibliography of stories studied, see Appendix. Figures 1 to 57 refer to the *SEP* and 101 to 168 to *Collier's*. On the difference between the *SEP* and *Collier's*, see Appendix, Tables 6.4, 6.5.

12. It will be very important to check how far the war situation confirmed, changed, or even reversed the trend. A few casual observations may be mentioned. (1) The *New York Times Magazine*, on July 12, 1942, published an article "Wallace Warns Against 'New Isolationism.'" The vice-president of the United States is photographed playing tennis. The caption for the picture reads "Mr. Wallace's Serve." This picture and its caption are a very revealing symbol. The world "serve" does not refer to social usefulness, but to a feature in the vice-president's private life. (2) This remark can be supplemented by quoting a few issues of the *SEP* and *Collier's*, picked at random from their publications during the summer of 1942. While everywhere else in this study we have limited ourselves to the analysis of strictly biographical contributions, we should like, by quoting some of the topics of the entire issues which we have chosen for this year, to emphasize the overall importance of the spheres of consumption. Not only has the selection of heroes for biographies not changed since America's active participation in the war, but many other of the nonfictional articles are also still concerned with consumers' interests. (3) Of the ten nonfictional articles in the *SEP*, August 8, 1942, five are connected with the consumers' world: a serial on Hollywood agents; a report on a hometown circus; a report on roadside restaurants; an analysis of women as book readers; and an essay on the horse and buggy. In an issue one week later, August 15, 1942, there is a report on the International Correspondence School; the continuation of the serial on the Hollywood agents; and a biography on the radio idol Kate Smith. Or let us look at *Collier's*, which as a whole, devotes a much higher percentage of articles to war topics than the *SEP*. Out of nine articles in the issue of July 4, 1942, five belong to the consumers' world. There is again one on the horse and buggy, another one on a baseball hero, a third one on an Army comedian, a fourth one on a Broadway producer, and finally, one on budget buffets. Three weeks later, on July 25, out of ten articles, again five belong to the same category. (4) In other words, out of 37 articles found in four issues of two leading popular magazines during the present crisis, not less than 17 treat the gustatory and entertainment features of the average citizen. (5) There appears to be some cause for concern in the fact that so much of the fare presented to the reading public during the times immediately preceding the war and during the war itself is almost completely divorced from important social issues.

13. We proceeded to collect all the passages in the 125 stories pertaining to our four categories. It is not intended here to analyze the 2,400 quotations exhaustively, but merely to present in the following chapters a few observations or hypotheses which their study suggested to us and which we hope may be stimulating to further research in content analysis.

14. D. G. Phillips, "The Right Hand to Pierpont Morgan," *Saturday Evening Post*, June 28, 1902.

15. Max Horkheimer, "The End of Reason," in *Studies in Philosophy and Social Science*, vol. IX, no. 3 (1941), p. 381.

16. Ibid.

17. The spectacle of success, hardships and accidents is attended in the biographies by an assortment of numbers and figures which purport to bestow glamour and exactness to the narration. Calculability is the ideal language of modern biographies. They belong to the scientific mentality which sees its ideal in the transformation from quality into quantity. Life's riddle is solved if caught in a numeric constellation. The majority of figures refer to income, to which may be added relatively few data on capital. The other figures pertain to the spectators of a ball game, to the budget of a city, to the votes of an election, etc.

18. A study of this writer on popular German biographies, which appears in this volume as Chapter 5, shows that the use of superlatives also characterizes them. These books by Emil Ludwig, Stefan Zweig and others, are on a different intellectual level, yet it seems probable that similar sociological implications hold for them as for magazine biographies.

19. Helen McGill Hughes, *News and the Human Interest Story*, p. 183, is aware of the fact that the association of "classical" names has a stimulating effect on what she calls "the city demos": "Stated in terms of his popular literature, the mind of modern man lives in the present. And as the present changes, so his news is voluminous and rapidly succeeded by more news. But what fascinates him is the news story—the true story—even though it may duplicate *Bluebeard* or *Romeo and Juliet* so exactly that the headline tells the news just by mentioning the familiar names. The human interest of the common man in the modern world will, and does, ensnare him into reading folktales or even the classics, dull and unreal as he finds them in themselves, if they are paraphrased as the careers of twentieth century Electras, Macbeths and Moll Flanders, for he is preoccupied with the things that depart from the expected and make news."

20. André Maurois, *Aspects of Biography* (New York: Appleton-Century, 1939), p. 203.

21. Franklin Bobbitt, "Major Fields of Human Concern," quoted in Gray and Munroe, *The Reading Interests*, p. 47.

22. *A qualitative study of magazines: Who Reads Them and Why* (McCall Corporation, October 1939).

Excursus C
SOME THOUGHTS ON THE
1937 EDITION OF *INTERNATIONAL*
WHO'S WHO

One might well ask whether the liberal belief in harmony is still valid today. Why, especially today, should our faith in the free development of the individual, in the individualistic doctrine of the vital rights and potentialities of each and everyone which has become common stock, have lost its social basis? Is it indeed true that people today are organized like herds, distinguished for their "breeders" only by the color of their skin, the cut of their wool: mere raw material without the gift of spontaneity? A cursory survey of the media of our times seems to refute any such theoretical propositions as the end or even the crisis of liberalism and individualism.

Individuality consists first of all in a name; it is insufficiently described, however, if it is only attributed to the human species. A proper concept of individuality only arises when defined as pertaining to the unique exemplar which is nothing else but itself. Our age seems to live in a literal frenzy of individual name-giving. We are told that the Renaissance was the age of the discovery of the individual. Adolescents, students and even adults continue to discover themselves according to this historical model. It is a familiar manner of expression among educated people to refer to the nature of a Cesare Borgia when they see someone excel in cunning, or to a Lucretia Borgia when they want to comment on spicy erotic fantasies. Equally familiar are testimonies of cultural sophistication on the part of those who in private and public see themselves surrounded by faces, limbs and souls reminiscent of brush strokes of Botticelli, Raphael, Dürer and Holbein or of the chisels and carving knives of Donatello and Riemenschneider, as if they were discovering reincarnations of those artistic creations. Such rhetoric, however, might still be seen as an expression of a sort of civilized modesty informed by a certain respect for the famous name which carried so much more weight than one's own. In addition, until recently the historical consciousness of the educated

237

was sustained by concrete historical concepts which were not limited to notions of antiquity or the Middle Ages but by very specific references such as the ages of absolutism, the counter-reformation, the French Revolution, or the nineteenth century. To mention Cromwell or Robespierre when actually the bourgeois revolutions were meant, was considered a somewhat precious affectation—as if one were on personal terms with the historically significant.

While we are not all brothers, we are also no longer strangers to each other in as much as we learn the names of many of our fellow men. Man steps out of the dark of history into the glaring floodlights seemingly illuminating his specifically named individuality. The worthiness and uniqueness of each individual involved in the making of a film finds expression in the film's credit lines. These indicate not only the names of the director and actors, but also of those who handled the lighting, manipulated the film in the darkroom, sewed the famous star's costumes and who pushed various pieces of equipment here and there, who engineered the sounds of railroad cars, cowbells and catastrophic explosions; all these are made dear to us and, for seconds at least, familiar. The press is not different in this regard. Where formerly the talk was of great powers, economic constellations and parties, these various issues nowadays are discussed in terms of the names of statesmen, party activists, economic leaders and their helpers who are constantly quoted with this or that statement. Today, the message of John: in the beginning was the word, is repeated a thousand times over. And the religious message that man is created in the image of God seems endlessly repeated on the front pages of newspapers where a daily history of creation is reported through the comments of Mr. Smith and Reverend Jones. The circle of those whose names are worthy of mention is no longer restricted to the members of the power elite. Rather, the very mention of a name in the media nowadays seems to bestow a semblance of worthiness to the countless members of insignificant technicians, dilettantes, amateurs, reporters, announcers, administrators, politicians; but their significance fades with the deluge of tomorrow's names.

This avalanche of a vulgarized *Who's Who* takes on ludicrous proportions. The fog of anonymity is seemingly lifted from the name- and faceless crowd of the work force. A sign in the window of a ticket counter names the agent, a sign on her desk the secretary, a nametag on his lapel that of the elevator operator, railroad conductor, barber, hairdresser, bartender, gas station attendant, convention participant. Who has not yet been delighted with the concern of his fellows when—on his birthday— he not only received greetings from his friends but also from his insurance agent? The "human touch" has dignified and ennobled the business of advertising and public relations. Out of the goodness of his heart the contractor or developer will build this lovely house for this couple; the loyal bank manager confides in you just how much your welfare and that of your loved ones mean to him. Modern printing equipment permits the reproduction of letters in such a way that each letter appears individually written on a typewriter so as to give it a "personal touch." The only individualized aspect of this procedure is the personal address of the recipient which can be executed on a typewriter without visible difference between the typed and printed parts of the letter. The trick is known to many of the recipients, but to many it is not. They believe that not only the greeting but the substance of the letter was intended for them alone.

The fiction of this individuality which demands that its name be noted by others, is certainly not limited to the described social spheres where the private becomes public and is turned into a ritualistic formula which has lost its social grounding. It is not without cruel irony, that the blows which the liberal political and cultural system is presently enduring find expression in totalitarian politics through a greeting that incessantly invokes the name of its "Führer." The people of a country which is a breeding ground of collectivism greet each other by pledging allegiance to the name of an individual while—paradoxically—the country which still prides itself on its individualism, is also the home of the most indiscriminate, faceless greeting, the "hello."

There is something terrifying in this lifting of anonymity. If previously a name meant the familiar and opened a friendly door through which we were invited to enter, the name of the person presented to us, of the artist whose work we were about to encounter, the productive person who has opened new vistas, now the name of the Führer has become a symbol of sinister muteness. The greeting invoking his name connotes the uniform, uniformity itself; caution is required, a retreat and withdrawal into the nameless shadow of the masses.

The trend to substitute the commitment to critical insight and careful analysis with the dropping of a name might also be detected among the emigrants who have escaped the totalitarian systems and yet seem compelled to compete with them. I mean the tendency to aggrandize themselves by invoking the names of great writers, philosophers, scientists or charismatic pacifists. Why, for instance, the proposal to name the umbrella-organization of all the diverse political and cultural exile groups the Hellmuth von Gerlach Organization rather than, e.g., the Association of Free Germany in Exile? This tendency has its precedence. It began during the French Revolution and continued throughout the history of the groupings and group conflicts of the leftist movements since the middle of the nineteenth century, as for instance in such designations as "Bakunists" and "Lassallians." A similar tendency to substitute names of leaders, founders, innovators for philosophical schools or religious movements has become more and more prevalent in our time.

In truth, this new world of names is nameless. There was once an immediate relationship between justification through faith and the believer, between the pietistic hymns of spiritual peace and the small craftsman, between the proclamation of the rights of man and the rights of this or that person, between classicism and romanticism and individual cultural needs. The object-related language of bygone centuries reflects a stronger and more authentic confidence in the potential of the individual than the noisy and cheap glorification of the multitude of names surrounding us today.

The tenuousness of this alleged individuality manifests itself in such minor responses as the irritation we experience if, for instance, our name is but slightly mispronounced or mistaken. In fact, the hypertrophy of the name-giving cult is but another reflection of the continuing disintegration of the individual whose unconscious is all too aware of the ever-increasing indifference of our fellow-man to which we are exposed. The ubiquitous name-cult is as inauthentic in its intimacy as it is inauthentic in its egalitarianism. The verbal reverence which today still refers to "a" Goethe and "a" Bismarck for instance, conceals the futile desire to acquire for oneself a small measure of uniqueness in a world in which the fate of the venerator is equal to that of the indefinite pronoun which actually denotes anonymity.

He who speaks of the leaders speaks of his own impotence. As we are increasingly overwhelmed with facts demanding unquestioned authority and subjugation of our independent judgments and feeling, names and more names, along with our own, are added to this authoritarian learning process. The names are to be forgotten as soon as they are learned. Looking at *Who's Who in 1937* these thoughts take on a terrifying aspect.

Part II
CONTRIBUTIONS TO
THE PHILOSOPHY OF
COMMUNICATION

Chapter 7
ON SOCIOLOGY OF LITERATURE
(1932)

I

History of literature is in a unique way subject to the difficulties which arise with every historical effort. Not only is it implicated in all theoretical discussions concerning the conceptual meaning and material structure of history, but, in additon, its object of study falls into the realm of numerous scientific disciplines. Over and beyond the techniques involved in the critical analysis of sources, numerous disciplines step forward with a variety of claims, among them philosophy, aesthetics, psychology, pedagogy, philology and even statistics. When we turn to day-to-day practice, however, we find that literary studies have become scientific jetsam. Everybody, from the "naive reader" to the presumably legitimate teacher with special expertise, is prepared to launch interpretations of literary texts in the most arbitrary and capricious ways. Knowledge of a language combined with the conviction that an adequate technical terminology can be dispensed with, are considered sufficient prerequisites to engage in such ventures. On the other hand, academics have thus far not developed methods of research and analysis which would do justice to the complexity of their object of study. This is not a wholesale indictment of every single specialized work; rather, what I am concerned with here are the prevailing principles underlying today's study of literary history and literary criticism.

Virtually all of the scholars who contributed to the collection of essays *Die Philosophie der Literaturwissenschaft*[1] (The Philosophy of Literary Studies) are in agreement that a "scientific" approach to the history of literature would lead nowhere. Not only do they believe—and rightly so—that each literary work contains some nonrational elements, they also consider any rational approach inadequate with regard to the very nature of the object under investigation. Consequently, the study of literature as it was founded in the nineteenth century is condemned and rejected as "historical pragmatism,"[2] as "historicizing psychologism,"[3] and as "positivistic method."[4] Certainly, Hermann Hettner's or Wilhelm Scherer's works lack absolute validity; indeed, they would never have claimed it. But all attempts to deal with literature which profess to a scholarly character have to draw critically on the scientific methods of the nineteenth century.

Isolation and simplification of a literary historical object is admittedly achieved in an exceedingly sublime process. Author and work become abstracted from the matrix of historical circumstances, and molded into a kind of predictable coalescence from which the diverse manifold of details and dimensions has been drained. Through this reification they acquire a dignity and worthiness which no other cultural phenomenon can boast. "In the history of literature acts and actors are 'givens,' whereas in world history we are presented with more or less falsified accounts of mostly shady dealings by rarely identifiable dealers."[5] True dignity is reserved only for such historical phenomena which are a manifestation of the mind, or may be perceived at least as existing in a unique domain.[6] Of course, only when an object of investigation is not considered part of inner and outer nature and its variable conditions, but instead has to be ontologically conceived as a creation of a higher kind, do positivistic methods prove fundamentally insufficient. With the confidence of a philosophical instinct, the concept of structure introduced by Dilthey, which was based on historical contextuality, is abandoned and replaced by the concept of the organic "that clearly, unambiguously and decisively characterizes the spiritual as the individualization in history determined by unity of meaning."[7] Ambiguous terms such as "work," "form," "content," proclaim a metaphysically grounded unity of author and work, transcending and negating all diversity. This radical estrangement from historical reality finds its purest expressions in concepts such as "classicism" and "romanticism" which are not only relegated to history, but also metaphysically transfigured. "Like the superordinate concept of eternity, both the concept of perfection and of infinity are derived from historical and psychological experience as well as from philosophical knowledge."[8]

This rigid and in itself irrational stance on the part of those representing literary scholarship today presumes its legitimation in the fact that the "methods of the natural sciences" analyze their object into bits and pieces, and when attempting to define its "vital poetic soul," these methods cannot help but miss entirely its "secret."[9] The significance of these statements is hard to grasp. For nobody has ever demonstrated why, and to what extent, an object would be harmed or distorted by a rational approach. Any study of a phenomenon can be mindful of its wholeness, its "Gestalt," while being conscious of a selective methodology. Admittedly, such an analysis will only yield the elements of a mosaic whose sum never represents the whole. But where on earth does scientific analysis exhaust itself in nothing but a summation of fractured parts? And are the methods of the natural sciences exclusively atomistic in nature? Certainly not, and neither do methods of literary analysis have to be, if they are inappropriate to a specific task. On their journey into the vagaries of metaphysics, the literary scholars also appropriated the concept of law. However, rather than to identify law with order and regularity which can be submitted to scrutiny and observation, the concept, from the start, is burdened with a troublesome new and vague meaning. Instead of the search for regularity there appears a "unity of meaning," and the "artistic personality" and the "poetic work"[10] are identified, among others, as the major problems of literary studies, problems which seem to be resolved before they have been investigated. Yet, *personality* and *work* belong to those conceptual constructs which thwart any theoretical effort precisely because they are opaque and finite.

In as much as these fashionable literary scholars point to the pitfalls involved in seeking to understand the relationship of author and work through, for instance, mere philological data analysis, I have no quarrel with this antipositivistic attitude. But precisely when it comes to an evaluation of a work of art and its qualitative aspects, an understanding of its intrinsic merit and its authenticity—questions so much at the center of the concerns of these scholars—their methods reveal their utter inadequacy. The question of whether and to what extent the literary artist consciously applies conventions of form, can only be explored by rational means. But the metaphysical mystification so prevalent in contemporary literary studies impedes any sober reflection and scholarship. Its tasks are not only historical in nature; I would like to refer to Dilthey's concept of *Verstehen* (understanding) and its particular emphasis on the relationship between the author and his work. Admittedly, the demystification of investigative approaches to literature cannot be achieved by means of a formal poetics alone. What is needed above all is a psychology of art, i.e. a study of the psychological interaction between artist, artistic creation and reception. What is not needed, however, is a psychology that places the "great work of art" in a mystical relationship "with the people," and that finds the "personal biography of the author . . . interesting and necessary, but unessential with regard to the act of artistic creation."[11]

II

In contrast to the vague declamatory statements so characteristic of Jungian psychology, the classical Freudian model of psychoanalysis has already made important theoretical contributions to a psychology of art.

Some of its proponents have discussed central questions of literature, particularly those dealing with the psychic conditions under which great works of art originate, specifically the origins and structure of artistic imagination, and last not least, the question of the relationship between the artistic work and its reception which so far has been ignored or at least insufficiently explored.[12] Admittedly, some of these psychoanalytic propositions are not yet polished and refined enough and remain somewhat schematic. But to reject the assistance of scientific psychology in the study of art and literature does not provide protection from "a barbarian assault of conquerers,"[13] as one contemporary literary mandarin put it, but rather is a "barbarian" argument itself!

Coupled with the condemnation of "historicizing psychologism," which cannot explore the secret of the "authentic poetic soul,"[14] is the repudiation of accepted historical methodology and particularly of any theory of historical causality, in short, what in modern literary scholarship is anathematized as "positivistic materialism."[15] But as in the case of psychology, the trend setters take liberties: modern literary scholarlship has no qualms and even consistently makes use of grand historical categories such as "folk, society, humanity"[16] or the "pluralistic, aspiring" and the "spiritualizing, articulating experience."[17] There is mention of "associations of essence and fate," of "perfection and infinity" as "conceptual basis" of "historical experience";[18] while the phraseology of the "age of Homer, Pericles, Augustus, Dante, Goethe"[19] is acceptable, any historically and sociologically oriented theoretical approach will meet with scorn and contempt when it attempts to understand literature as a social phenomenon in combination with the positivistic and materialistic methods which evolved out of the historical scholarlship of the nineteenth century. The bluntly stated objective is "the abandonment of the descriptive vantage point of positivism and the return to a commitment to the metaphysical character of the *Geisteswissenschaften* (humanities)."[20] We shall see that such "abandonment" is demanded with even greater determination once the theory of historical materialism replaces traditional historical description. Even the boundary between scholarship and demagogery is obscured when the anti-historical transfiguration of a work of art has to be maintained: "Historical pragmatism may perhaps conclude that syphilis led to the disappearance of Minnesang and its polygamous convention, or that the currency reform of 1923 gave rise to Expressionism. . . . The essence of Minnesang and Expressionism remains unaffected by such findings. The question here is not why is it but what is it? The 'why' would simply lead to an infinite regress: Why at the end of the Middle Ages was lues spread, why at the beginning of 1924 was the *Reichsmark* introduced, and so on until the egg of Leda."[21] This kind of rhetoric makes a caricature of any legitimate scholarly inquiry. By no means do causal questions require infinite regress; clearly stated they can be precisely answered, even if new questions might be posed by this answer. An investigation of the reasons for Goethe's move to Weimar does not require an investigation of the history of urban development in Germany!

Considering the current situation of literary scholarship as sketched in the preceding outline, its precarious relationship to psychology, history, and social science, the arbitrariness in the selection of its categories, the artificial isolation and scientific alienation of its object, one might agree with a modern literary historian who, dissatisfied with the "metaphysicalization" that has invaded his discipline, calls for the return to strict scientific standards, a passionate devotion to material, a deep concern for pure knowledge; in short, a new "appreciation of knowledge and learning."[22] If Franz Schultz, however, simultaneously rejects any over-arching theory,[23] he does not have the courage of his own convictions. In fact, it is possible to conceive of a theoretical approach to literature which remains faithful to "knowledge and learning" and interprets literary works historically and sociologically, avoiding the pitfalls of both either descriptive positivism or mere metaphysical speculation.

III

Such concern with the historical and sociological dimensions of literature requires a theory of history and society. This is not to say that one is limited to vague theorizing about the relationships between literature and society in general, nor that it is necessary to speak in generalities about social conditions which are required for the emergence of literature. Rather, the historical explanation of literature has to address the extent to which particular social structures find expression in individual literary works and what function these works perform in society. Man is involved in specific relations of production throughout his history. These relations present themselves socially as classes in struggle with each other, and the development of their relationship forms the real basis for the various cultural spheres. The specific structure of production, i.e. the economy, is the independent explanatory variable not only for the legal forms of property and organization of state and government but, at the same time, for the shape and quality of human life in each historical epoch. It is illusionary to assume an autonomy of the social superstructure, and this is not altered through the use of a scientific terminology claiming such autonomy. As long as literary history is exclusively conceived as *Geistesgeschichte,* it will remain powerless to make cogent statements, even though in practice the talent and sensibilities of a literary historian may have produced something of interest. A genuine, explanatory history of literature must proceed on materialistic principles. That is to say, it must investigate the economic structures as they present themselves in literature, as well as the impact which the materialistically interpreted work of art has in the economically determined society.

Such a demand along with the social theory which it presupposes, has a dogmatic ring unless it specifies its problematic. This has been achieved to a large extent in the fields of economics and political history, but even in the area of literary studies fledgling attempts have been made. Worthy of mention are Franz Mehring's[24] essays on literary history which, sometimes using a simplified and popular, sometimes a narrowly defined political approach, have for the first time attempted to apply the theory of historical materialism to literature. But as in the case of the aforementioned psychological studies, the work of Mehring and other scholars of his persuasion has either been ignored or even ridiculed by literary historians. A sociologist of culture recently referred to "such a conceptual framework not only as unsociological or incompatible with scientific sociology," but also comparable to "a parasitic plant" that "draws off the healthy sap of a tree."[25]

The materialistic explanation of history cannot afford to proceed in the simplifying and isolating manner so characteristic for the academic establishment of literary history, interpretation, and criticism. Contrary to common assertions, this theory neither postulates that culture in its entirety can be explained in terms of economic relations, nor that specific cultural or psychological phenomena are nothing but reflections of the social substructure. Rather, a materialistic theory places its emphasis on mediation: the mediating processes between a mode of production and the modes of cultural life including literature. Psychology must be considered as one of the principal mediating processes, particularly in the field of literary studies, since it describes the psychic processes by means of which the cultural functions of a work of art reproduce the structures of the societal base. In as much as the basis of each society in history can be seen as the relationship between ruling and ruled classes and is, in fact, a metabolic process between society and nature, literature—like all other cultural phenomena—will make this relationship transparent. For that reason the concept of ideology will be decisive for the social explanation of all phenomena of the superstructure from legal institutions to the arts. Ideology is false consciousness of social contradictions and attempts to replace them with the illusions of social harmony. Indeed, literary studies are largely an investigation of ideologies.

The often-voiced criticism that the theory of historical materialism lacks methodological refinement and possesses a crude conceptual apparatus can easily be countered: the proponents of this theory have never avoided the discussion of its flaws. Its findings and results have always been open to the scrutiny of other scholars, as well as to possible theoretical changes prompted by new experiences in social reality. Historical materialism has certainly not taken refuge in quasi-ontological imagery which, seductive and enchanting as it might be, connotes a spurious philosophy of knowledge. As long as a theory does not consider itself finite but rather continuously sustained and possibly altered by new and different experiences the frequent accusation that historical materialism ultimately contains an element of faith seems of little consequence.

IV

The following examples are intended to illustrate the application of historical materialism to literary studies and will address questions of form, motif, and content.

Beginning with the issue of *form* I should like to consider the problem of the encyclopedic novel as it exists in Balzac's *Comédie Humaine* or in Zola's *Les Rougon-Macquart*. Both seek to represent, through their all-encompassing narratives, the society of their time in its entirety with all its living and dead inventory, occupations, and forms of state, passions, and domestic furnishings. Their aim appears anchored in the bourgeois-rationalist belief that, in principle, it is possible to possess the world through thought and to dominate it through intellectual appropriation. In the case of Balzac, this rationalism is mediated by his adherence to a mercantilist model of the economy which supposedly allows government to regulate society in an orderly fashion—a Balzac anachronism rooted in his peculiar psychological infatuation with the *ancien régime*. In the case of Zola, however, one faces a critical orientation toward the capitalist mode of production and the hope of remedying its deficiencies through a critical analysis of the society it conditions. The breadth of each of these cyclic novels reveals just as much about the author and his place in a class society as it does about the theoretical and moral position he adopts toward the social structure of his time.

Social meanings present themselves in more specific issues as well. The same literary form, for instance, can have a completely different social meaning in different contexts. One example would be the emphasis on dialogue and the resulting limitation of the narrative voice or commentative inserts in the text. The works of Gutzkow and Spielhagen and the impressionist writers are paradigmatic for this style. Gutzkow was probably the first to introduce into German literature the modern bourgeois dialogue. The history of the dialogue in narrative texts is that of a development from a tradition of stiff conventions to the spontaneous, open conversational technique of the present. The dialogue is in reality the criterion of the varying degrees of psychological astuteness which the freely competing members of capitalist society, at least in its liberal epoch, are able to demonstrate. Those who are more adroit and possess superior insight into the response mechanisms of their interlocutors also have superior chances of economic success, so long as the situation is not controlled by crude power relations which would make any discussion impossible in the first place. The function of the conversational form in the literature of the *Junges Deutschland* (Young Germany: the liberal intelligentsia of the 1830s and 1840s), which was almost entirely oblivious of its social context, is only indirectly identifiable, and in Spielhagen appears burdened by a kind of theory. The epic narrative insert has been reduced to a minimum, creating the impression that the author's arrangement of events has been dictated by the demands of reality, i.e. the verbalized interactions of the novel's characters, and that he has drastically reduced authorial interference through actions, events, and incidents as well as their authorial interpretation. Beginning with the later Fontane and Sudermann up until Arthur Schnitzler's last novellas, the impressionist novella makes extensive use of the uncommented dialogue. But this "renunciation of the privileges of the interpreting and supplementing narrator"[26] has one meaning and function in Spielhagen and another in the German impressionists.

Spielhagen's technique is based on the conviction that through the conversations of people social reality becomes transparent to the reflective reader who then will discover their underlying theory about human and societal relations. A bourgeois idealist, Spielhagen believes in the power of the objective mind which materializes in the articulated thoughts of men so that the free exchange of dialogue can leave no doubt as to the substantive convictions of the author. In contrast, the ascetic absence of commentary characteristic for the impressionists, is an expression of the self-criticism liberal bourgeois society pronounced on itself since the beginning of the twentieth century. The inability to formulate a theory of society, the increasing insecurity, if not helplessness, of the German middle class, resulted in fact in a mentality of relativism, a loss of confidence in the subjective mind which believed in the possibility of universally applicable knowledge. While Gutzkow's groping increments in dialogue reflect the economic gropings of a liberal bourgeoisie in Germany in the first stages of upward mobility and while the novellistic technique of Spielhagen celebrates its social victory, the impressionist style reflects its crisis: it either hides this crisis with an ideological film or admits to it through pointless conversations which lead nowhere.

Other class relationships reveal themselves when one compares the technique of the narrative frame in the novellas of Theodor Storm and C. F. Meyer. This literary device fulfills radically opposed functions in the work of these authors. Storm assumes a posture of resignation, of renunciatory retrospection. He is the weary, petty bourgeois pensioner whose world has collapsed, a world in which he could hope to engage in affairs of social importance. Time has run out; the only sustenance the present still offers are "framed," idealized remembrances of the past. Memory is capable of recovering only those fragments of the past that do not immediately bear on the gloomy present and therefore do not have to be repressed. In the case of Meyer, on the other hand, the narrative frames of his novellas quite literally serve as the magnificent frames of a glorious painting, and as such function as indicators of the worthiness of the image they enclose and are meant to separate the unique, which is all that matters, from the indifferent diversity of appearances. The same stylistic device which in Storm's world symbolizes the modest, the small and the waning, is used by Meyer as the symbol of vital reality. While the petty bourgeois soul of Storm quietly mourns, Meyer thrusts his characters into a world that corresponds to the feudal daydreams of the German upper classes in the 1870s.

As a final example of the sociological implications in problems of form, I shall briefly consider the use of pictorial imagery. For Lessing the aesthetician, the pictorial has no place in literary arts. For Meyer it is a favorite artistic device. The progress of humanity in historical time, the development of mankind are the important issues for Lessing, who was a firm believer in the future. He was an early champion of a rising bourgeois society which saw in the tensions and resolutions of a drama the paradigm for the conflicts and possible resolutions in society. Meyer is the heir to this dramatic tradition, but the surviving victors are now limited to the members of the upper class. Where Lessing is a dramatist, Meyer has become a sculptor. Where the former animates, the latter in fact halts the motion of progress. If for Lessing art expresses a universalist morality binding for all men, a morality which transcends individual idiosyncracies, it is for Meyer the extraordinary and the unique in selected individuals that finds expression in art. Magnificently framed, the infinite diversity of reality is condensed into the great moments of great individuals and eternalized as in a painting, transcending time and place. This ideological position mirrors precisely the self-image of the dominant strata of the bourgeoisie in the last third of the nineteenth century, for which the social world is but an opportunity for the development of the great personality, in short, the social elite. Its members stand aloof from trivial everyday cares and live surrounded by significant people, great ideals and important affairs which all reflect and confirm their uniqueness.

A *motif* that likewise serves to glorify economic power positions is the motif of boredom in the novels of Stendhal. Boredom is as fatal as death for "the happy few" who alone are entitled to read his books and for whom alone he chooses to write. These happy few, far removed from the consequences of an economically limited existence, are entitled to pursue their happiness according to their own autonomous morality. Just as Stendhal is the supreme novelist of the bourgeois aristocracy in the age of Napoleon, so Gustav Freytag sings the praise of the German mid-nineteenth century bourgeoisie which he transfigures by denying any knowledge of its contradictions that are evident in the division, organization and remuneration of labor. In as much as Freytag applies an undifferentiated concept of "work" to the equally undifferentiated concept of "the people," (two concepts Stendhal would have never used) he successfully overlooked, in a literal sense, the antagonistic social order with its competing and feuding classes. Ideology comes to the fore at the very beginning of his major work *Soll und Haben* (Debit and Credit) which has as its motto the words of Julian Schmidt: "The novel ought to look for the German people where they are at their virtuous best, that is, at work."

I should like to touch upon the death motif as it is struck repeatedly in Mörike's *Maler Nolten* (Painter Nolten) and Meyer's *Jürg Jenatsch*. Mörike's world is that of the *Biedermeier* of the honest man, the not yet politically emancipated bourgeois in the period of the *Vormärz*, i.e. in the period between the Vienna Congress and the, in fact, abortive revolutions of 1848-49. In his novels, the death motif may be interpreted as a harbinger of the political defeat of the bourgeoisie in his generation. The motifs of transience, fate, and death serve as ideological metaphors for the political impotence of the middle class in his time of which he himself was a prototype. By contrast, in the stories of Meyer, death takes on the aspect of a highly intensified moment in the fullness of life. When Lucretia kills Jürg Jenatsch this deed marks also the beginning of her own physical destruction. What is in fact a violent double murder is presented as the expression of heroic lifestyles. Only Jürg and Lucretia are worthy of one another, they represent a rare and perfect balance of character and fate; only by virtue of this singular congruity do these two have the right to eliminate each other. The solidarity of the international ruling minority proves itself unto death.

Finally, turning to *content,* I once more refer to Freytag and Meyer. Both wrote historical novels and short stories. Freytag's collected works might be called the textbook of the conformist middle class, exhorting the virtues and perils of its members. The study of history is not seen as an occasion for intellectual enjoyment for its own sake, but for its pedagogic values. Either for the purpose of warning or emulation, it contains the history of individuals and groups intended to teach future generations lessons of social competence which might help them avoid the dubious fate of the aristocracy or the sordid fate of the lower classes. If this stance toward history is a manifestation of the self-image of a bourgeoisie struggling for its existence with tenacious diligence, then, by contrast, Meyer's selective approach to history may be dubbed a "historicism of the upper bourgeoisie." When history is constituted randomly from disjoint events, the abundance of historical phenomena is forced into a dim twilight and the chain of diachronic experiences itself has no significance at all. There is no continuum of events of any interpretable character, be it causal, theological or otherwise teleological in nature. Political, economic cultural changes carry no weight and the flow of history is in itself without importance. The historian turns spectator taking pleasure in observing the singular like a magnificent drama. Thus the category of play penetrates real history as much as historical research to the extent that history's diversity and complexity is reduced to a puppet theater of heroes whose lives and activities are reconstituted for the playful enjoyment of the spectator-interpreter. An upper-class bourgeois likes his favorite historian to be an aesthete.

Another example for the exploration of content is the question of politics. In Gottfried Keller we find an almost bold disregard for economic realities, but considerable emphasis is placed on the political sphere, whether in occasional caricaturization of armchair politics or in the informed and competent conversations of the burgher in the *Fähnlein der sieben Aufrechten* (The Seven Upright) on topics of general import. To identify politics as the supreme, if not exclusive arena for the confrontation and final settlement of public affairs, is characteristic for social groups which, on the one hand, experience themselves as economically secure, but whose social mobility, on the other hand, is limited. All through the nineteenth century the middle class is inclined to look at politics as a resource for arbitration between competing groups and individuals, as, literally, a "middle"-way. This notion of the middle station, incidentally, was already fervently glorified in the fictional and pamphlet literature read by the English middle class in the eighteenth century. In the case of Stendhal, politics does not function as an ideological device, rather, consciously or not, he acts as spokesman for the upper class of his time who considered political dealings part of economic transactions and conflicts, and governments nothing more than business partners of big business itself.

It has always been of great interest to me why a task as important as the study of the reception of literature among various social groups has been so utterly neglected even though a vast pool of research material is available in journals and newspapers, in letters and memoirs. A materialistic history of literature, unhampered by the anxious protection of the literary arts by its self-styled guardians and without fear of getting stranded in a quagmire of routine philology or mindless data collection, is well prepared to tackle this task.

NOTES

1. Emil Ermatinger, ed., *Die Philosophie der Literaturewissenschaft* (Berlin, 1930).
2. Herbert Cysarz, "Das Periodenprinzip in der Literaturwissenschaft" (The Principle of Periodization in Literary Studies), in *Die Philosophie,* p. 110.
3. D. H. Sarnetzki, "Literaturwissenschaft, Dichtung, Kritik des Tages" (Literary Study, Literary Work, Contemporary Criticism), in *Die Philosophie,* p. 454.
4. Ermatinger, *Die Philosophie,* passim.
5. Cysarz, op. cit.
6. See Werner Ziegenfuß, "Kunst" (Art) in *Handwörterbuch der Soziologie* (Encyclopedia of Sociology), (1931), p. 311.
7. Emil Ermatinger, "Das Gesetz in der Literaturwissenschaft" (Law in Literary Study), in *Die Philosophie,* p. 352.
8. Fritz Strich, *Deutsche Klassik und Romantik* (German Classicism and Romanticism), (Munich, 1924), p. 7.
9. Sarnetzki, op. cit.
10. Ermatinger, op. cit., pp. 363f.
11. C. G. Jung, *Psychologie und Dichtung* (Psychology and Literature), qu. in Musch (see n. 13 below), p. 330.
12. See the important publication of Hanns Sachs, *Gemeinsame Tagträume* (Shared Daydreams), (Leipzig, 1924), esp. pt. I.
13. Walter Musch, *Psychoanalyse und Literaturwissenschaft* (Psychoanalysis and Literary Study), (Berlin, 1930), p. 15.
14. Sarnetzki, op. cit.
15. Ibid.
16. Ziegenfuß, op. cit., p. 337.
17. Herbert Cysarz, *Erfahrung und Idee* (Experience and Ideal), (Vienna/Leipzig, 1922), pp. 6f.
18. Strich, op. cit.
19. Friedrich Gundolf, *Shakespeare* (Berlin, 1928), vol. 1, p. 10.
20. Ermatinger, op. cit., p. 352.
21. Herbert Cysarz, "Das Periodenprinzip," p. 110.
22. Franz Schultz, *Das Schicksal der deutschen Literaturgeschichte* (The Fate of German Literary History), (Frankfurt/Main, 1928), p. 138.
23. Ibid., pp. 141ff.

24. Franz Mehring, *Schriften und Ausfsätze* (Writings and Essays), vol. 1 (Berlin, 1929); vol. 2, *Über Literaturgeschichte* (On Literary History), (Berlin, 1929); *Die Lessinglegende* (The Lessing Legend), (Berlin, 1926).
25. Ziegenfuß, op. cit., pp. 330f.
26. Oskar Walzel, *Die Deutsche Literatur von Goethes Tod bis zur Gegenwart* (German Literature from Goethe's Death to the Present), (Berlin, 1918), p. 664.

Chapter 8
ON SOCIOLOGY OF LITERATURE
(1948)

The sociological interpretation of literature is not a favorite son of organized social science. Since the emancipation of the study of literature from the rigid research dicta and historically cogent laws of philology, almost everybody with a fair access to reading and writing feels entitled to offer historical, aesthetic, and sociological criticism and generalization. The academic disciplines which have been traditionally charged with the history and analysis of literature have been caught unaware by the impact of mass literature, the best seller, the popular magazine, the comics and the like, and they have maintained an attitude of haughty indifference to the lower depths of imagination in print. A field and a challenge have thus been left open and the sociologist will have to do something about them.[1]

The following remarks, making no claim to systematization or comprehensiveness, are intended as an attempt to survey work done and to be done.

AREAS OF ANALYSIS

Literature and the Social System

The problems envisaged under this heading are twofold. The primary aspect is to place literature in a functional frame within each society and again within the various levels of stratification of that society. In certain primitive as well as in some culturally highly developed societies, literature is integrated into other social manifestations and is not clearly differentiated as an independent entity apart from ceremonials of cult and religion. It is rather an outlet of these institutions as, for example, tribal chants, early Greek tragedy, or the medieval passion play. In contradistinction, literature in the middle-class world leads an existence clearly separated from other cultural activities, with many functional differentiations. It may become the escapist refuge of politically frustrated groups, as in early romanticism, or of social frustration on a mass scale, as in the current phenomenon of literary mass entertainment. Then again, literature may function as an ideological instrument in the proper sense of that word, by exalting a specific system of domination and contributing to its educational goals, as was the case with the Spanish and French dramatists in the era of absolutism.

A secondary aspect, perhaps less fertile in terms of research materials but no less rewarding in social perspectives, lies in the study of literary forms. The epic as well as lyric poetry, the drama like the novel, have affinities of their own to a particular social destiny. The solitude of the individual or the feeling of collective security, social optimism or despair, interest of psychological self-reflection or adherence to an objective scale of values, may be mentioned as starting points of associations that lend themselves to a reexamination of literary forms in terms of social situations.[2]

An example for studies in this area is taken from the field of mass communication. It deals with the role of the popular biographies that have become prominent features in magazines intended for large-scale consumption. In comparing the different "heroes" of biographies during the last forty years it could be ascertained that in the first fifteen years of the present century about 75 percent of the subjects were taken from political life, business and the professions, whereas in 1941 73 percent of the "heroes" come from the "spheres of consumption," that is to say, from the entertainment, sports and communication fields. It seems that this change of literary taste is closely connected with a change in the social situation of the reading public. Whereas forty years ago they bought information about the agents and methods of social production, today they buy information about the agents and methods of individual consumption. This change is reinforced by a parallel change in topical material. A generation ago the reader was told about the special political, business or professional activities of his heroes; today he is held spellbound by their private lives, their hobbies and food preferences, their friends and acquaintances, and so on.

The major sociological conclusion to be drawn from this change is that the little man, who has been expelled from the Horatio Alger dream, who despairs of penetrating the thicket of grand strategy in politics and business, finds comfort in seeing his heroes as "a lot of guys" who like or dislike highballs, cigarettes, tomato juice, golf and social gatherings—just like himself. He knows how to converse in the sphere of consumption and here he can make no mistakes. By narrowing his focus of attention, he can experience the gratification of being confirmed in his own pleasures and discomforts by participating in the pleasures and discomforts of the great. The large confusing issues in the political and economic realm and the antagonisms and controversies in the social realm are submerged in the experience of being at one with the powerful and great in the sphere of consumption.[3]

The Position of the Writer in Society

The creative writer is the intellectual per se, for whom objective source materials are merely an arbitrary arsenal of reference of which he makes use, if at all, according to his specifically aesthetic aims. He thus represents the prototype of intellectual behavior and the lively discussion among sociologists about the role of the intelligentsia could perhaps be extended to a more concrete level if it were supported by a historically documented analysis of both the socially relevant self-portrait and the specific functions of one of the oldest groups among the intellectual professions.

It must suffice here to enumerate a few points of departure and to mention under the heading of subjectivity the phenomena of the prophetic, the missionary, the entertaining, the strictly handicraft and professional, the political or money-making self-conceptions of literary producers. On the objective level we shall have to inquire into the sources of prestige and income, the pressure of institutionalized agencies of social control, visible or anonymous, the influence of technology and the market mechanisms, all with regard to the stimulation and dissemination of artistic writing and to the social, economic and cultural situation within which writers find themselves at various historical stages. The relationships of the princely courts, the academies and salons, the book clubs and the movie industry to the literary craft exemplify the relevant topics for systematic discussion.[4] Then there are problems which cross the subjective and objective aspects, such as, whether under conditions of modern book and magazine production the writer is still an independent entrepreneur or in fact an employee of his publisher and advertiser.

Society and Social Problems as Literary Materials

Here we enter the traditional area of sociological research in literature. There are innumerable books and papers on the treatment of the state or society or the economy or this and the other articulate social phenomenon by any number of writers in any number of countries and languages. These more or less reliable repositories of factual information, though written for the most part by literary people and therefore more or less haphazardous in matters of social theory, cannot be dismissed lightly. They evaluate literature as secondary source material for historical analysis and become all the more valuable the scarcer the primary sources for any specific period. Furthermore, they contribute to our knowledge of the kind of perception which a specific social group—writers—has of specific social phenomena, and they belong therefore to propaedeutic studies of a history and sociology of social consciousness.

Nevertheless, a sociologist with literary interest and analytical experience in the field of belles-lettres must not be satisfied merely to interpret literary materials which are sociological by definition; his task is also to study the social implications of literary themes and motives which are remote from public or publicly relevant affairs. The specific treatment which a creative writer gives to nature or to love, to gestures and moods, to situations of gregariousness or solitude, the weight given to reflections, descriptions or conversations, are all phenomena which on first sight may seem sterile from a sociological point of view but which are in fact genuinely primary sources for a study of the penetration of the most private and intimate spheres of individual life by the social climate, on which, in the last analysis, this life thrives. For times that have passed, literature often becomes the only available source of information about private modes and mores.

The shortcoming of fashionable biographies of today stem in part from their increasing attempt to explain literary figures (and for good measure the entire social situation in which they were created) by short-circuited conclusions made up of analogies with the psychology of present-day man. But women like Faust's Gretchen, Madame Bovary, or Anna Karenina cannot be interpreted by mere analogy: their problems simply cannot be experienced today because the atmosphere out of which their conflicts grew has passed. The social data of the period in which they were created and the social analysis of the characters themselves are the very material from which the meaning and the function of the works of art can be understood. If our would-be psychologists in the literary field were to be completely sincere, they would have to confess that every one of these women, if alive today, would be considered stupid, frustrated neurotics who ought to take a job or undergo psychiatric treatment to rid themselves of their obsessions and inhibitions.

It is the task of the sociologist of literature to relate the experience of the imaginary characters to the specific historical climate from which they stem and, thus, to make literary hermeneutics a part of the sociology of knowledge. That sociologist has to transform the private equation of themes and stylistic means into social equations.[5]

Some fifteen years ago, I made a study of Knut Hamsun which incidentally turned out to be a case of successful sociological prediction in the field of literature.[6] The particular task consisted of analyzing themes and motives having no direct connection with public issues, for they were domiciled in the private sphere. The study showed that Hamsun was intrinsically a Fascist. Events have proved that, this once at least, prediction is possible for a sociologist of literature. To the surprise of most of our contemporaries, Hamsun turned out to be a close collaborator of the Nazis.

Here only a few rather disjointed examples of this type of analysis can be given. Of special interest seems to be Hamsun's treatment of nature. In the authoritarian state, the individual is taught to seek the meaning of his life in "natural" factors like race and soil. Over and over again he is told that he is nothing more than nature, specifically, than race and "natural" community. The pantheistic infatuation with nature which Hamsun demonstrates and accepts leads to this dictated identity between the individual and "natural" forces. The route is circuitous in appearance only.

The shift from the dream world of naturalness to the social reality of Fascism is inherent in the forms in which the uproar of the elements, brutal nature, is experienced. Hamsun writes (and the following is merely a sample repeated in endless variations):

> A wind comes up, and suddenly it rumbles far and wide. . . . Then lightning flashes, and . . . the thunder rolls like a dreadful avalanche far beyond, between the mountains. . . . Lightning again, and the thunder is closer at hand; it also begins to rain, a driving rain, the echo is very powerful, all nature is in an uproar. . . . More lightning, and thunder and more driving rain.[7]

Immanuel Kant had defined his conception of the sublimity of nature in a storm in such a way that man, in experiencing his own helplessness (as a being of nature) in the face of the superior might of natural phenomena, simultaneously experiences the inferiority of the latter in the face of his own humanity, which is greater than nature. Man can indeed succumb to nature, but that is only incidental and external to the power of his soul and mind.[8]

Kant's social consciousness bids nature be silent, as it were, about what it experiences from man and what it can do for man. But for Hamsun the storm can hardly shout loudly enough to drown out individual and social impotence. The storm is the occasion for experiencing and formulating the insignificance of the individual—the exact opposite of Kant's conception:

> When a moment of sadness and realization of my own worthlessness in the face of all the surrounding powers comes over me, I lament and think: Which man am I, or am I perhaps lost, am I perhaps no longer existent!

And I speak aloud and call my name, in order to hear whether he is still present.[9]

Anxiety appears to be a sort of secret emotion bound up with this late pantheism. Kant's pride in human autonomy has no place for the sentimental uneasiness which is announced in every fear of a thunderstorm and which appears in Hamsun as a promiscuous jumble of mawkish sympathies for both natural objects and spiritual difficulties.[10] Hamsun's storm world foreshadows the affinity between the elements of brutality and sentimentality, which are united in Fascist behavior.

The law of rhythm is of particular significance for Hamsun's concept of nature. The rhythmic cycle of the seasons is noted in the novels incessantly, as if in imitation of the phenomenon itself. "Then came the autumn, then came the winter."[11] ". . . but the road leads on, summer follows spring in the world."[12] In the end, the rhythmic principle takes on a normative character. What is wrong with certain people is that "they won't keep pace with life . . . but there's none should rage against life."[13] Even sexual relationships are oriented to the regularity of nature. The shepherdess will walk past the hunter's cabin in the autumn just as infallibly as she comes to him in the spring. "The autumn, the winter, had laid hold of her too; her senses drowsed."[14]

We have attained the extreme opposite of human self-consciousness before nature if man can and must never disturb the natural cycle at any point. In this new ideology, which seeks to transfigure helplessness and subjection, the individual lays down his arms before a higher power in seemingly free volition. Man must expect the terrors of a meaningless life unless he obediently accepts as his own what may be called the alien law of nature. The social solution to the puzzle of natural rhythm is blind discipline, the rhythm of marches and parades.

Concerning love and womanhood one might say of Hamsun's attitude that woman attains her proper character and happiness when she unites the home with the naturalness of true existence in her functions as housewife and mother. We find in Hamsun unmistakable traces of the tendency to reduce the role of woman to merely biological functions, the duty to bear many children. This trend is part of his ideal counterpart to liberal society—the Fascist reality. "A real girl will marry, shall become the wife of a man, shall become a mother, shall become fertility itself."[15] The apotheosis of biological functions inevitably leads to bitter hatred of all reforms, emancipation, or spirituality which woman might desire,[16] to contempt for "the modern woman." Real individual satisfaction seems possible only in the sexual sphere, but not because sensual pleasure has a specific connection with the development of the personality. It is rather hatred and malice, associated with great disdain for woman, which are operative in this relationship.

> "Come and show me where there's cloudberries," said Gustaf. . . . And how could a woman say no? . . . Who would not have done the same? Oh, woman cannot tell one man from another; not always—not often.[17]

Hamsun dresses the role of promiscuous sexuality in all kinds of natural myths. There is a complete lack of interest in one's partner's happiness. Sexual relations are ruled by complete passivity, a sort of service which man obeys:

> He broke through all rules of propriety and was very friendly, picked the hay from her bosom, brushed it from her knees, stroked, petted, threw his arms around her. Some call it free will.[18]

Even when man is occupied with love, Hamsun maliciously reminds him of his mere naturalness, a true disciple of Fascism's moral relativism.

When we turn to his treatment of marginal figures, we soon discover that, next to the peasant, Hamsun has particular sympathy for the vagabond. In the prehistory of Fascism in Germany, yeoman work was done by a conceited, individualistic group of uprooted literati who played with the cult of the hero. In the anticipation of Fascism which we find in Hamsun's novels, the vagabond is a forerunner of the brutal man who weeps over a dry twig and bares his fist to his wife. Flirtation with the anarchistic vagabond is a coquettish and spiritualized expression of the veneration of heroic forces. There is abundant evidence from every period of Hamsun's career, as in a late novel in which the vagabond August longs "to shoot the knife out of the hand of a man who was trying to make off with his wallet" because that would be a thrill for the "children of the age" in their dreary existence;[19] or in his prewar writings where he plays the same romantic game without introducing heroic crime,[20] and where he ridicules the notion of bourgeois efficiency as poverty-stricken ("no thunderbolt ever falls");[21] or even in his earliest work, where he cries for "gigantic demi-gods" and blunders into a political program for which the way has been cleared by this very heroic ideology: "The great terrorist is greatest, the dimension, the immense lever which can raise worlds."[22] It is but a short step from here to the glorification of the leader.

Finally a word about Hamsun's relationship to mankind as a whole. It is most ironic that the biological comparison with the anthill, so popular in liberal reformist literature as a symbol of higher social aims

and organization, is completely reversed by Hamsun and made into the
image of the planlessness of all human existence:

> Oh, that little anthill! All its inhabitants are occupied with their own affairs,
> they cross each other's paths, push each other aside, sometimes they trample
> each other under feet. It cannot be otherwise, sometimes they trample each
> other under feet.[23]

This picture of life and of man's aimless crawling closes the ring of
antiliberal ideology. We have returned to the starting point, the myth
of nature.

Social Determinants of Success

By and large the legitimate business which the sociologist of literature
may have in the field of communications research consists in formulating
hypotheses for research on "what reading does to people."[24] But he
cannot simply pass the buck to his colleague, the empirical researcher,
after having done his historical, biographical and analytical work. There
are certain factors of social relevance which, though very decisive for
the measurement of effects, will have to undergo sociological exploration
on the level of theory and documentary study.

There is, first of all, the problem of finding out what we know about
the influence of all-embracing social constellations on writing and the
reading public. Are times of war or peace, of economic boom or depression
more or less conducive to literary production? Are specific types of the
literary level, literary form, and subject matter more or less preponderant?
What about the outlets of distribution, the publishing house, the circulation
figures, the competition between books and magazines in these various
periods? What do we know about readership figures in public and
university libraries, in the army and the hospitals—again broken down
according to changing social conditions? What do we know, qualitatively
and quantitatively, about the ratio between literature distributed and
consumed and other media of mass communication, or even nonverbalized
forms of organized entertainment?[25]

A second auxiliary source lies in the area of social controls. What do
we know about the influence of formal controls of production and reading?
We must deal with the worldwide phenomenon of the use of tax money
for public libraries, with the European practice of governmental sub-
ventions for theaters, with the American experience of supporting creative
writers out of public funds during the New Deal administration, to cite
a few examples. We have to study the impact of selective and cherished
symbols of public rewards, from the Nobel Prize for literature to the

contests arranged by publishing houses, from the Pulitzer Prize to the honors bestowed by local or regional communities on successful authors whose cradles were fortunately situated in particular localities. We should study "manipulated controls": publishers' advertising campaigns, the expectations of profit tied up with book clubs and film production, the far-flung market of magazine serializations, the reprint houses and so on. We must not forget the area of censorship, of institutionalized restrictions from the index of the Catholic Church to local ordinances prohibiting the sale of certain books and periodicals. And, finally, we would have to analyze and systematize what we know about the impact of informal controls, of book reviews and broadcasts, of popular writeups of authors, of opinion leadership, of literary gossip and private conversations.

A third, and certainly not the least, social determinant of success is connected with technological change and its economic and social consequences.[26] The phenomenal development of the publishing business, putting out literary products on all levels in the low price field is surpassed only by the still more spectacular modes of production in other media of mass communication. Thus, it would be worth studying whether the financial returns received by writers in the last few decades can be attributed in large measure to improved technical facilities, including the author's working instruments, and whether this change in technique has changed the social status of writers as a group. Relatively little is known about the cumulative effects of technological improvements from one medium to the other. Do more people read more books because they see more pictures or listen to more broadcasts or is it the other way around? Or is there no such interdependence?[27] Is there a relationship between the high degree of accessibility of printed material and the methods by which educational institutions avail themselves of this material at all age levels?

As an illustration for social determinants of success the broad, diversified and articulated response in Germany to Dostoevski may be cited. An examination of available material in books, magazines and newspapers showed that certain psychological patterns in the German middle classes were apparently highly gratified in reading Dostoevski.[28] Unlike the study of Hamsun, here we are not concerned with the work of the writer, but with the social character of his reception.

The peculiar fate of the German middle classes, which had never experienced any sustained periods of liberal political and cultural life, kept them wavering between the mechanisms of identification with an aggressive, imperialistic, domineering set of ruling groups and a mechanism of defeatism and passivity, which, despite all the traditions of philosophical idealism, constantly induced them to attitudes of willing submission to what they sensed to be superior leadership. The ensuing sadomasochistic reactions found pliable material for acts of identification in the self-torturing and torturing protagonists of Dostoevski's novels.

The active life process of human society, all its progressive forces, indeed, the whole compass of the productive forces in general, hit a blind spot in the vision of these German masses. This is apparent, for example, in their failure to notice a gap in Dostoevski's themes, namely, earthly happiness. Happiness, measured socially, presupposes an active transformation of reality, that is to say, the removal of its gross contradictions. That would require not only a complete transformation of existing power relations but also a reconstruction of social consciousness. Really to direct one's impulses toward the realization of social happiness is to enter sometimes into direct opposition to the existing power apparatus. The insignificant role which the category of happiness played in the social consciousness of the German middle classes can be understood only from the totality of their social relationships. A satisfying social organization was closed to them as a declining class and, therefore, it must also be shut out from consciousness in its true meaning as happiness.

It might be argued against this conception, which uses Dostoevski as evidence of a nonactivist ideology devoid of moral deed and social solidarity, that one must not expect such an approach from him, the apostle of love and compassion for mankind. Nearly all the literary critiques of Dostoevski do, in fact, revolve around the theme of love and compassion, whether in elegant formulations, like the "surpassing calm, through which only a sort of deeply secret sorrow vibrates, an endless compassion . . ."[29] or in painfully popular statements, like his "heart trembles with sympathy, compassion."[30] A very naive passage will serve to indicate the social significance:

> His predilection for the oppressed and the depraved gradually assumes the morbid form of . . . "Russian compassion," that compassion which excludes all upright, honest working men, and extends only to prostitutes, murderers, drunkards, and similar blossoms on the tree of mankind.[31]

This statement may be crude, but it points to something very true. The reception of Dostoevski was not bothered by the fact that in his works love remains a weak disposition of the soul, which can be understood only by prersupposing a frantic defense against all social change and a fundamental passivity in the face of every truly moral act. The demand for love and compassion could mean a realization of the existence of social contradictions and the need for change; it could be the effective approach to the activity of men in their thoughts and actions. Instead, it remains a matter of mere sentiment, a permission, not a demand. That is perhaps the clearest sign of the ideological role of such a concept of love. Demand and the power to act cannot enter into the social consciousness of relatively impotent social strata any more than they can accept a principle of justice which must destroy their solidarity with the rulers and point to their common interests with the ruled.[32]

SOME CHALLENGING TASKS

If a sociologist of literature wants to hold his claim to be heard in the field of modern communications research, the least he can do is to discuss a program of research that can be located within the areas proper to his field and at the same time joins up with the scientific experiences already accumulated for the other mass media. Four possible fields of research paralleling the four areas of analysis will be outlined here.

Functional Content

Obvious as it may be, the point must be made that the basic requirement for finding out what kind of gratification people expect from mass literature in a given social framework, or better, at a specific historical moment, is to have exact knowledge of the content of these works. What we need are qualitative and quantitative inventories of the contents of popular works on a comparative scale, beginning not later than the early nineteenth century. Studies made so far are scanty,[33] though speculative ideas about the assumed content are overabundant.

Take the commonly accepted notion that the main function of mass literature is to provide an outlet for the escapist drives of frustrated people. How do we know that this was ever true or is still true today? Perhaps the functional content of the novel today is much less escapist than informative: literature has become a cheap and easily accessible tool for orientation in a bewildering outside and inside world. The reader is looking for prescriptions for inner manipulation, an abridged and understandable psychoanalytical cure, as it were, which will permit him by way of identification and imitation to grope his way out of his bewilderment. Escape involves an attitude of self-reliance and is much more likely to be found in times of individual stability than in our present period, characterized by ego-weakness needing alien crutches for survival. Whether this hypothesis is justified or not, it might fruitfully be pursued in studying the patterns of identification and imitation offered by mass literature. One might find that, in contrast to earlier literary products, the contemporary novel has a much higher density and velocity of action and an accelerating recession of reflection and description.

It would be interesting, for example, to compare the popular historical novel of today and a generation ago. We would perhaps discover that the older works tried to transmit a panorama-like picture of a period in which the reader could sit restfully next to the historical protagonist around whom the panorama developed. Today, however, this picture dissolves into a multitude of figures, situations, and actions which leave the reader without the enjoyment of sitting invisibly with one selected protagonist, who used to be the measure and yardstick for the literary materials that a writer conjured up. The pressure of modern life, which produces the very weak egos who are in turn exposed to the pressure, makes it necessary to forego identification with just one figure, or with the inner processes of the soul, or with theoretical ideas and values. Thus the classical situation of literary consumption, in which the reader shares the solitude of choice or fate with the solitude and uniqueness of the one and unrepeatable work of art, may be replaced by collective experience of well-organized activity in the direction of adaptation and the acquisition of the tricks of self-manipulation. More and more studies are making source materials available,[34] but their systematic sociological exploration remains to be done.

The Writer's Attitude

What the reader is looking for in literary communication is one thing; what the author delivers beyond the conscious awareness of the reader is something else again. The case of Knut Hamsun illustrates this kind of problem.

Wheher and to what extent opinions and attitudes are influenced by the literary avalanche depends not only on its manifest content but also on its latent implications. It is true, to lift them from their formulated content is a task to be undertaken with untried tools. Nevertheless, an extremely inexpensive social laboratory might be suggested where no living beings need be interviewed with all the paraphernalia of money-and-time-outlay. More or less consciously, usually less, the author is a manipulator who tries to get over certain messages that reflect his own personality and personality problems. To find out where he stands, it might be worth while reviving him and the figures of his imagination with artificial respiration and subjecting them to questions and psychological experiments on the most advanced level.

With the help of standardized ideological questionnaires, for example, we might scan through a well-chosen sample of mass literature and find out about the author's attitudes, about his points of view on human nature, on group tensions, on historical and natural catastrophes, on sex, on masses versus great individuals, and so forth. We might then, in scoring the answers, get a qualitative and quantitative yardstick with which to locate the social position of the writer and thus be able to make predictions about his behavior as a person and about the kind of production with which he will follow up work previously done. If we enlarge our sample sufficiently we might learn much about the self-identification of these agents of mass communication and of the potential influence of these hidden self-portraits on the readers.

Such a laboratory experiment could be implemented by analyzing the character structure of the protagonists in the fictional material. Recent work in social psychology has furnished us with a set of structure syndromes to be gathered from responses to ideological and projective interview procedures, by which we can diagnose with a high degree of reliability whether a person is authoritarian or anti-authoritarian in type. These findings have an obvious bearing on prognostications of political, moral and emotional behavior. Surface descriptions are very often misleading and can be corrected by these new methods.[35]

Cultural Heritage

In studying the direct and indirect social content of popular literature the marginal media deserve far more attention than they have received so far, particularly the comics[36] and perhaps some other products the enjoyment of which is shared by adults and juveniles alike. A thorough-going content analysis of these materials should result in a number of valuable hypotheses on the continuing significance of ideas, values and emotions stemming from situations that have become completely obsolete.

It would be necessary to study not only the obviously archaic and infantile motives of the fairy world of subhuman and superhuman serials, but also those materials in which, under the guise of everyday misery or everyday enjoyment, values become visible which were associated with earlier stages of modern society, and especially with the more serene style of life in the nineteenth century. Measuring such material against the ideological and emotional content of traditional and respectable fiction, we might gain added insight into the wavering of modern readers between the necessity of learning the mechanisms of adaptation and conformity and the daydreams of a happier, though unattainable or historically impossible, way of life. Taking "adult" and "preadult" contents together we might be able to develop hypotheses that would open up systematic exploration of likes and dislikes on levels of awareness, as well as of deeper psychological levels.

The Role of Social Environment

In the area description three aspects of social determinants of success were noted, two of which should be referred to here in order to clarify the type of research envisaged.

There is first of all the problem whether different stages of the economic and political cycle leave distinguishing marks on literary products. The research task would involve a modification of the studies in functional content mapped out earlier in this section. An inventory should be taken of a literary sample in times of depression and boom, of war and peace. This inventory would not be limited to an enumeration of fictional topics, but would be particularly concerned with emotional patterns which may safely be assumed to be closely tied up with the specific gratifications and frustrations of the readers. As a very tentative example, the hypothesis is ventured that the use of happy or not so happy endings is a point of difference. At the height of an economic depression, escapist identifications with lovely daydreams of unchallenged happiness may characterize the literary scenery. Today, however, a pseudotragic ending on a note of unsolved problems is by no means rare because the relative prosperity permits fictional experiences with a higher degree of reality and even some insight into our psychological and cultural shortcomings.

Many other situations may have to be selected before one can construct an index of content and motive preference for various overall situations. A study comparing the two postwar booms and the two prewar depressions of the last thirty-five years might actually lead to a point from which future predictions of preferences in fiction would be possible. Educational and professional inferences which could then be drawn are so obvious that they need not be gone into here.

In the field of technological determinants it would be worth studying the reading ability of the average man and the way it has been modified by his experiences with auditory and visual media. We know a lot about clinical reading disabilities but we know relatively little about intellectual selectivity in reading.[37] Similarly it would be interesting to study what is read and remembered and what is more or less slurred over or not read at all. A more precise knowledge about "content-reading" abilities and disabilities could become a labor-saving device for writers; as for sociologists they would gain corroborating evidence to the findings of functional content analysis.

Blueprinting research tasks has all the shortcomings of any set of unfulfilled promises. The expert in communications research might, however, become interested in the troublesome achievements and tasks of a neighboring branch of study and its potential contribution to his own field.

I should like to conclude with a personal experience. A sociologist treating literature in the classroom is bound to encounter a divided reaction: Students will display an eager interest in a new scientific experience, but, as instruction goes on, some of them will protest against the analytical "dismembering" of poetic material. The students are eager for guidance in an uncharted sea since they never have been quite able to find out what is good and what is not so good. Somehow they look forward to getting possession of a foolproof formula that will set them straight once and for all regarding this vague and vast field situated somewhere between education and mere entertainment. What the students do not know is that their initial approach is already a manifestation of the particular stage at which sociological interpretation of literature still finds itself.

NOTES

1. Characteristically enough, the one existing bibliography in the field of the sociology of literature that aims at a comprehensive survey is available only in mimeographed form: "Annotated Bibliography on the Sociology of Literature, with an Introductory Essay on Methodological Problems in the Field," by Hugh Dalziel Duncan (The University of Chicago Press, 1947).
2. The most suggestive study of this aspect is unfortunately inaccessible in English: Georg Lukács, *Die Theorie des Romans* (Berlin, 1920). Thematically the problem has also been posed by Kenneth Burke, *The Philosophy of Literary Form* (Louisiana State University Press, 1941).
3. See Chapter 6 in this volume ("The Triumph of Mass Idols").
4. Valuable suggestions for the study of the objective aspects of this area may be found in Albert Guérard, *Literature and Society* (Boston, 1935).
5. I should say that the work of Eric Bentley, *The Playwright as Thinker* (New York: Reynal & Hitchcock, 1946), is a highly successful attempt to translate private into social scenes and then to interpret them in sociologically meaningful terms.
6. See Leo Lowenthal, "Knut Hamsun: Zur Vorgeschichte der autoritären Ideologie," *Zeitschrift für Sozialforschung*, vol. VI, no. 2 (1937).
7. *The Last Joy* (German edition), p. 310.
8. See Kant, *Critique of Aesthetic Judgment*, trans. J. C. Meredith (Oxford, 1911), pp. 110-11.
9. *The Last Joy*, p. 311.
10. See, for example, *Pan*, trans. W. W. Worster (New York, 1921), pp. 23-24: "I pick up a little dry twig and hold it in my hand and sit looking at it, and think my own thoughts; the twig is almost rotten, its poor back touches me, pity fills my heart. And when I get up again, I do not throw the twig far away, but lay it down, and stand liking it; at last, I look at it once more with wet eyes before I go away and leave it there."

11. *The Road Leads On,* trans. Eugene Gay-Tifft (New York, 1934), p. 46.
12. *The Ring is Closed,* trans. Eugene Gay-Tifft (New York, 1937), p. 152.
13. *Growth of the Soil,* trans. W. W. Worster (New York, 1921), vol. II, p. 246; cf. *Rosa,* trans. A. G. Chater (New York, 1926), p. 18: " 'What are you sitting here for?' 'Ah, young man!' he said, holding up the palm of his hand. 'What am I sitting here for? I sit here keeping pace with my existence. Ay, that's what I'm doing.' "
14. *Pan,* p. 164.
15. *The Last Joy,* p. 344.
16. Cf. *Chapter the Last,* trans. A. G. Chater (New York, 1929), pp. 105-7.
17. *Growth of the Soil,* vol. II, p. 92.
18. *Chapter the Last,* p. 102.
19. *The Road Leads On,* p. 409.
20. See *The Last Joy,* p. 298.
21. *Children of the Age,* trans. J. S. Scott (New York, 1924), p. 82.
22. *Mysteries,* trans. A. G. Chater (New York, 1927), p. 51.
23. *The Women at the Pump,* trans. A. G. Chater (New York, 1928), p. 5.
24. See the spadework study under that title by Douglas Waples, Bernard Berelson, and Franklyn R. Bradshaw (University of Chicago Press, 1940).
25. See Paul F. Lazarsfeld, *Radio and the Printed Page* (New York: Duell, Sloan & Pearce, 1940).
26. Theoretical groundwork for the study of modern technological change and its social consequences in the artistic field has been laid in the article by Max Horkheimer, "Art and Mass Culture," *Studies in Philosophy and Social Science,* vol. IX (1941), to whom the author is indebted in many ways for his thinking in the sociology of literature.
27. The impact of technological change on production and reproduction in the sphere of visible and audible artistic production has been exposed in a masterly fashion by T. W. Adorno in the field of music and by Walter Benjamin in the field of motion pictures. See, e.g., the former's article "On Popular Music," *Studies in Philosophy and Social Science,* vol. IX, no. 1 (1941), and the latter's "L'oeuvre d'art a l'epoque de sa reproduction mé- canisée," *Zeitschrift für Sozialforschung,* vol. V, no. 1 (1936). Valuable information on the interchange between films and literary production may be found in S. Kracauer, *From Caligari to Hitler: A Psychological History of the German Film* (Princeton University Press, 1947).
28. See Leo Lowenthal, "Die Auffasung Dostojewskis im Vorkriegsdeutschland," *Zeitschrift für Sozialforschung,* vol. III, no. 3 (1934). Reprinted as Chapter 4 in this volume.
29. Hermann Conradi, "Dostojewski," in *Die Gesellschaft,* vol. 6 (1889), p. 528.
30. L. Brehm, "Dostojewskis 'Dämonen'," in *Der Deutsche,* vol. 5 (1906), p. 346.
31. C. Busse, *Geschichte der Weltliteratur* (Bielefeld and Leipzig, 1913), vol. II, p. 595.
32. Books and articles on Dostoevski which have appeared in this country since the end of the war offer a good opportunity for comparison with European experiences. My impression is that several of these publications show an atmosphere of malaise and frustration which, for the sociologist, reveals trends of spiritual needs and confusion not unrelated to the European experience with Dostoevski a generation ago.

33. I am indebted to Ralph H. Ojemann of the State University of Iowa for bringing to my attention the excellent master thesis, written under his supervision, by Evelyn Peters: "A Study of the Types of Behavior toward Children Approved in Fiction Materials," 1946.
34. See, e.g., Frank Luther Mott, *Golden Multitudes* (New York: Macmillan, 1947); Alice Payne Hackett, *Fifty Years of Best Sellers* (New York: Bowker, 1945); Edward H. O'Neill, *The History of American Biography* (University of Pennsylvania Press, 1935), and so on.
35. These studies were published jointly in 1949 by the Berkeley Opinion Study Group and the Institute of Social Research, under the title *The Authoritarian Personality* (T. W. Adorno, Else Brunswick, Daniel Levinson and R. N. Sanford, authors).
36. See, however, the book by Coulton Waugh, *The Comics* (New York: Macmillan, 1947).
37. See Rudolf Flesch, *The Art of Plain Talk* (New York: Harper and Brothers, 1946).

Chapter 9
HUMANISTIC PERSPECTIVES
OF DAVID RIESMAN'S
THE LONELY CROWD

I

Titles as well as books have a significance that it behooves the critic to trace and interpret. What specific connotations the authors of *The Lonely Crowd* had in mind in electing for the title of their book a poetic image I do not know. But it is a rare social scientist indeed who has the courage to choose that conspicuous symbol of his contributions, a book title, from the humanities and, as if that were not daring enough, from poetry itself. In so doing, the authors of *The Lonely Crowd* have identified themselves with that small minority that cannot understand how social science, as a science of man, can be anything else but a profoundly humanistic endeavor.

While the relationship of the humanities and the social sciences is a problem extending beyond the work under discussion, it is nevertheless a significant document in the struggle to break through the narrow definitions of academic disciplines. It seems appropriate, therefore, to use *The Lonely Crowd* as a welcome opportunity for offering some observations about this relationship.

The discussion of the ordering of fields of knowledge can be traced back to Plato, who was concerned primarily with educational implications. Aristotle's concepts of "physics" and "metaphysics" guided the discussion into the theoretical sphere. During the Middle Ages the controversy over what comprised the scope and responsibilities of scientific specialties was blurred for a time by the use of a blanket term, "the seven liberal arts." But the development of mathematics and theoretical physics during the sixteenth and seventeenth centuries brought the boundary line issue surging back to life. With Descartes, reality was split into two distinct spheres, one subjected to insights of mathematics and the natural sciences and the other to those of philosophy—or, to use Descartes's terms, into extension and cogitation. This trend was apparent even in political theory, where thinkers were oriented toward one or another side of Descartes's dualism: toward the natural sciences (e.g., Hobbes) or toward applied moral philosophy (e.g., the French moralists of the seventeenth and early eighteenth centuries). The Cartesian demarcations of the sciences still remain discernible in the traditional division of higher learning in France into "sciences" and "letters."

Around the turn of the nineteenth century German philosophers and writers systematized the concept of political and intellectual history as a science. Concurrently, the concepts of culture and cultures, of *Zeitgeist* and *Volksgeist* (already introduced by Montesquieu and Herder), were further developed and the relationship among the sciences was reformulated: the pole occupied by mathematics and the natural sciences remained unchanged, but the substance of philosophy proper acquired a predominantly historical character in place of its erstwhile metaphysical aspect.

Dilthey, Windelband, and Rickert, the founders of *Geistes-* and *Kulturwissenschaften,* were the outstanding proponents of this redefinition. Though differing in minor respects, they agreed in principle: the natural sciences deal with the recurrent and are oriented toward the establishment of universally valid laws; the humanistic fields are concerned with individual events and persons, and are characterized by a view of the individual as the representative of prevailing value systems, changing from period to period, and, within an era, from one group to another. Simmel's concept of the "individual law" (an intentionally contradictory proposition), and Max Weber's dual role as sociologist and historian, are prime witnesses of this tradition.

The situation today is dominated by the intellectual innovations contributed by the American social (or behavioral) sciences. New disciplines are interposed between the humanities and the natural sciences, and, unlike the earlier phases of the discussion, few classification schemes have yet been proposed for defining and clarifying the interrelationships between the new and the old fields. That the need for redefinition of the scientific universe is strongly felt, however, is evidenced by numerous programmatic statements about the desirability of "cross-fertilization" of the sciences, and expressions (ritualized at times) of the need for interdisciplinary research.

Thus, we are entering an era of clarification of the relation between the scientific and the intellectual universe, though this trend has never been made an object of historical and systematic studies. The symptoms are unmistakable. Whether we think of the intertwining of medicine or religion with social and individual psychology, of aesthetic theory with sociology, of social research with anthropology, or whether we think of some of the learned institutions of technology introducing humanistic as well as social science courses in their curriculums, all this seems to indicate that we are experiencing again the old craving for a new concept of a *scientia universalis*.

It is characteristic of contemporary democratic society that these comparatively new intellectual programs and their applications are not justified by philosophical concepts, but by concepts of applicability—serving social as well as individual needs. This article of faith of the social scientist is consciously shared, in the United States, with practitioners in political and social institutions—witness, for example, the incorporation of psychology into the curriculum of clergymen, relationships between medicine and the theory and practice of social work, and the role of political science and economics in applied anthropology.

The heat of the discussion seems now to be generated not by the problem of the relationship between natural and "nonnatural" sciences, but by that between the social and behavioral sciences and the humanities. The natural sciences, ever since the seventeenth century, have searched for laws of the physical world sufficiently valid to allow for prediction; the behavioral sciences of today substitute a human for a natural realm, but keep constant the search for laws and reliable norms for prediction.

This has led to serious intellectual cleavages both here and abroad. With the exception of a few hesitant attempts to import the methodology and skill of American research into western and central Europe, European sociologists still move in the atmosphere of Dilthey and Rickert. By their concentration on problems that we usually subsume under the rubric "sociology of knowledge," they perpetuate the preoccupation with the history of ideas and the speculations about the hierarchy of values. Some European sociologists may believe that, in their historic orientation, they have made the "right" choice in accepting for their field Bergson's historical time, while in their opinion the majority of their American colleagues are dangerously close to applying physical time concepts. And they have a point.[1]

On this side of the Atlantic it is among the representatives of humanistic disciplines that we are likely to find concepts about modern social science resembling those prevailing in traditional European sociology. Their views on current social science, at the extreme, would probably be couched in terms of statistical gadgeteering and polling which ties up millions of dollars for research, which is lacking in historical and spiritual concepts, and which is void of any universal intellectual interest.[2] It is likely that many social scientists, for their part, reciprocate with the disdainful belief that all humanists do is to propound unverifiable generalizations on the basis of spurious evidence.

The current definitions of the two disciplines that seem to have the most bearing on the interrelationship are: (1) that the social sciences should strive for theorems as exact as those of mathematical and physical theory and for the formulation of findings in terms of predictions; and (2) that the humanities should work for meaningful analyses of important individualities, be they events, documents, or persons. But the boundaries are this clear-cut only on the most superficial level. Consider, for example, the disparate functions that such authors as Balzac, Taine, and Zola ascribed to literature—that it should comprise natural history, quasi-biological analyses, and universally valid prescriptions for the behavior of the human race. Or Wilhelm Dilthey's hopes that the final objective of the "cultural sciences" (*Geisteswissenschaften*), devoted to the hermeneutics of the individual, should be the planning and directing of social development. And one must not overlook the body of writing, centered around the idea of a cultural crisis, that followed in the wake of the French Revolution, represented by so varied a group as De Maistre, Carlyle, Nietzsche, and—in our time—Spengler, whose forays into the field of predictions should make many a social scientist envious. Such literary and philosophical approaches testify to a long tradition behind the notion that the humanist and social scientist must not necessarily be strangers to each other.

Or consider the problem of the socialization of the individual, in which the humanistic biographical arts excel and the social sciences do not. Freud is an exception. Psychoanalytical theory, at least in its classical period, describes the dynamics by which a specific social environment asserts itself in individuals. It is true that from a sociological point of view this model operates on rather limited extremes of the social continuum—at one pole an individual's family and at the other the archaic prehistorical stage of mankind. Nevertheless, the Oedipus complex is a good sociological model because it explains specific mechanisms by which an individual is related to social structures. Better, it serves to explain how the psychological structure of an individual manifests itself as, in part, a derivative of societal structures with which he interacts on various levels of consciousness. This psychoanalytical model illustrates by contrast the social scientist's shortcomings because (in spite of Freud's "naturalism") it synthesizes broad historical trends, in which the history of the species as a whole is a necessary but not a sufficient referent for the understanding of the unique moment of time represented by a specific individual. In this sense Freud's theory deals with more than psychology— it deals with culture, as did Dilthey. A concern with the historical dimension of societal structures, including a concern with the representation of these structures in individuals, constitutes a sociology of culture.

II

Riesman and his associates are American sociologists who deal in earnestness with problems of culture. Their work also joins with other contemporary studies on the effect of the development of mass or popular culture, and the impact of popular culture on the general cultural level of society. These two trends reverse the previous pattern, dominant in the social sciences in the late thirties and forties, of a preeminent concern with methodology and with the construction of theoretical models. The claim of positivistically oriented empiricists is that their endeavors, for which they coined the term of "hard" analysis, alone deserve to be called scientific. They leave no more than a condescending smile (if that) for the social theorist whose orientation is humanistic.

The Lonely Crowd offers a remarkable occasion to reopen the debate on the humanistic implications of social theory. The shift in emphasis that it represents looks back toward Plato and Aristotle; that is, toward an analysis of the individual in his society. *The Lonely Crowd* differs sharply from a-historical sociological studies, and its intellectual style brings it close to the European, particularly the German, "cultural sciences" in theoretical as well as empirical orientation. Unfortunately, the thinker to whom the methodology of the book is most closely related is fairly unknown in this country, and the translation of his principal works is still an unfulfilled task. This man, whose life work was dedicated to a synthesis of history and psychology, and to a scheme of interpretation in which individual human experience was to be correlated, in terms of psychological typologies, to historical epochs, was Wilhelm Dilthey. In his conception, the net woven of individual expression, cultural institutions, and political and religious modes was a manifestation of unique historical periods. Through this interpenetration of spatial and temporal constituents of the social universe Dilthey (and not he alone) countered the positivistic infatuation with general laws based on endless observations on the one side, and a mystic historicism (which has triggered the positivistic plague) void of any general concepts on the other.[3] This European tradition (with Dilthey as its most brilliant exponent) has continued, to some extent, in cultural anthropology, which undertakes to blend a study of cultures and their artifacts with a study of personality within a given social context. Indeed, *The Lonely Crowd* studies the universal trends of the age of industrialization by searching out the meaning of human behavior and character within this society, and in the last analysis it is a study of mass society (although the term itself is hardly used in the book) as the latest stage in the development of the industrial world.

Riesman and his coauthors face the same frustrations and perplexities that were encountered by the leading representatives of the "cultural sciences"—the difficulty of interpreting within one conceptual framework the uniqueness of an historical period and the general features of human behavior prevailing in it—features which, if they change at all, change at an infinitely slower pace than the events in the polity and many institutions of society. But this dilemma has to be faced if one wants to understand *uno actu* individuals both in their social roles and in their personal imagery. Today, the main feature of this nexus is the antagonistic display of individualistic estrangement and group identification.

The Lonely Crowd is a major contribution to the understanding of alienation and conformism. The generally observable features of only incidental relatedness of modern man to his work and his simultaneous eagerness to hide this estrangement behind a continual display of peer-oriented, optimistically toned behavior are explained by the objective roles that modern industrial society prescribes for its members. The problem posed by this book is: what is the impact of this society on the social and private experiences of individuals? While I referred to Dilthey, it is quite evident that the study of modern man as he becomes conditioned by industrial society has also a very specific sociological ancestry in Marx and Max Weber, in Veblen and Sombart, and above all in Simmel.

True, this body of theories had produced many vague symbolic references; and it is an easy, though I believe unworthy, pastime to dismiss European, and particularly German, philosophy of history and society during the nineteenth century as just so many manifestations of metaphysical double-talk. It is too readily forgotten that, during this century, history as a scene of social struggles and society as a product of historical trends and pressures became, for the first time, manageable scholarly concepts. However, we have learned in the meantime (and this is a great contribution of sociological theory in the first decades of the twentieth century) slowly to replace ambiguous theoretical and analytical notions with specific scientific approaches; and *The Lonely Crowd* participates in this process of scholarly specification, in which we are no longer satisfied to discuss the "spirit" of an epoch without at the same time specifying such components as consumption habit, education, group life, political behavior, and the like.[4] Indeed, *The Longely Crowd* adds new dimensions to the process of specification in its elaborate and enlightening references to specific contemporary institutions, such as the mass media, the political broker, the inside dopester, the nursery school, and so on.

The great question that always arises in connection with social theory is the scope of its applicability. *The Lonely Crowd* takes its material primarily from the American scene. To be sure, this approach is a bit on the parochial side. Granted that the United States today occupies the place of a model of Western society, as England did at the time of Marx. But we may be more general. If certain character types are determined by industrial society, then any such relationship must extend to this society as a whole and not only to one country. This is not to say that all the member cultures of our era display the same features, traits, and institutions at one and the same time with the same amount of intensity; but it does mean that related, if not identical, social characteristics must be found in some form or fashion at some time everywhere within the Western world. In addition, Riesman and his collaborators are subjected to a dilemma always encountered in theoretical constructs of the "cultural sciences." Such constructs tend to be static rather than evolutionary, and to focus the trends of an age as in a still picture. (This is, for instance, the case in various interpretations by other writers of seemingly monolithic, "timeless" periods, such as *the* Renaissance or *the* Greek World.) The static implications of *The Lonely Crowd*, however, are not so much apparent in a predilection for collapsing historical dynamic into an idealized portrait of a timeless age, as in a collapsing of worldwide trends into an insular portrait. True, this method has its rewards, because it allows for a minute elaboration of one clearly circumscribed area. In its concentration on the specific, the analytic methods of the book are close to those of Simmel.[5]

I do not wish to be censorious. On the contrary, a good case can be made (and I think this book implicitly makes it) for saying that while we deal here with phenomena that are not limited to a single country, nevertheless the peculiar situation of the United States, which in contrast to Europe did not have to assume the mortgages of various value systems inherited from feudal and absolutistic periods, allowed this country to adopt the style of life of a commercial society more quickly and with less friction than on the Old Continent—a phenomenon, by the way, which made many European observers both jealous and furious. I agree with the interpretation of Tocqueville by the authors of *The Lonely Crowd;* in stressing traits of conformity, he was not merely diagnosing the prevailing social climate of America in the 1830s but foreseeing certain developmental features that seemed to fit into a coherent picture of Western civilization as it was and as it was to become. As did every constructive theorist of human events, Tocqueville could perceive the almost imperceptible in human behavior. I think that there is a very high affinity between the mentality of a social theorist who is willing to take intellectual risks, and aesthetic creativity, the essence of which is the creation of something unique as a symbol of something general if not universal. It is hard to say whether we owe more to Tocqueville for diagnosis or for prognosis; for an understanding of the United States as a special historical phenomenon or as a breeding ground for special character types; for being a humanist who analyzes culture or a social scientist who analyzes people in the context of their social roles. I do not consider such questions very relevant, though in themselves they are a symptom of the larger process of alienation, since for most social scientists the study of the meaning of human existence, in general or at a given moment of time, has tended to become discredited as being meaningless, as has a critical evaluation of the relation of the individual to himself and his world of work and leisure.

III

The basic dichotomy of the autonomous personality and of other-directness, which, at least for a philosophy of contemporary society, is perhaps the most relevant concept in Riesman's work, has a venerable intellectual tradition, dating back to the Romantic period in England and Germany. It assumed the form of a concern over the threat posed by the emerging instrumentalities of conformist middle-class styles of life, including the products of popular culture, to the autonomous spirit and creative personality. Artists and writers feared that the public would lose its ability to discriminate between valuable cultural creations and mere merchandise designed to induce relaxation. Such concerns found expression in the public and private statements of Goethe and Schiller in Germany, and of Wordsworth and Coleridge as well. Other and more enterprising English literati, though politically opposed to the Tory spirit of the Lake Poets, expressed the same fears, mainly through the medium of the *Edinburgh Review.* What these artists and writers shared was the awareness of a threat to the artist as he embarked on an aesthetic and moral mission, subjected to no jurisdiction other than that of excellence.

The intellectual (most of all the artist) has been exposed to very significant cross-pressures ever since his separate status was established. At the turn of the eighteenth century philosophers and poets alike ascribed to themselves the mission of guardianship over the moral and aesthetic values of the nation, if not the human community as such. At the same time they, as well as other groups of intellectuals, gained increasing access into professional positions in the institutions of learning, in governmental agencies, and above all became producers for a market mediated by periodicals, publishing houses, public and private art galleries, and the like. Finally, in our own day, the stress is on an almost complete professionalization for intellectual skills. This development is characterized by the desire to reconcile the ethos of individual independence and integrity with the inexorable social power of a demand and supply economy. One of the consequences of the ambiguity in the social role of the intellectual has been the increasing tendency to claim the prerogative of an exempt situation and philosophy of life and to deny that the determinants of social stratification are equally applicable to the practitioners of intellectual pursuits. Karl Mannheim's concept of the free-floating intelligentsia is a case in point. The infatuation of a great number of intellectuals, from the Romantics to the present-day advocates of the New Conservatism, with the allegedly autonomous status of culture in feudal and aristocratic societies may be attributed to a tendency of intellectuals to locate themselves in some idealized utopia of the past;[6] intellectuals (like everybody else) are, in fact, located in the harsh realities of a social system whose prevailing character types are eloquently described in *The Lonely Crowd*. The debates on culture and taste, on public opinion and urbanization, that pervaded the writings of the literati, at least in western Europe, all through the nineteenth century comprise a telltale document for the dilemma of the intellectual. In this debate the artist, and particularly the critic, plays a key role. Once again I wish to point out the significance of the fact that, of all the possible symbols of reference, Riesman and his collaborators choose as their title emblem an artistic image. If there is any single phenomenon that most pointedly attests to what is called other-directedness, it is alienation from artistic experiences.[7]

I agree with most of S. M. Lipset's chapter in *Culture and Social Character*,[8] which traces trends of other-directedness back to American public and private behavior patterns in the nineteenth century, but I do not believe that these trends are exclusively and predominantly a phenomenon specific to the United States. What we are dealing with all through the nineteenth century and all over the Western world are the birth throes of the prevailing character types of our contemporary society, or better, the antagonisms and struggles between traditional, self-reliant human models on the one hand and group orientedness on the other. This is as true for Europe as it is for the United States. With reference to Mr. Lipset's observations, I would submit as a hunch that his quotations from European sources, testifying to observed features of other-directedness in America, could easily be counterbalanced by any number of American writers (I will just name Ralph Waldo Emerson and the whole school of New England Transcendentalism) who testify to the task of displaying independence and individualism as the foremost moral obligation of the citizens of the New World. More than that, the very same trends (whether formulated in terms of accusation or admiration) ascribed to America by European authors are continuously and consistently attributed by other European intellectuals to the behavior and attitudes of people in their own countries. From the point of view of historical psychology, I would assume that a good deal of the very interesting material for which we are indebted to Mr. Lipset must be interpreted as merely projective: observers are not free of the distortion of culturally determined perception, which makes them see elsewhere the very features of modernity to which they close their eyes in their own countries.

I take the liberty of inserting here an anecdote. In lecturing on the nature of the stereotype, I have frequently quoted the following excerpt from a letter of Abigail Adams, the wife of the second president of the United States; she wrote during a European journey on November 21, 1786:

> The accounts you gave me of the singing of your birds and the prattle of your children entertained me much. Do you know that European birds have not half the melody of ours? Nor is their fruit half so sweet, nor their flowers half so fragrant, nor their manners half so pure nor their people half so virtuous; but keep this to yourself, or I shall be thought more than half deficient in understanding and taste. . . . Far removed from my mind may the national prejudice be, of conceiving all that is good and excellent comprised within the narrow compass of the United States.[9]

Only that on first reading I falsify the source by claiming that the letter was written by a recent European newcomer to the United States, and I reverse the references to Europe and America. Invariably I encounter an indignant reaction among the native-born part of the audience and a snickering of agreement on the part of European-born people. This experiment has always struck me as a particularly suitable illustration for the mechanism of cultural projection.

This mechanism deserves attention. At least in a germinal form, nineteenth century writers understood it quite well. To give an example: one of the favorite pastimes of literary criticism in English nineteenth century journals was to develop a kind of proto-sociological chapter on personality and social structure. A journal such as the *Edinburgh Review* would abound in essays explaining what appears to the writers to be the most important trait in, for example, Goethe or Balzac as conditioned by the German or French "national character"—a term one finds in this periodical, with capitalized letters, as early as 1825. One contribution tries in all earnestness to explain *Wilhelm Meister* as primarily a typical manifestation of German taste and German habits. Yet while the author of this article goes to great length not only to analyze Goethe's novel as a product "made in Germany" but also his German critics as ruled by a spirit of "German idolatry," he admits (and thereby almost destroys his thesis) that

> different nations . . . will judge of their own productions and those of their neighbours, according to that standard of taste which belongs to the place they then hold in this great circle;—and that a whole people will look on their neighbours with wonder and scorn, for admiring what their own grandfathers looked on with equal admiration,—while they themselves are scorned and vilified in return, for tastes which will infallibly be adopted by the grandchildren of those who despise them.[10]

Incidentally, all through the century there is unanimity in looking at the newspapers as the most powerful equalizer of opinions and attitudes. While occasionally a timid attempt is made to burden America with the stigma of their "most pernicious influence," the main line remains that "the condition of our own Daily Press" is a "morning and evening witness against the moral character of the people."[11] To be sure, these very traits in Europe are overlaid by cultural tradition. Yet, modernity wins out. Incidentally, the historians of European culture and mores have neglected to comment on these new commonly shared quasi-cultural phenomena of the Western world. Why this is so is in itself a sociologically pertinent problem. Perhaps the mechanisms of self-defense are as operative in the intellectual as a professional as they are in his (as well as in anybody else's) private life.

For the spread of other-directedness in the old country, Wordsworth is a primary source in time and scope. In his preface to the 1800 edition of the *Lyrical Ballads,* and again in his "Essay Supplementary to the Preface" (1815), he speaks of the jeopardy in which the artist finds himself as he tries to ward off the effects of the mediocre bourgeois style of life. He looked upon his own work as "a feeble endeavor" to counteract a "tendency of life and manners" that is about "to blunt the discriminating of the mind and . . . to reduce it to a state of almost savage torpor." He regrets "the increasing accumulation of men in cities, where the uniformity of their occupation produces a craving for extraordinary incident, which the rapid communication of intelligence hourly gratifies." In drawing a fine line between the "people" and the "public" he defines the prevailing type of individuals as those who follow "a small though loud portion of the community" which manipulates "the changing humour of the majority."

This influence of opinion leaders, which subverts the spontaneity of individual judgment, becomes a leitmotif from now on. One finds classical formulations in the writings of John Stuart Mill, particularly in his critique of the "despotism of public opinion"[12] and of "society" at large, which

> practices a social tyranny more formidable than many kinds of political oppression, since, though not usually upheld by such extreme penalties, it leaves fewer means of escape . . . there needs protection also against the tyranny of the prevailing opinion and feeling; against the tendency of society to impose, by other means than civil penalties, its own ideas and practices as rules of conduct on those who dissent from them; to fetter the development, and, if possible, prevent the formation of any individuality not in harmony with its ways, and compel all characters to fashion themselves upon the model of its own.[13]

The reader will appreciate the similarity between Mill's characterization of the English social climate and Tocqueville's famous words about the cruel tyranny of public opinion in the United States. The very same Tocqueville and many of the writers treated in Lipset's article are quite ready to criticize the disfavor with which independent thought was regarded in America. But we should be cautioned against prematurely limiting generalizations to the United States. As early as 1811, a contributor to the *Edinburgh Review* bitterly complains that "the profounder and more abstract truths of philosophy . . . are apt . . . to fall into discredit or neglect, at a period when it is labour enough for most men to keep themselves up to the level of that great tide of popular information, which has been rising, with such unexampled rapidity, for the last forty years." The writer stresses the inclination of the contemporary reading public to forego "the pursuit of any abstract or continued study," which is now replaced by "the dissipation of time and of attention" where "various and superficial knowledge is now not only so common that the want of it is felt as a disgrace" but where it helps the average person to participate in "much amusing and provoking talk in every party."[14]

Such complaints about the atrophy of serious intellectual application find their most articulate expression in an article published in 1849; and I do not know of any more eloquent formulation of the entrance of the other-directed character into the modern world than these sentences, which, moreover, indict the gadget-minded style of life in an industrial civilization:

> The aids and appliances which are now multiplied . . . enfeeble them [modern society]. . . . The division of labour has forestalled the necessity

of intellectual self-reliance, and of that large yet minute development of faculties which was produced when, for the work of one man, the most opposite qualities were required. Industrialism, likewise—while the prosperity which is its just reward too often betrays it into selfishness,—is a sedative to the passions. A certain social uniformity ensues, exercising a retarding force like the resistance of the air or the attrition of matter, and insensibly destroying men's humours, idiosyncrasies, and spontaneous emotions. It does so, by rendering their concealment an habitual necessity, and by allowing them neither food nor sphere. Men are thus, as it were, cast in a mold. Besides—the innumerable influences, intellectual and moral, which, at a period of diffused knowledge like the present, co-exist and cooperate in building up our mental structure, are often completely at variance with each other in origin and tendency: so that they neutralize each other's effects, and leave a man well-stored with thoughts and speech, but frequently without aim or purpose.

In other words, the British national character has changed from "individual robustness," from "intellectual greatness," to one of complete conformity, wiping out the nuances of individuality. The writer of this article continues his argument in stating that the "tameness" of modern character is rooted in "subserviency to Opinion—that irresponsible life which makes little things great, and shuts great things out from our view." And he concludes by stating that the breakdown of individuality also ruins the great educational mission of art: "Art becomes decorative merely; and the poetic delineation of man, in losing its sublime nakedness, retains but a feeble hold of the true and the real."[15]

This statement is quoted here at some length because it leads us back to the most important theoretical aspects of *The Lonely Crowd,* pointed out earlier, namely, the correlation of specific psychological types of behavior with specific social institutions. One irritating mannerism of criticism a historical sociologist easily encounters is the facile comment that, after all, this or that construct of social correlates is nothing new, because it can also be observed in this or that period. The decisive question, however, lies always in the specificity of a social context in a given historical period. Trend analysis in historical sociology must learn from the historian to remain close and faithful to the singularity and uniqueness of data that accrue to a body of knowledge about a definite time span. Applying this observation to *The Lonely Crowd,* it is of course quite easy to point in a loose way to an endless number of historical phenomena that may easily be interpreted with the help of some of the basic categories of this book. People always have paid attention to what neighbors say or might think and have adjusted appearances and mores accordingly. This is as true for all peasant societies as it is conspicuous in aristocratic circles—particularly (as Stendhal has shown in some of his novels) when the latter have felt threatened by the middle classes. The significant contribution of Riesman and his associates lies in the very specific interpretation of prevailing social patterns. They are not speaking about human nature in general or recurring epiphenomena within the frame of a motley collection of social systems and subsystems. They analyze human existence under the condition of modern Western industrial society. In that respect—perhaps because of the background of the authors, or their focus of interest—they have leaned over backwards in the direction of caution and have more or less restricted themselves to data from the American scene. What I wish to suggest is that while they deserve credit for having resisted the temptation to apply their theories in the grandiose universal manner, they may—as I intimated earlier—perhaps be a bit parochial in restricting themselves to claim for the development of American society what rightfully, though with certain qualifications, extends to a wider area. It may very well be that the authors of *The Lonely Crowd* have achieved a richer return than they bargained for; their observations on the development of character types in American society may very well turn out to be a description of a secular trend of modern industrial society as a whole.

NOTES

1. What T. M. Knox has to say about certain English philosophers, apropos his brilliant discussion of the works of Collingwood, should be addressed to many an American sociologist: "It is not too much to say that after these books English philosophers will be able to continue ignoring history only by burying their heads in the sand." (See his preface to R. G. Collingwood, *The Idea of History* [New York: Oxford Galaxy, 1956], p. viii.)

2. See, e.g., Norman E. Nelson, "Popular Arts and the Humanities," *College English* (May, 1955), p. 482: "The sociologists may not be the monsters that literary people imagine them to be, but they may well be creating a monster that will overshadow the hydrogen bomb. They are building an impersonal machinery for analyzing human beings into standard interchangeable parts in order to sort them into handy pigeonholes and reassemble them to specification—at the behest of anyone with enough money or political power to rend or commandeer the machinery." There are, however, brilliant exceptions. Quite a few significant scholars in the field of English literature have made important contributions toward a synthesis of humanistic and social science approaches. I have only to mention the writings of Richard Altick, Harry Levin, and Ian Watt.

3. Dilthey, however, never tore himself completely loose from positivism. See Max Horkheimer, "The Relation between Psychology and Sociology in the Work of Wilhelm Dilthey," *Studies in Philosophy and Social Science,* 8 (1939), 430 ff.

4. I agree with H. Stuart Hughes' comment on the contributions of the "cultural sciences" to social theory: "The middle level of social study, however, the

level of careful synthesis and the modest testing of hypothesis, tended to drop out entirely." See his *Consciousness and Society* (New York: Knopf, 1958), p. 186.

5. See the profound observations of the relationship of Dilthey to Simmel in Collingwood, op. cit., pp. 174-75; also Horkheimer, loc. cit., p. 432.

6. Karl Mannheim calls it "false traditionalism." See his posthumously edited *Essays on the Sociology of Culture* (London: Routledge & Kegan Paul, 1956), p. 119.

7. See, for the beginnings of the alienation of a middle-class public from the autonomous experience of art, Leo Lowenthal and Marjorie Fiske, "The Controversy over Art and Popular Culture in 18th Century England," in *Common Frontiers of the Social Sciences,* edited by Mirra Komarovsky (Glencoe: Free Press, 1957). Reprinted as Chapter 3 in this volume. Also, with regard to Goethe, the section "World Literature and Popular Culture," in Leo Lowenthal, *Literature and the Image of Man* (Boston: Beacon Press, 1957).

8. S. M. Lipset, "A Changing American Character?"

9. Quoted from Philip Rahv (ed.), *Discovery of Europe* (Boston: Houghton Mifflin, 1947), p. 49.

10. *The Edinburgh Review,* vol. 42, article VII, August, 1825.

11. *The Edinburgh Review,* vol. 76, January, 1843.

12. See John Stuart Mill, *On Bentham and Coleridge* (1838), (London: Chatto & Windus, 1950), p. 85.

13. John Stuart Mill, *On Liberty* (1859), (New York: Oxford World's Classics), p. 9.

14. *The Edinburgh Review,* vol. 17, article IX, 1810-1811.

15. *The Edinburgh Review,* vol. 89, article III, April, 1849.

Chapter 10
POPULAR CULTURE: A HUMANISTIC AND SOCIOLOGICAL CONCEPT

If one speaks today about communication, one is almost forced into a controversy over the mass media. The media are, of course, merely the instruments of possible communication—they are the tools our technology has developed and whose right application is in question. Technology has extended our access to the world as never before. Yet despite telephones, radios, television, increased literacy, expanded circulation of books, newspapers, and periodicals we are lonelier than ever before—and certainly our common human need for world peace seems further removed than ever. Deterioration of our intellectual and moral heritage has not only accompanied the quantitative growth of mass media in modern society but has been a result as well. It is my contention that an awareness of these problems is essential to the preservation of the dignity and growth of the individual.

We have learned very little from the social sciences about how communication has affected man's humanity. In fact, the discussion of communications, precisely because it is mainly a discussion of mass media of communication, has seriously jeopardized productive discourse between social scientists and humanists. Yet stereotypes of the humanities to the contrary, there are now some social scientists who believe that to get at the meaning of communication in our time we had better turn toward the realm of symbolic expression—to the arts and religion. The humanists, sometimes quite rightly, suspect that all the social scientists care about are quantifiable aggregates of people and facts or rather people as facts. A temperamental illustration of the humanist's attitude we owe to W. H. Auden. To quote from his poem "Under Which Lyre":

> *Thou shalt not answer questionnaires*
> *Or quizzes upon World-Affairs*
> *Nor with compliance*
> *Take any test.*
> *Thou shalt not sit*

With statisticians nor commit
A social science.[1]

In prose, the poet is echoed by a worthy professor of English who wrote in *College English:*

> Little did I know, and my colleagues less: the social sciences have these many years been studying the popular arts as mass media of communication. In some vague way we had all heard of it, but what man of sensibility reading the words mass media and communication would attach any meaning to them: he would shudder at the vulgar jargon and turn away. I have since spent many a long hour over sociological monography, many of them as empty as they are execrably written. If I may say so without reflecting on any one—least of all myself—the study of mass communications does not attract the best minds.

Communication has been almost completely divested of its human content, a content suggested by the word itself. For true communication entails a communion, a sharing of innermost experience. The dehumanization of communication has resulted from its annexation by the media of modern culture—by the newspapers first, and then by radio and television.

That this dehumanization should have been brought to near perfection in a society that professes an ultimate commitment to the sanctity and autonomy of the individual is one of the grotesque ironies of history. When an individual appears in the media of communication he is insidiously separated from his humanity. Mass communication relies upon the ideological sanction of individual autonomy in the very process of exploiting individuality to serve mass culture. Note how, in the following advertisement of Young Readers of America, a branch of the Book-of-the-Month Club, Inc., Dr. Gallup's private achievement, his particularity, is annulled by his being made into an instrument of persuasion: "As Dr. George Gallup, a former psychology professor himself, points out in a recent article in the *Ladies' Home Journal,* if a child can acquire the habit of book reading, it will be invaluable in helping him to cope successfully with all his later experiences in life."

The passage borrows the halo of mass culture as reflected in public opinion surveys to make palatable the intake of high culture. In citing Gallup as an authority on the value of culture pursuits one relies for the "finer" things in life on the master mass diagnostician who knows what is in the mind of the "public" and, by implication, what is best for it. To identify him as a former psychology professor implies that he has a good educational background and a respectable professional career but invokes simultaneously the sanctions of the intellectual and the successful businessman.

There is a new venture named "Time Books." This enterprise promises a "Time Reading Program." The cost? Only $3.95 for each package of three or four books and for this monthly charge you will partake in "a planned approach," which guarantees that "though your time may be limited you will be reading widely and profitably . . . books which are truly timeless in style and significance." The reliability of the selection is beyond any doubt: "This plan draws its strength from the fact that the editors spent thousands of hours finding the answers to questions that you too must have asked yourself many times. . . . It is part of their job to single out the few books that tower over all others." Meaning, quality, and importance of these publications are assured: "In each case the editors will write special introductions to underline what is unique in the book, what impact it has had or will have, what place it has earned in literature and contemporary thought." In addition, a kind of religious sanction attaches to the wrappings of the enterprise: "The books will be bound in durable, flexible covers similar to those used for binding fine Bibles and Missals." This circular, which must have come out in millions of copies, claims that "this letter" was "written only to people whom we know to be thoughtful readers." The circular is called a "letter," the most personal genre of individual communication in writing—an example within an example of the perversion of communication in mass communications.

The social scientists of the last two generations have evaded moral commitment by pretending to engage in value-free research—something that exists neither in logic nor in history. In an era of increasing positivistic infatuation (which includes a large share of the teachers in humanistic fields, who should know better), the inalienable birthright of the intellectual as a critic, trivial as it may sound, must be energetically asserted. Plainly the communications set-up of the modern world has corrupted human communication, and its images have penetrated perniciously and painfully the private realms of individuals in their most intimate spheres of discourse. Conversation becomes "a waste of time." The coffee house, since Queen Anne's time the refuge of the most delicate or indelicate personal dialogue, has been observed to be on its way out in Europe and ironically to be on its way into the American scene—yet as an only slightly veiled version of the desolate Third Avenue bar, home of the homeless isolates who make up a significant part of the populace. And it would be parochial snobbery to characterize the decay of language as genuine experience, including the downgrading of unplanned conversation, as merely a phenomenon of American civilization.

Here is a response cited in a survey recently made in Japan:

> For example it is night and you are sitting alone at your desk with a
> textbook open. . . . So you switch on the radio, and without seeming to
> listen you begin to hear the late-late jazz program. And then the rhythm
> of the music appropriately puts a part of yourself to sleep and banishes
> excessive worry and longing; and riding to its pace as though mounted on
> a belt-conveyor, your studies begin to advance a little as though they were
> automates.

But memorizing one's homework is not cultivating one's memory. Memory
is man's receptacle of living language and language lived by him and
his fellow man through human history. Modern man, however, suffers
a shrinkage of memory. It often seems limited to the news of yesterday's,
if not today's, newspaper or television shows. Not only automobiles and
washing machines but also language itself suffers today the fate of planned,
or at least factual, obsolescence. What is remembered and what is forgotten
seem almost indistinguishable, left to chance without any significance.

Toward the end of the dialogue *Phaedrus,* Socrates tells the story of
the inventor-god Theuth, who boasts to Thamus, the king-god of Egypt,
about his innovations. They sound almost like the enumeration of the
basic features of our modern life style—an obsession with technology as
well as with organized leisure time. "He it was who invented numbers
and arithmetic and geometry and astronomy, also the game of checkers
and dice"—laying the groundwork as it were for the radiation laboratories
and the gambling casinos. What Theuth is most proud of is the invention
of the alphabet: "This invention will make the Egyptians wiser and will
improve their memories; for it is an elixir of memory and wisdom that
I have discovered." The wise king, however, spots in the invention of
writing the dismal seeds of rote, repetition, and renunciation of self-
reliance. Plato's genius discovers in the achievements of civilization its
very threat to culture. Not the spoken word but its written coagulation
contains the germ for scholarship and the literary arts, as well as for
the derivative products of mass communications—from newspapers to
comic books, from Time Reader leaflets to billboards (those frozen
highwaymen of our time). Thamus throws back at Theuth the concept
of the written alphabet as elixir (the *pharmakon,* as it is called in Greek)
and instead of accepting it as a medication predicts its potential deadly
powers:

> For this invention will produce forgetfulness in the minds of those who
> learn to use it, because they will not practice their memory. Their trust in
> writing, produced by external characters which are no part of themselves,

will discourage the use of their own memory within them. You have invented an elixir not of memory but of reminding and you offer your pupils the *appearance* of wisdom, not true wisdom, for they will read many things without instruction and will therefore seem to know many things, when they are for the most part ignorant and hard to get along with, since they are not wise, but only appear wise.

As if Plato had wished to tell us with emphasis that communication only exists as shared experience, shared with one's own self and the selves of others, he applies the technique of the dialogue within the dialogue: Socrates speaks to Phaedrus about Theuth and Thamus speaking to each other. This technique is an emblem of con-versation—turning to each other and striving for the common. It is the emblem of the open heart, the open mind, the very opposite of the prejudice and stereotype that are forever present in mass communications and their precipitations on modern man and his life style of borrowed experience. Memory is a bench mark for human, or better, humanistic behavior, as opposed to the quasi-biological, day-by-day, futile-moment-by-futile-moment existence to which modern man seems to have committed himself. The continuity of scholarship, the timelessness of the symbolic mementos of the arts, the tradition-laden connotations of religions, the faithful and solidary behavior of an individual—all these elements are variations on the theme of memory, which I am inclined to equate with communication truly understood, as Plato equated it with philosophy. All these concepts— memory, communication, philosophy—refer to genuine experience. After 2000 years John Smith, the Cambridge Platonist, restated in 1660 this Platonic credo: "As an organizing argument I suggest the need for the scrupulous education of man. There is no easy road. For our words must refer to our experiences if we are to know whereof we speak and they must evoke the experiences of our peers if we are to be understood."

I am tempted to say that the Platonic dialogue embraces the idea of the divine coffeehouse; in any case, Plato's insistence on the cultivation of memory as the touchstone of individuality and creative participation in human communication does not appear by chance in a dialogue whose essential theme is the philosophy of the beautiful.

True, the humanistic meaning of communication is not entirely forgotten and interred. Ezra Pound (who, in spite of his aberrations, retains the stature of the poet and humanist) writes: "As language becomes the most powerful instrument of perfidy, so language alone can riddle and cut through the meshes. Used to conceal meaning, used to blur meaning, used to produce the complete and utter inferno of the past century [and I may add the present as well] . . . against which, SOLELY a care for language, for accurate registration by language avails."

A story yet to be written is a social history of the intellectual debate on the style of modern life and more specifically on the fate and vicissitudes of the standards of culture, taste, and morality under the impact of urbanization and industrialization. This debate comes to a head in the critical analysis of the role and substance of the arts and their degraded counterparts or, to use these vague contemporary terms, on the relationship of high culture and popular culture. At least since Montaigne and Pascal and most articulately in individual works, in the magazines of the professional writers in England in the eighteenth and nineteenth centuries and also in Continental Europe, a lively discussion arose around the very same issue that Plato so provocatively put before Western man: What is going to happen to us when the very ego, this precious invention of idealistic philosophy, romantic poetry, and the spirit of capitalist enterprise, becomes increasingly enmeshed in the mechanisms of con- formity—the whole network of institutional and psychological controls? It would reflect a painful misunderstanding of the significance of this widely ramified discourse and debate if we filed it away under the rubric "problems of leisure time." The very fact that the concern of these eighteenth- and nineteenth-century writers again and again turns toward the social supplies of leisure time—the novels, the theaters, the magazines, the newspapers, sports and games, and what have you—means that the worried and troubled intellectuals examine critically that space of life within which man is supposedly free, his "free time." Although, of course, the supporters of conformity who sell their talents to the highest bidders are not absent among the intellectuals, the emphasis remains on the open wound, the wound of imitation—not the imitation of Christ but the almost mimetic imitation of what one is supposed to imitate. Whether or not the discussants consider a solution of the crisis of man and society possible, whether improvement of education or return to romanticized forms of agricultural society or withdrawal to the ivory tower or "No Exit" is the powerless recommendation of the critics—the essential verdict (long before Ezra Pound) is directed toward the decay of language, the limbo of human communication. This theme was as essential for Goethe as for Flaubert, for Wordsworth as for Eliot, for Coleridge as for Nietzsche— or for that matter for a large list of contributors to *The Edinburgh Review* as well as to other journals of sophisticated opinion.

This truly humanistic critique turns against instrumentalist language (as means to an end) and advocates the autonomous character of the human word as an end in itself. But as a human end indeed! Language *qua* language must retain the sacred dignity of the human condition. This paradoxical statement is made with intent. Language is indeed ideally the definitive logos. There is nothing else available to us for ultimate expression and true manifestation of the individual than language. In this view, I agree with Jakob Burckhardt, whom one cannot reproach for being insensible to nonverbal creative artifacts, who once said: "If it were possible to express in words the quintessence, the idea of a work of art, art itself would become superfluous, and all buildings, statues, and pictures could as well have been unbuilt, unsculpted, unpainted." The symbolic language of Judaeo-Christian religion has continuously emphasized the noninstrumental essence of language by endowing it with divine origin. Whether you look at Psalm 139 ("For there is not a word in my tongue, but, lo, O God, thou knowest it altogether") or at Sermon 79 of John Donne ("The Holy Ghost is an eloquent author, a vehement and an abundant author but yet not luxuriant; he is far from a penurious but as far from a superfluous style too"), man is viewed as created in the image of God because it is language that allows him to partake in the divine. There is a biblical passage that conveys archetypically the humanistic meaning of language. It is found in the First Book of Kings, chapter 19: "And, behold, God passed by, and a great and strong wind rent the mountains, and brake in pieces the rocks before God; but God was not in the wind. And after the wind an earthquake; but God was not in the earthquake; and after the earthquake a fire; but God was not in the fire; and after the fire a still small voice," the voice of the Lord. When we talk about communication today, we are inclined to mean the strong wind and the earthquake and the fire of the mass media of communication, of manipulation, of advertisements, of propaganda, mass circulation, and so forth. Yet human communication is truly the "still, small voice."

The meaning of the sacred in language is paradoxical. The instrumentalist concept of language (so frequently practiced in mass communications but, alas, in the scholar's world as well) conceives of language as a tool, and as such it must be as near perfect as any sophisticated technological product. Its ideal would be speed reading and writing, the teaching machine, the computer. But these ideals are—to turn a theological phrase—the ideals of the devil because language as the expression of the creative individual must also be the witness of his ever present incompletion. Mortal as we are, our language must reflect our limitations as well as the ever present tasks, possibilities, and potentialities before us. This function is exactly what is betrayed or at least denied in the products of popular culture. When the motion picture is finished or *The Reader's Digest* is read or the crooner's songs are heard, there is nothing to be said or seen or heard any more. Creative imagination has become muted. The patterned communications mechanism has as its logical and psychological end the switching off of the projector, the radio set, and the television box or the final mute grimace of the singer. But the true meaning of communication, which is upheld by the literary artists and above all by the poets, insists on productive imagination, on ambiguity, even on silence. Today the communications conscience of man is kept alive by the artist who communicates the very breakdown of communication: James Joyce, for instance, when he explores the archaic secrets of word and syntax, or the dramatists of the Theater of the Absurd when they explore the radical gulf that separates word and meaning.

There is no need, however, to take recourse to the messages of the avant-garde. The scene is as of old, and the witnesses are available in more familiar places.

One hundred and fifty years ago Coleridge wrote a letter to his friend Southey aiming at a harmless act of manipulation. He requested Southey to write a letter to his magazine *The Friend* in a "humorous manner" so that he, Coleridge, would be able to reply and explain his attitude toward style in the same periodical. What Coleridge wanted to achieve by this planted interchange of letters was "in the answer [to Southey] to state my own convictions in full on the nature of obscurity." Needless to say, "obscurity" is used here in an ironical manner. Coleridge's intent was to stress the commitment of the true writer, the genuine communicator, toward the connotative character or, to speak in aesthetic terms, the ambiguity of language. This letter of Coleridge, written October 20, 1809, is a classic and valid statement on the theme to which this paper addresses itself. Here are the main elements: the absence of a responsible cultural elite that would serve as the guardian and taskmaster of intellectual creativity; the decreasing intellectual demands made on the reading public at large; and finally the all-embracing emergence of a one-dimensional, nonconnotative, unambiguous language of efficiency and predigested derivative thought, which (as Plato stated) leaves no room for the unique and idiosyncratic, for productive imagination and the dissenting voice:

> No real information can be conveyed, no important errors radically extracted, without demanding an effort of thought on the part of the reader; but the obstinate, and now contemptuous, aversion to all energy of thinking is the mother evil, the cause of all the evils in politics, morals, and literature, which it is my object to wage war against. . . . Now, what I wish you to do for me . . . is . . . to write a letter to *The Friend* in a lively style, chiefly urging, in a humorous manner, my Don Quixotism in expecting that the public will ever pretend to understand my lucubrations, or feel any interest in subjects of such sad and unkempt antiquity, and contrasting my style with the cementless periods of the modern Anglo-Gallican style, which not only are understood *beforehand,* but, being free from all connections of logic, all the hooks and eyes of intellectual memory, never oppress the mind by any after recollections, but, like civil visitors, stay a

few moments, and leave the room quite free and open for the next comers. Something of this kind, I mean, that I may be able to answer it so as, in the answer, to state my own convictions at full on the nature of obscurity.

It is with consummate irony that Coleridge calls his philosophy of communication an act of Don Quixotism; he hardly could have found a more convincing metaphor to stress the productive ambiguity of artistic symbols than the reference to the noble knight who stands for the condemnation of banality and triviality and the unshakable commitment to the idea of men by artistically manipulating a world of trivial objects and persons—very much the archetype and pioneer of the modern absurdists. As if he had to answer the spurious arguments of the managers of the motion-picture industry and their confreres in other fields of mass entertainment who try to convince themselves that they have to follow the cues of the masses, Coleridge clearly indicts the manufacturers of information and entertainment for not "demanding an effort of thought on the part of the reader"—an issue as much with us today as it was in the time of Coleridge or of Goethe and Stendhal, to name two of his comrades-in-arms.

It is predominantly the poet who in our time has remained the committed spokesman for language as the ever given realm of human fulfillment and the ever present realm of human frustration, creating higher levels of aspiration and attainment. Earlier Ezra Pound and Eliot were mentioned. Eliot created definitive lines for "demanding an effort of thought on the part of the reader," as well as of the writer himself. In "East Coker" he reports "trying to learn to use words":

> *every attempt*
> *Is a wholly new start, and a different kind of failure*
> *Because one has only learned to get the better of words*
> *For the thing one no longer has to say, or the way in which*
> *One is no longer disposed to say it. And so each venture*
> *Is a new beginning, a raid on the inarticulate.* [2]

What comes to the fore in this generalized autobiography of the poet is the infinite care man owes to his most specific human endowment. It is important that we attempt to "raid" the inarticulate—that vast part of the self in which (it so often seems) the self most truly *is* and that is denied altogether by the pat, mechanical, and soporific oversimplifications of "mass communications." It is the "spiritual" dimension of life, the mystery at the very heart of being, that we betray by the hideous impoverishment of the vocabularies and instruments of our thought and feeling implicit in the mass enterprise of mass communications (to which we are all party in some measure).

Two thinkers as different as John Stuart Mill and Friedrich Nietzsche have voiced their sorrows over the style of modern life aided and abetted by literary mass production, which seems to leave the public no choice but an almost neurotic gobbling-up of an endless stream of sounds and sights and words—not to be remembered, not to be translated into productive enrichment, and not to be translated into "dreams," that "stuff" of which, according to Shakespeare, our world is made. In an article "Civilization," which appeared in the *London and Westminster Review* of April, 1836, John Stuart Mill wrote:

> The world . . . gorges itself with intellectual food, and in order to swallow the more, *bolts it*. Nothing is now read slowly, or twice over. . . . He . . . who should and would write a book, and write it in the proper manner of writing a book, now dashes down his first hasty thoughts, or what he mistakes for thoughts, in a periodical. And the public is in the predicament of an indolent man, who cannot bring himself to apply his mind vigorously to his own affairs, and over whom, therefore, not he who speaks most wisely, but he who speaks most frequently, obtains the influence.

And in a similar vein, though in a most different style, Nietzsche wrote in the preface of *The Dawn of Day:*

> I have not been a philologist in vain; perhaps I am one yet: a teacher of slow reading. I even come to write slowly. At present it is not only my habit, but even my taste, a perverted taste, maybe—to write nothing but what will drive to despair every one who is in a hurry . . . philology is now more desirable than ever before; . . . it is the highest attraction and incitement in an age of "work": that is to say, of haste, of unseemly and immoderate hurry-scurry, which is intent upon "getting things done" at once, even every book, whether old or new. Philology itself, perhaps, will not "get things done" so hurriedly: it teaches how to read *well:* i.e. slowly, profoundly, attentively, prudently, with inner thoughts, with the mental doors ajar, with delicate fingers and eyes.

To sum up what has happened in our day and age: Communication has become part of a consumers' culture in which those who produce and those who receive are hardly distinguishable from each other because they are both the serfs of a life style of conformity and regulation. It is the basic tragedy and paradox of modern civilization and particularly of our own phase that the sermon of individualism has turned into the practice of conformity, that the ideology of education and persuasion through the spoken and printed word has become the reality of insensibility and numbness to meaning, and that the professed belief of the powers that be in all spheres of public life—political or cultural or economic—in the persuasive influence of the worded message is answered by increasing skepticism if not outright disbelief in the world itself.

I don't have any prescriptions or utopias to offer, but I have summoned some of the witnesses who, although rather weak as social powers, are yet with us as the ever-present conscience of true human consciousness. If in the beginning I have intimated my pessimism in regard to the communications research we social scientists have been conducting, I should like in the end to regain at least some of the territory I have voluntarily ceded. None less than the great John Dewey, philosopher and social scientist as well, in his brilliant essay "Democracy and Education" presented us with a definition of communication that I predict will still live when many of the data of mass media communications research have collected dust:

> Society not only continues to exist *by* transmission, *by* communication. There is more than a verbal tie between the words common, community, and communication. Men live in a community in virtue of the things which they have in common; and communication is the way in which they come to possess things in common. . . . To be a recipient of a communication is to have an enlarged . . . experience. One shares in what another has thought and felt, and in so far, meagerly or amply, has his own attitude modified. Nor is the one who communicates left unaffected. . . . Except in dealing with commonplaces and catch phrases one has to assimilate, imaginatively, something of another's experience in order to tell him intelligently of one's own experience. All communication is like art.

NOTES

1. "Under Which Lyre," © 1946 by W. H. Auden. Reprinted from *Nones*, by W. H. Auden, by permission of Random House, Inc., and of Faber and Faber, Ltd.
2. This portion of "East Coker" reprinted from *Four Quartets*, by T. S. Eliot, by permission of Harcourt, Brace & World, Inc., and of Faber and Faber, Ltd.

CL

306
LOW